VIRGIL'S AUGUSTAN EPIC

VIRGIL'S
AUGUSTAN EPIC

*

Francis Cairns

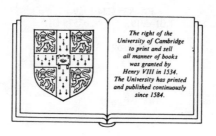

The right of the
University of Cambridge
to print and sell
all manner of books
was granted by
Henry VIII in 1534.
The University has printed
and published continuously
since 1584.

CAMBRIDGE UNIVERSITY PRESS

CAMBRIDGE

NEW YORK   PORT CHESTER

MELBOURNE   SYDNEY

Published by the Press Syndicate of the University of Cambridge
The Pitt Building, Trumpington Street, Cambridge CB2 1RP
40 West 20th Street, New York, NY 10011, USA
10 Stamford Road, Oakleigh, Melbourne 3166, Australia

First published 1989

Reprinted 1990

Printed in Great Britain by the
Athenaeum Press Ltd, Newcastle upon Tyne

British Library cataloguing in publication data

Cairns, Francis
Virgil's Augustan epic.
1. Epic poetry in Latin. Virgil, Aeneid -
Critical studies
I. Title
873′.01

Library of Congress cataloguing in publication data

Cairns, Francis
Virgil's Augustan epic / Francis Cairns.
p.   cm.
Bibliography: p.
ISBN 0 521 35358 0
1. Virgil. Aeneis.
2. Aeneas (Legendary character) in literature.
3. Kings and rulers in literature.
I. Title
PA6825.C34 1989
873′.01-dc19   88-203525 CIP

ISBN 0 521 35358 0

To Robin Nisbet

CONTENTS

PREFACE

This book explores Virgil's embodiment in the *Aeneid* of some of the political and literary ideals of early Augustan Rome, and in doing so tries to throw new light on the epic characters and action. Writing a book on Virgil has been, inevitably, a humbling experience. More than any other ancient writer except Homer, he defies expectation and generalisation, instantly deflating pretensions to define him.

It is assumed that the reader will have a copy of the *Aeneid* to hand, so that quotations from it are restricted to those vital for the immediate argument. They are based on Mynors (1969), as quotations of ancient works are generally based on the relevant Oxford Classical Texts, although I have reserved the right to vary readings and punctuation where necessary. I am grateful to the Delegates of the Clarendon Press for permission to use their copyright material in this way. Throughout Greek (but not Latin) quotations are translated or paraphrased, and my thanks are due to J.G. Howie for checking these renderings. Greek proper names are transliterated in the most commonly accepted way. The terms 'homeric', 'hellenistic', and the names of philosophical schools are not capitalised.

The almost infinite secondary literature on the *Aeneid* not only eludes adequate coverage, for all the sterling assistance given by Suerbaum (1980–1), but includes eminent contributions which have shaped the basic and often unrecognised assumptions with which we approach Virgil. Within this tradition of Virgilian scholarship the older commentators, as well as Heinze (1915), are in fact omnipresent in this book, although they are seldom cited. Pöschl (1977) has in the interval since its first edition (1950) come to enjoy virtually the same status. In contrast the frequent citation of Knauer (1964) may show how much remains to be absorbed of this truly fundamental work, even though it has already altered radically every modern scholar's perception of the *Aeneid*. The (more recent) writings of G.K. Galinsky rank very high too, and are cited accordingly. I am conscious of having benefited immensely from these scholars' labours, as from much other secondary literature on the *Aeneid*, and of having found particularly helpful among more recent publications those of G. Binder, V. Buchheit, E.L. Harrison, N.M. Horsfall, E. Kraggerud, M. Lausberg, P.R. Hardie, D. West, and A. Wlosok. Many specialist dissertations, monographs and papers, both of this century and of the last, and both on the *Aeneid* and on other matters, have also been invaluable; in recent non-Virgilian scholarship I have been especially aware of influence going beyond particulars from the writings of M. Dickie, C.W. Macleod, E. Kaiser, F. Millar, O. Murray, E. Rawson, N.J. Richardson, and W.J. Slater. Some of the scholars mentioned above have also provided stimulus in personal discussions, or correspondence; other enlivening factors have been the Virgilian Bimillenary, with its many conferences and conference proceedings (on which cf. Wlosok (1985)), and the appearance of some volumes of the *Enciclopedia virgiliana*.

I have sought in general to restrict references to secondary literature by citing only works of substance, and by giving preference to more recent treatments of longstanding problems, especially if the earlier bibliography is noted there; but citation has been fuller when necessary. Only on very large questions is Suerbaum (1980–1) invoked directly. Citations are usually of material in support of, or coinciding with, views advanced, although on occasion diametrically opposed views are cited for completeness. Silence then does not always indicate disagreement, or citation agreement. I regret any unintentional misrepresentation of other scholars' views, or failure to give due credit to a predecessor. It goes without saying that the List of Modern Works Cited (pp. 249–70) does not claim to offer a comprehensive bibliography on any of the topics treated. The Index Locorum includes all *Aeneid* passages cited; passages from other ancient works are listed only when there is some discussion. Where more general references to ancient authors or their works are made, these are covered in the General Index.

Virgil's Augustan Epic was written over the decade 1977–1987, and attempted to keep abreast with secondary literature appearing up to the end of 1987. During the period of composition, various chapters formed the basis of papers given in universities and conferences at Arezzo, Belfast, Birkbeck College London, Birmingham, Bristol, Calgary, Cornell, Jena, Ioannina, Leeds, Liverpool, Massachusetts (Amherst), McGill, McMaster, Newcastle, Ottawa, Pisa and Siena. I once again thank my hosts for their invitations, and my audiences for their comments. An abbreviated version of Chapter 4 appeared as Cairns (1985) and an earlier version of part of Chapter 5 as Cairns (1977).

It is a pleasure to record my warm gratitude to those friends who read the penultimate draft of the book, saving me from errors and infelicities, and bettering it in many ways: Ted Harrison, Nicholas Horsfall, Richard Thomas and David West commented on the whole book with an abundance of learning and sensitivity; and Oswyn Murray at an earlier stage brought to bear on Chapters 1–5 his unparalleled knowledge of kingship and kingship theory in the ancient world.

The referees for Cambridge University Press made some useful points which I have incorporated, and one referee suggested a better title than the book originally had. My wife Sandra not only typed and word-processed draft after draft but provided the academic *summa manus* and compiled the indexes. Robert Peden and Frederick Williams kindly acted as proof-readers. Despite all the help proferred by those mentioned above, there have inevitably been points at which I have resisted advice. I take full responsibility for remaining errors and inadequacies.

Birkenhead   F.C.
January 1988

1

DIVINE AND HUMAN KINGSHIP

A striking and neglected[1] feature of the *Aeneid*, and of its first book in particular, is the frequency with which references to kingship appear. In Book 1, royalty is an attribute of several gods, with Jupiter pre-eminent. He is *divum pater atque hominum rex* at 65; he is addressed by Venus as *rex magne* at 241, and she speaks of him 'ruling' (*regis*) at 230. His consort Juno appears as *regina deum* at 9. She calls herself *divum ... regina* at 46; she is addressed by Aeolus as *o regina* at 76; and at 443 she is *regia Juno*. The wind-god Aeolus plays a major role in Book 1 as proximate cause of the storm which brings Aeneas to Carthage; he is *rex Aeolus* in 52 and *rex* in 62 and 137; he has *sceptra* in 57 and a *regnum* and *sceptra* in 78; and he receives a command from Neptune *regnare* in 141.

It is however men who provide the bulk of kingship references in *Aeneid* 1. Among minor human characters Ascanius is *regius ... puer* (677f.) and he will transfer his *regnum* to Alba Longa (270f.). Ilia is *regina sacerdos* (273) and mention is made of the *reges Pelasgi* (624). Pygmalion had the *regna* of Tyre (346), and Hector's line will 'reign' for three hundred years at Alba Longa (272f.). Acestes is *rex* of Eryx at 558 and 570, while the kingdom of Carthage appears at 17 and 338, that of Libya at 226, of Troy at 268, of the Liburnians at 244, and of Teucer in 620.

But the characters most frequently designated as royal in *Aeneid* 1 are Aeneas and Dido. Aeneas is *Teucrorum ... regem* (38) in Juno's

---

[1] Matakiewicz (1930–1) regarded Virgil's emphasis on kingship as essentially a reflection of Homer. R.J. Murray (1964–5) noted the frequency of *rex* and related words in four Augustan poets, Tibullus, Propertius, Horace and Virgil, and correctly concluded that 'the word "king" can have created little animosity among Romans of the Augustan age' (244). He also highlighted Virgil's applications of *rex* to Aeneas and Iulus but did not carry his insights further; and, apart from the dismissal of his paper by Classen (1965) in a Korrekturzusatz (402 n. 59), his views have been ignored. The importance of the 'good king' theme in the *Aeneid* was briefly noted in Cairns (1977) 115; hints of interest in Dido's kingship appear in Pöschl (3rd edn 1977) 94, which goes back to the first edition of 1950 (pp. 116f.), in that of Aeneas in Galinsky (1969) 7f., in that of both in Thornton (1976) 85, and in the theme in Paschalis (1982) 344f. and Hahn (1984). The title of Baker (1980) appears to promise a relevant treatment, but handles Ascanius in general terms. Murray (1984) 236 notes that Philodemus' treatise 'points the way to the public poetry of the Augustan poets'.

reflections. He will 'reign' over Latium at 265. He is described by Ilioneus as the king of the fugitive Trojans in 544 (*rex erat Aeneas nobis*); and a little later he is again called *rex* at 553 and 575. His gifts are *regia* at 696. The royal status of Dido is even more frequently emphasised. She is *regina* eleven times, at 303, 389, 454, 496, 522, 594, 660, 674, 697, 717 and 728. Her royal status is stressed in other ways too: *regit*, 340; *regni novitas*, 563; *regnis*, 572; *regia ... / tecta*, 631f.; *regali ... luxu*, 637; and *regalis ... mensas*, 686.

One reaction to this stress on royalty in *Aeneid* 1, and indeed throughout the epic, might be to try to minimise the meaningfulness of Virgil's kingship references: its kings and kingdoms could, for example, be explained away as due to the temporal setting and literary ancestry of the *Aeneid*. Its events certainly take place in the heroic age, when kingship was the normal form of government; and, *qua* epic, it was written in conscious imitation of earlier epics, principally Homer's *Iliad* and *Odyssey* and Apollonius Rhodius' *Argonautica*, where many of the principal characters were kings. Thus the frequent references to kingship in the *Aeneid* would, on this view, not necessarily reflect a strong interest in it on the part of Virgil and his readers. It might be argued further that such interest is in any case unlikely, given the ingrained Roman dislike of kings, which dated from the regal period.[2] Indeed Roman republican sentiment might be thought to guarantee that kingship references in the *Aeneid* are literary reminiscence and not political comment; and conversely Virgil might seem to have been protected from any suspicion of fostering the hated notion of 'king' by its very omnipresence in his epic models.

It would be foolish to dismiss this approach out of hand. Virgil's particularly frequent emphasis on the royal status of Dido does seem to be linked with the fact that her city, Carthage, was to become Rome's arch-enemy. Here Virgil may be exploiting the negative associations of kingship to brand Carthage as a 'royal' city from its inception. But given the complex ways in which ancient political and moral concepts operated, this negative exploitation of kingship would not rule out more positive associations for it when Aeneas is in question, especially if, as I shall argue in Ch. 2, Virgil regarded Dido as a bad example of the genus king, and Aeneas as an excellent one. There are, too, several indications that Virgil and his readers had a more sophisticated attitude to kingship than is sometimes realised, and that the concept was a living and vital

[2] Cf. Wirszubski (1960) esp. 121f., 130–58; M.T. Griffin (1976) 141–8.

one in early imperial Rome. To begin with, the first item or section of an ancient literary work tends to be 'programmatic'. Thus the frequency of references to kingship in Book 1 (the statistics will be discussed shortly) implies that it was a significant theme for Virgil and that he expected his readers to keep it in mind when interpreting situations and personalities throughout the epic.

Again, the homeric epics certainly do make many references to kingship. But the frequency in Virgil is significantly greater than in Homer. Statistics of this sort are of course, on one level, crude and unsatisfactory tools for literary analysis.[3] But, on another level, if they are properly assembled, their very crudeness prevents the intrusion of subjective bias. The *Iliad* (15,693 lines) has 287 literal kingship references, i.e. uses of the words ἄναξ (king), βασιλεύς (king), σκῆπτρον (sceptre) and their compounds and cognates;[4] the *Odyssey* (12,110 lines) has 194. The shorter *Aeneid* (9,896 lines) has 342 uses of *rex* and its cognates and *sceptrum*.[5] 8 are parts of *regere* not referring to 'ruling'. Thus it has 334 kingship references, one per 29.63 lines, as against one per 54.67 lines in the *Iliad* and one per 62.42 lines in the *Odyssey*. The high concentration in *Aeneid* 1 also emerges: 56 in its 756 lines, i.e. one per 13.5 lines, more than double the average for the *Aeneid*. *Iliad* 1 (611 lines) has 30, i.e. one per 20.37 lines, also much higher than the *Iliad* average. Thus Virgil's kingship interest was certainly cued by the *Iliad*. *Odyssey* 1 (444 lines), with only 9 kingship references, i.e. one per 49.33 lines, again has more than the average for

[3] The principal difficulty is that, to avoid subjectivity, word frequency counts must be used. But the significance of these totals varies depending on the contexts and concentration of the key terms. However, as the examples increase in number, this problem diminishes. The concordances used in the word-counts are: *Iliad*: Prendergast (1962); *Odyssey*: Dunbar (1962); *Argonautica*: Campbell (1983); *Aeneid*: Warwick (1975). The line-counts for the works are taken from the respective Oxford Classical Texts.

[4] Because θρόνος (seat) is more general in meaning than 'throne', it and *solium*, which normally does refer to a royal throne, are both omitted. This biases the statistics slightly in favour of the hypothesis being argued. The inclusion of σκῆπτρον–*sceptrum*, where again the Greek term is more general than the Latin, may redress this bias. The details (in case anyone wishes to correct or refine them) are:

	Iliad	Odyssey	Argonautica		Aeneid
ἄναξ etc.	183	111	46	rex etc.	316
βασιλεύς etc.	74	69	33		
σκῆπτρον etc.	30	14	8	sceptrum	18
Book 1 total	30	9	Not useful		56

(Note: ἐμβασιλεύω is included with βασιλεύς etc.)

[5] R.J. Murray (1964–5) 245 tabulates all 'Virgilian' occurrences of *rex* and cognates (including those from the *Ciris*!). His total is 384.

the epic, but this is probably not significant given that the number is so small. For completeness it may be added that Apollonius' *Argonautica* (5,835 lines) has 87 royal references, i.e. one per 67.07 lines, which makes Apollonius less concerned with royalty than Homer and much less so than Virgil.[6] The pattern apparent in all this suggests that, although homeric kingship interest may have stimulated Virgil's concern with kingship, it cannot be explained away as non-significant homeric imitation. The statistics for the *Argonautica* reinforce this judgement, since the trend of Virgil's other model, Apollonius, was clearly in the other direction, so that Virgil here is departing from Apollonian practice. Kingship in the *Aeneid* is therefore not just an epic feature.

A third factor suggesting that Virgil's kingship references are meaningful is the link between kingship and Aeneas: he is at once the character most frequently and consistently treated in terms of kingship and the one who, as the ancestor of the Julian house, which Augustus had joined by adoption, ties the *Aeneid* most closely to the concerns of Virgil's contemporaries. Of course caution must be exercised in applying things said about Aeneas to Augustus, and the pair are to be seen as analogues rather than equated.[7] But any repeated attribute of Aeneas must to some extent have reflected on Augustus. Already in the forties BC Aeneas had a role in Julius Caesar's stress on the long, distinguished and divine ancestry of his family, the Iulii: a coin which he issued in 47 BC[8] showed, as a symbol of the issuer's *pietas*, Aeneas with the Palladium rescuing his father Anchises. This is not to say that Augustus, or Virgil, was trying to return to the heady days of the forties when Julius Caesar held supreme power and when he may, although this is disputed,[9] have flirted with the idea of kingship. Augustus was

---

[6] A further statistical bias against the view being argued may lie in the fact that Virgil sometimes uses a non-royal word like *imperium* (for which there is no Greek equivalent) of power which is actually royal. The word *tyrannus* has not been included in the statistics. It appears 7 times in the *Aeneid*: of Pygmalion (1.361), Mezentius (8.483), Turnus (10.448), and Aeneas (in the mouth of Turnus at 12.75), in all cases with hostile overtones; with more neutral reference, although perhaps with a suggestion of fear or awe, of the nomad sheiks (4.320), Latinus (7.342) and again Aeneas (in Latinus' mouth at 7.266).

[7] Its equation of them has led to the undue neglect of Drew (1927), otherwise a usefully stimulating work. For a recent and valuable exploitation of the analogue approach, cf. Nadeau (1982), although Nadeau (1984) is open to the same objections as Drew (1927); for a balanced major account of the Augustus–Aeneas analogue, cf. Binder (1971); and from a historical viewpoint Strasburger (1983) and most recently Wistrand (1984).

[8] Cf. Weinstock (1971) 253. The Trojan claims of the Iulii can of course be documented earlier, cf. Horsfall (1985) esp. 227–9.

[9] Cf. Weinstock (1971) Chs. 13–15; Rawson (1975) 148–50.

more cautious and more aware of public opinion. But this only highlights Virgil's decision to call Aeneas 'king' and to emphasise his royal status; and it confirms that he did not deem it offensive to his contemporaries. Had there been any problem here, Virgil could perfectly well have called Aeneas *dux* or *ductor* consistently, instead of intermittently,[10] or even, although this might have introduced an over-archaic flavour, have used the term *induperator* (i.e. *imperator*).[11]

The fact that he did not do so is a strong pointer to the reality of Augustan opinion about kingship. Augustus himself had no truck with the title *rex*, just as he avoided *dictator*, and was in general concerned after 27 BC that his titulature should sound republican.[12] But the idea that he and his successors were kings, although never officially accepted in the western empire, was increasingly realistic as time went on.[13] Egypt of course is a special case, in that the treatment of emperors as kings there was a natural carry-over from the Ptolemies. So Augustus appears as 'king of Upper and Lower Egypt' in his hieroglyphic representation,[14] while the old Graeco-Egyptian titulature of officials and their posts, including the 'royal secretariat', βασιλικὴ γραμματεία, remained in existence.[15] Neutral Latin uses of kingship terminology for the emperors appear in non-official sources from the second century AD on;[16] but since kingship, far from being suspect in the cultures of the eastern empire, was rather the ideal form of government, the Greeks were, not surprisingly, quicker to describe the emperors as 'kings'.[17] Examples appear freely from the mid-first century AD on. But, apart from the

[10] Sometimes (e.g. 4.124, 4.165, 7.107, 8.496, 10.156) Aeneas is literally 'leading'; elsewhere (e.g. 6.348, 6.562, 8.470, 8.513, 9.675, 10.602, 10.814) *dux/ductor* refers to status rather than activity.

[11] Nisbet (1978–80) calls attention to Virgil's exploitation of Roman expectations of the *imperator*, and also to links between Aeneas and Augustus. *induperator* appears twice in Lucretius (4.967, 5.1227) without obvious archaic overtones. That Virgil was in no way averse to using *imperium* in the *Aeneid* is shown by the word's frequency (40), although it often means just 'instruction' or 'direction'.

[12] Cf. Millar (1977) 613f.; Paschalis (1982) 344f.; Kienast (1982) 171–263 esp. 171–8.

[13] Cf. Millar (1973), of which the final words are worth quoting: 'The victory of Actium, the death of Antonius and the stabilization of affairs in Rome all marked steps towards, not away from, the establishment of a monarchy; and no good evidence suggests that anybody at the time claimed, or supposed, otherwise.' (67); Millar (1977) 613–20; Wallace-Hadrill (1982). Grimal (1986) 253–9 now examines valuably the ways in which the image of Augustus on the *clupeus virtutis* was in effect a royal one.

[14] Cf. Gardthausen (1891–1906) II.1.241 n. 18; Mommsen (1887–8) II.764. I am indebted to Dr David Thomas for advice on matters relating to Augustan Egypt.

[15] Cf. Mommsen (1887–8) II.764 n. 2; Marquardt (1881–5) I.450 and n. 2.

[16] Cf. Mommsen (1887–8) II.764 n. 4.

[17] Cf. Mommsen (1887–8) II.764f. and n. 3; Mason (1974) 120f.; Millar (1977) 613–20.

ambivalent[18] anecdote of Macrobius about the dancer Pylades, in which the latter casually addresses Augustus as βασιλεύς (king), there is an extraordinary example where the term βασιλεύς is applied publicly to Augustus: Antipater of Thessalonica, *AP* 10.25 = Gow–Page 40, dating probably from 9/8 BC,[19] reads:

Φοῖβε Κεφαλλήνων λιμενοσκόπε θῖνα Πανόρμου
ναίων τρηχείης ἀντιπέρην Ἰθάκης,
δός με δι' εὐπλώτοιο πρὸς Ἀσίδα κύματος ἐλθεῖν
Πείσωνος δολιχῇ νηὶ συνεσπόμενον,
καὶ τὸν ἐμὸν βασιλῆα τὸν ἄλκιμον εὖ μὲν ἐκείνῳ   5
ἵλαον εὖ δ' ὕμνοις ἄρτισον ἡμετέροις.

(Phoebus, watcher of the Cephallenians' harbour, dweller on the shore of Panormus opposite rough Ithaca, grant me to voyage to Asia through calm waves in the wake of Piso's warship. And make my warrior king gracious to him and gracious to my songs.)

It is quite certain that the 'king' (βασιλεύς) is Augustus and that the word does mean this, and not 'patron' (cf. Latin *rex*), because in the final couplet Antipater's real patron, L. Calpurnius Piso Frugi, is also mentioned, and the βασιλεύς is asked to favour him. Antipater's epigram may well be the surviving representative of many Greek literary works describing Augustus as 'king'.

A further point is that, even in the last two centuries of the Roman republic and even in quarters usually associated with 'republicanism', kingship was not always regarded in an uncomplicatedly hostile way. There were in fact two distinct views.[20] On the one hand Romans knew the Greek belief that the rule of a king was the best form of government, and were aware of its philosophical justifications.[21] In addition their own kings, with the exception of the last, Tarquinius Superbus, were in general thought to have been good rulers: they were regarded as the founders of important institutions and as moral exemplars, and were

---

[18] *idem cum propter populi seditionem pro contentione inter se Hylamque habita concitatam indignationem excepisset Augusti, respondit:* καὶ ἀχαριστεῖς, βασιλεῦ. ἔασον αὐτοὺς περὶ ἡμᾶς ἀσχολεῖσθαι (How ungracious you are, basileus! Do let them get worked up about us!) (*Saturnalia* 2.7.19). Here βασιλεύς may simply mean, as *rex* can, 'patron', particularly since Pylades was a freedman of Augustus.

[19] Cf. Millar (1977) 613 n. 19.

[20] This and succeeding paragraphs are indebted to and documented from Rawson (1975) (*q.v.*). The positive Roman attitude to kingship was sketched earlier by R.J. Murray (1964–5). Cf. also, for the details of Roman republican ambivalence about Romulus and kingship in general, Classen (1962) and (1965).

[21] Rawson (1975) 151.

honoured in history and literature and with statues on the Capitol.[22] Prominent Roman families claimed royal descent.[23] Contemporary kings could be seen as important and enviable figures, and they were at times valued allies of the Roman people.[24] On the other hand kingship and freedom could also be seen as mutually exclusive and kingship declared identical with its philosophical opposite, tyranny.[25] But expression of this latter view was reserved for specific situations. It was a useful pretext for removing or opposing kings whose actions were contrary to Rome's interests;[26] and it was excellent propaganda in political infighting both against real kings and against Romans, especially Julius Caesar, who were thought to be behaving like kings.[27]

Out of this conflict of views developed a complex attitude towards kingship on the part of important Romans. They could see that the power and influence of the highest Roman magistrates, and even of leading senators, was as great as that of kings. When in contact with kings they behaved as their equals or even demanded precedence.[28] It was no wonder that they developed 'ideas which suggested that they were themselves equal to kings, or even, in a sense *were* kings'.[29] As early as the late third century BC P. Cornelius Scipio Africanus Maior was modelling himself either on Alexander or on Cyrus, and, like Caesar later, was 'refusing' the title of king.[30] In the second century BC P. Cornelius Scipio Aemilianus was a reader of Xenophon's *Cyropaedia*. One of the standard works on kingship in the hellenistic world, it was read regularly as such by Roman nobles in the first century BC.[31] In this context the action of the epicurean philosopher Philodemus, attached to the household of L. Calpurnius Piso Caesoninus, consul in 58 BC and proconsul of Macedonia in 57 BC, in writing and dedicating to his patron a work entitled *On the good king according to Homer* can be seen as normal for its period.[32] The precepts which earlier had been offered to hellenistic kings could now, with due attention to cultural differences, and with full exploitation of the distancing factor inherent in the homeric background, be addressed to Roman politicians.

---

[22] Rawson (1975) 152f.; for the statues 153 n. 47; cf. also Martin (1982) Chs. 6, 7.
[23] Cf. Wiseman (1974); Rawson (1975) 152f.   [24] Rawson (1975) 151–3, 158.
[25] Rawson (1975) 149–52.   [26] Rawson (1975) 150–2, 158.
[27] Rawson (1975) 148–50, 157.   [28] Rawson (1975) 152, 154, 157f.
[29] Rawson (1975) 152, 154f.   [30] Rawson (1975) 154; Grimal (1986) 250.
[31] Rawson (1973) 164f.; (1975) 154.
[32] Cf. Rawson (1975) 154. Murray (1965), whose understanding of Philodemus remains fundamental and is in general confirmed by Dorandi (1982), claims (178) that Philodemus was doing something novel in equating Roman nobles with homeric kings. On 'multiple kingship', cf. also now Grimal (1986) 252f.

Interest in kingship among important Romans had material effects. Royal trappings were given to or used by Roman generals: L. Aemilius Paullus sailed up the Tiber in a Macedonian royal galley[33] and Ti. Gracchus was allegedly presented with royal dress by a Pergamene ambassador.[34] In the opposite direction, gifts of triumphal and magisterial insignia to kings by the Senate and by Roman generals, although perhaps not intended to do so, must have created an impression of equivalence in both directions,[35] particularly since the insignia themselves were in origin and in Roman attitudes associated with royalty, either Roman or Etruscan. It would hardly be surprising, when *triumphatores*, *imperatores*, consuls and even ordinary senators[36] were seen by others and by themselves as *de facto* 'kings', if the positive view of kingship was thought applicable to the *princeps* Augustus. This is particularly likely if a recent conclusion about the essential compromise adopted by prominent Republican figures, and even by Julius Caesar, is accepted,[37] namely that such men were eager to stress to the limit advantageous royal associations, while drawing back at the last moment from the actual name of king, with its residual disadvantageous concomitants.[38]

It is the ease with which Virgil takes for granted a positive view of kingship, and indeed a positive reaction to it from his audience, which argues loudest for the thesis offered here about his exploitation of ancient kingship theory. Explicit signs of his assumptions appear in his treatment of the kings of Rome in Book 6 (cf. pp. 60–62). Another striking signal comes in the programmatic prologue of the *Aeneid*, where Virgil introduces Juno and her reactions to destiny; there Virgil speaks of the *populus Romanus* as wielding 'royal' power (1.21f.), referring to the Roman republic, which destroyed Carthage: *hinc populum late regem belloque superbum / venturum excidio Libyae.* Juno's bias against Rome is allowed to tinge this account of destiny. But, although slightly paradoxical and malevolent, it remains creditable to Rome; and Virgil later, as is his way, takes up the concept again and purges it of its unpleasant undertone by placing it in modified form in the mouth of Anchises at *Aeneid* 6.851: *tu regere imperio populos, Romane, memento.*[39]

---

[33] Rawson (1975) 154. [34] Rawson (1975) 157. [35] Rawson (1975) 155f.
[36] Rawson (1975) 156. [37] Rawson (1975) 148–50.
[38] Cf. above, p. 5 nn. 12, 13. Grimal (1986) esp. 239ff. (*q.v.*), now makes the vital point that increasing Roman willingness to think in these terms, and to take a more positive view of kingship, is derived in part from 'evolutionary' views of political history.
[39] Cf. R.J. Murray (1964–5) 244f., who also notes as further confirmation *Aen.*

8

As an epic writer Virgil may have drawn some inspiration in this area from the father of Roman epic, Ennius. An examination of Ennius' views of kingship has revealed the same ambivalence found throughout the whole period under discussion.[40] Although conscious of kingship as, on one level, an antithesis to Roman republican government, Ennius is favourable not only towards most of the early kings of Rome but also towards the early royal enemies of Rome. In this he is characteristic of his age; and his influence upon Virgil must certainly be seen in Virgil's treatment of the early kings of Rome and perhaps more broadly. The fact that *pater Ennius*, the Roman Homer, had been interested in and had felt positively about kings must for Virgil have reinforced the epic associations of the theme as well as given a lead to his attitudes.

In Chs. 2 and 3 Virgil's characterisation of his principal actors, Aeneas, Dido and Turnus, will be examined in the light of his interest in kingship; and the hypothesis will be advanced that Virgil was acquainted with the standard works on kingship,[41] in which the virtues of good kings and the vices of bad kings were described, or at the very least that he was abreast of current popular conceptions of the matter, and that in consequence he portrayed these, and some minor characters in the *Aeneid*, in the light of the ancient stereotype of kingship. In these terms Aeneas is the 'good king', with his main actions and motivations flowing from this concept. Similarly Dido begins with the best of intentions and behaviour as a 'good king', but deteriorates and becomes a 'bad king'.[42] Turnus displays fewer of the characteristics of the 'good king' and more of those of the 'bad king'. Among minor characters Mezentius is an out-and-out monster, a tyrant, the very antithesis of the 'good king'.[43] Anchises, Evander and Latinus, in their various ways, are older versions of the 'good king' and Ascanius a younger version. It will be suggested that this approach throws light on some traditional pro-

[40] and points out that the same sentiment appears in Juno's mouth at Hor. *O.* 3.3.37–9, esp. 39: *regnanto. Aen.* 1.206 and 253 offer yet more support.
[40] Cf. Classen (1965) 388–90.
[41] The main surviving (perhaps hellenistic, cf. below, pp. 13f.) texts on kingship have been edited by Delatte (1942) with commentary, and by Thesleff (1965), and Philodemus' work on kingship by Dorandi (1982) with commentary. Fragmentary works, evidence for lost works, and later material are also discussed by, among others, Aalders (1975), Barner (1889), Born (1934), Burkert (1972), Delatte (1942) 137–63, Farber (1979), Fraser (1972) I.485 and nn. 53–9, Goodenough (1928), Höistad (1948), Murray (1965) and (1967), Schubart (1937), Thesleff (1961) and (1972), Walbank (1984), Wallace-Hadrill (1981).
[42] 'King' covers 'queen' also, sex difference having no significance in ancient kingship theory.
[43] On Mezentius, cf. esp. Martin (1978); also Thome (1979); Glenn (1981); Basson (1984); Gotoff (1984).

blems about the character and characterisation of Aeneas and refutes some of the criticisms made of him. The kingship ideals of antiquity also reveal more clearly how Virgil's first readers must have felt about Dido and her love affair with Aeneas; and they are equally useful in clarifying the parallel confrontation between Aeneas and Turnus in the second half of the *Aeneid*. Thus kingship is relevant to some of the central concerns of the epic.[44] The remainder of the present chapter will prepare for Chs. 2 and 3 by analysing the ancient stereotype of the good king and by examining briefly the kingship of the gods in the *Aeneid*.

The concept of the good king had a long history in Greek literature, philosophy and rhetoric. From time to time different strands of it can be related specifically to one tradition. But little is to be gained for the present study from such distinctions, since the three areas were subject to constant mutual influence and Virgil's knowledge of the concept was indebted to all three. It will be argued (pp. 31–8) that Virgil's treatment of Aeneas as the good king may owe something of particular substance to one specific philosophical approach to kingship. But even here there is no question of making a sharp distinction: if Virgil leans to a particular philosophical approach, he does so as an intelligent layman and not as a professional philosopher, so that his penchant does not cut him off from other influences. Hence in what follows evidence from all convergent literary, philosophical and rhetorical sources will be used without distinction to reconstruct the concept of the ancient 'good king'.

There is no doubt that literature took precedence in establishing it. The homeric epics may not initially appear to have kingship as a principal theme, although they contain explicit treatments of it.[45] Ancient readers of Homer, however, who correctly regarded his work as morally educative, clearly did see kingship as one of his chief concerns. The fragments of Philodemus' *On the good king according to Homer* show that homeric comment on kings and kingship was felt to involve a large number of passages, many of which in fact contain only implicit reflections on the subject.[46] In consequence Homer's contribution to the

---

[44] Although neglected by most modern students of Virgil (cf. above, p. 1 n. 1) this did not escape the notice of the renaissance, when the 'perfect prince' was again in vogue. The sixteenth-century Scottish poet, Gavin Douglas, read and translated the *Aeneid* in these terms: cf. Dearing (1952) 853–62.

[45] Delatte (1942) 126f. notes some of the explicit homeric and Hesiodic references. Dvornik (1966) (on which, cf. Murray (1968)) Ch. 4 treats, on a broad front and with bibliography, 'Political Philosophy' from Homer to Isocrates.

[46] Cf. Murray (1965).

tradition was thought to be large. It was supplemented by Hesiod's *Works and Days*, an explicitly paraenetic treatise condemning the injustice of the 'kings'. Homer and Hesiod[47] influenced the praise of leading men in the choric poets, notably Pindar, Simonides and Bacchylides; and Pindar's own contribution, in terms of both material and presentation, also seems to have been substantial.[48] Kings and other important men were not always distinguished sharply in this early period, so that the encomium and paraenesis addressed to both classes may encompass topics which later became specifically kingship topics.

In the fourth century these topics can be seen employed extensively and schematically in prose, although there is little trace of fifth-century predecessors.[49] It is true that the beginnings of formal rhetorical instruction go back to early in the fifth century;[50] but the first preserved full-scale rhetorical idealisations of kingship are Isocrates' prose laudations of Euagoras, Nicocles, Philip of Macedon and others.[51] In the same period Xenophon composed a 'laudation' of Cyrus the Younger in his *Anabasis* (1.9) and his *Agesilaus* is an encomium of that king; his *Hieron* is a more theoretical treatment of kingship.[52] More important for later theory is his *Cyropaedia*, with its idealised portrait of Cyrus the Elder, the founder of his dynasty. This work immediately became a standard treatise on kingship: it not only influenced hellenistic idealisation of kings, but was a textbook of statesmanship for important Romans in the second and first centuries BC (cf. p. 7), well before the rule of a single man became an acceptable permanent system of government for Rome.[53]

Fourth-century rhetorical and historical writings, including those

[47] The political commitment of Archilochus, Sappho and Alcaeus is indubitable: but they were strongly opposed to 'monarchy'.

[48] Cf. Fraustadt (1909) 21–41. Attic tragedy is an unsatisfactory source for contemporary concepts of kingship, since at any point homeric influence may be in play.

[49] Their existence could seem to be implied by the attack on the μούναρχος at Hdt. 3.80f., alᵗhough this would not necessarily mean, as some older commentators thought, that Herodotus was simply borrowing his material directly from a sophistic source, cf. How and Wells (1912) *ad loc*. But this line of argument is tenuous. The same subject matter is handled by fifth-century tragedy, e.g. Eur. *Suppl*. 399–455 and Aesch. *P.V.*, esp. 186ff., in contexts where, naturally, democracy is thought of as a preferable form of government, but cf. above, n. 48.

[50] Cf. Radermacher (1951) 11–35; Kennedy (1963) 58–61.

[51] Cf. Fraustadt (1909) 57–67, 70–3; Walbank (1984) 75f.

[52] On *Anab.* 1.9, cf. Fraustadt (1909) 56f.; on *Ages. id.* 67–70; in general Walbank (1984) 75.

[53] Farber (1979) is valuable on the *Cyropaedia*; but on the ps.-pythagorean texts (for their problems, cf. below, pp. 13f.) he adopts (497 n. 5) the views of Delatte (1942) without reference to later discussions.

now lost,[54] established the full canon of topics. Fourth-century philosophy also contributed: although, as an Athenian, Plato tended to think primarily of the city (πόλις), even in contexts where the ideal form of rule was in question, he demonstrates interest in kingship in a number of works, notably *Republic, Politicus, Laws*, cf. [*Alcibiades Major*].[55] While kingship and aristocracy are not, for him, rigidly separated, many topics of kingship theory are already present in Plato.[56] Aristotle likewise handled kingship, along with many other political and constitutional questions. His Περὶ βασιλείας (*On Kingship*) has not survived; but *Politics* 3 contains a critique of some standard elements of fourth-century kingship theory and there are occasional items elsewhere.[57] Only after the absolute rule of single individuals within large territories had become the norm over the expanded Greek world, i.e. after the death of Alexander, could controversies about the best form of rule be replaced with the assumption that this was kingship; and only then could philosophers turn whole-heartedly to theorising about the virtues of the good king.

Hellenistic discussions of kingship were of course by no means confined to philosophy. Within the relatively small percentage of hellenistic poetry which survives, Theocritus *Idyll* 16 contains lengthy praise of Hieron II of Syracuse which draws on a number of standard kingship topics,[58] while *Idyll* 17 is a full-scale βασιλικὸς λόγος, i.e. a rhetorical-style encomium of king Ptolemy II Soter incorporating a homericising yet thoroughly contemporary view of royalty.[59] There are other less extensive indications of kingship interest in hellenistic poetry;[60] and doubtless, if more hellenistic poetry survived, examples would be multiplied. Again, many documents from the hellenistic world show that the concepts associated with kingship theory were incorporated into royal propaganda and the vocabulary of administration.[61] But kingship does seem greatly to have occupied the attention of hellenistic philosophers, not surprisingly, given the contemporary

---

[54] Cf. Fraustadt (1909) 70–7.
[55] Cf. Delatte (1942) 131–5; Walbank (1984) 75f.
[56] Cf. Goodenough (1928) 66f., 84, 87.
[57] Cf. Delatte (1942) 135f.; Farber (1979) 500f. On ps.-Archytas cf. below, p. 13 and n. 66. On 'Hellenistic Political Philosophy', cf. Dvornik (1966) Ch. 5 (with bibliography), again a discussion on a broad front.
[58] Cf. Meincke (1965) 62–6, 73–8.
[59] Cf. Meincke (1965) 89–140; Cairns (1972) 100–12, 114f., 119f.
[60] E.g. Theocr. *Id.* 14.58–65, 15.22–4, 44–9, 106–11; Call. *Hymn* 1.79–90 (cf. Meincke (1965) 180f., 190–3), 2.26f.; *Aet. Fr.* 110 (Pf.); Lloyd-Jones–Parsons (1983) 254–69.
[61] Cf. Schubart (1937); Fraser (1972) I.485 and n. 58.

political situation. There were peripatetic treatises on kingship, including works by, or ascribed to, Aristotle and Theophrastus, and some of them were associated with the Macedonian or Ptolemaic courts.[62] There were several stoic treatises on kingship, and much stoic theorising about political institutions and the place of kingship in society; in addition a number of important stoics were advisers to kings.[63] Later stoics appear to have regarded kingship as the ideal form of government; but the views of the Old and Middle Stoa are unlikely to have been so clear-cut.[64] The Academy was interested in political theory: Xenocrates, second in succession to Plato as its head, wrote a work on kingship in four books addressed to Alexander the Great;[65] and there was also cynic theorising about kingship (cf. pp. 33–6).

But, strangely enough, it is the neo-pythagorean movement which can claim to have transmitted the most striking philosophical texts about kingship, if their dating to the hellenistic period could be substantiated. One fragment bearing on the topic and attributed to Archytas is certainly hellenistic.[66] But there are acute dating problems with the three principal neo-pythagorean writers on kingship, 'Diotogenes', 'Ekphantus' and 'Sthenidas'. The last fifty years have seen them attributed both to the first or more probably the second century AD[67] and to the third century BC.[68] More recently the position has become even more confused.[69] Fortunately however the dating problems may

---

[62] Goodenough (1928) 57–9, 91f.; Aalders (1975) 5–12; Fraser (1972) I.484ff. and nn. 50, 56, who suggests that the Macedonian court was more significant as a centre than the Ptolemaic court (I.485 n. 53); Walbank (1984) 76f. Recently Grimal (1986) (*q.v.*) has valuably resurveyed the whole question of hellenistic philosophical interest in kingship.

[63] Cf. Aalders (1975) 76–8, 88–91; Reesor (1951) 13–20; Henrichs (1984) 146f.; Walbank (1984) 77; Grimal (1986) 246–50.

[64] Cf. Aalders (1975) 75–93, 97–112; Barker (1956) 204–9; Brunt (1975) esp. 18f.; Raimar Müller (1984) esp. 309–11.

[65] Cf. Aalders (1975) 11f.

[66] Thesleff (1965) p. 36.1–10. The word used is ἄρχων (ruler) not βασιλεύς; but the terminology is the standard hellenistic one for royalty, although ps.-Archytas normally treats the πόλις (city), cf. Aalders (1975) 28f.

[67] By Delatte (1942), whose conclusions (contrary to those of Goodenough (1928) for whom they were early third-century BC texts) were based on studies of their dialect (59–87), vocabulary (88–109), syntactical and stylistic traits (110–19) and (in the commentary) conceptual basis.

[68] By Thesleff (1961), who surveyed the history of scholarship in this area and argued against the late dating of the texts by Delatte (1942).

[69] Fraser (1972) II.701f. n. 55 regards the objections of Thesleff (1961) to Delatte (1942) as not seriously weakening them; cf. also Wallace-Hadrill (1982) 34; Walbank (1984) 78–81. A later dating (late second or early third century AD) was again proposed by Burkert (1972). Thesleff (1972) was prepared, in response to Burkert's arguments, to admit the probability of a date in the latter part of the second century BC for 'Sthenidas' and 'Diotogenes', but preferred to retain an early hellenistic date for 'Ekphantus'. The

13

not be particularly significant for the present enquiry; for whether some or all of these texts are hellenistic or not, the many connections between their content and other evidence for hellenistic views of kingship gives good ground for thinking that in general they reflect the latter, although particular emphases may belong to a later date.[70] In any case these texts exist through an accident of survival and they do not show that their neo-pythagorean authors were more concerned with kingship than the hellenistic or post-hellenistic political theorists of most other philosophical schools.

It might have been expected that the epicureans, who were professedly political quietists, would be a prominent exception to hellenistic philosophical interest in kingship; and indeed Epicurus in his Περὶ βασιλείας prohibited his followers from consorting with kings.[71] But the work in itself shows his interest in the topic, and elsewhere he offered at least some advice to kings; and there is further evidence that overall epicurean practice was out of step with precept, and that various early epicureans were fairly close to rulers.[72] Only in the first century BC however, in the work of Philodemus, do we have an epicurean treatise on kingship intimately linked with contemporary politics.[73] The minor schools, the cyrenaics, megarians and sceptics, show a low level of interest in political theory.[74] But it must be emphasised that these

discussion in *Pseudepigrapha* I (1972) 88–102, which followed these two papers, reveals continued divided opinion; and in any case its subject was all the pseudo-pythagorean texts and not just the kingship treatises. Another tendency has been to connect the pseudo-pythagorean texts as a group with Eudorus of Alexandria (on whom cf. Dillon (1977) 115–35 and, in a general pythagorean context, Schneider (1967–9) II.615–22 esp. 620). Prof. Thesleff writes to me in a private letter (2 March 1985): 'I am now even more convinced than I was before that the ideas reflected in the texts (including some of the alleged Peripatetic and Stoic details) derive essentially from the Early Academy.' I am grateful to him for his additional advice on these matters.

[70] Cf. Goodenough (1928); Thesleff (1961); 'the contents could, on the whole, be fitted into a hellenistic context' (Thesleff (1972) 59); Dvornik (1966) I.245–61; Chesnut (1978), an otherwise useful summary, may have been written before 1972, since it makes no reference to Thesleff (1972) and Burkert (1972).

[71] Cf. Plut. *Mor.* 1127A; Diog. Laert. 10.28 for Epicurus' work of kingship; also Aalders (1975) 39–45.

[72] Cf. Plut *Mor.* 1095A for Epicurus' advice to kings; on the overall epicurean situation Grimal (1986) 260–6 (also 279: contribution of O. Gigon to the subsequent discussion).

[73] Grimal (1966) argued the view that Philodemus' tract dates from the mid-forties BC and is a pro-Caesarian allegory, in which the homeric heroes stand for various contemporaries. In general however an earlier date has been favoured: Murray (1965) 177–82 suggested 59 BC; more recently Dorandi (1982) 39–47 esp. 44–6 would tentatively place it in the late seventies BC. On Philodemus again, cf. most recently Grimal (1986) 265–73, with further valuable reflections on the influence of epicureanism in the Augustan period.

[74] Aalders (1975) 50–3.

schools were the exceptions. The general picture for the hellenistic period is of a proliferation of books about kingship, written from all viewpoints, including philosophical ones, but on the whole converging in their conclusions; only in this context can Plutarch's anecdote about Demetrius of Phaleron's advice to Ptolemy Soter be meaningful even as an anecdote:[75]

Δημήτριος ὁ Φαληρεὺς Πτολεμαίῳ τῷ βασιλεῖ παρῄνει τὰ περὶ βασιλείας καὶ ἡγεμονίας βιβλία κτᾶσθαι καὶ ἀναγινώσκειν. "ἃ γὰρ οἱ φίλοι τοῖς βασιλεῦσιν οὐ θαρροῦσι παραινεῖν, ταῦτα ἐν τοῖς βιβλίοις γέγραπται."

(Demetrius of Phaleron advised king Ptolemy to get and read the books on kingship and leadership, saying: 'The things royal ministers do not dare tell kings are written in those books'.)

Similarly many diverse hellenistic treatises on kingship and many portrayals of political and social customs in works of history must lie behind ps.-Aristeas' *Letter to Philocrates* (c. 100 BC), with its Judaeo-Hellenic cultural synthesis.[76]

The first century BC saw not only the Greek treatise of Philodemus written for a Roman audience, but also Latin political theory. Both reflect that interest which had begun in the second century BC and had expressed itself in the study by Roman statesmen of Greek text books on kingship. The most significant Latin contributions were made by Cicero in his *De Republica, De Legibus* and *De Officiis*.[77] These works reflect various philosophical influences, mainly Platonism and the Middle Stoa, and also Cicero's practical experience of a lifetime in Roman politics. It is small wonder then that no cut-and-dried internally consistent summary can be offered of Cicero's views on political questions and that the works are typical of his age in their diversity and self-contradictions. But some points are clear: Rome in Cicero's day was not a monarchy; his interests therefore were closer to those of fourth-century BC Athens, and hence the *polis*-based approaches of Plato, and to a lesser extent Aristotle, were the main ultimate theoretical influences. This led Cicero to settle on the whole for the 'mixed constitution' as the ideal, although neither he nor any other Roman had ever experienced it in reality. Cicero however knew the hellenistic

[75] Plut. *Mor.* 189D; cf. Aalders (1975) 5f., 11f.; Fraser (1972) I.485 and n. 54.
[76] On Aristeas, cf. Murray (1967); (1975); (1987); Speyer (1971) 163; Mendels (1979); on Hecataeus of Abdera and kingship, cf. Murray (1970).
[77] Cf. Barker (1956) 185–204. Dvornik (1966) Ch. 8 (with bibliography) offers a wide-ranging discussion of the impact of hellenistic ideas of rulership upon the Roman world.

world; and his preference for the 'mixed constitution' is combined with a strong interest in leadership and an attitude towards kingship which is not hostile. But naturally, when he thinks of leadership, his main emphasis is not on kings and their virtues but on the leading men of the Roman state and on the virtues desirable in them as a group, an emphasis consistent with Cicero's ideal of a 'mixed constitution', given that such a regime must be guided by virtuous *principes*.

But again, since the virtues of leading men were identical with those of kings, Virgil's generation could easily have found in Cicero's political works material to supplement and reinforce what they had learnt from hellenistic texts and contemporary thought about the rule of a single *princeps*, the king. However Virgil did choose to call Aeneas and other prominent characters *rex* or *regina* rather than use a near-synonym. So his and his generation's interest in kingship must have been rooted in Greek political theory, as well as in Cicero's romanised versions of it. Virgil and his audience must therefore have faced up to kingship as an institution inherently different from their own republican constitution and must have come to terms with it, rather than simply drawing on late republican adaptations of kingship theory to Roman society.[78]

The establishment of the Roman empire led to more Greek treatises on kingship and, in addition, Latin ones, since both philosophers and rhetoricians now had the incentive to blend earlier ideas about royal rule with the new facts of power in the Graeco-Roman world. These writings of the imperial period, although later than Virgil, frequently confirm and round out the picture built upon the pre-Virgilian evidence. They are therefore worth brief discussion before the standard concepts found in many ancient texts about kingship are listed.

The earliest post-Virgilian writer with interesting ideas about kingship is Philo Judaeus,[79] a product of the same hellenistic Jewish background as the author of the earlier *Letter to Philocrates*. Then, on the Latin side, Seneca the Younger provides ample evidence of mid-first-century AD attitudes to power in the later Julio-Claudian empire. Seneca's testimony might be expected to have particular value because of his practical experience as one of Nero's ministers. There is some such influence; but to a great extent Seneca's material and emphases in his principal political work, the *De Clementia*, are philosophical and show

---

[78] The Περὶ βασιλέων of that troubled contemporary of Virgil, Timagenes, may also have contributed: cf. Gigante (1984) 287.

[79] Cf. Barner (1889) 11f.; Goodenough (1938) Ch. 5.

heavy dependence on the hellenistic treatises on kingship.[80] After Seneca Latin political theory surfaces most frequently in the practical oratory of the *Panegyrici Latini*, with the Younger Pliny as an early and influential exponent of the genre.[81] On the Greek side Dio Chrysostom (mid-first century AD on) provides copious documentation of kingship theory.[82] In Dio rhetorical and philosophical standpoints blend or appear indifferently. In the same period Plutarch is more philosophical in his approach, while Aelius Aristides (second century AD) offers a more rhetorical standpoint.[83] During the fourth-century revival of learning Themistius, Libanius and the emperor Julian all took up and developed older ideas on kingship at some length.[84] With Libanius the impetus is mainly rhetorical, while Themistius, and to a lesser extent Julian, unite philosophical and rhetorical influences. Imperial iconography became in the second and succeeding centuries increasingly important as an expression of imperial ideology, so that the theory of kingship found its most potent encapsulation in the ritual of *adventus* and in court ceremonies, with their rhetorical and poetic concomitants.[85] Kingship of course remained a popular topic for twelve hundred years or more after the fall of the western empire; and there are many texts from later antiquity, the Carolingian period, the middle ages and the renaissance which bear on the subject.[86] The ideals of kingship which originated in antiquity continued in fact to play a real part in the political life of Europe up to the nineteenth century; but in many essentials they were already established by the hellenistic period; and they can be documented perfectly adequately from material earlier than 400 AD. Hence later sources are ignored for the purpose of this study.

From the different traditions then, philosophical, literary and rhetorical, up to the fourth century AD, a composite picture of the hellenistic 'good king' can be drawn. The 'good king' is a stereotype;

---

[80] Cf. Adam (1970); M.T. Griffin (1976) skilfully links *De Clementia* with the circumstances of composition and with Roman imperial ideology (133–71). But the influence of the hellenistic kingship treatises also emerges clearly (143–8). Senecan drama, like its Attic predecessors, is not an easy source for contemporary views of kingship.

[81] Cf. Born (1934) and Seager (1984) for surveys of the conventional although flexible ideological content of the panegyrists.

[82] Barner (1889) 12–24.

[83] Barner (1889) 25–30.

[84] Barner (1889) 30–46; Dvornik (1966) Chs. 10 and 11 (with bibliography) surveys monarchic thought from this period up to Justinian.

[85] Cf. esp. MacCormack (1976); (1981); Godman (1987).

[86] MacCormack (1981) has a valuable bibliography containing many items relevant to the late Latin and early Byzantine period; Kleinschmidt (1974) has an excellent medieval bibliography. For the renaissance, cf. the bibliography of Gilbert (1938).

and to modern eyes he might appear wooden and uninspiring.[87] But the moral concerns of the ancient world revolved very much around stereotypes rather than precepts;[88] and this is what gave models like the 'good king' such wide currency and influence. The principles in accordance with which the elements of the stereotype have been assembled are these:

(1) The list is not intended to be complete. A few, but only a few, elements, e.g. 'the king avoids immoderate laughter and buffoonery'[89] or 'the king is not susceptible to flattery',[90] seldom exemplified and irrelevant to the *Aeneid*, are omitted. One very significant and relevant element, the king's function as promoter of concord among his people, is given little prominence here because it will be dealt with fully in Ch. 4.

(2) The list is not ordered logically nor are its categories necessarily mutually exclusive. The king's generosity, for example, could easily be seen as part of his role as the benefactor of his people; but the two concepts are recorded separately since they often crop up in isolation. This procedure is in part practical and in part a recognition that there are genuine differences between Greek and Roman ways of thinking about the cardinal and other virtues and also that there were disagreements, both Greek and Roman, about the headings under which a particular minor virtue might fall.[91]

(3) A single item in the list may embrace two genuinely different concepts: e.g. K5 vii covers both 'the king is law-abiding' and 'the king is law embodied'. But they are conjoined since the main point is the relationship between the king and the law.

(4) Later writers, and sometimes earlier ones, may subdivide and amplify single elements, e.g. the king's self-control may be specified as operating in the spheres of food and drink, or sex, or anger etc.

[87] It is interesting to compare part of the influential (although no longer acceptable) assessment of Aeneas by T.E. Page (1894–1900) I/II.xviif. (which draws on earlier judgements): 'Moreover, Virgil is unhappy in his hero. Compared with Achilles his Aeneas is but the shadow of a man. He is an abstraction typifying the ideal Roman, ...'.

[88] The *locus classicus* is Hor. *Sat.* 1.4.105–31. On the Roman tradition of *exempla*, cf. Litchfield (1914).

[89] Cf. Barner (1889) 13, 39; Murray (1965) 167.

[90] Cf. e.g Pliny *Paneg.* 41. The notion is of course linked with the concept that the king has good advisers and ministers, i.e. K9.

[91] Wallace-Hadrill (1981) is most informative on questions of both classification and development in this area, and reveals the pitfalls into which any list of this type must fall. Reference has not been made to it in the list (pp. 19–21) since the material is distributed over the whole paper.

Attention is not paid to such subdivisions here, although they may be referred to separately in connection with the *Aeneid*.

(5) As the imperial period advanced, the good king stereotype modified itself to fit what had become the only possible political system for the whole Roman world. Inevitably the ideal of the 'good emperor' came to have a different flavour and substance from that of the hellenistic 'good king'. But even so, the principal elements of the late imperial stereotype remain the principal hellenistic ones; at the beginning of the empire this continuity was even more in evidence and it is to this that the list directs attention.

(6) The elements are documented from some of the modern secondary works on ancient kingship so as to avoid lengthy and repetitious primary documentation, which in any case could be useful only if analysed fully. They are:[92] Aalders (1975); Barner (1889); Bieler (1935); Born (1934); Farber (1979); Goodenough (1928); Murray (1965); Murray (1967); Schubart (1937); Walbank (1984). Where there is no ambivalence, the date is omitted.

The elements of the good king stereotype, with references in alphabetic order, are as follows. The good king is:

K1 pre-eminent in virtue: Aalders 35f.; Barner 10; Born 22; Farber 499–501; Goodenough 57; Schubart 5

K2 a model for imitation in virtue: Barner 18, 22, 29f.; Born 22; Goodenough 57, 88f., 92

K3 the imitator of god to reach virtue: Aalders 26, 32, 34; Barner 15, 22, 31, 42, 49; Goodenough 68, 73f.; Murray (1967) 353, 355, 357, 360

K4 possessor of the four cardinal virtues:

i justice, δικαιοσύνη, *justitia*: Born 26; Farber 502–5; Goodenough 65–7, 86; Murray (1967) 353, 355; Schubart 6f.

ii self-control and abstinence from pleasure, σωφροσύνη: Barner 10, 12, 14–16, 19f., 28–33, 37, 39, 42, 49; Born 22f.; Goodenough 69f., 87–9, 95; Murray (1967) 356; Schubart 6

iii wisdom, φρόνησις, *sapientia*: Goodenough 62, 67, 73–5, 94

iv warlike ability and courage, ἀνδρεία, *fortitudo*: Barner 16f.; Born

---

[92] Kloft (1979) collects some of these, and includes other useful papers. Its full bibliography is also helpful. Nauhardt (1940) contains some relevant material, but is so ordered as to make citation difficult. Fears (1981) esp. 875–924 sketches the history of the cult of imperial virtues, while Fears (1977) has much, mainly imperial, material slanted (naturally) towards the concept of divine election. Philodemus' contributions are here mainly referred to in their treatment by Murray (1965), since for the most part its hypotheses are accepted in the broader-ranging discussion of Dorandi (1982).

22f.; Goodenough 66, 70; Murray (1965) 168f.; Murray (1967) 354f.; Schubart 5; Walbank 66, 82f.[93]

K5 possessor of other virtues:

i piety, εὐσέβεια, *pietas*: Barner 16, 18f., 28f., 31, 34f., 37, 42, 49; Farber 501f.; Goodenough 66; Murray (1967) 357; Schubart 4–6

ii mercy, mildness, gentleness, pity, κατοίκτισις, ἐπιείκεια, ἡμερότης, πραότης: Barner 38; Born 22f.; Farber 509f.; Murray (1965) 168, 176f.; Murray (1967) 355f.; Schubart 5, 8, 10–13

iii kindness, φιλανθρωπία, εὐεργεσία, εὔνοια (and thus 'the source of benefits to his people'): Aalders 23; Barner 9, 17f., 29, 31, 34f.; Born 22, 27; Farber 509, 511–13; Murray (1967) 353f.; Schubart 10f., 14–17; Walbank 83[94] – cf. also K5 v

iv hard work, σπουδὴ καὶ προθυμία, πόνος, *labor*: Barner 20, 27, 37, 42, 49; Born 23; Farber 505f.; Murray (1967) 357

v generosity, especially towards his friends: Barner 24, 26, 33; Born 23f.; Farber 512; Murray (1967) 354; Schubart 5 – cf. also K5 iii

vi foresight, πρόνοια, *providentia*: Farber 506f.; Murray (1967) 353, 356; Schubart 8

vii observance of the law and being the living embodiment of the law and supreme lawgiver: Aalders 15, 27; Barner 23, 26, 34, 38; Born 22; Farber 502–5; Goodenough 57–73; 94; Murray (1967) 356 (cf. also Murray (1986) 676f. for reservations about the views of Dvornik (1966) on this topic); Schubart 7f.

viii care for his people, μέριμνα, φροντίς, ἐπιμέλεια, *cura*: Barner 27; Farber 507; Schubart 8, 18f. (sleeplessness of subordinates)

K6 because of his care etc. for his people:

i their father: Aalders 23; Barner 8f., 12f., 29, 31, 37, 42, 49; Born 22; Farber 506f., 511; Goodenough 84

ii their shepherd: Aalders 14, 23–5; Barner 12–14, 31–3; Goodenough 67, 84f.; doctor, steersman, 'leader of the flock': Barner 9, 12f., 28f., 31–3, 37, 42

---

[93] The claim of Aalders (1975) 22 that in hellenistic political theory extensive attention is not 'paid to the duties and required qualities of the king in war-time' is probably to be discounted in view of the prominent treatment of the topic at Theocr. *Id.* 17.90–4, 98–103 (in a highly rhetorical βασιλικὸς λόγος, cf. above, p. 12), and its reappearance in the late rhetorical prescription for that genre (Menander Rhetor ed. Spengel III.373.8 – 374.25). Cf. also Walbank (1984) 82, 66 (on 'spear-won territory'), and, for emphasis on military leadership, Goodenough (1928) 66. Murray (1965) 168 notes that courage could be demonstrated in hunting, and Horsfall (1971) 1110f. perceives that hunting involves not only courage but also hard work (K5 iv) and sleeplessness (K5 viii); cf. also for later imperial material on hunting Aymard (1951) 492–502, 523–58 and, on the inspiration of Xenophon, 470f.

[94] On cynic concepts in this area, cf. esp. Moles (1983) 108 n. 38, 112–15.

iii their saviour, σωτήρ, *salus populi*: Aalders 26; Farber 510f.; Goodenough 67; Schubart 13f.

iv a lover of his city and its people, i.e. feeling ἔρως τῆς πατρίδος, *amor patriae*: Barner 10, 25, 29; Schubart 12

v possessor of the love of his people as his best bodyguard and as the surest foundation of his kingdom: Aalders 33; Barner 20f., 33, 42; Born 22f., 27; Farber 506, 508; Murray (1967) 353, 359

K7 a lover of peace and harmony, ὁμόνοια, *concordia*: Barner 16f.; Murray (1965) 169; Murray (1967) 353, 355; Walbank 82

K8 of good appearance: Bieler 49–56; Born 22; Goodenough 72; Murray (1965) 171f.

K9 endowed with good advisers and ministers–officials: Barner 17, 23f.; Born 22, 29; Farber 500f.; Murray (1967) 358; Schubart 19–26

K10 seeing and hearing everything, often through his agents: Barner 11f., 24, 27, 39

K11 ensuring that the citizens go about their several tasks: Barner 10f.; Born 23

K12 deriving his kingship from Zeus–Jupiter: Barner 35, 38; Goodenough *passim*.

This chapter began by drawing attention to divine 'kingship' in the *Aeneid* and by noting that among the gods Jupiter is most prominently *rex*. The association of divinity with royalty, and Jupiter's status as king of the gods and the universe in particular, in part explain, and also enhance, the significance of human kingship in the epic. In one set of terms king Aeneas and king Jupiter were for Virgil equivalents on earth and in heaven in times past, just as in his lyrics Horace could portray Augustus as Jupiter's contemporary terrestrial regent and viceroy:[95]

> gentis humanae pater atque custos,
> orte Saturno, tibi cura magni   50
> Caesaris fatis data: tu secundo
> Caesare regnes. (*Odes* 1.12.49–52)

The origins and meaning of such equivalences lie in hellenistic philosophy; and as kingship itself interested many hellenistic schools, so

[95] Cf. Nisbet–Hubbard (1970) *ad loc.*; Hor. *O.* 3.1.5f., 3.5.1f.; Pietrusiński (1980); Grimal (1986) 243, 249f. The deification of kings and other important individuals in the hellenistic world and of emperors and members of the imperial family later, together with the philosophical justifications of this activity and its literary manifestations, constitutes a large subject which constantly impinges on kingship. For the interaction, cf. e.g. Dvornik (1966) *passim*. The subject has however for the most part been excluded from consideration here for reasons of space.

the human king's equivalence with Zeus was widespread. The most dramatic picture is offered by the neo-pythagorean kingship texts, which may of course be later.[96] But in this area the value of these texts as testimony, at least in their essentials, to earlier thought is confirmed by the analogous views found in hellenistic stoics (cf. p. 24).

'Diotogenes', in a long discussion of the king's role as the embodiment and administrator of justice and law, makes a direct comparison between the king and 'God':[97]

> καὶ μὰν τό τε δικασπολὲν καὶ διανέμεν τὸ δίκαιον, ξυνᾷ μὲν καθόλου ἰδίᾳ δὲ καθ᾽ ἕκαστον, οἰκῆον βασιλέως ὥσπερ θεῶ ἐν τῷ κόσμῳ <ᾦ> ἀγεμών τε καὶ προστάτας ἐντί, ... (Thesleff 72.9–11)
>
> In judging and in distributing justice, whether as a whole in Public Law, or to individuals in Private Law, it is right for the king to act as does God in his leadership and command of the universe (Goodenough 67)

Next 'Diotogenes' introduces a concept often linked with the king–'God' comparison, ἁρμονία (concord). The king is to bring his kingdom, both as a whole and in its parts, into a 'harmony' (Thesleff 72.11–14). The 'God'–king association is reintroduced by 'Diotogenes' when he deals with the king's piety: the worship of the gods is a fitting duty for the king: 'For the Best must be honoured by the best man, and the Governing Principle by one who is a governor' (Thesleff 72.16–18; Goodenough 68). This is explained as follows:

> τῶν μὲν οὖν φύσει τιμιωτάτων ἄριστον ὁ θεός, τῶν δὲ περὶ γᾶν καὶ τὼς ἀνθρώπως ὁ βασιλεύς. ἔχει δὲ καὶ ὡς θεὸς ποτὶ κόσμον βασιλεὺς ποτὶ πόλιν· καὶ ὡς πόλις ποτὶ κόσμον βασιλεὺς ποτὶ θεόν. (Thesleff 72.18–20)
>
> So just as God is the Best of those things which are most honorable by nature, likewise the king is best in the earthly and human realm. Now the king bears the same relation to the state as God to the world; and the state is in the same ratio to the world as the king is to God. (Goodenough 68)

'Diotogenes' then reintroduces 'harmony' to explain the connection further:

> ἁ μὲν γὰρ πόλις ἐκ πολλῶν καὶ διαφερόντων συναρμοσθεῖσα

---

[96] These works are quoted in the text of Thesleff (1965). I have used the translations of Goodenough (1928), omitting the occasional Greek word which he included for emphasis.
[97] Cf. Aalders (1975) 25f., 32f.

22

κόσμου σύνταξιν καὶ ἁρμονίαν μεμίμαται, ὁ δὲ βασιλεὺς ἀρχὰν
ἔχων ἀνυπεύθυνον, καὶ αὐτὸς ὢν νόμος ἔμψυχος, θεὸς ἐν
ἀνθρώποις παρεσχαμάτισται. (Thesleff 72.21-3)

For the state, made as it is by a harmonizing together of many
different elements, is an imitation of the order and harmony of the
world, while the king who has an absolute rulership, and is himself
Animate Law, has been metamorphosed into a deity among men.
(Goodenough 68)

Other passages of 'Diotogenes' linking the king and 'God' are Thesleff
73.15-19, again in the context of 'harmony', and Thesleff 75.8-16,
where the attributes of 'the gods and especially Zeus' are set out and
royalty is seen as an imitation of divinity.

The divine–human link is also found in 'Sthenidas', who views some
other standard elements of the good king stereotype, i.e. 'the king is the
imitator of god to reach virtue' and 'the king is the lawgiver', as part of
an overall parallelism between the king on earth and 'God' in heaven:

οὗτος γὰρ καὶ φύσει ἐστὶ καὶ πρᾶτος βασιλεύς τε καὶ δυνάστας, ὁ
δὲ γενέσει καὶ μιμάσει. καὶ ὁ μὲν ἐν τῷ παντὶ καὶ ὅλῳ, ὁ δὲ ἐπὶ γᾶς,
καὶ ὁ μὲν ἀεὶ τὰ πάντα διοικεῖ τε καὶ ζώει αὐτὸς ἐν αὐτῷ
κεκταμένος τὰν σοφίαν, ὁ δ᾽ ἐν χρόνῳ ἐπιστάμαν. (Thesleff
187.11 – 188.2)

For God is the first king and ruler by nature, while the other is so
only by birth and imitation. The one rules in the entire universe, the
other upon earth; and the one lives and rules all things forever and
possesses wisdom in himself, the other is temporal and has only
understanding. (Goodenough 74)

'Ekphantus' expresses the most striking ideas about the divinity of
kingship. He sees the question in vast cosmic terms: every living thing
should be in harmony with the whole universe; man is the highest form
of earthly life and the king is the most divine among men; in making the
king, 'God' used himself as an 'archetype'. The earthly ruler and the
ruler of the universe have a 'communion' (Thesleff 81.13). As for the
'harmony' (φιλία) of the political unit, this is an imitation of the
'concord' of the universe; and the king's rule is necessary to produce this
ideal condition (Thesleff 81.21 – 82.3). In another fragment of 'Ekphantus' the importance of the king's 'sacred and divine mentality', the
role of God as the φρόνησις (mind) of the universe and the vital
function of the king's φρόνησις in allowing him to possess other virtues
are emphasised (Thesleff 84.4–8); and in yet another he discusses at

23

length the king's imitation of 'God' (Thesleff 82.17–83.17). No summary of the views of 'Ekphantus' can do justice to the tone of the fairly extensive surviving passages. It is clear that he was putting forcefully a view of the nature of kingship which was typical of his school but which he chose to work out more fully than his fellow neo-pythagoreans.

If even the basic ideas of these texts can be deemed hellenistic, they offer a valuable corrective to assessments of the encomiastic literature, and of the royal and imperial titulature of the hellenistic and Roman periods, as insincere or sycophantic; and they are the clearest pointers to the cosmic background to kingship theory as a factor which led Virgil to be so concerned about divine kingship, especially that of Jupiter, as an essential correlative to his interest in human kingship in the *Aeneid*.[98] That these texts' underlying concepts are indeed hellenistic seems confirmed by the fact that they can be seen in embryo in academic and peripatetic discussion of kingship.[99] The stoics too may have arrived, as early as the hellenistic period, at an elevated view of the 'God'–king relationship. Later stoics certainly did relate 'God' and the king clearly as analogues,[100] and there is some probability that earlier stoics did likewise: it has been pointed out[101] that the terminology used by Cleanthes to describe 'the work of God in governing the universe' is the standard language used from the fourth century BC on to describe the work and virtues of the monarch. Moreover Cleanthes' concern in his *Hymn to Zeus*[102] with the role of Zeus as 'harmoniser' and creator of order in the universe resembles the neo-pythagorean interest in this topic in association with the 'God'–king identification (cf. esp. line 10). Chrysippus' descriptions of Zeus as 'the common nature of all things, fate, necessity, orderliness, justice, concord and peace' and of the gods as benefactors and lovers of the human race again show that early stoic accounts of 'God' drew on standard elements of kingship theory; there are also further confirmatory touches in his work.[103]

Early stoic kingship theory was thus probably not inconsistent with

[98] On Virgil's cosmic interests see now Hardie (1986) and (1986a). The present chapter was completed before the appearance of these learned and stimulating works; it should be read against them, although detailed cross-reference is not practical here.

[99] Cf. Goodenough (1928) 74–7.

[100] Cf. Aalders (1975) 26f., 89f.; Henrichs (1984) – for such associations in general from the fourth century BC onwards. The 'God'–king link is of course very old in Graeco-Roman culture, cf. Mondi (1980); Nisbet–Hubbard (1970) on *O*. 1.12.50.

[101] Reesor (1951) 18f.; Aalders (1975) 89–93.

[102] Cf. Arnim (1903–24) I *Fr*. 537 (pp. 121–3); Powell (1925) *Fr*. 1 (pp. 227–9).

[103] Cf. Reesor (1951) 18f.

the views later expressed by the neo-pythagoreans; and some scholars have gone further, arguing that similar concepts were also current among pre-stoic cynics. This latter view is based on passages of Dio Chrysostom's *Orationes* (late first – early second century AD), which do indeed associate Zeus and the king in as elevated a fashion as the neo-pythagorean texts and which are claimed to be cynic in origin. But these claims are highly controversial;[104] and it is safer to see Dio as confirming hellenistic stoic interest in cosmic approaches to the 'God'–king relationship, which may, but need not, also be indicative of hellenistic cynic attitudes, in so far as the distinction can be made. Evidence of stoic interest in the 'God'–king link is of course valuable for the *Aeneid*: for although, as will be argued later (pp. 31–8, 78–84), Virgil is 'eclectic' in his philosophical borrowings, an essentially stoic 'Fate' has been shown to play an important role in the epic, interacting radically with Jupiter and with its hero.[105] In general then the links made by several hellenistic philosophical schools between king and 'God' mean that kingship belongs not only to the political side of the *Aeneid* but also to its philosophical and religious dimensions.

As has often been observed, the Jupiter of the *Aeneid* is, because of intervening hellenistic developments, close to being a monotheistic 'God' and far away from Homer's Zeus. The distribution of references to Jupiter's kingship is significant in this respect: they are missing from Books 5, 8, 9 and 11 and most concentrated in Book 10, with five examples. Thus, although some do simply have local significance only, the position of many relates to Jupiter's role as the cosmic promoter of reconciliation, peace and concord, a power united in will and purpose with fate. Of the two in Book 1, Juno's reminder to Aeolus that *divum pater atque hominum rex* has appointed him controller of the winds (65) is a persuasive *suggestio falsi* (for Jupiter would not approve of her request) and it is yet another implicit comment (cf. p. 27) on Aeolus' failure to control his subjects. Balancing it is 229ff., where Venus reminds Jupiter of his cosmic rule and relationship with destiny. Book 2 contrasts two exercises of Jupiter's power of deciding the destiny of two individuals, Anchises (648f.) and Creusa (778f.). Both show Jupiter as directing the fate of significant characters at significant points. At 4.268f. this is seen again: when Jupiter sends Mercury to intervene directly and to command Aeneas to leave Carthage, the god reinforces

---

[104] Cf. Höistad (1948) 89, 190–4.
[105] Cf. esp. Otis (1963) General Index *s.v.* Fate (*fatum*); on the relationship of fate and 'compulsion' to kingship, cf. Goodenough (1928) 90.

his message by referring to Jupiter and to his role as ruler of the universe.

The Giants' attack on Jupiter's kingdom at 6.582–4 probably has more to do with contemporary political allegory than with the plot of the *Aeneid*,[106] especially since Book 6 is more concerned with the royal status of Dis, the Jupiter of the Underworld. But Juno's dismissal of Allecto, after her work is done, with the comment that her further presence on earth would not please *summi regnator Olympi* (7.557–9) is an admission that their joint activities breach the order of things. Book 10, with its five examples, portrays Jupiter in his role as cosmic ruler and reconciler at its beginning (2). Although he later professes neutrality as between the Trojans and the Italians (*rex Iuppiter omnibus idem. / fata viam invenient*, 112f.), the setting and atmosphere of the opening council of the gods and the consciousness of future history which attends it anticipate the final solution of the conflict in Book 12. This is why the kingship of Jupiter accompanies two interventions by him in Book 10 over important individuals (437, 621), in both of which contexts the role of the *fata* is directly or obliquely stressed (438, 624); and this is why Jupiter's kingship appears even in the mouth of the *contemptor deum* Mezentius (743). The last example in the *Aeneid* again involves intervention by Jupiter, this time to end Juturna's aid to Turnus (12.849). Interestingly Virgil abstains from exploiting kingship verbally during the ultimate divine reconciliation of Book 12. Instead, and to stress the genuineness of the reconciliation, he exploits the familial aspects of the renewed concord between his royal protagonists, Jupiter and Juno (cf. pp. 104f.).

The kingship of other gods in the *Aeneid* is not unimportant; but its importance is limited. Whereas Jupiter's kingship is universal and monarchical in a true sense, that of the rest is local and subordinate. Such emphasis as is placed on other gods' kingship reflects in part the *Aeneid*'s homeric background, and in part its overall desire to give prominence to kingship. A brief summary will suffice. Of the other gods, Juno is naturally referred to most frequently in this role after Jupiter;[107] and her progression as a 'king' reverses that of her protégée, Dido. While Dido, as will be seen, deteriorates as a monarch, Juno improves as such, lays aside her *ira*, which is the principal divine

---

[106] Cf. Nisbet–Hubbard (1978) 189–92; Hardie (1983) and (1986) Chs. 3, 4.

[107] *regina deum* etc.: 1.9, 1.46, 7.620; *o regina*: 1.76; *regia Iuno*: 1.443, 4.114, 7.438, 10.62; others: 4.102, 7.560.

obstacle to the fulfilment of the will of Jupiter and Fate, and so is ultimately reconciled with Jupiter and takes her place as Juno Regina in the highest ranks of the Roman pantheon. This formulation can stand despite the facts of future history, when Juno will be ranged against Rome in the Punic wars. Recent scholarship has rightly insisted that nevertheless the reconciliation in the *Aeneid* is in essence genuine.[108] In contrast to Juno's progress, the *furor*, i.e. the excessive amorous passion of Dido, which like *ira* breaches the royal virtue of self-control (σωφροσύνη) (cf. Ch. 2), brings Dido to destruction.

Aeolus is described in Book 1 as a *rex* established by Jupiter to control and harmonise his subjects, the winds (1.52–63). Aeolus is then deceived by Juno into allowing the great storm of Book 1 to arise; his words at 1.78f., *tu sceptra Iovemque / concilias*, show his belief that his own superior, Jupiter, approves of Juno's request (cf. 65f.). In this sense his kingship is not vitiated, even though the simile at 1.148–53 (cf. pp. 93–5), which equates the storm with discord, is, on another level, an oblique comment on Aeolus' failure to preserve a king's concord among his subjects.[109] Again 'king' Dis and his kingdom are mentioned a number of times in Book 6 and once at 8.244. The examples in Book 6 (106, 154, 252, 269, 396, 417) mark significant points in the progress of the living Aeneas through the kingdom of Jupiter's nether equivalent, such as being about to enter it (106) or being at the very door of it (396). There is a cosmic emphasis here: through the kingship of *Iuppiter infernus* the Underworld, which for the *Aeneid* is the key to the future as well as the past, is integrated into the universe ruled by Jupiter and the fates.[110] Other gods too are kings in their own spheres. So Saturn and his kingdom, i.e. Latium in its golden age, appear at 6.793, 8.324 and 11.252 (cf. pp. 63f.); Neptune is king of the sea at 5.792 and 800; Diana is queen as huntress at 11.845; and Mars is *rex Gradivus* at 10.542. Here, after Pallas' death, Aeneas sacrifices (*immolat*, 10.541) Haemonides, priest of Phoebus; and Serestus carries off Haemonides' arms and armour as an

---

[108] The complexities of this question are indicated by Harrison (1984a) and Feeney (1984); their insistence, with different emphases, that there is a reconciliation, albeit beyond the limits of the epic, and that Jupiter and Juno move together (even though remaining in tension) is persuasive.

[109] Cf. also Venus' words (10.37f.): *quid tempestatum regem ventosque furentes / Aeolia excitos?*, where *regem* (in combination with *furentes*) points up Aeolus' failure to do his royal duty.

[110] The equivalence is not however stated in the actual words *Iuppiter infernus*. The nearest is 12.199: *vimque deum infernam et duri sacraria Ditis*, although interestingly the Sibyl refers to Persephone as *Iuno inferna* at 6.138. Presumably the intention is to link Juno rather than Jupiter with the powers of Hades.

offering to Mars. In context the cult title alludes to Mars as god of the *ancilia*, while his status as 'king' reflects his primary Augustan roles as ancestor of the Iulii and *Ultor* of Rome and Caesar.[111]

[111] Cf. Kienast (1982) 200–2 on the dedication by Augustus in 2 BC of the temple of Mars Ultor in thanksgiving for Rome's vengeance on Parthia for the defeat at Carrhae, and for his own vengeance for the murder of Caesar.

2

KINGSHIP AND THE LOVE AFFAIR
OF AENEAS AND DIDO

Accompanying the emphasis on divine and human kingship in *Aeneid* 1 is an explicit portrait of Aeneas as a 'good king'. Aeneas has been separated by the storm from a large party of his men, who, led by Ilioneus, have made their way to Dido; and as Aeneas and his group stand concealed by a divinely generated mist, Ilioneus appeals for help to Dido, giving her an account of the adventures of the Trojans (1.522–43), and then of their unseen king:

> rex erat Aeneas nobis, quo iustior alter
> nec pietate fuit, nec bello maior et armis.   545
> quem si fata virum servant, si vescitur aura
> aetheria neque adhuc crudelibus occubat umbris,
> non metus, officio nec te certasse priorem
> paeniteat. sunt et Siculis regionibus urbes
> armaque Troianoque a sanguine clarus Acestes.   550
> quassatam ventis liceat subducere classem
> et silvis aptare trabes et stringere remos,
> si datur Italiam sociis et rege recepto
> tendere, ut Italiam laeti Latiumque petamus;
> sin absumpta salus, et te, pater optime Teucrum,   555
> pontus habet Libyae nec spes iam restat Iuli,
> at freta Sicaniae saltem sedesque paratas,
> unde huc advecti, regemque petamus Acesten. (1.544–58)

The first word of the first line of the passage is *rex*. The past tense is used of Aeneas' kingship (*erat*, 544) because Ilioneus fears Aeneas dead. The rest of lines 544f. rapidly stamps Aeneas as a good king by attributing to him three of the ideal monarch's major virtues, justice (*iustior*, K4 i), *pietas* (*pietate*, K5 i) and courage (*bello et armis*, cf. *virum*, 546, K4 iv). It is no accident that two of the four cardinal and royal virtues, self-control and wisdom (K4 ii and K4 iii), are here omitted. Thus Virgil subtly modifies the stereotype in anticipation of the events of Books 1–4, which will show Aeneas at first failing in self-control and abstinence from pleasure, and only subsequently acquiring this virtue

29

and greater wisdom through divine guidance.[1] Ilioneus then reveals
Aeneas as the 'salvation of his people' (*sin absumpta salus*, 555, K6 iii).
Earlier he had declared that the Trojans had no fear if Aeneas was still
alive (546–8); earlier too Ilioneus had implied that Aeneas showed the
proper kingly generosity and gratitude to his friends and benefactors
(K5 v): if Aeneas is safe, he says, Dido will not regret having taken the
initiative in helping the Trojans (546–9), a statement full of dramatic
irony but meant sincerely. Two further motifs of the good king
stereotype follow the *salus populi* theme in the words *et te, pater optime
Teucrum* (555): the good king is the father of his people (K6 i); and the
'best' among the citizens (K1).

A little later (588–93) this portrait of Aeneas is continued when the
concealing cloud is lifted and he stands revealed to Dido. Now Virgil
says of him:

> restitit Aeneas claraque in luce refulsit
> os umerosque deo similis; namque ipsa decoram
> caesariem nato genetrix lumenque iuventae   590
> purpureum et laetos oculis adflarat honores:
> quale manus addunt ebori decus, aut ubi flavo
> argentum Pariusve lapis circumdatur auro. (1.588–93)

All this of course in part accounts for Aeneas' personal impact on Dido.
But in conjunction with Ilioneus' speech it also completes the depiction
of Aeneas as a good king. Aeneas is 'godlike' (589), i.e. of handsome
appearance; and his good looks are enhanced by the source of all
beauty, his divine mother Venus (589–91). Good appearance was a
standard kingly quality (K8); and the Romans laid particular stress on
the appearance of important statesmen, a number of whom, it would
seem, considered themselves strikingly goodlooking.[2] Such self-images
could be connected with aspirations to divinity (cf. *deo similis*, 589).
Interestingly Julius Caesar claimed to have received his youthful
appearance from Venus; and Augustus, according to Suetonius, had
bright and piercing eyes and liked it to be thought that there was divine
vigour in them.[3]

---

[1] Bowra (1933–4) 11–16 points usefully to some of Aeneas' failings in terms of the four
virtues scheme; but his findings are partially vitiated by his hypothesis of a stoic basis for
the characterisation of Aeneas, which leads him, in the face of the evidence, to assert that
Aeneas lacks courage (13f.)!

[2] On this and related matters, cf. Weinstock (1971) 23–6; Woodman (1977) 97–9; and,
on the appearance of the θεῖος ἀνήρ (god-like man) in general, Bieler (1935) I.49–56.

[3] Nadeau (1982) 102f. offers an ingenious explanation of *Aen.* 6.460 in terms of the
caesaries–Caesar etymology also implicit at *Aen.* 1.590; *caeseus* (as an eye colour) also

This portrait of Aeneas marks him explicitly as a good king; and it directs attention all the more to the apparently contrasting way in which he is introduced into the epic named after him, i.e. as a suffering and toil-weary figure.[4] It is true that the *Aeneid* prologue does call Aeneas 'hero' (1.1), and it does reveal his role in helping to found the city which will rule the world (1.5–7, 33). But nevertheless its main emphasis is on the labours and endurance of Aeneas. Thus in line 2 Aeneas is *fato profugus* ('exiled by destiny'); at 3f. he is said to have been tossed on land and sea by the power of the gods; and at 5 he has suffered a great deal also in war. In the next lines (8–11) the poet asks why *insignem pietate virum* ('a hero distinguished for piety') was impelled by Juno *tot adire labores*; and when Aeneas makes his first personal appearance, he gives the impression of a man worn down by suffering: *extemplo Aeneae solvuntur frigore membra; / ingemit et duplicis tendens ad sidera palmas / talia voce refert* (1.92–4). Subjected to chill terror, he groans and wishes he had died at Troy.

Now on one level all this can be explained readily: toils are an exercise of royal virtue; and indeed it is no accident that Aeneas' *labores* (K5 iv) appear in the same line (1.10) of the *Aeneid* prologue as his *pietas*, that essential kingly quality (K5 i). The same could be said about Aeneas' actions once the storm is over, when he shows his talent for hard work (K5 iv), foresight (K5 vi), and care for his people (K5 viii). He brings the remnant of his forces to shore (170–4), climbs to a vantage point and tries to glimpse the rest of his fleet (180–3), and, seeing deer, hunts them to feed the Trojans (184–93). Indeed the last is a particularly royal act: Aeneas is not only caring for his distressed subjects, but by hunting he undertakes an activity more generally associated with kingship, and one which specifically evokes the royal qualities of courage (K4 iv), hard work (K5 iv), and wakefulness[5] – the last also manifested by Aeneas at 1.305. Having shared this food, with wine, among his people (194–7), Aeneas makes a speech to restore their spirits (198–207), presumably successfully, since his comrades turn eagerly to preparing food and

played its part. On all this, cf. also Weinstock (1971) 25f.; Woodman (1977) 98; Suet. *Aug.* 79.2: *oculos habuit claros ac nitidos, quibus etiam existimari volebat inesse quiddam divini vigoris.*

[4] It is not fully clear when the kingship implications of Aeneas' sufferings would have dawned on a contemporary reader; perhaps at *Aen.* 1.38, when Juno first identifies him as a king.

[5] Cf. Horsfall (1971) 1110f., *inter alia* for a specific Virgilian espousal of these concepts at *Aen.* 9.605. On hunting in the *Aeneid*, cf. Rocca (1983) 145–51; for general Roman attitudes to hunting, cf. Aymard (1951) esp. 469–558; on hunting in the *Aeneid id.* 116–28; cf. also above, p. 20 n. 93.

drink (210ff.). But the words in which Virgil sums up all this activity show that Aeneas has remained throughout in a state of worry and misery: *talia voce refert curisque ingentibus aeger / spem vultu simulat, premit altum corde dolorem* (1.208f.); and a little later (220–2) he is seen bewailing the fate of his lost companions.[6] So it could be argued that these passages exemplify Aeneas' royal ability to labour and suffer for his people, and thus add further, less glamorous, touches to the portrait of king Aeneas as caring shepherd and leader (K6), a role which naturally involves an enormous burden of worry and suffering (K5 viii); and it could be observed in this connection that Virgil reiterates the link between Aeneas' burdens and his *pietas* (K5 i) at 1.305, in connection with Aeneas' ceaseless care for his people as demonstrated by his sleeplessness:[7] *at pius Aeneas per noctem plurima volvens.* Again, the sufferings of Aeneas could be seen as also relevant to contemporary political thought: one standard description and justification of imperial rule in the Julio-Claudian period was that the *princeps* undertook the enormous burden and cares of the *imperium*. In *Epistles* 2.1 Horace, who goes on to use further motifs from the good king tradition, opens by addressing Augustus as follows: *cum tot sustineas et tanta negotia solus, / res Italas armis tuteris, moribus ornes, / legibus emendes ...* (2.1.1–3).[8]

But Virgil's strong emphasis on these motifs, their appearance in the programmatic prologue of the epic, and the fact that they precede the more imposing regal portrait of Aeneas at 1.544ff. and 588ff., all this suggests that something more significant may be involved, namely that Virgil might be presenting in Aeneas a king whose portrayal looks not simply to the generalised stereotype of the ancient monarch, but to a more specialised variant, a toiling and suffering ideal monarch. In this case the first impressions given of Aeneas would be designed to colour and modify the more formal portrait which follows. But where might Virgil have found inspiration for such a notion? No clear-cut answer is possible, but the question is worth exploring because other points of interest emerge en route. A first hypothesis might be that Virgil's inspiration is stoic, since the stoics did regard φιλοπονία (love of toil) as

---

[6] McGushin (1964) usefully discusses Aeneas' endurance and *labor* in the context of the Trojans' *duritia*; Binder (1971) 13–16 has valuable remarks on Aeneas' *curae* at *Aen.* 8.26–35 and their connection with Augustus.

[7] It should be emphasised that these activities of Aeneas are not just 'programmatic' but continue; his restless night leads to further exploratory activity on behalf of his people; 'watchfulness to save those who are asleep' is 'a favoured cynic antithesis' (Höistad (1948) 98). Cf. also below, p. 36 n. 25.

[8] Cf. Brink (1982) 35–57 esp. 44f.

a virtue;[9] and this hypothesis might be thought to draw strength from other indubitable stoic influences on the *Aeneid*, particularly where fate, the gods, and *furor* are concerned.[10] But in general the 'stoic *Aeneid*' is less plausible than it once seemed; and it is increasingly difficult to believe in Aeneas as a stoic hero, or in Virgil as committed to a single brand of philosophy. More particularly, stoic φιλοπονία seems to have been a generalised virtue of all 'wise men' (σοφοί), not just of stoic kings, and the portrait of Aeneas as a suffering and toiling king does not automatically and exclusively suggest stoic influence.

This is not to say however that ideas mediated to Virgil and his contemporaries through stoicism may not have played a significant part in determining Aeneas' portrayal as a king. This seeming contradiction may be resolved when a possible alternative source is suggested, namely 'cynicism': for the contrast in *Aeneid* 1 between the two sides of Aeneas' royal *persona* could be 'cynic' in inspiration, if the evidence that hellenistic cynics conceived the king as a suffering hero manifesting his virtues through his sufferings is deemed reliable.[11] Now all evidence about ancient cynicism, including that relating to its history in the late hellenistic and early imperial periods, tends to be highly controversial. So it should be stressed at the outset that the notion of 'cynic' influence on the portrayal of Aeneas does not depend on any particular view of the history of cynicism. A minimalist approach might see cynicism as having disappeared (or as having been eclipsed) as a school in the later hellenistic period, to be revived only in the early empire, mainly from stoic sources.[12] On this view, seemingly cynic elements in Virgil could be

[9] For the few and generalised early stoic references to φιλοπονία, cf. Arnim (1903–24) IV Index verborum etc. *s.vv.* πόνος, φιλοπονία, φιλόπονος.

[10] Cf. e.g. Pöschl (1977) Index *s.v.* Stoa; Otis (1963) Index *s.vv.* Stoicism (Stoic), Fate (*fatum*); on *fatum–fata*, cf. Pötscher (1977); Bowra (1933–4); Bonds (1978). For useful qualifications, cf. also Horsfall (1976) 77–82.

[11] Cf. Höistad (1948) Indices I *s.v.* πόνος, 195–204. There is unresolved controversy about whether stoic and cynic attitudes to monarchy were different (cf. Moles (1983) 106 and n. 26), but this affects the present discussion minimally. Aeneas' sufferings etc. are handled by Bowra (1933–4) in stoic terms with some forcing of the evidence. It is interesting that *Aen.* 1.92: *extemplo* etc. may derive from Livius *Fr.* 30 (Büchner): *igitur demum Ulixi cor frixit prae pavore* (cf. Galinsky (1969) 16f.), and thus link Aeneas directly with the archetypal cynic hero Odysseus; cf. also below, p. 35 nn. 18f.

[12] This formulation combines at least three views, for which cf. Moles (1983) 120–3. For the least radical hypothesis, i.e. survival at a low level, cf. also Dudley (1937) esp. Ch. 6. For the second view, that cynicism died out altogether and was reborn out of stoicism, cf. also recently Billerbeck (1982). The third view is that cynicism died out and was revived independently of stoicism. Curiously, the explanation in Dudley (1937) 118f. of why (in his view) cynicism was uncongenial to late republican Rome would make it equally uncongenial for the early empire. The overall implication of Moles (1983) is survival, with much evidence lost.

explained as deriving from commonplace ideas about hellenistic philosophy which were certainly current at Rome at all times in the popular moralising of teachers proclaiming themselves stoics, but following cynic lines. Varro's *Menippean Satires* provide evidence of such popular cynic interest in the late republic and Virgil could also have drawn on such works.[13] This approach would explain too the role of stoic φιλοπονία in the character of Aeneas.

At the other end of the spectrum, there have been recent claims that cynicism continued to exist throughout the period of its alleged disappearance or eclipse;[14] and further, if indirect, support may be forthcoming for these claims.[15] If cynicism did survive in some institutional form, then such Virgilian exploitation of 'cynic kingship' as could be established would reflect more than philosophical commonplace; and certainly a living tradition of real cynicism (as opposed to stoic reconstructions) would be a powerful help in explaining Augustan interest in it. But these historical problems are in a sense doubly irrelevant to the present enquiry, since there is a third route (that is, apart from popular philosophy and the survival of the school), by which knowledge of cynicism could have come to Augustan writers. This was provided by the Greek philosophical teacher, life-long friend of Augustus and member of the circle of Maecenas, Areius Didymus of Alexandria. Although stoic in his own tendencies, Areius was (and this was typical of his school) more concerned with the scholarly propagation of philosophical doctrines from a wide variety of sources.[16] It needs little imagination to speculate that cynic doctrines were among the many subjects which he expounded to select palace audiences including the *princeps*, Maecenas, Virgil and Horace.

But, as well as the problematic history of cynicism, there is a further, and even more central, area of uncertainty – about nothing short of cynic concepts of kingship in themselves. Did the cynics ever really hold to the ideal of the 'suffering king'? And, if it truly was a cynic stereotype,

[13] Cf. the testimonia at Bücheler (1904) 164; Macrob. *Sat* 1.11.42; *RE* Suppl. 6.1268–76. Whether Varro was in any real sense a cynic is however another question, cf. Dudley (1937) 119f.; Boyancé (1955).

[14] Cf. esp. Moles (1983) 103, 120–3. As noted above (p. 33 n. 12), this important paper also documents more orthodox viewpoints fully.

[15] The distinction between 'literary' and 'philosophical' cynicism must be upheld (cf. Moles (1983) 121f.). But the increasingly clear influence of cynic thought on Augustan literature (on which, cf. most recently Moles (1986)) raises even more insistently the question of cynicism's survival into that period, since, if 'real' cynicism was dead, its 'literary' presence in strength becomes all the more paradoxical.

[16] Cf. *Kl. P. s.v* Areios Didymos; Fraser (1972) I.490f.; Kahn (1983).

does it go back to the hellenistic period? The arguments for and against these possibilities cannot be reviewed here.[17] But, as with the historical problem, decisions about these matters are not fundamental for the interpretation of the *Aeneid*. If the cynic ideal was indeed a suffering king, then some aspects of Aeneas' personality and experiences would bring him into that orbit. But conceivably all that can be attributed to the cynics, or to hellenistic cynicism, is a way of thinking about the virtues, not of the ideal king, but of the ideal cynic, based on the paradeigmatic figures of Heracles, and (to a lesser extent but more characteristic for the school) Odysseus.[18] Even so, however, an approach to the kingship of Aeneas based on the hypothesis of cynic influence still has something to tell us about the *Aeneid*, in view of the great importance in it of those same two heroes as models and prototypes for Aeneas, Heracles in Book 8 (cf. pp. 84, 101f.),[19] and Odysseus throughout (cf. pp. 86–8, 184–8). Both Heracles and Odysseus are also linked with the concept of concord,[20] which has a major role in the *Aeneid* (cf. Ch. 4). Heracles was seen as an embodiment of the virtue of φιλανθρωπία (love of one's fellow men, K5 iii),[21] a frequent feature of Aeneas' royal *persona* also. Heracles' φιλανθρωπία was manifest mainly in the destruction of vicious monsters, treacherous men, tyrants and persons full of outrageous pride (ὕβρις), who allegorically represented the vices which plague mankind.[22] In this respect Heracles was a 'most just killer', 'the best of men' (cf. K1), and a benefactor of man (K5 iii).[23] Aeneas' destruction of Mezentius and Turnus should be seen in the same terms (cf. pp. 84, 105). Heracles was a wanderer and an exile

[17] Most of the reviews of Höistad (1948), a bold and speculative work, are brief, and either bland or positive. For a long and generally critical review, cf. Minar (1951), whose position on cynic kingship is that 'there were many changes between Diogenes of Sinope and Dio the friend of Hadrian' (438). References below to Höistad (1948) are primarily to its collected material, and do not necessarily imply acceptance of its conclusions about early cynicism.
[18] *Heracles*: Höistad (1948) 22–73, 150–70, 180–2, 195–7, 215–18. *Odysseus*: Höistad (1948) 94–102, 196f.; Kindstrand (1973) 137, 183f., 210. In the epicurean context of Philodemus, cf. Gigante (1984) 294–7.
[19] The link is well understood, cf. e.g. Buchheit (1963) 116–32; McGushin (1964) 232–42; Galinsky (1966); Binder (1971) Namen- u. Sachregister *s.vv.* Aeneas–Hercules, Hercules.
[20] Cf. Höistad (1948) 105–15. On the cynic as reconciler, cf. also Moles (1983) 109, 112 and n. 73, 115.
[21] *Heracles as king*: Höistad (1948) 34, 56, 63, 151–4; *Heracles as* φιλάνθρωπος (a lover of mankind): Höistad (1948) 23f., 27f. On φιλανθρωπία as a cynic virtue, cf. also Höistad (1948) Indices I *s.v.* φιλανθρωπία; Moles (1983) 108 and n. 38, 112–15.
[22] Cf. Höistad (1948) 23f., 42, 49.
[23] *Most just killer*: Höistad (1948) 24, 49; *Best of men*: Höistad (1948) 26, 28; *Benefactor*: Höistad (1948) Indices I *s.vv.* εὐεργέτης, σωτήρ.

deprived of his country for the sake of his divinely inspired mission; in this respect too he is comparable to Aeneas,[24] who in addition is often characterised as a solitary, a feature which also recalls the standard epithets signalling cynic virtue, 'alone' (μόνος), 'self-sufficient' (αὐτ-άρκης) and 'resistant to emotion' (ἀπαθής).[25] Aeneas' exile is something his enemies gibe at. Cynic heroes could be abused in the same way,[26] and because of the malice and falsehood of the gibers, such attacks turn into praise of their victim.[27]

Heracles' whole life was regarded by the cynics as ἄσκησις (training).[28] His physical labours were the equivalent of ethical labours and thus became a positive experience.[29] As one whose life was a continuous process of self-improvement and instruction in virtue,[30] Heracles is very similar to Aeneas, particularly since Heracles' labours were allegorised by cynics as his struggle against pleasure and desire.[31] In cynic thought Heracles was compelled to make a choice of life.[32] Aeneas' emotional experience in Carthage also forced such a choice on him. Again, Heracles was seen as a hero submissive to fate, which is the most striking aspect of Aeneas' character too.[33] Some of these same features were also noted by cynics in the character and experiences of Odysseus and interpreted in the same ways.[34] Finally Aeneas' strong interest in hunting may be worth emphasising in passing, since this was a characteristic of the king in cynic thought.[35]

There is no intrinsic reason why Virgil should not have sought cynic influence, from whatever source. As noted, the hypothesis of a 'stoic *Aeneid*' is over-narrow; and Virgil in truth seems to have been fairly

[24] Cf. Höistad (1948) 34; Moles (1978) 96–100.
[25] Cf. Höistad (1948) 195–203; Moles (1983) 111f. Another minor but noteworthy resemblance between Aeneas and Heracles is their sleeplessness, cf. Höistad (1948) 53f., and also 98 (Odysseus' watchfulness on behalf of those asleep!). For an interesting discussion of the representation of Heracles (and Aeneas) in the *Aeneid* in connection with Apollonius' treatment of Heracles, cf. Feeney (1986a).
[26] Cf. Höistad (1948) 34, 196–9, cf. 202; on gibes against Aeneas, cf. below, pp. 120f.
[27] The inspiration is, of course, from Homer, where Thersites, Irus and the suitors gibe at epic heroes. The principle, that attacks by unworthy persons function as praise of their victim, is of wide application in ancient literature and is exemplified by poets as disparate as Pindar and Propertius.
[28] Cf. Höistad (1948) Indices I *s.vv.* ἄσκησις, παιδεία.
[29] Cf. Höistad (1948) Indices I *s.v.* πόνος.
[30] Cf. Höistad (1948) Ch. 3 and Indices I *s.v.* παιδεία; Stewart (1972) 650: 'The essential subject of the *Aeneid* is the "education" of a political leader.'
[31] Cf. Höistad (1948) Indices I *s.v.* ἡδονή.
[32] Cf. Höistad (1948) 31–3, 46.
[33] Cf. Höistad (1948) 25, 63; cf. also above, p. 25 and n. 105.
[34] Cf. above, p. 35 and n. 18; Moles (1978) 97; below, pp. 86–8, 185f.
[35] Cf. Dickie (1986) 188, and, for the overall picture, 182–205.

broad in his philosophical attitudes. Ch. 3, for example, will introduce peripatetic views important for the characterisation of Aeneas;[36] and Virgil's use elsewhere of stoic positions is perfectly consistent with the hypothesis that in his treatment of Aeneas' kingship he was exploiting the views of a related movement, the cynics. In his 'eclecticism' Virgil was a typical Roman of the late republic and early empire. Such approaches to morality do not imply imprecision. They were simply characteristic Roman ways of adapting alien philosophies to native needs. By becoming an 'eclectic' a Roman citizen could view himself as adhering to a reasoned version of the *mos maiorum* rather than to any particular Greek philosophical sect, and so could borrow freely from all of them whatever reinforced his Roman way of life, automatically rejecting anything which ran counter to the *mos maiorum*, including philosophical technicalities. Virgil's 'eclecticism' probably also reflects the influence of the 'eclectic' Alexandrian schools of philosophy of the first century BC.[37] Areius Didymus, who was active in Rome during Virgil's lifetime, has already been mentioned as a member of one such school, and there were others (including possibly a neo-pythagorean group),[38] and prominent teachers within them; they created, among Greeks as well as Romans, an 'eclectic' climate.

There is too an interesting contemporary parallel for Virgil's hypothesised combination of cynic, stoic, and other approaches; Horace in his *Epistles* exploited the more moderate moral views of Panaetian stoicism, probably as mediated through Cicero's *De Officiis*, to humanise the more austere traditional stoic approach.[39] Virgil may be using cynic moral theories for the same purpose. It would have been difficult for him to portray Aeneas as the stoic 'wise man', for although, as a *sapiens*, Aeneas would automatically have been a good king with all the royal virtues, he would also have been a perfect man, and could only have been portrayed as such, which would have made for a dull hero and plot. Even if Virgil had made Aeneas a stoic προκόπτων (one making progress),[40] this would have left inadequate room for develop-

[36] Cf. Lyne (1983) and below, pp. 78–84.

[37] Cf. Fraser (1972) I.485–94.

[38] For the neo-pythagorean kingship texts in relation to the *Aeneid* cf. Ch. 1; the suggestion that the ps.-pythagorean texts in general may be linked with Eudorus (Ch. 1 n. 69) should be noted in this context.

[39] The full situation is more complex and so more reminiscent of Virgil's practice, in that Horace also admits further additional stoic and non-stoic influences and is sympathetically aware of contrasting viewpoints; on these questions, cf. McGann (1969) esp. Ch. 1.

[40] This was argued as plausibly as it might be by Bowra (1933–4).

KINGSHIP AND THE LOVE AFFAIR OF AENEAS AND DIDO

ment on his part,[41] because, even at that stage of the stoic path towards perfection, Aeneas would have had too few faults to make him realistic as a character. But as a cynic king Aeneas can develop morally step by step through his experience and 'training'. His labours thereby acquire a positive moral value, although he himself need not be faultless at any point. The cynic element thus allows Virgil more freedom as poet and narrator than would a purely stoic version; and some of the distress which the 'stoic Aeneas' has inflicted on his modern interpreters can be relieved. It is no longer necessary to imply that Aeneas is faultless, which he clearly is not, in order to show that Virgil in general approves of Aeneas and his mission.

By the end of Book 4 Aeneas has achieved a moral status reminiscent of Dio Chrysostom's king:

ὁ γὰρ βασιλεὺς ἀνθρώπων ἄριστός ἐστιν, ἀνδρειότατος ὢν καὶ δικαιότατος καὶ φιλανθρωπότατος καὶ ἀνίκητος ὑπὸ παντὸς πόνου καὶ πάσης ἐπιθυμίας. (*Oratio* 4.24)

(For the king is the best of men, the bravest and the most just and the most kindly, and he is unvanquished by any toil or desire.)

But, as noted, the first portrait of Aeneas (1.544ff.) omits wisdom and self-control. The love affair which follows is considerably clarified once the role of kingship in it is recognised. Both Aeneas and, as will be seen, Dido are represented in Book 1 as good monarchs. In Book 4 Dido deteriorates into a bad monarch, while Aeneas emerges at its end as an improved good king. Aeneas' progress in the royal virtues begins during the fall of Troy in Book 2 (earlier in the narrative sequence than Book 1 and Book 3); it then continues throughout Book 3, Book 1 and Book 4. Dido, on the other hand, is already on the slippery slope by the end of Book 1.

Before Dido's kingship and her love affair with Aeneas are treated in detail, those aspects of Aeneas' kingship which antedate Book 1 can be surveyed briefly. Prior to the fall of Troy, Aeneas was neither king of the Trojans, nor heir to the throne.[42] This is why Virgil describes how, on the night of the fall of Troy, the ghost of Hector, who, if he had lived, would have succeeded Priam as king of Troy, appeared to Aeneas

---

[41] For a summary of earlier views of the character of Aeneas and of his 'development', cf. Liebing (1953) int. iv–vii and, more recently, Pöschl (1977) 35–84.

[42] On this topic and its effects in the *Iliad* and *Aeneid*, cf. Harrison (1981) 213f.

(2.268–97). Hector entrusted to Aeneas the gods of Troy and gave him a commission to found the successor city to Troy: *sacra suosque tibi commendat Troia penates; / hos cape fatorum comites, his moenia quaere / magna pererrato statues quae denique ponto* (2.293–5). Aeneas' dream initiates his kingly role, but he does not at first understand its import and he continues to behave as though he were still a private citizen. Awakened by the din of the sack of Troy he snatches up his arms and wants to die in battle. He is motivated by *furor* and *ira* (2.314), emotions generally[43] inconsistent with the virtues of the good king, especially self-control (K4 ii). A little later (2.353) Aeneas urges his comrades to die in the midst of arms; the result is that they catch his 'madness': *sic animis iuvenum furor additus* (2.355). Again at 2.588 Aeneas has a *mens furiata*, just before Venus comes to calm him. These actions and motivations, while they show that Aeneas has not appreciated properly his royal destiny, do of course emphasise his bravery, another royal virtue (K4 iv) stressed at 2.431–4, where Aeneas calls on the ashes of Troy to bear witness that he shirked no danger. Aeneas' fury and suicidal rage end when he sees the corpse of Priam and thinks of his own father, wife and son in danger (2.560–4), a reflection confirmed by what Venus says to him a little later (2.594–600). Aeneas now shows proper kingly *pietas* (K5 i) by trying to rescue his father, son and wife. But in fact Creusa is spirited away by Cybele in the confusion, appearing in ghostly form at the end of the book to assure Aeneas of his royal destiny (2.783f.): *illic res laetae regnumque et regia coniunx / parta tibi.*

In Book 3 Aeneas' role as king is not heavily emphasised. This may be because that book is unfinished. But another consideration is that his *pater* Anchises is still alive in Book 3, physically recovered from his weakness at the fall of Troy and so able to assume an active role, giving commands to the fleet and providing Aeneas with guidance.[44] Since Anchises, like Latinus in Books 7–12, is an older kingly figure whose example and affection inspire Aeneas, the greater energy of Anchises may explain Aeneas' comparative subordination in Book 3 and its lack of emphasis on his kingship. However, at its end Anchises dies and Aeneas is able to assume the fuller kingly role in which he appears at the beginning of Book 1.

Dido's status as a 'good king' is first hinted at in the speech of Venus

---

[43] Cf. Bowra (1933–4) 16–19; Lyne (1983); and below, pp. 77f.

[44] On the character of Anchises, cf. esp. Lloyd (1957), whose subtle insistence on Anchises' consistency is valuable; also Harrison (1980) 361f.

disguised as a huntress at 1.338–70.[45] Her account of Dido's rule over Carthage tends at many points to make Dido's history and situation seem analogous to those of Aeneas himself.[46] Dido 'rules' the Tyrian colony of Carthage (*regna*, 338; *regit* – but its object is *imperium*, 340). Like Aeneas she was not the heir to the throne of the mother city (346f.), and like him, she was appointed ruler of the colony by a ghost, that of her husband, which also appeared to her in a dream (353–9). Like Aeneas Dido fled overseas (360–4); and she has already done what he hopes to do, set up her new city in a foreign land (365–8). These analogies, and the general tenor of Venus' speech, anticipate the later explicit identification of Dido as a 'good king'; and this mode of presentation creates another resemblance, for just as the full description of Aeneas as a good king is not given on his first mention or appearance but awaits his arrival at Carthage, so these first hints of Dido's role are confirmed only in that same scene of Aeneas' arrival at Carthage. In the interval, what Aeneas observes on his way into the city adds another touch to her portrait: the Carthaginians are hard at work upon their city (*instant ardentes Tyrii*, 423). The detailed account of their work (421–9) reveals them as the typical hardworking citizens of the good king (K 11); and their comparison to bees again brings the topic to mind, since the bees conventionally, and in discussions of kingship, owe their industry and organisation to their 'king'.[47]

Then, at the start of the scene in which Dido will first meet Aeneas, a direct description of Dido partly paralleling the earlier portrait of Aeneas establishes her firmly as a good king:

> regina ad templum, forma pulcherrima Dido,
> incessit magna iuvenum stipante caterva.
> qualis in Eurotae ripis aut per iuga Cynthi
> exercet Diana choros, quam mille secutae
> hinc atque hinc glomerantur Oreades; illa pharetram   500
> fert umero gradiensque deas supereminet omnis
> (Latonae tacitum pertemptant gaudia pectus):
> talis erat Dido, talem se laeta ferebat

---

[45] The figure of *Venus venatrix* has many ramifications, including the hunting associations of kingship (cf. above, p. 20 n.93 and below, p. 46). Cf. e.g. Harrison (1972–3) and (1979).

[46] Cf. Horsfall (1973–4) 6f.; G. Williams (1983) 14f. and Dyck (1983) 239–41 on these and other similarities between Dido and Aeneas.

[47] Cf. Virg. *Georg.* 4.210–18 and Dahlmann (1954). Prof. R.F. Thomas points out to me that further comparison between the *Aeneid* and the *Georgics* in terms of kingship theory (which would also take in *Georg.* 4.87–102 on the two bee 'kings') would yield more fruit.

> per medios instans operi regnisque futuris.
> tum foribus divae, media testudine templi,   505
> saepta armis solioque alte subnixa resedit.
> iura dabat legesque viris, operumque laborem
> partibus aequabat iustis aut sorte trahebat. (1.496–508)

The first word of the first line is *regina*, just as *rex* will begin Ilioneus' account of Aeneas as a good king (1.544). Dido's kingship[48] shows in her fine appearance (K8); she is said to be very beautiful (496) and the comparison with Diana[49] not only endows her, like Aeneas, with divine pulchritude, but specifically confirms that she is tall, since Diana stands out at least 'head above' her nymphs (500f.) as Dido does above her attendant youths (497, 503).[50] Dido therefore is 'beautiful' and 'tall' (καλὴ καὶ μεγάλη), and so has two qualities which characterise one ideal of femininity in antiquity.[51] The words *ad templum* which immediately follow *regina* (496) allude to her royal piety (K5 i). In line 504 Dido is hardworking (K5 iv) and takes thought for the future of her realm (K5 vi). In 505–8 she sits on her royal throne (506) and exercises other kingly roles, dispensing justice and laws and equitably assigning tasks to her people (K4 i, K5 vii, K11). The topics stressed in Dido's description are renewed and supplemented in Ilioneus' speech to Dido:

> o regina, novam cui condere Iuppiter urbem
> iustitiaque dedit gentes frenare superbas,
> Troes te miseri, ventis maria omnia vecti,
> oramus: prohibe infandos a navibus ignes,   525
> parce pio generi et propius res aspice nostras. (1.522–6)

Ilioneus notes that Jupiter, the source of kingship (K12), and also the protector of strangers, has permitted Dido to found her new city and to control *gentes superbas* through her justice (K4 i) (522f.). Thus he reiterates the last theme of the preceding description (505–8). Ilioneus then asks for help on behalf of the Trojans since they are a *pium genus* (526), appealing indirectly to her own royal *pietas* (cf. 496, K5 i) and directly to her φιλανθρωπία (K5 iii) and mercy (K5 ii).

---

[48] As noted above, p. 1 n. 1, Pöschl (1977) 94 briefly mentions Dido's royal characteristics as detailed here.

[49] On this comparison, cf. Conrardy (1904) 29–31; Clausen (1987) 19–21; and below, pp. 129–31.

[50] *Pace* West (1969) 44. That Dido's height is indeed in question is shown by Ap. Rhod. *Arg.* 3.876–84, a subsidiary source, where, in a simile describing Medea, Artemis stands (i.e. higher than her companions) in her chariot. For another significant emphasis on height in the *Aeneid*, cf. 8.162f.: *sed cunctis altior ibat / Anchises.*

[51] For evidence and modifications, cf. Jax (1933) 8f., 42, 68f., 183.

41

The rest of Ilioneus' speech first deals with the misfortunes of the Trojans (527–43) and then introduces the description of Aeneas as a good king (544–58). This sequence is doubtless intended to invoke the reply which it does. Dido feels herself challenged to display her own royal qualities and so match those of the absent Trojan king; and her reply shows that she does indeed possess kingly virtues. She behaves towards the Trojans with kindness (K5 iii) and generosity (K5 v) (562–71). She explains (563f.) the cautious behaviour of her coastguards towards the Trojans in terms of her cares and responsibilities for her new kingdom (K5 viii, K6). She offers the Trojans help if they wish to depart (569–71) but demonstrates further concern for her kingdom by trying to recruit for it Ilioneus and his group, whom she knows to be a lost remnant of the Trojan fleet (572–4). Here she again shows her justice (K4 i) by offering them equal citizenship in her city and treatment on a basis of complete impartiality with the Carthaginians. Thus, significantly, Dido makes a gesture identical with Aeneas' later and ultimately successful offer of reconciliation and common citizenship between Trojans and Latins (12.189–91, cf. pp. 104f.).[52] This last analogy between the royal pair will of course emerge only in time; but Dido is already aware of their similarity in fortune, emphasising it at 1.628f.: *me quoque per multos similis fortuna labores / iactatam hac demum voluit consistere terra.* At 1.731–3 another theme of this encounter will be confirmed when Dido, addressing Jupiter as the protector of strangers, confirms the hospitality and protection which she is giving to the Trojans, and thus further demonstrates her royal φιλανθρωπία (K5 iii) and *pietas* (K5 i).

The portrait of Dido as a good king is however incomplete, and it contains hints of the changes to come in her character. As with Aeneas, self-control and abstinence from pleasure (K4 ii) and wisdom (K4 iii) are not attributed to Dido. Again, in the first passage which reveals her kingship, the speech of Venus at 1.335–70, there are various ominous notes. The ferocity of the Libyan neighbours of Carthage in war (1.339) might simply be an allusion, by indirect means, to the royal virtue of courage in war (K4 iv) of Dido who controls this area (cf. 1.522f.). But this hint of hostilities confirms other unfriendly aspects of Carthage

---

[52] Dido's offer however derives from Hypsipyle's at Ap. Rhod. *Arg.* 1.827–31, made in an ominous context (cf. 1.834f.), and leading shortly to the intervention of Heracles at 1.865ff. (cf. Mercury in the *Aeneid*) and to the paired propemptikon–syntaktikon of Hypsipyle and Jason of 1.888–908 (with which contrast those of Dido and Aeneas at *Aen.* 4.305–87, cf. Cairns (1972) 128, 131–5).

which stand in contrast to the generally friendly reception which the Trojans receive (cf. p. 134) and which will cause Venus to take precautions for Aeneas' safety while he is at Carthage; and there are further indications that all is not well. The murder which has taken place within Dido's family (348–52) contrasts with the *pietas* dominant in the family of Aeneas. Dido's *amor*, albeit for her husband Sychaeus (1.344, especially 350, 352), and Pygmalion's *amor* for gold (349) are juxtaposed as a warning that Dido is subject to this vice, which negates royal self-control (K4 ii).[53]

Dido's deterioration proceeds rapidly. At 1.712–22 she begins, in accordance with Venus' plan (1.657–90), to forget her love for Sychaeus. Paradoxically, in some ancient moral terms this might have been considered venial. But she also starts to fall in love with Aeneas. No excuse could be made in ancient morality for this sort of love (cf. pp. 54–7), which certainly breaches royal self-control (K4 ii). By the beginning of Book 4, when Aeneas has completed for Dido his moving tale of the fall of Troy and of his adventures there and since, the damage has been done irreversibly. Dido is in love with him:

> At regina gravi iamdudum saucia cura
> vulnus alit venis et caeco carpitur igni.
> multa viri virtus animo multusque recursat
> gentis honos; haerent infixi pectore vultus
> verbaque nec placidam membris dat cura quietem. (4.1–5)

That Dido's love is due to Aeneas' virtues of heroic courage (K4 iv), noble descent (cf. K12) and good appearance (K8, cf. *vultus*, 4) only makes her plight worse.[54] Initially she struggles to exercise self-control; she reveals her love, at first hesitatingly, to her sister Anna at 4.9–23, and in these lines Aeneas' courage and good appearance recur (4.11). She stresses also that Aeneas is of divine descent (4.12, cf. K12) and has suffered toils and labours (4.13f., K5 iv). At this point Dido professes to be thinking only in terms of marriage: if her first marital love had not ended as it did, and if she had not sworn to be faithful to Sychaeus' memory, she might contemplate marriage with Aeneas. The vocabulary

---

[53] The contribution of Hypsipyle to Dido's character must again be borne in mind here, cf. Conrardy (1904) 25–8.

[54] Comparison with Ap. Rhod. *Arg.* 3.453–8 reveals that Virgil has substituted an 'ethical' description of Aeneas for Apollonius' physical description of Jason; but he has taken the hint of *Arg.* 3.455: ὥς θ' ἕζετ' ἐπὶ θρόνου (how he sat on his seat) (understanding θρόνος as 'royal throne', although this was not its actual meaning), and has made the ethical qualities which he attributes to Aeneas reminiscent of royal ones.

is carefully chosen to make clear the direction of her expressed attitudes: *vinclo iugali* (16), *thalami taedaeque* (18), *coniugis* (21). But Dido is, as the introductory lines of Book 4 have made clear beyond doubt, deeply in love with Aeneas. Her claimed antipathy to marriage is a smoke-screen. So is the resolve which she had expressed to remain faithful to the dead Sychaeus (24–9). Virgil signals this, and also the hopelessness of her situation, in the irony with which he speaks of Dido's *cura* (4.1) and sleeplessness (4.5). Whereas Aeneas felt *cura* for his people (K5 viii) as a good king should (1.208) and was wakeful through care for them (1.305), Dido now feels the *cura* of love[55] and experiences sleeplessness because of love,[56] as no good king should.

Anna responds to Dido's confession by proffering advice which shows that even she is not deceived by Dido's protestations. One characteristic of the good king is that he has good ministers and counsellors (K9); and Anna's advice to Dido is couched in terms of the interests of the Carthaginian state. She points out (4.39–43) that Dido's new city has fierce neighbours and reminds Dido of the continuing danger from Tyre (4.43f.). She therefore advises Dido to marry (*coniugio*, 48) Aeneas as a means of obtaining added protection (4.45–9). This advice has the initial appearance of soundness, and all the more since it echoes Dido's own first reaction to Ilioneus' Trojans, when she thought they had lost their king, Aeneas, and so invited them to settle in Carthage (1.572–4). However the context in which the advice is given, one in which Anna understands Dido's real motivations (cf. *placitone... amori*, 4.37) but pretends to accept the version Dido gives, along with the spurious emphasis by both Dido and Anna on marriage, and the deceit proposed in 4.51–3, where Aeneas' stay in Carthage is to be protracted by special pleading about wintry weather, all these factors reveal that Anna's advice is in fact the counsel of self-indulgence. Anna's real status is not therefore that of the good royal adviser she purports to be, but that of the evil counsellor of the bad, or potentially bad, king. Her function is similar to that of the nurse in Seneca's *Phaedra*.[57] Both, albeit in the nurse's case after an initial attempt at truly moral persuasion, something which Anna did not even attempt,

---

[55] *Cura* becomes the technical term both for 'love' and 'the beloved', cf. Pichon (1902) *s.v.*.

[56] For sleeplessness as a symptom of love, cf. Hölzer (1899) 48; Pichon (1902) *s.v. Vigilare*; Preston (1916) 11f.; Lier (1914) 32.

[57] On the Euripidean precedents, cf. Barrett (1964) 35–9. The tragic aspect of Dido's receipt of advice from Anna is of course part of the tragic dimension of her story, on which cf. pp. 135, 150 and n. 86

encourage the immoral aspirations of the person they are advising. It is therefore a sign that Dido is declining from her status as a good king that at this important juncture she receives bad advice from her sister.

The immediate results of Anna's advice, and the terms in which Virgil describes them, confirm that this is his view:

> his dictis impenso animum flammavit amore
> spemque dedit dubiae menti solvitque pudorem.   55
> principio delubra adeunt pacemque per aras
> exquirunt; mactant lectas de more bidentes
> legiferae Cereri Phoeboque patrique Lyaeo,
> Iunoni ante omnes, cui vincla iugalia curae. (4.54–9)

Dido and Anna now go to the temples to pray and sacrifice in order to seek the gods' pardon (cf. *veniam*, 50) and goodwill (*pacemque*, 56) for Dido's decision to break her faith to Sychaeus. There is an ironic contrast between this scene and the one in which Dido first appeared, when she was going specifically as queen to the temple of Juno (1.496) to perform her royal duties (1.505–8). This contrast is intensified by the placing of Juno at the end, and so in the most prominent position, of the list of gods whose temples Dido and Anna now visit; it is strengthened further by the phrase *ante omnes* (59), and by the emphasis on Juno's role as goddess of marriage (59). The result of their visits to temples is contrary to their hopes. While Dido inspects the entrails of beasts (63f.) love makes further inroads into her own body (66f.). She falls deeper and deeper in love with Aeneas, becomes 'mad' – as no self-controlled good king should be – and displays further symptoms of love (68–85); and shortly the results of her passion begin to manifest themselves in her kingdom. The Carthaginians, whose industry had aroused Aeneas' admiration when he arrived at Carthage (1.421–9), now begin to slacken their efforts:

> non coeptae adsurgunt turres, non arma iuventus
> exercet portusve aut propugnacula bello
> tuta parant: pendent opera interrupta minaeque
> murorum ingentes aequataque machina caelo. (4.86–9)

The line which immediately precedes this passage (85) ends with the word *amorem*. This is Virgil's signal that the Carthaginians' slackness results directly from Dido's love. They had formerly worked hard under the direction of their good king; now they share with Dido the idleness commonly associated with love in antiquity,[58] as well as that failure to take proper defensive precautions which conventionally resulted from love.[59] The implication is that Dido is no longer a good king.

Juno, observing Dido's plight, plans that Dido and Aeneas should marry, in the hope of frustrating Aeneas' mission. In a confrontation with Venus, Juno reiterates Dido's own marriage aspirations at 4.99f. and 103-5, and ends by declaring:[60] *conubio iungam stabili propriamque dicabo. / hic hymenaeus erit* (4.126f.). Venus pretends to acquiesce (107f., 127f.), just as she pretends to be uncertain about Jupiter's attitude (110-14), an objection which Juno brushes aside in a clever but unsatisfactory fashion (115). It is clear from the bad faith of both goddesses that nothing said by either has any bearing on the real status of Dido and Aeneas' relationship; but their design is put into effect nevertheless. Significantly, it is to be fulfilled while Dido and Aeneas are hunting together. Hunting has at least two relevant implications in this context: the first (exploited here ironically) is the link between hunting and kingship, in which hunting is a sign of royal 'bravery' (K4 iv), hard work (K5 iv) and wakefulness (K5 viii). This is why Dido enters the hunting scene as *reginam* (133), and Aeneas as *ante omnes pulcherrimus* (141, K8) and as comparable to Apollo (143-50, especially *tantum egregio decus enitet ore*, 150),[61] and also why Ascanius, as befits a young prince, rides about eager to encounter a wild boar or a lion (156-9). The irony of all this lies in the second association of hunting: it turns out here, as frequently,[62] to be an occasion for love-making. In the midst of the hunt the storm scatters the hunters and Dido and Aeneas end up together in a cave. Tellus and Iuno Pronuba give the signal; lightning flashes and *aether* is witness to the 'marriage'; nymphs wail on the peaks (166-8).

The question of how Virgil's contemporaries were intended to regard the union of Dido and Aeneas in legal terms, i.e. as a marriage or as an affair, is a vexed one, and it is not even easy to report the attitudes of

---

[58] Cf. André (1966) Index rerum notabilium *s.vv. Amor* (amour-passion), *Otium:-* galant.

[59] Cf. Fraenkel (1957) 211-14; André (1966) Index rerum notabilium *s.v. Otium:-* sens «correlatif» de: a) *militia*.

[60] For the interpretation of this scene, cf. Harrison (1981) 219-21.

[61] Curiously enough this simile derives from Ap. Rhod. *Arg.* 1.307-10 (but cf. also 1.536-9 and Conrardy (1904) 31f.), where Jason is setting out from home to begin his voyage. Such alterations can seemingly lack logical significance and simply exemplify a hellenistic poetic technique practised for its own sake.

[62] Cf. Kölblinger (1971) 87-122 and below, pp. 142f.

different scholars to it without distortion.[63] The difficulties are due in part to the conflicting viewpoints of the characters themselves, and in part to the heroic setting of the plot – at a time before Rome or Roman law existed. In Dido's eyes the 'wedding' was clearly a valid one; and the public continuation of the relationship by Aeneas, his functioning as Dido's consort, and such small touches as hanging up his arms in Dido's bedroom (4.495), all this might have led the Carthaginians and Trojans, as well as Dido, to see Aeneas as her lawful husband; and Roman marriage, as has been pointed out,[64] could exist without ceremony or formality. But on the other hand Virgil explicitly tells us that it was not a marriage (4.172, cf. p. 48); and throughout he plays off the details of the coupling of Dido and Aeneas in the cave against the expectations of a formal Roman marriage ceremony, as well as against the literary antecedent of the event in the *Argonautica*. The bad omens which surround it, its restriction to love-making, the macabre attendance of a *Iuno Pronuba* malevolent towards the 'bridegroom', and the lack of ceremony or witnesses (except for *aether!*), would all have told Virgil's upper-class and bourgeois Roman readers that no true marriage (*iustae nuptiae*) was in question. Moreover, there is a decisive obstacle to such a marriage in Roman terms: Dido was of a different nation (*peregrina*) from Aeneas and as such she did not have the legal right of *conubium* with him. Their union, even celebrated in a more formal way, would have had no legal standing at Rome.[65] In contrast, the marriage which Aeneas will ultimately contract with Lavinia will have such standing, since by that time the Trojans and Latins will have become one people, the ancestors of the Romans, so that their marriage will be between two *cives* and so will be *iustae nuptiae*.[66]

Virgil's use of his literary prototype, the marriage of Jason and Medea in a cave (Apollonius Rhodius *Argonautica* 4.1131), located, interestingly, in the analogue of Carthage, Phaeacia,[67] amply confirms this interpretation. All the circumstances are the reverse of those in the *Aeneid*. There is sacrifice and libation (4.1128f.); witnesses are present in

[63] Among other useful recent discussions, cf. Monti (1981) 45–50, 104f. n. 17, 106f. n. 29; Harrison (1984) 21; G. Williams (1983) General Index *s.v.* Dido: her 'marriage' etc.; Feeney (1983) 204f.; Moles (1984). Most recently Clausen (1987) 23–25 has a good account with emphasis on the Apollonian background.

[64] This analysis in the main follows G. Williams (1968) 377–89.

[65] Cf. Buckland (1963) 112–14.

[66] *Qua* marriage, that of Aeneas and Lavinia echoes implicitly the emphases found in Apollonius Rhodius, where Medea's virginity and the legality of her marriage were essential in saving her from the Colchians.

[67] Cf. G.P. Rose (1969); De Vries (1977); and below, pp. 131–4.

the shape of all the Argonauts and more; the cave is 'holy' (4.1131); and the Golden Fleece is spread on the marriage bed 'so that the wedding might be full of honour and celebrated in song' (4.1141-3). The nymphs gather flowers for the pair (4.1143-5); Hera honours Jason (4.1152); all sing the marriage song to the accompaniment of Orpheus' lyre (4.1159f.); and the necessity of celebrating the marriage away from Jason's paternal home is regarded as a minor nuisance only (4.1161-9). Next day the nymphs repeat the marriage song with the same accompaniment (4.1196f.), and Alcinous ratifies the marriage (4.1201-3), which had to be valid if Medea was not to be given back to the Colchians. In Virgil however everything is otherwise: storm, earthquake (if that is what is intended) and lightning are unfavourable signs (167f.),[68] and the flashing and glittering of the lightning in Virgil replaces the glow of the Golden Fleece in Apollonius. The wailing of the nymphs in Virgil is another unfavourable omen (168);[69] it stands in place of the approving activities of three classes of nymphs in Apollonius (4.1149-51), and Virgil hints at the two classes which he has omitted (Naiads and 'Dryads from the plains') in his rushing rivers (164) and in his *agros* (163). In Virgil, Orpheus' lyre is absent. So, as noted, are all human witnesses.

Finally, Virgil takes more explicit pains to prevent misunderstanding of the status of Aeneas and Dido's relationship both before and after its inception. There was first the earlier counterpointing of Dido's talk about marriage with the reality, her love for Aeneas (4.1-85). Then the passage immediately following the union of Aeneas and Dido is even more damning in its implications:

> ille dies primus leti primusque malorum
> causa fuit; neque enim specie famave movetur   170
> nec iam furtivum Dido meditatur amorem:
> coniugium vocat, hoc praetexit nomine culpam. (4.169-72)

For a marriage to be 'the first day of death and of evil' is a travesty of its anticipated implications; *furtivus amor* and marriage are totally opposed to each other; and Virgil characterises as *culpa* (a 'love affair') what Dido calls a marriage. Thus the superficial resemblances between the marriage of Jason and Medea and the union of Dido and Aeneas only

---

[68] The comments of Pease (1935) on these matters are judicious throughout: *Storm*: on 4.160 *interea* and 4.167 *dant signum*; *Earthquake*: on 4.166 *Tellus*; *Lightning*: on 4.167 *fulsere* etc.

[69] Cf. Pease (1935) on 4.168: *ulularunt*.

serve to underline the real differences between them. The outcome of the two events will also be piquantly different. Whereas Jason will falsely repudiate his true marriage (not in the *Argonautica*, but prominently in Euripides' *Medea*), Aeneas will truthfully declare that what happened between himself and Dido in the cave was not a marriage (4.338f.).

To underline the public implications of this event, the next section of Book 4 reintroduces the theme of kingship in explicit form. Rumour (*Fama*) instantly begins to circulate the news of the pair's union in Africa, and she does so in terms which emphasise that both Aeneas and Dido are kings. *Fama* claims (4.193f.) that they are spending the winter *luxu quam longa*, have put both their kingdoms out of their minds (*regnorum immemores*) and are enslaved to base lust (*turpique cupidine captos*). Thus they are being criticised in the language normally used to evaluate kings: they lack the royal virtues of self-control (K4 ii) and care for their people (K5 viii).[70]

Jupiter's response to these rumours, brought to his notice by the jealous prayers of Iarbas (4.206–18), is to form a correct assessment of the situation. Jupiter naturally knows what Virgil has already told the reader, that *Fama* is only partly accurate. She is *tam ficti pravique tenax quam nuntia veri* (4.188) and *pariter facta atque infecta canebat* (4.190). So although Jupiter now takes action to ensure that Aeneas is not deflected from the path of fate, his judgement is less crude than that of *Fama*.[71] He turns his eyes to Carthage (described as *moenia ... / regia*, 4.220f.) and to the *oblitos famae melioris amantes* (4.221). This combination of phrases, with its reproving but urbane summary, alludes to the ideals of kingship and to the breach of them by Dido and Aeneas. But it soon emerges that the state of the two *amantes*, as Jupiter thinks of them, is far from parallel. *Fama* has been truthful as far as Dido is concerned: Juno herself has already admitted at 4.101 that Dido is hopelessly in love. But Aeneas, although one of two *amantes*, is not an *amator*.[72]

---

[70] G. Williams (1983) 86 notes that the untruths spread by *Fama* correspond in reverse to the true news of the marriage of Jason and Medea spread by Hera at Ap. Rhod. *Arg.* 4.1184f.

[71] For useful remarks about alterations of emphasis in this scene, cf. Harrison (1984) 17–28.

[72] Pichon (1902) *s.v. Amans* distinguishes the emphasis of the singular and the plural; *s.v. Amator* he makes other distinctions. Cicero (*Tusc. Disp.* 4.27) is clearer: *ut inter ebrietatem et ebriositatem interest, aliudque est amatorem esse, aliud amantem.*

It was realised long ago,[73] but is sometimes forgotten, that there is a stark contrast between the innumerable statements and expressions of Dido's love for Aeneas and the very slight hints that Aeneas recipro-cated her feelings. The question is complicated because *amo* and its cognates cover the whole range from 'like' to 'love' in all senses of 'love'.[74] Nevertheless it is striking that, apart from this conjunction of Dido and Aeneas as *amantes*, which could be a purely physical description, there are only two passages in which Aeneas 'loves' Dido. Neither – and this must be significant – belongs to the period of their love affair. The first comes when Aeneas has given up Dido and she is no longer a threat to his mission; he leaves her *multa gemens magnoque animo labefactus amore* (4.395). The second is when Dido is dead and Aeneas meets her in the underworld and speaks *dulci ... amore* (6.455). Virgil obviously wanted to avoid suggesting that Aeneas felt love for Dido, at least until his 'love' was in the past and so no longer a threat to the fates.[75] Once the danger has receded, however, Aeneas' rejection of temptation can be enhanced by hinting at the strength of his feelings. His decision to abandon Dido can now be seen as a heroic and kingly choice of virtue, a thoroughly cynic phenomenon. But at the actual point when *Fama* is accusing him of being, like Dido, a lover, no evidence is presented that Aeneas really is one, or that he has, like Dido, abandoned his role as good king.

Jupiter's sophisticated understanding goes beyond his description of Aeneas and Dido. He sends Mercury to Aeneas with a sarcastic message ending with a brusque one-word command to leave Carthage: *naviget* (4.237).[76] The tone of this message and the partly contrasting real situation in Carthage are underlined by what Mercury finds there: *ut primum alatis tetigit magalia plantis, / Aenean fundantem arces ac tecta novantem / conspicit* (4.259–61). Aeneas' activities in Carthage are of course ominous and threaten the fulfilment of his true destiny as 'founder' of Rome. Indeed they are a perversion of that destiny, since he

---

[73] Cf. De Witt (1907) Ch. 3; in confirmation, cf. Kaiser (1964) 210f. for the same feature seen in Odysseus, and Nicolaus of Damascus *FGHist*. 90.F127 (V) alleging it in Augustus! On the traditional views of the date of Nicolaus' biography of Augustus (late twenties BC), its links with Augustus' autobiography and its political functions, cf. Kienast (1982) 223f. This dating has however been challenged by Toher (1985), who places the work later and probably after Augustus' death. His redating would reduce the interest for the present study of those parts of Nicolaus' biography which reflect kingship topoi.

[74] Cf. Fischer (1973) *passim*.

[75] Virgil confirms his intent at 6.474: *respondet curis aequatque Sychaeus amorem*, where her dead husband 'now fills the role that Aeneas could not': Dyck (1983) 244.

[76] On the syntax in this area, see Harrison (1984) 22.

is 'founding' (*fundantem*, 4.260) the citadel of Rome's arch-enemy. But at this same time Aeneas' activities contrast with those of the Carthaginians, who because of Dido's fall from kingly virtue have ceased to labour on their city (86–9; contrast 1.421–9). Aeneas however retains his royal industriousness and social commitment (K5 iv, K5 viii), even when working for an alien city.[77] Virgil is indicating that although Aeneas' royal self-control (K4 ii) has been partly undermined by his concessions to pleasure, he has not become an idler, i.e. a lover. In spite of finding evidence of some continuing virtue in Aeneas, Mercury is, as instructed by Jupiter, rough with him, all the more so since he finds Aeneas clad in a cloak of Tyrian purple worked by Dido's own hand and wearing a sword given him by her (4.261–4).[78] Mercury stresses that Aeneas is laying the foundations of Carthage and calls him *uxorius* for doing so (4.266), a multiply barbed remark, predominantly in its allusion to Dido's pretensions about marriage. Next Mercury repeats the accusation of *Fama* (but not Jupiter) that Aeneas has forgotten his own kingdom and responsibilities (4.267). Both gods, then, in order to move Aeneas to action, exaggerate in different ways Aeneas' lapse from the ideal of the good king.[79] But there is no denying that Aeneas has indeed lapsed; this is as clear as was his lapse during the sack of Troy, when, after his investiture as king by Hector, he was seized with *furor* (2.316f.).

Such lapses by Aeneas, which would be difficult to explain if Aeneas were a stoic 'wise man', are less troublesome if he is a cynic king, for then such failures in virtue and corrections are educative, with Aeneas at each point moving further towards the full ideal of kingship. His lapse in Carthage is more significant for his moral progress than his lapse at Troy because it offers him the opportunity to make a choice of life parallel to that of Hercules and Odysseus.[80] Hence the affair with Dido and the emotions experienced and to some extent yielded to by Aeneas are not simply an impediment to his mission but are a necessary stage in his development as a good man and king. The finality and

---

[77] Rudd (1976) 37 maintains that renewed activity on Dido's part too is implied. But the collocation of this passage, of 1.421–9 (where the Carthaginians were hard at work), and of 4.86–9 (where they cease to work) speaks against him.

[78] Cf. Harrison (1984) 20f.

[79] The differences here and elsewhere (both in the *Aeneid* and the *Iliad*) between the messages of Jupiter and those actually delivered by Hermes–Mercury are studied with acuteness and ingenuity by Harrison (1984).

[80] See above, p. 32. Such choices are of course an epic commonplace too, the first being the choice of Achilles.

strength of Aeneas' choice are reflected in his unhesitating response to Jupiter's command: *ardet abire fuga* (4.281). But he is faced with a problem: the queen, whom now, in his reformed state, he perceives as *furentem* (4.283) in her lack of self-control (K4 ii), might well object to his departure. His concern here is not for himself (or indeed for Dido) but for his people (K5 viii), and in this he once more acts like the ideal monarch, as he does in his foresight (K5 vi). He calls together his closest comrades and tells them to prepare for a secret departure (4.288–91). This decision is not cowardly or furtive but is Virgil's signal that Aeneas has once more resumed with full energy his role as good king. In fact he intends to speak to Dido about his departure when the opportunity presents itself (291–4).[81]

The exchanges which follow between Dido and Aeneas once Dido has anticipated his approach to her and has guessed what is going on (4.305–30, 333–61, 365–87),[82] together with the narrative context in which they are set, reveal how far Dido and Aeneas now differ in their states of mind and in their perception of their duty towards their two peoples. Virgil first characterises Dido as a lover (4.296), then as mad (*furenti*, 4.298), and tells us that she rages round the town (4.300f.). This wandering through the streets is a new and intensified form of her behaviour after she first fell in love with Aeneas but before their affair began (4.68f.); and it confirms the nature of her love for him. When Dido speaks she openly acknowledges that she has harmed her people by her actions (4.320f.) and damaged her reputation (4.322f.). But her only concern is to persuade Aeneas to change his mind and stay in Carthage.

Aeneas, in contrast, displays royal self-control (K4 ii). He remains calm and dignified, although we are told that he feels strong emotions, which he represses (4.331f., 360, 393–6). He expresses his gratitude towards Dido (4.333–6), denies that he had simply been planning to leave in secret (4.337f.) – a denial pre-indicated by Virgil (4.291–4) – and states the reality about what Dido wrongly considers to be their 'marriage': *nec coniugis umquam / praetendi taedas aut haec in foedera veni* (4.338f.). Aeneas reaffirms his duty towards his *patria*, by which he now means Italy (4.345–7), and declares his love for it, a royal trait (K6 iv). Finally he pleads the orders of his father Anchises' ghost, his duty to his son, and the direct commands of the gods (4.351–9). These last four

---

[81] On the truthfulness of this, cf. Feeney (1983) 207.

[82] On these cf. *op. cit.* above, p. 42 n. 52 and Feeney (1983) 204–10, a detailed and sensitive analysis.

topics sum up the Roman concept of *pietas* and are a manifesto of Aeneas' possession of that royal virtue (K5 i). Virgil underlines this in typical fashion: when Dido answers Aeneas by accusing him of lack of feeling and lack of gratitude to her (4.365–75), accusations which, if true, would tell against his status as a good king (K5 iii, K5 v), Virgil resumes his narrative, at the end of Dido's tirade and after her subsequent collapse, with the words: *at pius Aeneas* (4.393). By doing so, Virgil is referring back to 4.345–61, and is stressing that, despite Dido's accusations, Aeneas has indeed acted, as a good king should, in accordance with *pietas*, his duty to country, father, son and gods.[83]

Aeneas' sympathy for Dido throughout this whole scene, even though she is accusing him bitterly, is another feature worth noting. It can be explained partly in terms of Aeneas' *amor*, mentioned in 4.395, although this is clearly not strong enough to alter his resolve. It should be seen more as revealing in him the royal virtue of pity (K5 ii). The interview between Dido and Aeneas ends with Virgil emphasising Aeneas' determination to forward his mission: *iussa tamen divum exsequitur classemque revisit* (4.396). On the contrary Dido is now in the grip of an insane love which has taken full control of her. Her last desperate effort to retain Aeneas, and Aeneas' response to it, intensify the contrast between the two monarchs. Anna, whose initial bad advice to Dido at 4.31–53 encouraged her not to resist love, moves into the centre of action again at the end of the affair. Dido asks Anna to beg Aeneas on her behalf to delay his departure (4.416–36). Anna carries out this request, and conveys Dido's message to Aeneas (4.437f.). But Aeneas, the good king, is deaf to the advice of Anna, the bad counsellor (4.438–49), a response which contrasts with Dido's eager acceptance of Anna's bad advice at the beginning of the book. The simile comparing Aeneas to an oak blasted by the winds is followed by two lines (4.448f.) underlining Aeneas' royal *curae* (K5 viii) and his self-control (K4 ii) in the face of pressure.

In consequence, frustrated of her wish and further impelled by love-madness (4.465, 474f.), Dido wishes for death (4.451). Her speech on the night before her death, although disjointed and querulous, refers to kingship themes already prominent in Book 4. She reflects on her relations with neighbouring peoples (4.534– 6), a motif also present in Anna's advice to her (4.39–49). She considers accompanying the

---

[83] Cf. the similar underlining of Aeneas' royal *pietas* at *Aen.* 1.305 (above, p. 32), where care for his people was again involved.

Trojans, and repeats her earlier charges about their ingratitude (4.538f.);[84] then she blames Anna for her advice (4.548f.).[85] Here Virgil explicitly confirms what he had implied earlier about that advice. Then, once Dido discovers that the Trojans have gone in response to Mercury's warning (4.560–83), she first turns to threats and ill wishes (4.590–629) and then kills herself. Book 5 begins with Aeneas at sea on his way to Sicily, looking back at the flames which, unknown to him, rise from her funeral pyre.

This reading of the relationship between Aeneas and Dido and the interpretation of Dido's love for Aeneas as a breach of royal self-control may seem austere, exaggerated and unsympathetic. It is however confirmed by what we know of ancient attitudes to love (*amor*–ἔρως). Whereas the ancient world tended to regard sexual activity as in itself morally neutral and as acquiring moral significance, if any, from its context, love was always a moral matter. There was no single assessment of love in antiquity: naturally some love poetry (particularly lyric) presented it as a good thing. In moral philosophy and in social life however, as in other literature and even in some love poetry (elegy in particular), love was generally seen as a vice.[86] Of course distinctions were sometimes made between good and bad sorts of love. These overlap, and their genesis and history is not clear. Platonic discussions of love in the *Phaedrus* and the *Symposium*,[87] distinguishing sexual and non-sexual love in the homosexual sphere,[88] gave rise to some of the various distinctions made in hellenistic philosophy between 'rational' and 'irrational' love, which seem to have been mainly stoic in their expressions.[89] A second and certainly heterosexual distinction between good and bad love appears in Euripides: in the prologue of his *Stheneboea*, Bellerophon refuses to accept the advances of Stheneboea,

---

[84] Cf. *Aen.* 1.546–9, where Ilioneus declared that Dido would not regret helping the Trojans.

[85] Although (as noted) Virgil is here confirming the badness of Anna's advice, Dido's reproach is unjustified: she took it.

[86] Fischer (1973) assembles much material about 'love' in antiquity, including information about distinctions in this area. Her concern however is lexical and semantic rather than moral. Dover (1978) 39–54, 161–3 also has useful information.

[87] Cf. Dover (1978) esp. 153–70.

[88] The principal difficulty for the Greeks in this area appears to have lain in accepting that anything but physical love could be felt for a woman. This view goes back at least to the fifth century BC; see Dover (1978) 162–4.

[89] Cf. Preston (1916) 8f. Such distinctions were partly mediated to the Augustans through Cic. *Tusc. Disp.*, cf. Pohlenz (1906), esp. 349–51. The famous attack on *amor* at Lucr. 4.1037–191 distinguishes between love-madness and the enjoyment of sexual pleasure and thus is in line with traditional Roman morality.

who offers her husband Proetus' kingdom as his reward. Bellerophon explains that he does so

μισῶν ἔρωτα δεινόν, ὃς φθείρει βροτούς.
διπλοῖ γὰρ εἶσ᾽ ἔρωτες ἔντροφοι χθονί·
ὁ μὲν γεγὼς ἔχθιστος εἰς Ἅιδην φέρει,
ὁ δ᾽ εἰς τὸ σῶφρον ἐπ᾽ ἀρετήν τ᾽ ἄγων ἔρως
ζηλωτὸς ἀνθρώποισιν, ὧν εἴην ἐγώ. (21–5)[90]

(detesting that terrible love, which destroys mortals. For there are two loves nurtured on earth – one is deadly and leads to Hades, while the other love leads to self-control and virtue. This is what men aspire to, and may I be among them.)

The 'love which leads to self-control and to virtue' (24), as opposed to the 'terrible love, which destroys mortals' (21) and which 'leads to Hades' (23), is sexual but marital, and it is opposed here to vicious extramarital sexual love. A similar distinction appears both in his *Medea*, where at 627–41 marital love is linked with self-control, and in his *Iphigeneia in Aulis*, cf. especially: μάκαρες οἳ μετρίας θεοῦ / μετά τε σωφροσύνας μετέ- / σχον λέκτρων Ἀφροδίτας (blessed are those who share the bed of moderate love with self-control) (543–5).[91] These Euripidean passages are particularly relevant for the love affair between Aeneas and Dido, since Stheneboea and Medea (and Phaedra) formed part of that group of 'mad' women in love who contributed towards the literary tradition in which Dido was created.[92]

Another division between different kinds of love is exemplified at Catullus 72.3f.: *dilexi tum te non tantum ut volgus amicam, / sed pater ut gnatos diligit et generos*. The parallels offered by Kroll (1968) *ad loc.* suggest that at this point Catullus has in mind a division between familial, i.e. non-sexual love, and sexual love,[93] which is close to, but not identical with, some of the philosophical distinctions discussed above,

[90] Page (1941) no. 16. *TGF* Adesp. *Fr.* 187 (Nauck) δισσὰ πνεύματα πνεῖς, Ἔρως (Twin are the blasts you blow, Love) could reflect any type of distinction.

[91] Cf. also Kaibel (1878) no. 811.

[92] All three appear in a group of twenty-three women in ps.-Hyginus (Rose (1933)) Ch. 243, headed *Quae se ipsae interfecerunt*. In their cases *propter amorem – Bellerophontis* (Stheneboea) and *Aeneae* (Dido) – or *ob amorem* (Phaedra) is specifically given as the cause of their suicide. *propter amorem* (for their lovers) is also given as the cause for Canace, Byblis and Calypso, *propter desiderium Protesilai* for Laodameia and *propter Demophontem* for Phyllis. Others of them too (including Evadne) were lovers. These groupings are suggestive, especially since at *Aen.* 6.445–51 Phaedra heads a group of heroines in Hades (including Laodameia and Evadne) who have died from love, and Dido too is among them.

[93] Cf. also Fischer (1973) 40–5.

where however the element of family did not enter into the question. A fourth distinction which overlaps with the others is found in Aristotle,[94] where marital love, for all that it is sexual, is regarded as a type of φιλία, i.e. familial love, rather than e.g. being classed with 'intercourse' (συνουσία) or 'love' (ἔρως).

These distinctions (particularly the Euripidean one) are analogous to the distinction which Dido seeks at various points to make in connection with her own loves. She wants to represent herself as having felt marital love for Sychaeus (4.28f., cf. 1.343–52), and as feeling marital love for Aeneas (cf. 4.18f. and the later passages in Book 4 already discussed where Dido views her love affair as a marriage). The reader knows, however, from innumerable indications, that Dido's *amor* for Aeneas is not the love which, in Bellerophon's words, 'leads to self-control and virtue' (24), but is in truth for Dido the 'terrible love which destroys mortals' (21) and 'the most vicious love which leads to Hades' (23). The reader also suspects that even Dido's love for Sychaeus was not in fact the self-controlled marital kind but was uncontrolled and excessive.

Thus even in terms of these ancient distinctions Dido's self-defence fails; and the overall background must always be kept in mind. It was one of general moral disapproval of love: when no distinction is made between good and bad love, the implication is that all love is bad. Far from sharing the modern assumption that love in general, and the sort of passionate sexual love felt by Dido in particular, has a privileged status and is intrinsically good, antiquity regarded it as a spiritual disease, a form of madness akin to other passions such as greed and anger.[95] Such love was a dangerous, anti-social and censurable affliction even in an ordinary citizen, since it might well lead to neglect of property and to shirking of duties towards one's country as soldier, parent, and participant in the legal and administrative responsibilities of the state. The Roman elegists, who portray themselves as lovers, frequently simultaneously portray themselves as culpably negligent in those areas.[96]

If love was a serious vice in a private citizen, it was many times more so in a public figure; and it was unforgivable in a king. It should not be

---

[94] Cf. Arist. *EN* 1162A.16–19.

[95] Cf. Ringeltaube (1913) esp. 85. On Dido as a lover by nature, and for further reflections on *amor* and morality, cf. below, pp. 140f. and nn. 41–4. On marriage and love, cf. now Griffin (1985) Ch. 6.

[96] Cf. e.g. Boucher (1965) Ch. 1.

forgotten that the Roman world had in the decade before Virgil began writing the *Aeneid* seen two conspicuous examples of rulers who like Dido[97] – or so the propaganda of the Augustan age declared – had brought themselves and their followers to destruction through 'love', the triumvir M. Antonius and his consort Cleopatra, Queen of Egypt. It is well understood that Virgil to some extent modelled Dido upon Cleopatra.[98] But her consort in the *Aeneid* is not another bad king, a M. Antonius to equal the Cleopatra figure in vice, but the good king, Aeneas.

---

[97] Cf. Anna's words at 4.682f.: *extinxti te meque, soror, populumque patresque / Sidonios urbemque tuam.*

[98] Cf. e.g. Pease (1935) introd. 24–8.

3

KINGSHIP AND THE CONFLICT
OF AENEAS AND TURNUS

The two characters who interact most significantly with Aeneas, in terms of kingship (as in other ways), are Dido and Turnus. Since Dido dies at the end of Book 4 and Turnus, although alluded to at 6.89f., named at 7.56, and referred to at various places in the next few hundred lines, makes his first personal entry only at 7.413ff., Books 5 and 6 naturally concentrate less on kingship than do Books 1 and 4, and the stretch from 7.413 to the end of the epic. In addition the treatment of kingship in 7.1–412 mainly concerns Aeneas' interaction with another king, Latinus. But in 5 and 6 Aeneas is nevertheless developing as a king in unspectacular and situational terms, just as in general in this period, when he lacks the guidance of the living Anchises but has surmounted the temptations of Carthage, he is growing into the role which he will fulfil in Italy. This neglected aspect of Aeneas' development deserves some preliminary attention.

At 5.42ff., when the Trojan fleet has reached the shores of Sicily and has been welcomed by Acestes, Aeneas summons his followers to an assembly (*in coetum*, 5.43, cf. *e concilio*, 5.75). His action is perfectly normal, since he wishes to initiate funeral games in honour of his dead father, to whose tomb the Trojans have, by the hand of destiny, returned on the first anniversary of his death (5.46–57). But this formal assembly of the Trojans is the first held in the *Aeneid*. Thus it anticipates the later councils of the gods (10.2ff.) and of the Italians (11.234ff.), as well as foreshadowing the various Roman assemblies with their long and significant history. Its anticipatory function therefore gives it particular weight. This is increased by the fact that games are discussed at it. Games in general had great importance, both secular and religious, in the Roman cultural tradition; and the games of Book 5 are linked with Augustus' own innovations and revivals in this sphere.[1] Again the games play a weighty part in the narrative structure of the *Aeneid*: they are the static set-piece which divides off, both historically and

---

[1] Cf. Williams (1960) xf.; Mähl (1974) 33–5; Kienast (1982) Register: Namen u. Sachen *s.v.* Spiele.

58

symbolically, the two halves of the epic action and which embodies the communal unity of the Trojans on the eve of their arrival in Italy.

All this makes it worthwhile to note that councils, and the king's behaviour in them, were a matter of comment within ancient kingship literature. This appears from Philodemus' treatise: much of the emphasis of his most pertinent passage, coll. XIII.22–XV = coll. XXXI.22–XXXIV (Dorandi), was, it seems, on the king's role in and relationship to councils, and on the need for good counsel (εὐβουλία) and prudence (φρόνησις, K4 iii) on the part of the king.[2] It has been suggested also that it was the importance of the Roman Senate which led writers of the hellenistic period to place considerable stress on the council and its relationship with the king.[3] In *Aeneid* 5 the council is a general assembly of the Trojan people rather than a meeting of a smaller body like the Senate. But at it Aeneas proposes that funeral games should be held for his father, and the assembly assents, albeit without discussion, so that it is, in an attenuated sense, a 'council', and as such a meaningful context for Aeneas' proposal. As king he demonstrates good counsel and prudence in his *concilium* (K4 iii); these are accompanied by *pietas*, for he acts not just as a pious son but as a pious king (K5 i). This comes out in his speech, which evinces his devotion to Anchises (49f.), and makes much of Aeneas' *patria*, by which at this point is meant the Trojan race, and its cohesion (45, 58–63). Emphasis is also laid on the gods, from whom the Trojans are descended (45), and with whom Anchises is now associated as *divini ... parentis* (47), the recipient of sacrifice (54) and the future dedicatee of a temple at Rome (60). The role of the gods in bringing Aeneas back to Sicily and to his father's tomb at this particular time is prominent (56f.); and finally, the *patrii penates* and those of Acestes will all be present at the sacrifice to Anchises (62f.). *Pietas* in all its manifestations is thus the leitmotiv of Aeneas' speech; and this is aptly prefigured at line 26, where it was *pius Aeneas* who gave the order not to keep on course for Italy when the weather was contrary, having recognised through his royal foresight (K5 vi) that the Trojans should at this point be heading for Sicily.

In the remainder of Book 5 certain incidents allow Aeneas to display royal qualities. Twice during the games he rewards deserving losers: Sergestus, who had saved his ship and crew in spite of striking a rock (5.282–5) and Nisus and Salius, who, through accident and obstruction,

---

[2] Cf. Murray (1965) 170; Dorandi (1982) 184–90.
[3] Cf. Murray (1965) 176, but also Born (1934), which suggests that a regular body of advisors was the norm.

had failed to gain one of the first three places in the foot-race (5.348–61). These actions demonstrate Aeneas' royal justice (K4 i) and mercy (K5 ii) and also his royal concern for concord (K7). But on the whole Book 5 resembles Book 3 in playing down Aeneas' kingship. Book 3 did so because Anchises was still alive and active. In Book 5 the reasons are different. First, the Trojans are now in the domain of their fellow Trojan, king Acestes, whose kingdom (*regno*, 5.757) Aeneas 'founds' later in the book (5.755–61), and Acestes is '*senior*'. More importantly kingship, and Aeneas' kingship in particular, becomes prominent at turning points and moments of danger, since Aeneas is never represented as glorying in the pomp of royalty for its own sake. Rather he comes to the fore as king only when his country needs him – like a Roman dictator or, more pertinently, like Augustus in his own propaganda. Book 5 is a generally peaceful book dominated by the theme of concord; and, a paradox in view of the link between kingship and concord, this seems to be a major reason why Aeneas is never called *rex* in it.[4]

Book 6 however is a major turning point and kingship therefore becomes more prominent. At its beginning Aeneas acts typically and like a good king by undertaking an important task on behalf of his followers (6.9ff., K5 viii). The introductory formula *pius Aeneas* (6.9) emphasises, as elsewhere, that Aeneas is acting in accordance with his royal duty to gods and country (K5 i) when he visits the Sibyl's cave. But the most striking occurrence of kingship in Book 6 does not relate solely to Aeneas. In the underworld, he sees some of his successors and descendants, many of whom are kings, and he is thus confirmed in his kingship. In the process the temporal order of Roman history is distorted: Aeneas' distant descendants, Julius Caesar and Augustus, are inserted among the kings of Rome so that the republican section, which chronologically intervenes, comes later and separately in the text. Anchises' speech describing the procession of Aeneas' successors (6.756–853) first mentions Aeneas' unborn son, the child of Lavinia, Silvius, whom he describes as *regem regumque parentem* (6.765). Then Anchises details the later descendants of Aeneas through Silvius who will rule in Latium, with the list culminating in Romulus, associated in the succeeding lines with the rise of Rome (6.777–87). Immediately after this Anchises mentions his successors in the other branch, Julius Caesar and all the descendants of Iulus (*hic Caesar et omnis Iuli / progenies,*

---

[4] Aeneas' unobtrusiveness in Book 5 is comparable with Augustus' overt policy after 28 BC, also in a peaceful context; cf. below, Ch. 9.

6.789f.),[5] before moving on to introduce in the next lines *Augustus Caesar, divi genus* (792). This has the effect of associating Julius Caesar and Augustus both with Aeneas and with the material founder of Rome, Romulus.[6] An appended laudation of Augustus' achievements, analogous to but longer than that allotted to Romulus (6.792–807), modulates back at 6.808 into a set of brief descriptions of the other good kings of Rome, Numa, Tullus and Ancus, and only then does Anchises proceed via the Tarquins to the great men of the republican period (6.817–46). The speech culminates in the injunction to the Roman people *regere imperio* (6.851–3).

The details of this temporal distortion, which is typical of Roman poetic accounts of history,[7] can be represented schematically:

TEMPORAL ORDER	ACTUAL ORDER
(1) Aeneas	(1) Aeneas
(2) Descendants of Aeneas through Silvius	(2) Descendants of Aeneas through Silvius
(3) Romulus	(3) Romulus
(4) Numa	(8) Julius Caesar (and his ancestors from Iulus)
(5) Tullus	(9) Augustus
(6) Ancus	(4) Numa
(7) Republican heroes (the Roman people)	(5) Tullus
(8) Julius Caesar (and his ancestors) from Iulus	(6) Ancus
(9) Augustus	(7) Republican heroes (the Roman people

The juxtaposition of Julius Caesar and Augustus with Romulus gives them the divine aura of Romulus–Quirinus; and the triad Romulus–Julius Caesar–Augustus now forms the centrepiece of the whole list.

[5] Whatever else *Aen.* 6.789f. implies, the combination *Caesar ... Iuli* must (*pace* Austin (1977) on 788: *gentem*), refer to Julius Caesar, who thus stands in the centrepiece of both temporal distortions (cf. below, n. 7). Hence *hic vir* etc. (791) marks the introduction of a new character, i.e. Augustus. The double appearance of Julius Caesar, i.e. with Pompey and with Augustus, is unproblematic, given that the scenes are not static, but a 'parade', cf. Harrison (1977–8).

[6] Cf. Cairns (1979) 71–3 on the problems of this pair as 'founders'; and, on the whole subject of founders, Cornell (1983). Augustan poets appear to exploit the ambivalence of Aeneas' and Romulus' positions, regarding now one, now the other as founder, as they find it convenient (Evander too becomes, momentarily, *Romani conditor arcis* at *Aen.* 8.313). Dr T.J. Cornell draws my attention to the parallel situation at Croton where both Heracles and Myscellus (neither of them however the eponym) appear to have been regarded, in different circumstances, as founder.

[7] They are also more broadly typical of hellenistic poetry; cf. e.g. Cairns (1979) 114f., 176–81, Ch. 8. In *Aen.* 6, the section on republican heroes (818ff.) is also distorted temporally in several ways. Starting from Brutus, the first consul, it moves to the fourth century BC with the Decii, Torquatus and Camillus. But *Drusosque* (first or second or, if

Thus the logic of ancient ring-composition[8] compels comparison of them with the outermost elements of the structure, where Aeneas stands in first position and the Roman people, in its royal role (*regere*, 851), in the last. There could be no more striking proof of the favourable status of kingship in Augustan and Virgilian thought. Aeneas, the legendary kings of Rome, Julius Caesar, Augustus, the great republican heroes and the Roman people itself are all linked through kingship, with the implication that the whole of Roman history can be interpreted in royal terms. It has already been argued (pp. 5–8) that Augustan attitudes to kingship were more complex and positive than is sometimes assumed. The content and structure of Anchises' summary account of Roman history in 6.756–853 speak for the perceptions of some modern students of Augustan history,[9] who have held that, in addition to the official self-image of the Augustan regime as the restored republic, with the *princeps* just another magistrate and at most *primus inter pares*, there was a second, unofficial attitude, subscribed to by many in the inner councils of power and expressed most fully in literature, particularly at the beginning and end of Augustus' reign. This unofficial view saw the rule of one man as a permanent necessity; that man was a god-to-be, if not a god on earth, as well as a king.

The confirmation of Aeneas' kingship in the procession and in the speech of Anchises anticipates the return to greater emphasis on kingship in Book 7. From then on it remains a potent theme, appearing mainly in interactions between first, Aeneas and Latinus, and then, Aeneas and Turnus.[10] Latinus,[11] as Aeneas' future father-in-law, is the

M. Livius Salinator is being referred to, third century BC) is temporally anomalous and is a compliment to a descendant, Livia. Then the list jumps on to Julius Caesar and Pompey as antagonists in the civil war, before moving back in time and conflating, in no particular chronological order, a group of republican heroes of the third and second centuries BC. The effect is parallel to that of the other distortion: it provides a ring-compositional frame for the Caesar–Pompey section with its important overtones of concord (cf. below, pp. 95–8), and creates the impression of a long and interwoven chain of family distinction among the great men of the republic. This underpins the section's other emphasis, on the Julian family, whose distinction goes back further, to the foundation of Rome and beyond. On the historical section of *Aen.* 6, cf. most recently Feeney (1986).

[8] Cf. e.g. Cairns (1979) Ch. 8 with the sample bibliography at 194f. n. 4; and, in particular on the conceptual importance of the central position, Moritz (1968).

[9] Cf. Getty (1950) 9; Pietrusiński (1980); Kienast (1982) Ch. 4, Register Namen u. Sachen *s.v.* Divus Augustus; Weinstock (1971) Chs. 13–18 (on the Caesarian background); Taylor (1931) esp. Chs. 6–10; Millar (1973); cf. also above, pp. 9f. and n. 13.

[10] One natural progression in poetic technique can be observed in Books 7–12: by the beginning of Book 7 the motif of kingship has appeared so frequently that Virgil expects his readers to detect it easily; hence allusions to it are less explicit than they were in Books 1–6. Decreasing explicitness of this sort is standard in all ancient use of topoi, genres and conventions: cf. e.g. Giangrande (1967); Cairns (1972).

[11] For an extensive treatment of Latinus, cf. Balk (1968); cf. also Boas (1938) 69–78.

analogue and successor to his dead father, Anchises.[12] The complex modelling of Latinus not only on the homeric Nestor but also upon the iliadic Priam and the odyssean Laertes[13] increases the poignancy of the substitution. As a second Anchises, Latinus can display the virtues of a good king more extensively, since he functions as, and is named, king;[14] and it is to allow Latinus to be presented in these terms in the first half of Book 7 that Aeneas' kingship is given less attention there, just as the need to portray Turnus in a diverse light explains the lack of concentration on Aeneas in the latter half. Although at the beginning of *Aeneid* 7 Aeneas appears as his typical and kingly pious self (he is *pius* at 7.5, when raising the funerary monument and performing the funeral of his nurse Caieta), it is Latinus whose royalty and virtues are stressed most. When he is first described in the epic, he is *rex... Latinus* (7.45). He is said to have ruled his cities for a long time in peace (7.45f.), that standard characteristic of the good king (K7). Then Latinus' divine ancestry is detailed and, in an interesting variant on the normal linkage of the king with Jupiter (K12), Latinus' line is traced, as befits an Italian king of Latium, to Jupiter's father, Saturn (7.48f.), the aetiological and etymological 'founder' of Latium.[15]

This lineage not only stresses the autochthonous condition of the Latins but creates a link between Latinus and Aeneas, who is soon characterised as *rex ipse Iovis de gente suprema* (7.220). All kings are of course descendants of Jupiter; but the closeness of 7.220 to 7.45–9, and even more to 7.203, where the Latins are *Saturni gentem*, together with the further address to Latinus at 7.212 as *rex, genus egregium Fauni* (Faunus was the grandson of Saturn) and the mention of a relationship between the Trojans and the Latins through Dardanus (7.240–2), all these hints may show that the Saturnus–Latinus Jupiter–Aeneas parallel is meaningful, and is intended to foreshadow the destined assumption by Aeneas of his 'father' Latinus' rule in Latium, just as Jupiter, in one version of the myth, took over peacefully from Saturn.[16]

[12] Significantly it is the dead Anchises who first names Latinus (6.891).

[13] For the principle and for other examples, cf. Knauer (1964) Register *s.v.* Vergils Homerumformung etc.: Vereinigung etc.; (1981) 875, 881–4.

[14] Heinze (1915) 280 describes Latinus as almost the ideal of a king: 'fromm, besonnen, freigebig, gerecht, mildherzig; nur eines fehlt ihm: die *constantia*'.

[15] On Virgil's interest in 'etymology', cf. esp. Bartelink (1965); Due (1973); and for further bibliography Suerbaum (1980–1) 192f.; for the etymology of Latium in the *Aeneid*, cf. *Aen.* 8.322f. and Ahl (1985) 47f., noting *maluit* (323) as an anagram of *Latium* (322); for the specific principle employed at *Aen.* 8.322f., cf. Varro *LL* 5.6. See also below, n. 16, and p. 118 and n. 19.

[16] The role of Saturn in the *Aeneid*, as in Augustan literature in general, remains controversial, cf. e.g. Schiebe (1981) Personen- und Sachregister *s.v.* Saturn; Cairns (1979)

Mention of Latinus' distinguished ancestry in 7.47–9 is followed by a display of his piety (K5 i): in lines 58–80 he is shown as a respecter of portents forbidding the marriage of his daughter to Turnus; and he had already preserved unharmed a sacred tree growing in the courtyard of his palace (59–63).[17] The theme of the king's piety continues in the consultation by Latinus of the oracle of Faunus (81–101), who is, significantly, his father. There can be little doubt that Virgil's prominent emphasis on Latinus' royal *pietas* is meant to bring him closer to '*pius Aeneas*', who was described as such at 7.5 in part so as to stimulate awareness of their shared virtuous kingship.

When the Trojan envoys come to Latinus, his initial reception of them exemplifies the generosity (K5 v), gentleness (K5 ii) and kindness (K5 iii) of the good king, cf. esp. *placido ... ore*, 7.194. Offering them hospitality, he declares that the Latins are just (203). Then, as if he is trying to emphasise that his own royal justice (K4 i) is part of this – although his statement will turn out to have other, less positive, implications too (cf. pp. 65f.), Latinus specifies that they are just, not by constraint or through laws, but by consent and by obedience to the practice of the ancient god Saturn, from whom they claim descent (202–4), a notion which echoes earlier and later statements about the lineage of Latinus and the Latins. The scene involves many deliberate reminiscences, both direct and inverse, of the first confrontation between the Trojans and Dido (1.520–636).[18] In contrast to their arrival at Carthage, the Trojans have come to Italy, not driven by storm, but by free choice and divine will (7.213–18, 231f.). They want to settle there

General Index *s.v.* Saturn. Schiebe (1986) argues that the reign of Saturn in Latium is Virgil's own invention. Whatever the case, it looks as though Virgil had two versions of the Saturn–Jupiter succession myth in mind, one a peaceful Euhemerist transition variant in which Cronos–Saturn gave way voluntarily to Zeus–Jupiter; cf. e.g. Diod. Sic. 5.70.1: καί τινες μέν φασιν αὐτόν, μετὰ τὴν ἐξ ἀνθρώπων τοῦ Κρόνου μετάστασιν εἰς θεούς, διαδέξασθαι τὴν βασιλείαν, οὐ βίᾳ κατισχύσαντα τὸν πατέρα, νομίμως δὲ καὶ δικαίως ἀξιωθέντα ταύτης τῆς τιμῆς (and some say that, subsequent to Kronos' migration from men to gods, <Zeus> succeeded to his kingdom, not after overcoming his father by force but after being found worthy of this honour by due process of law and justice) – following a statement that there is no agreement among sources about the matter and followed by the usual myth. Cf. Roscher *Myth. Lex. s.v.* Kronos III.1466f. If this is so, then the *maluit* anagram/etymology (cf. above, p. 63 n. 15) may be intended as a confirmation of the peaceful transfer theory. But when Virgil makes Evander narrate the myth at *Aen.* 8.319ff., it is clear from 320 that the conflict and exile version is present.

[17] For some of the implications of this passage, cf. Stat. *Silv.* 1.3.59-63, with Vollmer (1898) and Frère–Izaac (1961) *ad loc.*

[18] Cf. Knauer (1964) 229-31. The link claimed by Latinus at *Aen.* 7.202-4 between the Latins' justice and their former king, Saturn, involves a modification of the standard idea that good kings produce voluntary conformity with the law in their subjects. Cf. Goodenough (1928) esp. 91; and below, pp. 65f.

because it is their ancient home (7.219–21, 240–2). Both monarchs receive the Trojans in a temple, Dido in that of Juno at Carthage, with its gates representing the battles at Troy (a glance back at the past and at Trojan defeat), Latinus in that of Picus in Latium, which is decorated with ancient Italic images and triumphal spoils (a hint of the future and of the victories of Rome). Latinus, unlike Dido, recognises the strangers as Trojans, and is also aware of their ancestral links with his own people. As at Carthage, Ilioneus is the spokesman of the Trojans, and, as there, he addresses a king, this time Latinus, whom he calls *rex* with his first word of his first line (7.213), just as *o regina* began his speech to Dido at 1.522.[19] Ilioneus once more mentions the Trojan king Aeneas, *rex ipse* (7.220), and again speaks of Aeneas' royal qualities, although this time more obliquely: Aeneas is descended from Jupiter (220, K12) and Ilioneus swears an oath: *fata per Aeneae iuro dextramque potentem, / sive fide seu quis bello est expertus et armis* (7.234f.), thus referring to Aeneas' justice (K4 i) and bravery (K4 iv). A further contrast with the Carthage scene is the frankness of Ilioneus about the Trojan situation and aims, possible because the Trojans indeed want to remain in Italy, whereas Carthage was only a stopping-off point on their way there.

Latinus' response to the ambassadors' message continues the trend of his initial reception: he shows his royal love of peace and concord (K7), generosity (K5 v), pious respect for kin (K5 i) – for it is as kin that the Trojans present themselves to him (cf. esp. pp. 119f.), and Latinus already acknowledges them as such (195f., 205–11); he also shows a pious attitude to the gods' will concerning Lavinia's marriage (cf. p. 64 and esp. 7.254–8). He offers to the Trojans territory, friendship, and hospitality, and to Aeneas the hand of his daughter (7.259–73). He gives them gifts in return for theirs (7.274–83), which he accepts (7.261). Latinus' royal virtue of self-control (K4 ii) is stressed in 251f. (*nec purpura regem / picta movet* etc.): he is not motivated in this transaction by greed for the Trojans' gifts, but by obedience to Faunus' oracle and to fate.

But although Latinus is unmistakably characterised as a good king, he is not flawless, and in this respect too he resembles Aeneas as he was at Troy and at Carthage. Latinus is either something of a fantasist, or over-eager about public relations, or both. His claim that the Latins are virtuous without constraint of laws (7.202–4) is anachronistic, since

---

[19] Cf. also the use of this position in the first descriptions as kings of Aeneas (1.544) and Dido (1.496), and cf. above, pp. 29, 41. On the contrasting frankness of Ilioneus in the present scene, cf. Harrison (1984) 4–6.

Latium is no longer in its golden age; rather it exists in the iron age, and there is permanent war between the Latins and Evander's Arcadians (8.55). In any case law was generally in antiquity insisted upon as the basis of true freedom.[20] Hence Latinus lacks wisdom (K4 iii); and he also lacks foresight (K5 vi), as is most clearly shown by his bland assumption that Turnus will stand by idly and see himself deprived of his promised bride. The lack of these royal qualities does not make Latinus a bad king, especially since, like Aeneas, he will acquire the virtues he lacks through suffering. But it is because of his flaws that he is forced to yield, for all the admirable self-control he shows throughout, in the face of Amata's inflammatory urgings (7.373f.), together with the upsurge of popular feeling created by Allecto and Turnus (7.586ff.).

Paradoxically, however, Latinus is not replaced as effective king by a better; and it is his own good kingly qualities that are cast aside by his people, a fact which stigmatises the Italians' cause as the worse one. Hence Latinus' change of status, signalled by his abdication of power at 7.594ff. and by Virgil's declaration at 7.600 that *rerumque reliquit habenas*, does not mark an abandonment by him of his royal virtues. Latinus will remain calm when war-fever attacks his people (7.586–90), so again showing his self-control; and his *pietas* will allow him to characterise the Latins as sacrilegious and to prophesy that Turnus will pay the penalty for his crime (7.596f.). Latinus will also refuse to open the gates of war against the Trojans (7.616–19), evincing again his love of peace and his perception that the Trojans and Latins are one people among whom, as a good king, he wishes there to be concord.

The fall of Latinus coincides with the rise of Turnus. Recently Turnus has provoked major scholarly studies[21] and dramatically diverse reactions, ranging from condemnation of him as a *hostis publicus*, an out-and-out M. Antonius analogue, to more or less sympathetic treatment of him as a tragic hero, or even as an anti-hero incorporating an anti-Augustan trend in Virgil's thought.[22] In Turnus' case, as always

---

[20] Cf. Wirzubski (1960) Ch. 1, esp. 7–9; Cic. *De Rep.* 1.3.

[21] Viz. Schenk (1984) and Renger (1985), written independently of one another. They are referred to below for major discussions and coincidences of view but not for all details.

[22] Interpretations more favourable to Turnus, which often involve also the 'tragic hero' view, gained strength in the 1960s and 1970s, partly because of contemporary political events. Although now less in vogue, they were perhaps more widespread and influential than might appear from Schenk (1984) 7–19, 337ff.; cf. e.g. Mackay (1957); Putnam (1965) Ch. 4; Quinn (1968) 271–6; Nethercut (1968); Wilson (1969); Boyle (1972) – cf. Boyle (1986) Chs. 4f.; Di Cesare (1974) 218, 238; Pöschl (1977) 122–69 (but a more complex approach). The whole matter is well discussed by Stahl (1981) 157–9. The anti-Aeneas/anti-Augustan approach reappears full-blown in Farron (1981), (1982) and

with Virgil, attempts to distil the poet's complexities into a simple formulation fail, particularly because Turnus is primarily none of these things; rather he is the second major foil to Aeneas, replacing Dido, who had played this role in the first half of the *Aeneid*.[23] Turnus' strengths and weaknesses complement and sometimes echo those of Aeneas, as did Dido's in Books 1–4. Kingship is one major and neglected area in which Turnus functions as a foil to Aeneas, and examination of it will underpin some aspects of traditional interpretations of his character, while giving it more light and shade.

In essence Turnus is a bad king. His name in itself indicates this, for whatever other etymologies antiquity may have offered for it, the true derivation, from the Etruscan version of Greek τύραννος ('tyrant'), will surely have been known in the circle of Virgil's patron, the Etruscan Maecenas, so that 'Turnus' would have suggested the interplay between 'king' and 'tyrant'.[24] As a bad king Turnus resembles Dido in her latter period, but in the nature, level and development of his failings in kingship he differs from her, and this is indicated in the manner in which the pair are introduced. Whereas Dido was designated as a queen almost from her first mention, i.e. not at 1.299 but at 1.340 (*imperium Dido ... regit*) and 1.389 (*reginae ad limina*), Turnus has to wait until 8.17 before being called *rex*. This delay must be significant because Turnus is so prominent in the interval, replacing both Latinus and Aeneas in the forefront of action: he was first mentioned by name at 7.56; he subsequently played the leading role in the scene at Ardea, where he was inflamed by Allecto with martial madness, which he then transmitted to the Rutulians (7.406–74); and finally he stood out in the aftermath of the skirmish which began the war between Latins and Trojans, making bad worse with his false accusations of ill-treatment by the Trojans (7.577–9).

Now of course another reason for the delay in naming Turnus 'king' is the importance of Latinus' kingship in Book 7, which helps suppress Turnus' royal role, just as in Book 3 Anchises' prominence overshadowed Aeneas' kingship. But the delay, and the difference in this

(1985); cf. also Gillis (1984) 339–41. For a useful summary of all views of Turnus, including his own, cf. Schenk (1984) 7–24; also cf. Renger (1985) 21–43.

[23] Concentration on the antagonistic relationship of Aeneas and Turnus is a major strength of Renger (1985); but cf. also Schenk (1984) esp. Ch. 3.

[24] On etymologies of 'Turnus', cf. *RE s. v. ad init.* (W. Brandenstein), who also notes the historically false (but in antiquity perfectly credible) etymology from Τυρρηνός (Etruscan). More fantastic is: *Turnus enim Grece quasi turosnus dicitur, id est furibundus sensus* (Fulgentius *Virg. Cont.* (ed. Helm) p. 105.13f.), drawn to my attention by Dr R. Maltby. On *tyrannus* in the *Aeneid*, cf. above, p. 4 n. 6.

respect between Virgil's treatments of Dido and Turnus, may be designed to mark their different moral status. Dido begins as a good king and she has many royal virtues, some of which, in particular her hospitality and kindness towards the Trojans (K5 ii, K5 iii), contribute towards her destruction. Now Turnus is not without good royal qualities; when he first appears, he is *ante alios pulcherrimus omnes* (7.55, cf. 7.473, 7.649f., K8), and also of noble ancestry (7.56, 7.476, cf. K12); that he is (for the most part) brave (K4 iv) is stated (7.474f.) and is indubitable, even though his *furor* in battle may in part counteract this virtue. But Turnus' vices are more numerous and more pronounced than his virtues, and they exceed the vices of Dido; in fact he cannot be said ever to have been a good king, and that is one reason why Virgil delays so long before calling him 'king'. Moreover the first naming of Turnus 'king' (8.17) comes in a misleading and ambivalent context damaging to Turnus. The Latins send an embassy to Diomedes, inviting him to join the war against the Trojans. In order to increase the attractiveness of the invitation to Diomedes, himself a *rex* (11.294), the message is falsely alleged to come jointly from *rex Turnus* and *rex Latinus*, when in fact (since Latinus gave up power at 7.600) it comes from Turnus alone: *manifestius ipsi / quam Turno regi aut regi apparere Latino* (8.16f.). These two kings who supposedly agree are juxtaposed with Aeneas, who is denied the title 'king' and described as an imposter at 8.12f.: *advectum Aenean classi victosque penates / inferre et fatis regem se dicere posci*. The embassy will fail, and the implications for Turnus' own kingship of this manner of introducing it are damning.

Equally damning, both generally and in terms of kingship, is the entire portrayal of Turnus from the first allusion to him. The dying Dido prophesies that Aeneas will reach Italy, but be *bello audacis populi vexatus et armis* (4.615). When Dido, Turnus' analogue in the first half of the *Aeneid*, speaks of the *audax populus* (of which Turnus is in fact king), and of the war against Aeneas (which he will lead), the reference to Turnus is unmistakable. The second allusion to him is more precise and more ominous: the Sibyl refers to him as *alius Achilles* (6.89), an identification which he himself later accepts explicitly at 9.742.[25] On Turnus' first mention by name (7.55-7), Amata's feelings about him are noted (56f.): *quem regia coniunx / adiungi generum miro properabat amore*. Now Amata's *mirus amor* is not for Turnus, but for acquiring

---

[25] Cf. Schenk (1984) Register 1 *s.v.* Turnus – Homerische Vorbilder – Achilleus. For the contrary view, cf. e.g. Mackay (1957); Nethercut (1968); and below, p. 119 and n. 21. A valuable analysis is offered by Galinsky (1981) 999–1001.

him as a son-in-law. But given that *amor* has already appeared in the epic as a destructive force, and as opposed to royal self-control (K4 ii), this phrasing is bound to recall Dido's self-destructive *amor* for Aeneas; and it foreshadows the later revelation that Turnus himself is also a lover. A second negative factor follows immediately at 7.58, where the gods' opposition to the designs of Turnus and Amata is stated crushingly: *sed variis portenta deum terroribus obstant.* Good kings enjoy divine favour and are led by their *pietas* to accord with divine will.

Then, on his first personal appearance, his confrontation with Allecto, Turnus is shown seized by divinely inspired *furor*, in a scene reminiscent of Dido's conquest by the love god disguised as Ascanius (1.715–22).[26] It is to Turnus' credit, as it was to Dido's, that he tries to resist temptation. But even in his manner of resisting, he displays the faults of a bad king. Allecto comes to him disguised as Calybe, the elderly priestess of Juno. A *rex pius* would have shown respect for her age, sacral status and role as divine messenger (7.416–20). But Turnus laughs at the Fury (7.435); he says that he already knows what she has told him; he is presumptuously confident of Juno's help; and he derides 'Calybe' as senile and deceived: she should confine herself to religious activities and leave warfare to men (7.436–44). The incident occurs in a dream, but Turnus acts in character. In terms of homeric imitation his response brands him as an analogue of Hector.[27] The exchange also recalls Callimachus *Hymn* 6.40ff., where Demeter, disguised as her own priestess Nicippa, tells Erysichthon to stop cutting down her sacred grove (41–9). Erysichthon responds with threats (53–5), whereupon the

---

[26] Both incidents involve well-known problems about how moral decision-making is represented in ancient poetic texts. It is assumed here that Virgil and his readers would have had little interest in a world of puppets and that, for the *Aeneid* to be meaningful in human terms, divine machinery must be understood as symbolising the forces of passion at work in men and women. Thus divine intervention in no way negates the 'free will' with which individuals believe they make moral decisions; and it does not release the epic characters from responsibility for what they do and its consequences. Modern observers are perhaps better placed to understand the practical limitations of human 'free will' than their eighteenth- or nineteenth-century predecessors and may see the divine personifications in Virgil's temptation scenes as producing a greater realism, both practical and psychological, than other, more rational models of moral decision-making. For the homeric basis of all this, cf. Harrison (1960) esp. 78–80; on its application to Turnus, cf. Schenk (1984) Ch. 3.

[27] On the Hector–Turnus equation, cf. Schenk (1984) Register 1 *s.v.* Turnus – Homerische Vorbilder – Hektor. Richardson (1980) 273f. *q.v.* summarises the homeric scholia's treatment of Hector; they overstress his faults and must have contributed to Virgil's portrait of Turnus. For Hector's high-handed attitude to omens, cf. *Il.* 12.199–250; but Hector is also in other terms conspicuously pious (cf. *Il.* 24.34f. and 66–70) and is rewarded after his death by divine protection of his body (*Il.* 23.185–91, 24.18–21).

goddess reveals herself, mocks him, and places upon him the curse of her own hunger (57–64). Similarly Allecto responds to Turnus' discourtesy by revealing herself (7.447–51), mocking him, and afflicting on him her own *furor* (7.452–62).[28] Subject to it, Turnus feels such martial rage and anger as Aeneas did on the night of the fall of Troy (2.314): *arma amens fremit, arma toro tectisque requirit: / saevit amor ferri et scelerata insania belli, / ira super* (7.460–2, cf. also *furit*, 464; *nec se iam capit unda*, 466);[29] and his emotions carry over to his subjects. Here Virgil makes ironic use of the kingship stereotype. Whereas Turnus' violence conflicts with royal self-control (K4 ii), Virgil notes that the Rutulians were inspired to war by Turnus' kingly qualities – his youthful good looks (K8), royal ancestry (cf. K12) and bravery (K4 iv): *hunc decus egregium formae movet atque iuventae, / hunc atavi reges, hunc claris dextera factis* (7.473f.).

These indications of Turnus' moral status are, however, moderate and mixed compared with the portrait of him which emerges once he is at last named *rex* at 8.17. The succeeding lines (18ff.) reveal a further reason for the delay in so naming him: there Aeneas again comes to the forefront, and the scenes which open Book 8, and which preface the war between Trojans and Latins, begin to exploit Turnus fully as a foil to Aeneas, particularly in respect of kingly qualities to do with war and peace. A few lines earlier Turnus had given the signal for war (8.1ff.). As a result the Latins' minds were *turbati* (8.4), so that here the bad king's fault is again transmitted to his subjects (cf. K2); the Latins swear oaths of allegiance *tumultu / ... trepido* (8.4f.) and their youth 'rages savagely' (*saevitque iuventus / effera*, 8.5f.). This scene ends with the joint reference to Latinus and Turnus as kings already noted (8.17). *Rex Turnus*, the man of war, is thus undercut by *rex Latinus*, the man of peace; and there is sharper undercutting in the next lines, where Aeneas *cuncta videns magno curarum fluctuat aestu* (8.19). Aeneas' tumult is internal, not external; and, as in the storm scene of Book 1 and thereafter, emphasis is placed on the *curae* of the suffering good king (K5 viii). It is night and Aeneas is asleep, but *tristi turbatus pectora bello*

---

[28] For a comparison of the two texts, cf. Schenk (1984) 45f.

[29] On this simile and on 2.355–8 where Aeneas and his Trojans in the grip of *furor* at the fall of Troy (cf. also 2.314) are compared to wolves, cf. Schenk (1984) 194–9; and, on the details of the simile, cf. S. Harrison (1986) 99f. See just below for the comparison of Turnus to a wolf. On Turnus' *ira-furor*, cf. (extensively) Schenk (1984) Ch. 2 and Register 1 *s.v.* Turnus – *furor*; Renger (1985) esp. 25–9, with a useful collection of Ciceronian parallels; and, most recently, Clausen (1987) Ch. 6, which includes a valuable discussion of Turnus' *audacia* and *violentia*.

(8.29). Here, the ironic contrast of *turbati* (8.4: of the Latins inspired by Turnus) and *turbatus* (8.29: of Aeneas) glances at the theme of peace and concord, (K7, cf. p. 101), since a *triste bellum* is specifically a 'civil war'. Appropriately, it is to Aeneas, not Turnus, that the river Tiber subsequently appears in a dream to offer comfort and advice.[30]

As the war runs its course unchecked from Book 9 on, bellicose rage and madness become constant features of Turnus' character.[31] In Book 9 he is *turbidus* in front of the Trojan camp as he seeks entry (57); and he is like a wolf *asper et improbus ira*, who *saevit* (62f.);[32] his *irae* burn (66). Later in the same book Turnus' lack of self-control leads him to a serious misjudgement: had he opened the gates of the Trojans' camp, he could have destroyed them (757-9); but *furor* and *caedis insana cupido* prevent him (760f., cf also *Turno diversa in parte furenti*, 9.691). As if to point up the contrasts in this book between Turnus and Aeneas and between Turnus and the royal stereotype, Virgil twice more calls Turnus 'king' (9.327, 369). The constant antithesis being created between Aeneas the lover of peace (K7) and Turnus the lover of strife[33] is linked both with Turnus' identification at 6.89 as an *alius ... Achilles* and with the kingship tradition. The real Achilles was stigmatised, both in the *Iliad* and in the kingship literature, as a lover of strife; and lovers of civil strife were attacked in that literature.[34] Philodemus also dealt specifically with the theme that the good ruler must be a lover of victory but not a lover of war and battle; and Zeus and Agamemnon's reproach of Ares and Achilles respectively for loving strife (cf. *Iliad* 5.891, 1.177) was, apparently, part of this same complex.[35] The criticism of Achilles for this fault within kingship literature therefore lies close to the surface of Virgil's handling of Turnus.

But although Turnus' *furor* and *ira* are the most prominent of his unkingly vices throughout, they are not his only vices. Others are revealed, or reappear, at strategic points. The most notable is his lack of

---

[30] Cf. *Aen.* 10.217f., where Aeneas, again calm but caring in the midst of troubles, contrasts with Turnus in these respects, and is again rewarded by a divine epiphany, when on his way to relieve Ascanius in the camp. There too it is night; but Aeneas is sleepless and attending to the rudder and sails of his ship. In this context his royal foresight (K5 vi) is also brought to mind: the cautious orders which he gave to the Trojans at *Aen.* 9.40-3, that on no account should they leave the camp to give battle, prove to be their salvation.

[31] Cf. esp. Schenk (1984) Ch. 2: 'Der *furor* und Turnus'.

[32] Cf. above, p. 70 n. 29.

[33] Cf. Schenk (1984) Register 1 *s.vv.* Aeneas – Friede, Krieg; Turnus – Friede, Krieg.

[34] Cf. Murray (1965) 169 = Coll. XXVII-XXIX (Dorandi) and Dorandi (1982) 173-9.

[35] Cf. Murray (1965) 169 = Col. XXVII.13-17 (Dorandi), with the modifications of Dorandi (1982) 172f.

pietas (K5 i), already manifest in his scene with Allecto (7.415–562),[36] which now reemerges as a strong and permanent feature of his character, causing him to be constantly deceived and maltreated by hostile gods. It involves presumption of divine assistance and culpable ignorance of fate, and signals more clearly than all his other faults his function as foil to *pius Aeneas*. One particularly shocking indication of Turnus' 'impiety' appears in Book 8, where Evander describes the worst king mentioned in the whole *Aeneid*, Mezentius.[37] Mezentius was a wicked tyrant, barbarous, proud, savage, a mass murderer and torturer (481–8). His people at last rose up against him, slaughtered his associates and burnt down his palace (489–91). But he himself slipped away and is protected *Turni ... hospitis armis* (492f.). The hospitality of the good king is an expression of his piety, gentleness, kindness and generosity (K5 i–iii, K5 v); and the good king has good friends (cf. K9). But Turnus has and protects as friend and guest a monster of depravity and wickedness; thus he perverts these linked royal virtues. Turnus' lack of piety surfaces again, at 9.133f., where, in another imitation of the iliadic Hector,[38] he blandly brushes aside a portent: *nil me fatalia terrent, / si qua Phryges prae se iactant, responsa deorum*. It is worth remembering that the Romans, with their long tradition of public attention to portents and auguries, would have found Turnus' impious behaviour in this area even more horrifying and dangerous than Homer's audience would have deemed Hector's parallel impieties in the *Iliad*.[39] This is why the good kings, Aeneas, Anchises and Latinus, always behave with great piety in the face of portents.

Turnus shows yet more impiety when, before killing Pallas, he wishes that Evander were present to witness his son's death: *cuperem ipse parens spectator adesset* (10.443). Turnus' wish recalls *Aeneid* 2.526–32, where Neoptolemus killed Priam's son Polites before his father's eyes. The curse which Priam then uttered against Neoptolemus reveals that this action was specifically considered contrary to *pietas*: *at tibi pro*

---

[36] Turnus responds 'piously' to the message of Iris at 9.6–13 only because it stimulates him to the war on which he is already set, and his acceptance of an omen at 9.18ff.: *sequor omina tanta* (21) is immediately undercut by what follows: *quisquis in arma vocas* (22), i.e. the omen points the way he wants to go! On this scene, cf. most recently Schenk (1984) 51f., 56.

[37] Cf. above, p. 9 n. 43.

[38] Cf. above, p. 69 and n. 28.

[39] On *prodigia* etc., cf. Wülker (1903); Luterbacher (1904), and in contrast Steinhauser (1911); for late republican and Augustan material, cf. Weinstock (1971) Index I *s.v.* Portents; Kienast (1982) 179–84. Cf. also above, p. 69 n. 27. For contrasting genuinely good relations between Turnus and (some) deities, cf. below, p. 76.

scelere ... pro talibus ausis / di, si qua est caelo pietas quae talia curet, / persolvant grates dignas et praemia reddant / debita (2.535-8). Less horrific but equally serious is the impiety shown by Turnus a little later in Book 10: he has been preserved by divine intervention and carried out to sea in a boat (653-65). Far from showing gratitude to the gods, Turnus is *ignarus rerum ingratusque salutis* (666); and he even cries out in angry protest against Jupiter (668f.). It is perhaps to contrast with these repeated impieties of Turnus in Books 9 and 10 that Aeneas is shown at the beginning of Book 11 not only as especially pious in the things he does, but also as both prudent and pious in the very order (*primo*, 4; *tum*, 12; *interea*, 22) in which he does them: first Aeneas pays his vows to the gods (4-11); then he tries to give encouragement to his people (12-21); and only finally does he take thought for the burial of the dead (22-8). The reader was alerted to notice Aeneas' particular piety and prudence in this exercise at 11.2f., where the diverse pressures on Aeneas were mentioned so as to recall the suffering king motif.

A clear division in the epic action is visible in Book 11. Up to its beginning the war had progressed unchecked. But now the losses on both sides, and more on the Italian side, bring about a truce and a council of the Latins to discuss their future. The potential advent of peace allows the contrasting portrayals of Aeneas and Turnus to be more sharply focussed, and further light is thrown on them by Latinus' return to an active role. When the Latin ambassadors ask a truce for the burial of their dead, Aeneas, like the virtuous king he is (cf. esp. *bonus Aeneas*, 11.106), offers them a permanent peace (11.108-19). He follows up his offer by proposing the means to peace, single combat between himself and Turnus; and the response of the principal Latin ambassador, Drances, is to laud Aeneas in terms of two important royal virtues, justice (K4 i) and bravery (K4 iv): *o fama ingens, ingentior armis, / vir Troiane, quibus caelo te laudibus aequem? / iustitiaene prius mirer belline laborum?* (11.124-6). The consequence of Aeneas' offer is seen in the Latins' council, that scenario significant for kingship in ancient thought (cf. p. 59). In it Latinus tries unsuccessfully to reassert his royal authority and Turnus' faults as a king are damningly revealed. Drances, admittedly for mixed motives (cf. 11.336-41) but nevertheless rightly,[40] appeals to Turnus to give ground, declaring him to be the sole author of strife (*Latio caput horum et causa malorum*, 11.361). He accuses Turnus

---

[40] Cf. also below, p. 74. Drances represents a partial Virgilian 'correction' of Homer's Thersites: as opposed to Thersites, Drances is right in his proposal (*consiliis habitus non futtilis auctor*, *Aen.* 11.339), but he retains Thersites' quality of being *seditione potens* (*Aen.* 11.340); cf. Schenk (1984) 123-36.

of bringing his people into danger and, alluding further to the *salus populi* motif (K6 iii), declares: *nulla salus bello, pacem te poscimus omnes, / Turne* (11.362f.). But Turnus shows his usual *violentia* (11.376), is scathingly sarcastic, and treats the idea of peace with contempt (11.378–444). Thus he displays another characteristic of the bad king by rejecting good advice (cf. K9). The emphasis in Book 4 on the attitudes of good and bad kings to good and bad counsel (cf. pp. 44f., 53) guarantees that this motif is significant here also. Turnus might have some justification for not responding to this ill-motivated advice of Drances; but Latinus, who feels great goodwill towards Turnus, has already called for peace to be negotiated (11.302–35); and the frequent reference to Latinus as king in this context (cf. below) is intended to underline the point. Finally, when the approach of Aeneas' army creates panic throughout the town (11.451–5), Turnus seizes the opportunity to put the council once more into a fighting posture. His biting gibes reveal what he really thinks of peace (11.459–61); and he returns to a posture of warlike *furor: cingitur ipse furens certatim in proelia Turnus* (11.486), cf. *ille furens* (11.901). In this council Latinus, once again a figure of authority (11.237ff.), provides a counterforce to Turnus' violence. Diomedes, in a message to the Italians rendered *placido ... ore* (11.251, cf. 7.194, where the phrase was used of Latinus), had advised that the Latins and Trojans should make peace. The ambassadors, in reporting this to Latinus, indicate that they have come to an end by saying: *et responsa simul quae sint, rex optime, regis / audisti* (11.294f.). The implication of *rex optime* and the polyptoton *rex... regis* is that Diomedes, who is now a good king and a lover of peace, is sending his message to another good king and lover of peace.

The renewed violence which breaks up the council only proves once more that for the Latins war is a route to disaster. But Book 12 will see more fighting, and in it the contrast in kingship between Aeneas and Turnus will achieve its sharpest focus, with Latinus emerging even more prominently as the third of a balanced royal triad, and Turnus' old vices reappearing in extreme forms. At 12.1ff., although compelled by the war-weariness of the Latins to fight with Aeneas a duel which will resolve the conflict, Turnus is even more under the control of *furor: ultro implacabilis ardet / attolitque animos* (12.3f.); and at 12.45ff. he rejects with rage Latinus' kindly advice to withdraw from this single combat. Again, in the run-up to the planned duel of Book 12 Turnus is full of bellicose madness and anger: *his agitur furiis, totoque ardentis ab ore / scintillae absistunt, oculis micat acribus ignis* (12.101f., cf. also *irasci,*

104). In the same context Aeneas must deliberately arouse his warlike fury; but, even so, he retains enough composure, concern for his people and *pietas* to console his son and companions, expound the dictates of fate and explain this combat as the route to peace, and think about the negotiations for peace (107–12, and cf. pp. 78, 80). The contrast between Aeneas and Turnus in terms of love of peace/war then comes to a head at 12.311ff., where Aeneas, again appositely *pius* at line 311, tries unarmed to stop the fighting (*discordia*, 313), which the Latins have restarted. He is rewarded with a cowardly arrow wound (319). Turnus immediately restarts the battle (324ff.); and when he recovers from his wound with his mother's help, Aeneas rightly declares that Turnus is the *caput* and *belli summa nefandi* (572). Turnus' *furor* is even more clearly in play, along with other destructive emotions, before the single combat which leads to his death: *aestuat ingens / uno in corde pudor mixtoque insania luctu / et furiis agitatus amor et conscia virtus* (12.666–8 cf. *turbidus*, 671).[41] It is wholly in character when Turnus then refuses his sister's protection and insists at 12.680: *hunc ... sine me furere ante furorem*. Aeneas too, as will be seen, is capable of *furiae* and martial rage; but for him this is an exceptional condition, while it has become Turnus' invariable state.

Along with *furor* Turnus' other vices surface in these scenes: just as he rejected Drances' good advice with *violentia*, so, as noted above, he similarly rejects that of Latinus: *haudquaquam dictis violentia Turni / flectitur; exsuperat magis aegrescitque medendo* (12.45f.). This is diagnostic of Turnus' deterioration, since against Drances' malice *violentia* might have been partly excusable, while in the face of Latinus' well-meant advice it is not so. Again Turnus' impiety is prominent, for even though his fortunes are constantly in decline, understanding of the gods' power is very long in coming to him: just before the final battle, he casually dismisses Venus' powers: *longe illi dea mater erit, quae nube fugacem / feminea tegat et vanis sese occulat umbris* (12.52f.), showing that he does not understand the difference between the Virgilian Venus and the homeric Aphrodite.[42] Only when his death is imminent does Turnus become aware of the realities of divine intervention in his conflict with Aeneas: *ille caput quassans: 'non me tua fervida terrent / dicta, ferox; di me terrent et Iuppiter hostis'* (12.894f.).

But the portrait of Turnus is not unrelieved: *conscia virtus* (12.668)

---

[41] 12.666f. repeat 10.870f., which describe Mezentius. The repetition is clearly intentional and speaks against Turnus; cf. above, p. 72.

[42] Cf. Harrison (1981) 219–23.

stresses one royal quality not denied to Turnus, bravery (K4 iv),[43] which also manifests itself near his end in the words just quoted (12.894f.). Combined unobtrusively with his *conscia virtus* at 12.666-8 was his final royal fault, but one which rounds off his character in human terms, his *amor*. This first appeared earlier in Book 12, when Turnus was led to reject the advice of Latinus (and even of Amata!) to make peace simply by the sight of Lavinia: *illum turbat amor figitque in virgine vultus; / ardet in arma magis* (70f.). Before this Virgil had not revealed that Turnus was an *amator*, but in both these passages he is portrayed unmistakably in this role; and the language of both (esp. *turbat amor*, 70 and *furiis agitatus amor*, 668) underlines the uncontrolled nature of his passion, and its links with his *ira-furor*. The revelation of Turnus' *amor* only when it becomes the motive for his last suicidal decision to fight Aeneas is highly effective because it spotlights, just before the crisis of the epic, the symmetry in character and circumstances of Aeneas' two great foils, Dido and Turnus. Thus, although a vice, Turnus' *amor* helps to soften his image near his end by aligning him with Dido, that other bad king who nevertheless was much less vicious than Turnus. A last minor touch in Book 12 further rounds and softens Turnus' character in another area where he was previously very defective, *pietas* and relations with the gods. When all other deities have abandoned Turnus and when even his sister Juturna will, at the command of Jupiter, be driven off the field of battle by the *Dira*, Turnus is not forsaken by one divine helper, Faunus, grandson of Latian Saturn, and god of the Italian countryside (12.776-83, cf. p. 123).[44]

The resurgence of Latinus in Books 11 and 12 adds further depth to the contrast between Aeneas and Turnus. This is not to say that all is sweetness and light between Aeneas and Latinus. Aeneas reproaches Latinus at two points: when speaking to the Latin envoys at 11.113f., where he charges him with abandoning his friendship with the Trojans and preferring Turnus; and at 12.579ff., when Aeneas comes up to the walls of Latinus' city and accuses Latinus of twice breaking a compact of peace with the Trojans (cf. also 12.567, where Latinus' city is *causa*

---

[43] Turnus also feels *pudor* (*Aen.* 12.667). Although sometimes felt by the Trojans and their allies in moments of military stress, *pudor* is never attributed to Aeneas. Dido's sexual *pudor* appears at 4.27, 4.55, and 4.322. The concept appears not to be part of the good king stereotype, perhaps because αἰδώς (shame) was (in Aristotelian terms) a πάθος (emotion) rather than an ἀρετή (virtue); cf. Arist. *EN* 1128A.10–35. Erffa (1937) treats αἰδώς in an earlier period but is not helpful on this topic.

[44] It is worth emphasising that the view that Virgil intended Turnus to attract sympathy at his death is not mere modern sentimentality. The homeric scholia attributed the same motive to Homer over the death of Hector; cf. Richardson (1980) 274.

belli). Virgil does not of course intend the reader to hold Latinus responsible, since Turnus' guilt has already been established and Latinus could not have prevented the war. But a king and his people are, in ancient thought, closely linked, so that what the people does is ultimately the responsibility of the king. That is why Latinus, at an interval after Aeneas' first accusation, reproaches himself for not having gone ahead and made Aeneas his son-in-law (11.471f.), and why Aeneas' second accusation of Latinus is followed almost immediately by a personal tragedy for Latinus, the suicide of his wife, Amata (12.595–603), which reduces him to complete wretchedness (12.609–11).

But, despite these differences, Latinus and Aeneas are in essence of one mind. This emerged clearly in Book 7 and was hinted at again in the reply of Diomedes[45] to the Latins' embassy, when he aptly combined praise of the Latins (11.252–4) with that of Aeneas and lauded Hector and Aeneas as equal in spirit and bravery, but Aeneas as superior to Hector in *pietas* (11.289–92), a strong quality of Latinus also (cf. pp. 64f.). The consensus between Aeneas and Latinus reappears fully only at 12.161ff., where the two kings meet to agree the terms for Aeneas' duel with Turnus. Throughout the scene Aeneas' *pietas* (K5 i) is stressed: he is *pius* at 12.175 as he begins his oath; his prayer (12.176–82) shows cosmic *pietas*, addressing the sun, the deified land of Italy, Jupiter, even Juno as *iam melior* (12.179), Mars, the gods of fresh water and those of air and sea.[46] Aeneas then shows his love of peace (K7) by swearing that, if he is killed, the Trojans will retire in peace; he shows his justice (K4 i) by promising that, if he is victorious, he will treat Italians and Trojans as equals under an eternal compact, with Latinus remaining in his previous station (12.183–94). Latinus then immediately echoes these sentiments and swears that the Italians will keep their agreement inviolate (12.197–211). The truce is in fact quickly violated (12.257ff.); but this is a temporary setback, since the gods themselves will renew its terms (12.791–841; cf. pp. 104f.).

It has been argued that Turnus is stigmatised by Virgil as subject to *ira* and *furor*, love of strife and impiety. He could also be regarded as cruel for his killing of Pallas and so as lacking in royal φιλανθρωπία (K5 iii). But how can all this be regarded as significant when Aeneas appears to be subject to some of the same 'vices'?[47] This is an old problem, which

---

[45] On Diomedes in Virgil, cf. esp. De Grummond (1967); *Enciclopedia Virgiliana s.v.* Diomede; and above, p. 74, below, p. 122.

[46] On these oaths and Latinus' response, cf. esp. Fontenrose (1968).

[47] For other recent treatments of this problem, cf. below, p. 78 n. 50; the most satisfactory to date is Lyne (1983).

has been approached in a number of useful ways. That Aeneas is not a woodenly perfect hero, but has humanising faults throughout, is clear and is a tribute to Virgil's artistic realism. That Aeneas improves morally as the epic proceeds is again likely, although it is sometimes denied.[48] Thus both his irrational behaviour during the fall of Troy and his tarrying in Carthage, although reprehensible, can be seen as lapses in self-control of the less experienced and less mature Aeneas of the early books. Again, Aeneas later yields, as is human, to emotion in situations of stress, while presenting a virtuous attitude in general and when he is not under stress.[49] But as well as these general considerations, advances in thinking about particular aspects of the problem have been made in recent years:[50] the philosophical and ethical background to Aeneas' characterisation has been clarified, so that it now seems hard to believe that in the last books of the *Aeneid* Virgil is portraying Aeneas as anything other than a virtuous king. These advances make a brief reexamination of the problem worthwhile.

Aeneas' anger has already been touched on (p. 75) when a distinction was made between Turnus, who is constantly angry and belligerent, and Aeneas, who is only occasionally so and under extreme provocation; and it has been noted that the actions of Aeneas as he prepares for his duel with Turnus are particularly instructive on this point: *nec minus interea maternis saevus in armis / Aeneas acuit Martem et se suscitat ira* (12.107f.). Aeneas' *ira* is not an involuntary or uncontrolled passion, nor is it identical with *furor*; it is a conscious instrument with which he prepares himself for war,[51] and so is different from his emotion at the fall of Troy. Elsewhere in the last books Aeneas' anger is at times less deliberate; but the paradigm case at 12.107f. indicates that, as has in part been understood,[52] philosophical approaches to anger other than the standard stoic one[53] lie behind Virgil's accounts of the anger of Aeneas. Whereas the stoics saw anger as entirely vicious, the peripatetics regarded it as the 'whetstone of courage'.[54] This view appears

---

[48] Cf. Lyne (1983) 202. [49] Cf. Lyne (1983) 198f.

[50] Diverse treatments of the problem have independently pointed in the same direction. As well as Lyne (1983) (cf. above, p. 77 n. 47), Stahl (1981) notes that in the *Aeneid* not all violent emotion is represented as bad; he analyses in detail the implications. Wlosok (1980) stresses in passing that Aeneas' anger is justifiable. Cf. also Galinsky (1966) 41f.; (1981) 991. Thornton (1976) devotes a very perceptive appendix to '*ira* and *furor*' (159–63). The discussion of the death of Turnus by Renger (1985) 72–103 is also worthy of close attention.

[51] Cf. Schenk (1984) 218.

[52] Cf. esp. Thornton (1976) 159–63, concluding (162): 'Virgil's views of anger are Aristotelian or perhaps Platonic rather than Stoic'; also Lyne (1983).

[53] Cf. Ringeltaube (1913) 32–81, 83–90. [54] Cf. Lyne (1983) 189f.

e.g. in Cicero *Tusculan Disputations* 4.43ff., and so was obviously current in Virgil's day. But the problem of anger in relation to virtue was much discussed in antiquity; and Virgil was relying on his readers' knowledge of even earlier treatments of it.[55] The peripatetic solution derives from Plato, whose 'guardian' (*Republic* 375Aff.) had to be θυμοειδής ('high-spirited' or 'passionate'), which implies a certain pugnacity and ferocity against aggressors. The Platonic approach was formalised by Aristotle, who had some verbal difficulty in creating his distinctions,[56] but whose moral position is comparatively clear. For Aristotle absolute lack of anger and excessive anger were both vices. On the linguistic front this led to the apparent paradox that the πρᾶος, the 'mild man', whose behaviour was the virtuous mean between these two faults, was in fact an 'angry' man (*Nicomachean Ethics* 1125B.31–3): ὁ μὲν οὖν ἐφ' οἷς δεῖ καὶ οἷς δεῖ ὀργιζόμενος, ἔτι δὲ καὶ ὡς δεῖ καὶ ὅτε καὶ ὅσον χρόνον, ἐπαινεῖται· πρᾶος δὴ οὗτος ἂν εἴη, i.e. his virtue consisted in choosing 'the right things to be angry over, and the right people to be angry with, and the right extent of being angry, and the right occasion, and the right length of time'. Later peripatetics were following Aristotle faithfully when, partly in reaction to the stoics' absolute condemnation of anger, they regarded it as a natural faculty useful as a stimulus to bravery and as a spur towards self-defence and the punishment of evil-doers.[57] The epicureans entered this controversy; and for us they are represented mainly by Philodemus (Ch. 1 dealt with his importance for kingship theory), who claimed to be taking a view intermediate between that of the stoics and the peripatetics. The epicureans tried to pretend that while the stoics considered all anger to be evil, which in fact they did, the peripatetics regarded all anger as good, which in fact they did not. By creating this false dichotomy the epicureans could claim to hold the middle ground by advocating what was in fact the peripatetic position, namely that moderate anger was good and immoderate anger bad.[58]

Hence there exists a philosophical justification of Aeneas' anger; but

---

[55] The statements about anger in antiquity in this paragraph are indebted to discussions with and papers given by Mr J.R.G. Wright on stoic and other approaches to virtue and vice in the years 1965–74, and also to his unpublished work, to which he generously gave me access. For the Platonic origin of the peripatetic position, cf. further *Rep.* 411B.1ff.

[56] Cf. Arist. *EN.* 1108A.4–9 and 1125B.26–1126B.10.

[57] Cf. above, and Ringeltaube (1913) 33–8, 88f.; Dillon (1977) General Index *s.v.* passions, moderation of etc.; and esp. Arist. *Pol.* 1327B.38ff.; *EN* 1126A.4ff.

[58] Cf. Ringeltaube (1913) 38–50, with the warning that Philodemus' epicurean orthodoxy should not be taken for granted. He knew well that some peripatetics held a view similar to his: cf. Περὶ ὀργῆς (On Anger) Col. XXXI.31–9.

it is not a stoic one, and here again it is impossible to read the *Aeneid* as a consistently stoic epic. Virgil's treatment of anger is yet another indication (cf. pp. 36f.) that he was seriously committed to morality and moral philosophy but, as the educated man of the hellenistic–Roman age that he was, an eclectic in the best sense,[59] he was open to ideas from a number of philosophical schools, The deliberate self-stimulation of Aeneas to anger at 12.107f. is thus the morally justifiable act of a good king arousing his bravery to punish an evil-doer and to protect the innocent. He is a Platonic guardian, an Aristotelian πρᾶος and, in epicurean terms, he does not suffer disturbance.[60] The next lines confirm this: *oblato gaudens componi foedere bellum. / tum socios maestique metum solatur Iuli / fata docens* (12.109–11). They show that, far from having lost his self-control and being mad for war and destruction, Aeneas is his normal peace-loving and prudent self, glad that war is about to be terminated and wanting to fight Turnus only to promote permanent peace (cf. pp. 75, 78).[61] Aeneas goes on in 12.111f. to mention *pacis leges* immediately after referring to Latinus as king: *regique iubet responsa Latino / certa referre viros et pacis dicere leges.* Thus the entire context reveals that Aeneas' anger is not a fault but a manifestation of his royal qualities.

A number of passages in the latter books of the *Aeneid* show Aeneas acting, by modern standards, cruelly. Thus he might appear to lack the mercy and kindness (K5 ii, K5 iii) of the good king. The incidents are: Aeneas' capture of prisoners for human sacrifice after Pallas' death (10.517–20, cf. 11.81f., where they are sent off bound for sacrifice); Aeneas' slaughter in the field of the helpless and suppliant Magus (10.521–36); and his sacrificial killing (*immolat*, 10.541) of the prone Haemonides.[62] The fact that these incidents are modelled on Achilles' behaviour after Patroclus' death in *Iliad* 21 in no way exonerates Aeneas, since Achilles (cf. pp. 68, 71, 85ff., 185f.) is a poor model both in the epic and in the kingship traditions. Nor does the fact that human

---

[59] For the tradition derived from Eudorus through Areius Didymus, which, it is suggested, influenced Virgil and his contemporaries, cf. above, pp. 34–7

[60] Cf. Ringeltaube (1913) 41f.; there is a confirmatory hint of such a view at Arist. *EN* 1125B.33–5: βούλεται γὰρ ὁ πρᾶος ἀτάραχος εἶναι καὶ μὴ ἄγεσθαι ὑπὸ τοῦ πάθους κ.τ.λ. (for the mild man wishes to be free of disturbance and not to be led on by emotion etc.).

[61] This was of course the standard Roman justification of war: cf. Lyne (1983) 188f.

[62] Cf. e.g. Farron (1985). The argument of Renger (1985) 62f., following Donatus, that Haemonides is 'sacrificed' because of various derelictions of priestly duties, if accepted, would remove this deed from the catalogue but would leave the others as problematic; more interesting is the use of the same term of Pallas' 'killing' of Turnus (12.949).

sacrifice was a rare but recurrent feature of Roman religious practice, being commemorated here in antiquarian fashion.[63] There is some basis however to the view[64] that Aeneas' human sacrifice and slaughter of helpless enemies (including Turnus) are meant to show his feelings for Pallas and so to underline the importance of Pallas. Furthermore, the ancient epic hero need not have as an attribute 'humaneness' in the modern sense;[65] and ancient royal φιλανθρωπία and related virtues were not displayed in battle.

But a more satisfactory approach would look at the difference between the homeric and Virgilian heroes' accounts of their motives under similar circumstances. Achilles offers two explanations for his action in killing the helpless Lycaon, the loss of Patroclus and his own expectation of early death (*Iliad* 21.99–113). Aeneas' justification for his killing of Mago is couched in more impersonal and legalistic terms: *belli commercia Turnus / sustulit ista prior iam tum Pallante perempto. / hoc patris Anchisae manes, hoc sentit Iulus* (10.532–4). The hiatus derives from the cultural differences between seventh-century BC Greece and first-century BC Rome. The best (and near contemporary) commentary on Virgil's attitude is *De Officiis* 1.34ff.,[66] in a section derived from Panaetian stoicism, where Cicero is discussing the practice of justice in war. He begins: *atque in re publica maxime conservanda sunt iura belli*; then he explains that force should only be resorted to if discussion fails and only with a view to peace: *nam cum sint duo genera decertandi, unum per disceptationem, alterum per vim, cumque illud proprium sit hominis, hoc beluarum, confugiendum est ad posterius, si uti non licet superiore. qua re suscipienda quidem bella sunt ob eam causam ut sine iniuria in pace vivatur* (34f.). Up to this point Cicero's words could almost be a commentary on Aeneas' motives and behaviour in war: he preserves the *iura belli* and makes war to achieve peace.

Cicero proceeds: *parta autem victoria conservandi ei qui non crudeles in bello, non immanes fuerunt, ut maiores nostri Tusculanos, Aequos, Volscos, Sabinos, Hernicos in civitatem etiam acceperunt, at Karthaginem*

---

[63] The vexed question of human sacrifice in antiquity (on which cf. Schwenn (1915) for material and older views) has yet to be resolved; most recently Henrichs (1981) takes a sceptical approach. But whether there ever was a genuine historical tradition of human sacrifice in Graeco-Roman culture, the hellenistic and Roman periods believed in one and sometimes imitated their belief, cf. e.g. Weinstock (1971) 79, 399; Renger (1985) 60–9. The *arae Perusinae* may also lie somewhere in Virgil's mind, cf. Stahl (1981) 158f., but also, more recently Kraggerud (1987), much more sceptical.

[64] Cf. Renger (1985) 75–81; Schenk (1984) 347–62.

[65] Cf. Stahl (1981) 159.

[66] Partly quoted and discussed by Lyne (1983) 188 in a different connection.

et Numantiam funditus sustulerunt (1.35). The distinction made here between enemies who have and have not been 'cruel' and 'monstrous' in war is fundamental to *Aeneid* 10.517ff. Turnus has been both: he has abrogated the *belli commercia* (12.532) = *iura belli* (*De Officiis* 1.34); this is why he and his people must now pay the price. Cicero goes on equally appositely: he speaks of accepting the surrender of enemies who yield 'even when the battering-ram has struck their wall' (*De Officiis* 1.35).[67] His discussion is thus a virtual blueprint for the last books of the *Aeneid* and its aftermath: the Latins do come to terms when almost in such a plight and Aeneas does protect them, except of course for the 'cruel' and 'monstrous' Turnus, who cannot be exempted from punishment. Aeneas' own exceptionally cruel behaviour at 10.517–41 should be seen partly in these terms, and partly also in terms of the standard use in the ancient world of cruelty as an instrument of public order and political power.[68] To a society accustomed to public crucifixions and tortures and to the butchery of the arena, Aeneas' actions must inevitably have been less shocking.

Finally, the question of Aeneas and *furor*, most starkly raised at the climax of the epic, must be treated; for if anger can be justified in the good man and cruelty accepted as part of Roman ethics and practice, the same cannot be said of *furor*. In all ancient philosophic and moral systems *furor* was unmistakably a vice. That is why Virgil, when he represents Aeneas recounting his *furor* and *ira* at the fall of Troy, makes Aeneas condemn his own emotions:

> arma amens capio; nec sat rationis in armis,
> sed glomerare manum bello et concurrere in arcem   315
> cum sociis ardent animi; furor iraque mentem
> praecipitat, pulchrumque mori succurrit in armis. (2.314–17)

Here not just *amens*[69] (314) but also *nec sat rationis in armis* shows that

---

[67] Cf. esp. Aeneas' threat to destroy Latinus' city (12.567–9) *ni frenum accipere et victi parere fatentur* (568).

[68] Cf. Wiseman (1985) 5–10; MacMullen (1986).

[69] Aeneas is also *amens* at 2.745, and again at Carthage on the appearance of Mercury (4.279). The Trojan Panthus is *amens* at 2.321, at the fall of Troy, Andromache at 3.307, the mother of Euryalus at 9.478, and Nisus at 9.424. Turnus is *amens* five times (at 7.460, 10.681, 12.622, 12.742, 12.776). *insania* and its cognates are not applied to the Trojans, except while they are still at Troy, i.e. to the community at 2.42, to Aeneas at 2.776, where it is Creusa who speaks, and to Coroebus, whose *insanus amor* for Cassandra brought him to Troy and to doom (2.343, cf. his *furiata mens* at 2.407 and his death at 2.424–6). They are applied in later books to Dido, Turnus, Allecto, Mezentius and Latinus. Neither set of terms has the force of *furor* etc.; but their distribution in the epic is confirmation of Virgil's self-conscious application of moral and philosophical terminology.

the *furor* and *ira* which Aeneas felt at that time were irrational and vicious. Divine intervention by Venus gives further confirmation of this (cf. p. 39). But what then of the end of the *Aeneid*, where Aeneas, having glimpsed on Turnus' shoulder the baldric of Pallas (*saevi monimenta doloris*, 12.945), reacts by becoming *furiis accensus et ira / terribilis* (12.946f.)? Is Aeneas being condemned again, this time by Virgil, and in the final scene?

At this point an interesting set of lexical facts should be brought into play. Virgil employs in the *Aeneid* the cognates *furor*, *furo/furens*, *furiae* and *furibundus*, but these do not have the same moral evaluative force: there seems to be a distinction between *furor* and *furibundus* on one hand, which are always condemnatory, and *furiae* and *furo/furens* on the other. These latter terms may be condemnatory, but need not be. The best demonstration of this is 8.494: *ergo omnis furiis surrexit Etruria iustis.* Here *iustis* establishes that the Etruscans' *furiae* were good.[70] When the distribution of the various terms is studied, the implications emerge. *furor*, always with a negative force, ranges from excessive folly, for example of the Trojans making a breach in their walls to admit the wooden horse (2.244), through the frenzied loves of Dido and Amata, to the bellicose insanity of Aeneas in Book 2 and of Turnus in later books. However, *furor* is never attributed to Aeneas except (as noted) by himself at 2.316, where he condemns it. Likewise the pejorative *furibundus* is reserved for Dido and Amata (4.646, 7.348). But *furo* and *furens* cover a much wider range. They can be morally neutral or even positive, cf. e.g. *furit Aeneas tectusque tenet se* (10.802), where Aeneas is being bombarded by missiles. *tenet se* suggests that Aeneas is not out of control: by sheltering behind his shield rather than rushing out berserk-wise, he shows himself paradoxically to be both *furens* and σώφρων (self-controlled). Martial rage of this sort appears also in Aeneas at 10.545 (*furit*), and 10.604 (*furens*). Being *furens* in battle is thus, if it is Aeneas who is in this state, equivalent to being righteously angry. At other times *furo/furens* does have a condemnatory sense, when it is used of Dido, Amata and Turnus. *furiae* has the same range as *furo/furens*. Indeed, as has been seen, *furiae* can even be *iustae*; elsewhere, for example when attributed to Turnus (12.101), *furiae* is apparently the equivalent of *furor*. The pattern of usage of *furor* and its cognates is curious but explicable. All might have been expected, like other moral vocabulary, to range in application from the highly evaluative to the

[70] Cf. Pötscher (1983) 368f. for parallels to the phrase and for discussion. Thornton (1976) 162f. distinguishes the noun *furor* and the verb *furere*, but not *furor* and *furiae*.

highly descriptive, with the proportion of evaluative and descriptive content varying considerably. The group does behave in this way, with the exception of *furor* and *furibundus*. *furor* is different because it had become a technical term of ancient moral philosophy and had thus acquired a fixed, pejorative force.[71] Virgil seems to be using *furibundus* idiosyncratically, as though it were the adjectival form of *furor* in its technical sense.

It is therefore highly significant that in 12.946 Aeneas is fired by *furiae* and not by *furor*, since *furor* is beyond the moral pale, but this is not the case with *furiae*. If further proof is needed, the parallelism between Aeneas' *furiae* before he kills Turnus and the *furiae* of his great predecessor and exemplar Hercules should be observed. Hercules' reactions to Cacus are described at 8.219f.: *hic vero Alcidae furiis exarserat atro / felle dolor*, cf. *non tulit Alcides animis* (256), just before he kills Cacus. It is well understood that Aeneas' experiences in Book 8, when he learns about Hercules' killing of Cacus, are among his most formative;[72] and structurally Aeneas' education there as a second Hercules parallels his Herculean choice of life between *pietas* and *amor* in Book 4. Aeneas' learning about and from Hercules begins at 8.102ff.: it is on Hercules' feast-day that he arrives at Rome as Evander's guest. At 362–5 Aeneas is welcomed into the house which had welcomed Hercules and urged to emulate Hercules' moral qualities. The link continues in Aeneas' offering to Hercules (541ff.) and in the Herculean lion-skin motif, first emerging at 177f., where it covers Aeneas' couch, and then at 552f., where it covers Aeneas' horse. But in Book 8 Hercules is above all the destroyer of Cacus (185ff.); the hymn to Hercules stresses his destruction of similar monsters (293–302); and, like Hercules, Aeneas will destroy a 'monster' threatening the peace of Italy.

So the *furiae* of Aeneas and Hercules are virtuous, while the *furor* of Turnus is evil. The summing-up of Dido in Book 4 at the moment of her death (696f.) had contrived to indicate the limits of ambivalence permissible in judging her: she was both a queen to be condemned and a woman to be pitied. A similar, though less tormenting, ambivalence, accompanies Turnus: he is a bad king, but in some human and epic terms he is not unworthy of sympathy.[73]

[71] Cf. Hare (1952) for a full treatment of the sort of usage of moral vocabulary suggested here.

[72] Cf. Buchheit (1963) 116–33; Galinsky (1966); Binder (1971) 141–9; Galinsky (1972) 132–52, which analyses the assimilation of Aeneas to Hercules throughout the *Aeneid*.

[73] Cf. Di Cesare (1974) 230–3; Schenk (1984) Register 1 *s.v.* Turnus – Homerisches Heldentum, Mitleid.

4

CONCORD AND DISCORD

The previous chapter suggested various factors which lead to a positive assessment of something which has shocked some modern critics, Virgil's ending the *Aeneid* with Aeneas' killing of Turnus.[1] But a twinge of doubt may remain: could not Virgil have arranged matters differently, e.g. by sending Turnus off safe with consolatory reflections before the final battle, as Latinus tried to do (12.19–45), or by displaying Aeneas as the merciful victor, as he himself was fleetingly tempted to be (12.940f.)? This chapter will advance a further reason why Virgil did end the epic with the death of Turnus, and in doing so will investigate a vital but neglected thematic nexus in the *Aeneid*, that of 'concord' and 'discord'.[2] Their presence in it can best be approached indirectly through Horace's account of the *Iliad* and *Odyssey*:

> fabula, qua Paridis propter narratur amorem
> Graecia Barbariae lento collisa duello,
> stultorum regum et populorum continet aestus.
> Antenor censet belli praecidere causam:
> quid Paris? ut salvus regnet vivatque beatus   10
> cogi posse negat. Nestor componere litis
> inter Peliden festinat et inter Atriden;
> hunc amor, ira quidem communiter urit utrumque.
> quidquid delirant reges plectuntur Achivi.
> seditione, dolis, scelere atque libidine et ira   15
> Iliacos intra muros peccatur et extra.
> rursus quid virtus et quid sapientia possit
> utile proposuit nobis exemplar Ulixen,
> qui domitor Troiae multorum providus urbis
> et mores hominum inspexit, latumque per aequor,   20

---

[1] The main points revolved around Aeneas' Herculean *aemulatio*, the Roman view that particularly cruel enemies should be destroyed, and the legalistic Roman approach to the war–peace antithesis: for 'anti-Augustan' treatments of the death of Turnus cf. above, pp. 66f. and n. 22.
[2] For some earlier hints cf. e.g. Grant (1963–4); Hošek (1967) esp. 159–61, a paper concentrating mainly on Ovid; Binder (1971) 248f., 276–8; Harrison (1981) 211f.; Horsfall (1982) 12, on the links between Camillus, Augustus and Concordia; Cairns (1985), for a broader discussion incorporated in this chapter.

dum sibi, dum sociis reditum parat, aspera multa
pertulit, adversis rerum immersabilis undis.
Sirenum voces et Circae pocula nosti;
quae si cum sociis stultus cupidusque bibisset,
sub domina meretrice fuisset turpis et excors,　　　　25
vixisset canis immundus vel amica luto sus. (*Epistles* 1.2.6-26)

Horace's moralising view of Homer is of course sophisticated and part
of a witty conceptual triangle made up of rhetoric, philosophy and
literature. But it is based on a standard ancient way of interpreting
Homer:[3] Horace's generation and many before it accepted that Homer
was a moralist, and that the *Iliad* was primarily a story of how moral
faults caused discord (*seditio*), both between the Greeks and Trojans
and within each of their two camps, the internal strife (6-16) being
almost the more significant. Moralising interpretations of Homer have
been out of fashion for the last hundred years, but there is no reason to
think them necessarily untrue to the poet;[4] and this particular topic was
clearly of vital interest to Homer: the first lines of the *Iliad* show that
conflict is its dominant theme. The wrath of Achilles is to be recounted
(1.6f.) ἐξ οὗ δὴ τὰ πρῶτα διαστήτην ἐρίσαντε / Ἀτρεΐδης τε ἄναξ
ἀνδρῶν καὶ δῖος Ἀχιλλεύς (right from the time when they first fell out
in strife, Agamemnon son of Atreus, king of men, and godlike Achilles);
and Homer immediately picks up ἐρίσαντε with line 8: τίς τ᾽ ἄρ σφωε
θεῶν ἔριδι ξυνέηκε μάχεσθαι; (But which of the gods was it who set
them to battle in strife?). So Horace is following Homer's own
emphasis. The moralising account of the *Odyssey* which follows in
Epistles 1.2.17-26 complements that of the *Iliad*. Odysseus' *virtus* and
sapientia (17), his *providentia* (cf. *providus*, 19), his endurance (21) and
his self-control (23-6), are implicitly contrasted with the *amor* (13),
aestus (8), *stultitia* (cf. *stultorum*, 8), madness (cf. *delirant*, 14), discord
(15), dishonesty (cf. *dolis*, 15), *scelus* (15), *libido* (15) and *ira* (13, 15) of
the protagonists of the *Iliad*.

Horace's contemporaries would inevitably have seen the *Aeneid* in
similar terms and would have realised that Virgil is combining a part-

---

[3] Cf. e.g. Kaiser (1964) 109f.; Ronconi (1972); Di Benedetto (1966); Gigante (1984)
295-8. The most interesting fact in this context is that Philodemus seems to offer a similar
analysis of this aspect of the *Iliad*, cf. Murray (1965) 169; Dorandi (1982) 172-9. For
detailed discussion of the philosophical aspects of Hor. *Ep.* 1.2, cf. now Moles (1986)
34-41.
[4] For the moralising of the *Iliad* scholia, cf. Richardson (1980). Griffin (1976) and
(1980) argue for the truth to Homer of the emotional values detected by the scholia; the
truth to Homer of at least some of the moral values could equally be argued.

analogue of the virtuous hero of the *Odyssey*, Aeneas (cf. pp. 184ff.), with a part-analogue of the strife-ridden situation of the *Iliad*, i.e. the war between the Trojans and the Latins – a piece of typical hellenistic *contaminatio*.[5] In the outcome of the *Aeneid* Virgil is practising equally typical hellenistic *oppositio in imitando*, since the *Aeneid* leads to permanent peace and concord between Trojans and Latins while the *Iliad* brings no end to the war at Troy. Evidence that Virgil was conscious of all this comes at 1.458, where Aeneas sees on the gates of Juno's temple at Carthage *Atridas Priamumque et saevum ambobus Achillem*. Here not only is the duality of the iliadic strife motif recognised, but Virgil alludes covertly to *Iliad* 1.7 (part of the epic's programmatic prologue where strife is proclaimed as its main theme) by echoing the distribution of proper names found in that line: Ἀτρεΐδης τε ἄναξ ἀνδρῶν καὶ δῖος Ἀχιλλεύς (Atreides king of men and god-like Achilles). Virgil also makes the cause of the main conflict in the *Aeneid* (between the Latins and the Italians) resemble (and in the exaggerations of Aeneas' enemies become identical with) the causes both of the Trojan War and of the quarrel between Achilles and Agamemnon, that is, the theft or withholding of a 'wife'; for Briseis is spoken of by Achilles at one point as his wife (*Iliad* 9.335–45). Hence the Latins are often assimilated to some or all of the Greeks at the siege of Troy.[6]

Horace's other emphasis in *Epistles* 1.2, on kings and kingship (8, 10, 14), is reminiscent of Virgil's stress on the same topic; and the discussion of strife and kingship in combination by both writers is no accident. In ancient thought the most natural way for concord to be achieved was through the action of a king (K 7, CII 1 j). This idea goes back at least to Isocrates, who applied it to Philip, describing him also as the new Heracles (cf. CII 3 a). The link between kingship and concord then crops up in two of the pseudo-pythagorean kingship texts,[7] where the king is compared in this respect with Zeus, ruler of the gods, who harmonises the universe. It is prominent in cynic thought (cf. p. 35 and n. 20), and significantly it is linked with the cynic view of Odysseus; it is also found obliquely in Diodorus' account of the Utopia of Iambulus,[8]

---

[5] For *contaminatio*, cf. West–Woodman (1979) General index *s.v.*; for a more detailed account of Virgil's *contaminatio* of the two homeric epics, cf. below, Chs. 8 and 9. A further relevant fact is that the *Odyssey* does result in concord, both political and familial, cf. Knauer (1964) 322–7 and below, pp. 188f.

[6] The main vector for the identification is Turnus: cf. Schenk (1984) Register 1 *s.v.* Turnus – Homerische Vorbilder – Achilleus, Agamemnon etc.

[7] Cf. Tarn (1948) II.403, 409–11 and above, pp. 22f.; Momigliano (1942) 119 n. 1 – on Gorgias.   [8] Cf. Tarn (1948) II.411–13.

and it recurs in a Sibylline prophecy about Cleopatra (p. 41K), as well as in Cicero's *De Re Publica* and various texts of the principate.[9] On the politico-religious front it would generate *Concordia Augusta*.[10] The connection between kings and concord thus explains Horace's stress on the failure of the iliadic kings to do their duty by creating concord. In the *Aeneid*, by contrast, it is the initiative and virtues of the good king, Aeneas, which will produce concord.

Indeed this contrast raises the suspicion that Horace may actually be alluding to the *Aeneid* in his moralising account of the *Iliad* and *Odyssey*. The chronology and situation fit: *Epistles* 1 was probably written between 24 and 19 BC. Horace was a close friend of Virgil; there are many links between their oeuvres;[11] and in any case the composition of the *Aeneid* as the improved Roman equivalent of Homer was general knowledge long before its 'publication'. Another poet under the patronage of Maecenas, Propertius, had hailed it as *nescio quid maius...* *Iliade* in 28–25 BC (2.34.66); and Horace had anticipated its appearance in more oblique terms in *Odes* 1.3,[12] which appeared in his three-book collection of odes in 23 BC. Horace's description of Ulysses in particular brings the *Odyssey* and the *Aeneid* close together. Horace translates part of the *Odyssey* preface (*Epistles* 1.2.19–22 = *Odyssey* 1.1–5) but represents with '*sapientia*' Homer's qualification of Ulysses as πολύτροπος (*Odyssey* 1.1) – often rendered as 'cunning' – thus following the more flattering interpretations of homeric scholarship,[13] and adds *virtus*, doubtless on the basis of the hero's sufferings. This oblique invocation of the cynic Odysseus makes Horace's Ulysses look remarkably like Aeneas; only *domitor Troiae* = *Odyssey* 1.2: ἐπεὶ Τροίης ἱερὸν πτολίεθρον ἔπερσε (when he had sacked the sacred citadel of Troy), is inapplicable to Aeneas, since besides possessing *virtus*, *sapientia*, *providentia*, self-control and endurance, Aeneas, like Odysseus, survived the war at Troy, saw many cities, and sought for himself and for his *socii* a *reditus* (νόστος) – in the Trojans' case a return to their ancient homeland Italy (cf. Ch. 5). Indeed he bettered Odysseus by achieving not just his own νόστος but that of his companions, cf. pp. 206f. Even if Horace is not alluding to the *Aeneid*, *Epistles* 1.2

---

[9] Cf. Tarn (1948) II.414f.; Skard (1932) 198–202; Weinstock (1971) 260–6.
[10] Not however before 7 BC: cf. Hölscher (forthcoming) Katalog Nos. 111, 117, 118 – and cf. below, pp. 107f.
[11] Cf. for bibliography Suerbaum (1980–1) B IV 4 = 54–6.
[12] Cf. Lockyer (1967–8); Cairns (1972) 231–5; Santirocco (1986) 27–30.
[13] Cf. Eustath. on *Od*. 1.1f. = 1381.34–56 and cf. below, pp. 191f.

nevertheless gives an unmistakable indication of how Virgil's contemporaries would have viewed its related themes of concord and kingship.

It may be convenient at this point to sketch the history of 'concord' (and by implication of its opposite, 'discord') in antiquity before investigating its workings in the *Aeneid*. There are a number of Greek and Latin terms for the concept: ὁμοφρονέω, ὁμονοέω, ὁμόνοια, *consensus, concordia, concorditas*; στάσις, *seditio, discordia, discorditas, dissensus*, with date and literary form determining which are used.[14] That is why the English words 'concord' and 'discord' are used predominantly in this chapter. The ancient concept, however, formed itself especially around the words ὁμόνοια and *concordia*. Concord first appears in Homer,[15] who uses ὁμοφρονέω of private relationships, particularly marriage, in contexts where ὁμονοέω and ὁμόνοια were later used. The word ὁμόνοια seems to have arisen in fifth-century sophistic political theory to cover the relationship between different cities and between the citizens of a single city.[16] Hence it acquired moral associations and was linked with virtues from the four-fold canon, entering the familial sphere in which ὁμοφρονέω had operated.[17] The concept appears in Aristotle,[18] and it was taken up by the stoics and linked with the harmony of the universe.[19] In its original political sense ὁμόνοια (between the citizens of a single city or realm) was a catchword both in Athenian fourth-century democratic propaganda[20] and in the monarchic propaganda of Philip, Alexander[21] and their successors.[22] *Concordia* was adopted as the slogan of various parties in the Roman republic,[23] and ended up in the platforms of Julius Caesar and Augustus.[24] In the allied religious sphere ὁμόνοια was deified in fourth-century BC Greece,[25] as was *Concordia* at least by the late third century BC at Rome.[26] The appearance of Ὁμόνοια as a goddess in Apollonius

---

[14] For modern studies of concord etc. cf. below, p. 90. Funke (1980) approaches the question from a historical rather than a conceptual view.
[15] Kramer (1915) 8f. [16] Kramer (1915) 13f.; Aalders (1975) 15f.
[17] On the virtues cf. below, p. 92 (CII 1 2); on familial links cf. Kramer (1915) 45–9.
[18] Cf. Aalders (1975) 16 n. 47; Bonitz (1870) *s.v.* ὁμόνοια.
[19] Kramer (1915) 36 n. 1; Reesor (1951) 18f.
[20] Kramer (1915) 14–30; Momigliano (1942) 119 n. 2.
[21] Tarn (1948) II.399–409. [22] Kramer (1915) 47f.; Tarn (1948) II.409–11.
[23] Cf. Skard (1932); Weinstock (1971) 260f., 267–9; Hellegouarc'h (1963) 116–37, esp. 125–7. This last work in the main approaches these questions from a different but equally valuable viewpoint.
[24] Skard (1932) 207f.; Weinstock (1971) 260–6. [25] Kramer (1915) 50–3.
[26] But probably from 367/366 BC: cf. Weinstock (1971) 260 and n. 4 for a summary of the question; Hölscher (forthcoming) Katalog Nos. 112, 113.

Rhodius *Argonautica* 2.717f., where the heroes erect a temple to her, offers a piquant precedent for Virgil's interest in concord. The cult continued up to and beyond Virgil's time, with Julius Caesar's *Concordia Nova*[27] and the later Augustan *Concordia Augusta*[28] as innovations.

Momigliano (1942) distinguished between Greek and Roman practical applications of ὁμόνοια–*concordia*, but found no distinction on the theoretical side. He wrote: 'the Roman notion of Concord is almost entirely under the influence of the static ὁμόνοια' (p. 119) and: 'I have examined the material collected in *Thesaurus* s.v. 'concordia' and 'discordia' and in Skard, cit., and have not been able to discover (as far as political doctrines of the Republican and Augustan times are concerned) any relevant difference between Roman texts on *concordia* and Greek texts on ὁμόνοια, the more rigid class-distinction ('ordines') of Rome excepted.' (n. 4, pp. 119f.). Hence the concept of concord in the *Aeneid* can properly be illustrated, in the theoretical area, from Greek and Latin sources indifferently. A table of the spheres of application and associations of concord will most economically allow Virgil's frequently oblique reference to it to be treated. As with the 'good king' stereotype, and for the same reasons, the various aspects of concord will be documented from secondary works which handle the topic. These are, in the first place: Delatte (1942); De Romilly (1972); Fuchs (1926); Goodenough (1928); Höistad (1948); Hölscher (forthcoming); Kramer (1915); Momigliano (1942); *RE s.vv.* Concordia (5) (IV, 1900, 831–5 – Aust), Homonoia (VIII, 1913, 2265–8 – Zwicker); Skard (1932); Tarn (1948); Weinstock (1971); and (to a lesser extent) Aalders (1975); Dorandi (1982); Flory (1984); Jal (1961); Reesor (1951); and Wheeler (1930). These works are cited without dates in the list below.[29]

CI Sphere of action
1 Political
(a) between cities: Kramer 44f., 50f.

(b) between important people (e.g. royal family, *principes*): Kramer 46f. (cf. also CI 3 a iii)

(c) within a state between citizens, sometimes of different classes or parties: Momigliano; Kramer 16–45; Skard 191 (cf. also CII 1)

---

[27] Weinstock (1971) 260–6.

[28] Weinstock (1971) 266; Flory (1984); Hölscher (forthcoming) No. 111.

[29] For convenience reference is made to the page numbers of the partial reprint of Skard (1932) in Opperman (1967).

2 Personal
  (a) blood relations, esp. brothers: Kramer 46-8
  (b) husband and wife: Kramer 9, 11, 45–53; *RE s.v.* Homonoia 2266; Weinstock 263 n.4; Wheeler 214 (cf. also CI 3 a ii)
  (c) *amor* and *amicitia*: Kramer 45-9; Skard 189

3 Religious
  (a) Όμόνοια-*Concordia* as deity: *RE s.vv.* Concordia 5), Homonoia; Skard 174-7, 207f.
    i ὀμόνοια-*concordia* of citizens or states: Kramer 50-3 = *concordia civium*
    ii ὀμόνοια-*concordia* of marriage: Flory; Kramer 52f.; Momigliano 120 n.1; *RE s.v.* Homonoia 2266; Wheeler 214
    iii association with Emperors: Flory; Hölscher; *RE s.v.* Concordia
  (b) the ὀμόνοια of the gods–the universe: Aalders 32f.; Goodenough; Jal 222f.; Kramer 10; Reesor 18f.; Tarn II.410f.

4 Philosophical
  (a) stoic: Aalders 90f.; Kramer 36 n.1; Reesor 18f.; Skard 188-92; Tarn II.420-6
  (b) cynic: Höistad 106-15; Tarn II.404-9
  (c) other schools: Goodenough (cf. also CI 3 b)

5 Rhetorical–Declamatory: Skard 197

CII Associations
1 Political (cf. also CI 3 a i)
  (a) peace: Aalders 91; Fuchs esp. 167-205; Jal; Skard 205, 207f.; Weinstock 266-9
  (b) equality: Kramer 34, 36; Tarn II.400, 423, 429
  (c) freedom: De Romilly 207f.; Kramer 31f., 35f.
  (d) absence of revolution: Kramer 27f.; Skard 184–6
  (e) democracy: De Romilly esp. 200f.; Kramer 27f.; Momigliano 119 n. 1
  (f) defence and holding of territory: Kramer 27f., 36
  (g) facing a common enemy: Kramer 44f.; Tarn II.403
  (h) colonisation: Kramer 42f.
  (i) 'there are no victors in a civil war': Kramer 16
  (j) the action of a king: Aalders 32f., 46; Dorandi 177f., cf. Murray (1965) 169; Goodenough 67-73, 83f., 91; Reesor 18f.; Skard 201-7; Tarn II.403, 409-17, 423
  (k) among the virtues of a good citizen: Kramer 18

(l) law and obedience to the laws: Kramer 18, 28; Momigliano 119 n. 1; Skard 181

(m) sharing of resources, especially by rich with poor: Kramer 16f., 32, 34; Momigliano 119 n. 3 (cf. also CII 1 o)

(n) μὴ μνησικακεῖν (not bearing a grudge), i.e. wiping off of old scores and debts, and return of exiles: Kramer 22, 24

(o) φιλανθρωπία–humaneness: Tarn II.403 (cf. also CII 1 m)

(p) world conquest: Weinstock 263 n.8

(q) between races (cf. CII 1 b)

2 Personal Virtues

(a) σωφροσύνη–self-control: Kramer 23, 37; Skard 178, 182, 189; Tarn II.326; Weinstock 263 n.7; including avoidance of πλεονεξία (greed): Kramer 37; Skard 180f., 183, 187

(b) ἀνδρεία–bravery: De Romilly 206f.; Kramer 31, 33–36; Skard 178, 188f., 203

(c) δικαιοσύνη–justice: Goodenough 91; Momigliano 119 n. 1; Skard 202

(d) αὐτάρκεια–self-sufficiency: Goodenough 86f.; Skard 180

3 Heroes–Great men

(a) Hercules: Höistad 127f.; Tarn II.403

(b) Romulus–Numa: Tarn II.415; Weinstock 261, 264

(c) Alexander: Aalders 91; Tarn II Appendix 24 and 25; but cf. also Höistad 206–20

(d) Augustus: Hölscher; Jal 221, 227; Tarn II.415f.; Weinstock 266

There can be few periods in the history of Rome when concord had more immediate significance than in the years succeeding Actium. The final achievement of peace after a century of civil strife became a dominant motif in the literary and historical work of the time. Often the focus of interest, for reasons which will be mentioned (p. 108), was the term *pax*.[30] But in Virgil's case the philosophically and culturally richer concept of *concordia* (for all that it may have been less favoured at this time in the political arena, cf. pp. 107f.), appears to have offered more scope for moral meditation. It is hard to see how contemporary readers could have failed to grasp the importance of *concordia* in the *Aeneid*, since, to begin with, it is triply inherent in the epic action. The second half describes a 'civil war' which will end with concord between the

---

[30] Cf. e.g. Taylor (1931) index *s.v.* Pax; Syme (1939) Index *s.vv* Pax, Pax Augusta; Kienast (1982) Register. Namen u. Sachen *s.v.* Pax Augusta; Stahl (1985) Subject Index *s.v.* Peace etc.

Latins and the Trojans, the joint ancestors of the Romans. This war is a clear analogue of the recent civil wars of Rome; and the first half offers two further conflicts with significantly different resolutions. Diametrically opposite to the Trojan–Latin conflict, with its outcome in concord, is the strife between Rome and Carthage which begins with the breach between Aeneas and Dido. Dido herself spells out the bitter Punic wars which will result from it (4.622–9), predicting unremitting strife which, the reader knows, ended only with the destruction of Carthage. Between these extremes lies the conflict between Greeks and Trojans. Its temporary climax, the destruction of Troy, comes in *Aeneid* 2. But this struggle was also seen by Augustan readers as continuing in more recent history, in Rome's wars with Pyrrhus of Epirus (allegedly a descendant of Achilles), Macedon, the Achaean league and Mithridates. The outcome of this conflict was less savage than the end of Carthage: Rome conquered Greece, a victory which Virgil treats as delayed revenge for the destruction of Troy (6.836–40, cf. 1.283–5 and 2.192–4 – Sinon's lying prophecy in part fulfilled). But Greece was allowed to survive under Roman domination, and the *Aeneid*, while preserving vestiges of this Graeco-Roman conflict throughout, anticipates its more merciful solution in various episodes: in the *clementia* of the Trojans to Achaemenides (3.588–691) incorporating the μὴ μνησικακεῖν topos from the concord stereotype (CII 1 n), in the Trojans' alliance with Evander's Arcadians (8.102–74), and in Diomedes' late-won wisdom (11.243–95).

As well as being immanent in the narrative, concord features frequently in the detailed texture of the *Aeneid*. In Books 1–6 the Trojans have not reached Italy, so that their eventual concord with the Italians is not yet in question. But the theme is prominent in two important contexts in *Aeneid* 1 and 6. Concord first appears near the beginning of the epic. After an eleven-line preface and twenty-two more lines describing the wrath of Juno, the *Aeneid* leaps straight *in medias res* (34ff.). Troy has fallen and the Trojans are sailing from Sicily to Italy, when Juno stirs up a storm to detain them, and Neptune (124ff.) calms the sea again. Neptune's action is illustrated by a simile:

> ac veluti magno in populo cum saepe coorta est
> seditio saevitque animis ignobile vulgus
> iamque faces et saxa volant, furor arma ministrat;   150
> tum, pietate gravem ac meritis si forte virum quem
> conspexere, silent arrectisque auribus astant;

93

ille regit dictis animos et pectora mulcet:
sic cunctus pelagi cecidit fragor ... (1.148–54)

The role of Virgilian similes in adding depth and detail to the main narrative is much better understood nowadays than it was twenty years ago.[31] This one is the first in the *Aeneid*, and that gives it and its theme of political concord–discord extra significance, which is enhanced by Virgil's preparation for it. At an earlier point (1.52–63), the normal role of 'king' Aeolus in controlling the winds *foedere certo* (1.62) was emphasised. It derived from Jupiter's dispensation (1.60–3) and was a means of preventing the universe falling into confusion.[32] When Aeolus subsequently, under Juno's influence, withholds his control over the winds and allows the storm to begin, it is natural, given the standard ancient analogy between concord in the state and the harmony of the universe (CI 3 b), for the lack of concord among the elements to be compared with a breach of the normal harmony of a political community; and this natural tendency is reinforced by the verbal echoes between the earlier description of Aeolus and the later simile.[33]

In the simile discord, involving vices (*furor* and *saevitia*) inconsistent with concord (CII 2 a), comes upon the *ignobile vulgus*;[34] and it is repressed by an orator of *pietas* and *gravitas*, who has *merita*, who is a *vir*, i.e. possesses *virtus* in general and bravery specifically (CII 2, esp. b), and who 'rules the minds' of the seditious mob with his words. The scene probably does not allude primarily to a particular event or individual.[35] But the simile is relevant to the internal workings of the *Aeneid* and also to the recent history of Rome.[36] The storm–*seditio* of Book 1 anticipates the war of Books 7–12, for in Book 1 Juno stirs up a storm suppressed by Neptune, just as in Book 7 Juno stirs up the 'civil'

---

[31] Cf. below, p. 110 and n. 3.

[32] For the role of Zeus–Jupiter in cosmic harmony, cf. above, pp. 22–5. *Aen.* 1.58f. is in effect a description of a state of primordial chaos which preceded the world. On the simile, cf. now esp. Hardie (1986) 204–7.

[33] Viz. *vasto ... antro* (52) / *magno in populo* (148); *rex* (52), *imperio premit* (54) / *regit* (153); *furentibus* (51), *indignantes* (55), *iras* (57) / *furor* (150); *magno cum murmure* (55), *fremunt* (56) / *silent* (152); *mollitque animos et temperat iras* (57), *et mulcere dedit fluctus* (66) / *regit dictis animos et pectora mulcet* (153).

[34] This emphasis may echo the traditional Roman conservative use of the slogan (cf. esp. Skard §IV); it also recalls the contemporary phrase of Dion. Hal. 5.67.4: ἐὰν μὲν οὖν τῆς βουλῆς τὸν ἄφρονα δῆμον ἄρχειν ἐῶσιν (if they allow the senseless people to rule the senate).

[35] Although, since Aeneas is the *vir* par excellence in the *Aeneid* – cf. *arma virumque* (*Aen.* 1.1) and, most recently, S. Harrison (1986) 102, we may also be meant to think of him.

[36] For the principle, cf. Camps (1969) Ch. 10.

war between Latins and Trojans.[37] The storm underlines this parallelism in two ways: it is the proof of Juno's irrational hatred for the Trojans and is mentioned later by Venus as such (5.789–92); and the discord of Books 7–12 between Trojans and Latins is suppressed by Aeneas, a hero whose royal *pietas* and other kingly virtues match those of the virtuous orator in the simile.[38] In terms of recent Roman history the simile at least recalls the civil war 'stirred up' by M. Antonius, the virtuous suppressor of this *seditio* being Augustus.

The second key passage involving concord appears near the end of Book 6. Like the first, it adumbrates the events of Books 7–12. Among the future Roman heroes shown by Anchises to Aeneas in the Underworld are Julius Caesar and Pompey.[39] They are not named but are described obliquely:

> illae autem paribus quas fulgere cernis in armis,
> concordes animae nunc et dum nocte premuntur,
> heu quantum inter se bellum, si lumina vitae
> attigerint, quantas acies stragemque ciebunt,
> aggeribus socer Alpinis atque arce Monoeci   830
> descendens, gener adversis instructus Eois!
> ne, pueri, ne tanta animis adsuescite bella
> neu patriae validas in viscera vertite viris;
> tuque prior, tu parce, genus qui ducis Olympo,
> proice tela manu, sanguis meus! (6.826–35)   835

A number of points require emphasis. First, the pair, who are armed (826), are said to be *concordes animae nunc et dum nocte premuntur* (827). Their harmony in the centuries before their birth thus foreshadows the outcome after Actium of the series of civil wars which their conflict began; and it suggests that their enmity in life was an aberration. In contrast, and as if to confirm that Virgil intends the difference between attitudes in life and out of life to be meaningful, the good king Ancus was earlier said to possess prior to incarnation (*nunc*, 816) the same character he would have in life (*quoque*, 816). The concord in the underworld of Pompey and Caesar is obliquely anticipated earlier in

---

[37] The parallelisms between Books 1 and 7 are well known: cf. e.g. Knauer (1964) 229–33 and, on the two 'prayers' to Aeolus and Allecto, 231f.; Pöschl (1977) 24–33.

[38] The role of Neptune in this episode is all the more significant because Poseidon was an ally of Juno and the Greeks in the *Iliad*, and an enemy of Aeneas' analogue Odysseus (cf. below, pp. 188–90) in the *Odyssey*. Poseidon's help for the Trojans in *Aen.* 1 indicates both their moral rectitude and the support for their mission of the fates and Jupiter. Virgil will have been acutely conscious of the god's change of sides, given that at *Aen.* 2.610–16 Neptune helps Juno to destroy Troy.

[39] On this passage, cf. esp. Camps (1969) 96f.; Horsfall (1982).

Book 6: before Aeneas entered the underworld he saw excluded in its vestibule a number of horrible personifications (273–81), the last of which are *Bellum* and *Discordia* (279f.). This implies that *Discordia* has no place in the nether world – and to reinforce the point, the description of Actium, the climax of Rome's most recent civil war, on the shield of Aeneas in Book 8 portrays *Discordia* (8.702) and *Bellona* (8.703) in action.

Following the description of the prenatal harmony of Caesar and Pompey Anchises explicitly depicts the war between them as a civil war (832f.). Then Caesar, addressed by Anchises as *sanguis meus* (835), is urged to make the first move towards peace (834f.). This links him with Aeneas, because Aeneas actually does this later in the epic (11.108–19). The impact of Anchises' injunction is strengthened by the climax of his prophetic speeches later in Book 6, the reign of Augustus in which the Golden Age, with its implications of peace and concord, will be achieved together with Rome's world empire (6.791–805, cf. CII 1 p).

Lastly, the relationship of Caesar and Pompey as *gener* and *socer* appears in lines 830f., evoking the familial and marital links of *concordia* (CI 2 b) so important for the *Aeneid* (cf. pp. 105–7). It also recalls the hopes of the Roman people in the fifties BC for concord as a result of the marriage of Pompey and Caesar's daughter Julia, hopes dashed when Julia, whom Velleius calls *concordiae pignus*, died in 54 BC.[40] Virgil's interest in this topic is further and contrastingly shown in Book 11, when Drances, urging peace between Latins and Trojans, speaks to Turnus:

> quid miseros totiens in aperta pericula civis   360
> proicis, o Latio caput horum et causa malorum?
> nulla salus bello, pacem te poscimus omnes,
> Turne, simul pacis solum inviolabile pignus. (11.360–3)

miseros ... civis (11.360) suggests that a specifically 'civil' war (i.e. a *triste bellum*, cf. pp. 100ff.) is going on, as does the oblique evocation of the 'no victors in a civil war' concept (CII 1 i) in *nulla salus bello* (362). The marriage of Aeneas to Lavinia will be the *pacis ... pignus* (363) and (unlike that of Pompey and Julia) will achieve its purpose (cf. *solum inviolabile*, 363).

---

[40] Cf. Weinstock (1971) 263 and n. 4. On the *gener–socer* motif in Roman 'history', cf. Boas (1938) 86f.; for its presence in the *Aeneid* (and elsewhere) cf. Fordyce (1977) on *Aen.* 7.317 – oversceptical however about its significance; on these scenes, cf. also below, pp. 118ff.

This final motif from the Caesar–Pompey passage, that of *gener–socer* at 6.830f., gains deeper resonance from its many later appearances in the *Aeneid*, which often involve or imply Aeneas and Latinus in these roles. The first is soon after the arrival of the Trojans in Italy. Latinus was expecting a 'foreign' son-in-law (*externi ... generi*, 7.98); and when Aeneas landed he immediately sent a message of peace to Latinus (*pacemque exposcere Teucris*, 155), an action which relates obliquely to Anchises' enjoining Julius Caesar to take the initiative towards peace in the civil war (cf. p. 96). Latinus in reply offered Aeneas hospitality and the hand of his daughter, recognising him as his fated *gener* (7.259–73, cf. also 255–8). Juno too was aware of the situation in these terms: intent on strife, she declares *hac gener atque socer coeant mercede suorum* (7.317, cf. also 7.555f.); and when (again echoing the injunction of Anchises to Caesar) Aeneas proposes peace to the Latins after war has broken out (11.108ff.), the *gener–socer* theme appears once more (11.105: *parceret hospitibus quondam socerisque vocatis*), as it does finally at 12.192f. (contrast 11.440f.). Book 8 contributes to this development of the *gener–socer* theme with a scene on the shield of Aeneas (a construct which, through its complementary picture of the future history of Rome, reinforces those prophecies of Anchises in Book 6 from which the Caesar–Pompey passage comes):

> nec procul hinc Romam et raptas sine more Sabinas   635
> consessu caveae, magnis Circensibus actis,
> addiderat, subitoque novum consurgere bellum
> Romulidis Tatioque seni Curibusque severis.
> post idem inter se posito certamine reges
> armati Iovis ante aram paterasque tenentes   640
> stabant et caesa iungebant foedera porca. (8.635–41)

Here another 'civil' war between father-in-law (Tatius) and son-in-law (Romulus), not only the eponym of Rome but a second forerunner of Julius Caesar and Augustus (whose name suggested among other things Romulus' *augustum augurium*),[41] also leads to concord and the unification of two peoples, in this case the Romans and the Sabines. The two kings (*reges*, 639) stand before the altar after their sacrifice, holding *paterae* and making their alliance. Like Caesar and Pompey (cf. *paribus*

---

[41] Cf. Weinstock (1971) Index I *s.v.* Romulus; Kienast (1982) Register. Namen u. Sachen *s.v.* Romulus. For Romulus as the creator of Roman ὁμόνοια, cf. Dion. Hal. 2.11 and, in the context of his agreement with the Sabines, Weinstock (1971) 261 and n. 5. On Romulus and 'Augustus', cf. Kienast (1982) Register. Namen u. Sachen *s.v.* Augustus-name.

CONCORD AND DISCORD

... *fulgere* ... *in armis*, 6.826) Romulus and Tatius are *armati* (8.640). The importance of this scene lies also in its anticipation of the attempt of Latinus and Aeneas to make a *foedus* (12.286, 290) as they stand before the altars with *paterae* (12.173f.), preparing and offering the victims (12.213–15). To this latter ceremony Aeneas goes *sidereo flagrans clipeo et caelestibus armis* (12.167) and sacrifices *stricto ... ense* (12.175). Although the *foedus* is disturbed and the altar overthrown (283ff.), peace is finally assured by the death of Turnus (cf. pp. 104f.); and, perhaps to foreshadow this, Latinus is not armed but crowned (12.162–4) and is carrying his royal sceptre (12.206, *forte* there being emphatic, not dismissive), and Aeneas, when fighting breaks out, tries to stop it by stretching out his *dextram ... inermem* (12.311), *nudato capite* (12.312).

Besides the two key passages in Books 1 and 6, there are a few other references to concord in the first half of the *Aeneid* which mainly involve the original familial and marital context of ὁμοφρονέω–ὁμόνοια. These can be treated briefly in order of appearance. Book 1 contains the first of several prophecies about the future greatness of Rome (1.257–96). Jupiter comforts Venus by confirming that Aeneas will found Rome, which will have *imperium sine fine*. Juno, he reveals, will change her attitude towards the Romans and join Jupiter in favouring them. The future concord between the two gods will be both marital and familial, since Jupiter and Juno are brother and sister as well as husband and wife, as will later be stressed in the final achievement of concord between them at 12.793–842 (cf. pp. 104f.). This dual relationship of Jupiter–Zeus and Juno–Hera and its significance in terms of concord was already an explicit part of Ptolemaic royal propaganda. Theocritus had written of Ptolemy II and his sister–wife Arsinoe:

αὐτός τ᾽ ἰφθίμα τ᾽ ἄλοχος, τᾶς οὔτις ἀρείων
νυμφίον ἐν μεγάροισι γυνὰ περιβάλλετ᾽ ἀγοστῷ,
ἐκ θυμοῦ στέργοισα κασίγνητόν τε πόσιν τε.   130
ὧδε καὶ ἀθανάτων ἱερὸς γάμος ἐξετελέσθη
οὓς τέκετο κρείουσα Ῥέα βασιλῆας Ὀλύμπου·
ἐν δὲ λέχος στόρνυσιν ἰαύειν Ζηνὶ καὶ Ἥρῃ
χεῖρας φοιβήσασα μύροις ἔτι παρθένος Ἴρις. (*Idyll* 17.128–34)

(the king and his noble wife – no better woman embraces a husband in his halls, loving with all her heart her brother-spouse. Even so was brought to pass the sacred marriage of the immortal gods, those two whom Rhea brought forth to be rulers of Olympus; and Iris, still a virgin, her hands purified with myrrh, spreads a single couch for Zeus and Hera to pass the night.)

98

So close will the concord of Jupiter and Juno be that another of the three major thematic conflicts of the *Aeneid*, between Greece and Troy–Rome, will be resolved through Rome's victory over Greece, consented to by Juno, even though it means that Rome will dominate Argos, one of Juno's own most favoured cities (1.283–5, cf. 1.24). The subsequent apotheosis either of Julius Caesar or of Augustus[42] will be followed by universal peace: *Fides*, Vesta, Romulus, and Remus, will rule together, i.e. justice and concord will prevail (292f., cf. 293–6).[43]

After a brief interval the theme appears again in Book 1 in a balancing description of discord between another brother and sister (cf. p. 43). At lines 335ff. Venus, disguised as a Punic girl, offers Aeneas a brief account of Dido's kingdom, founded when Dido fled from her brother, who had murdered her husband. This discord in the royal family of Tyre–Carthage was brought about by that standard cause of discord, greed (349, 363f.).[44] Here Virgil implicitly contrasts the circumstances of Dido's exile with that of Aeneas, brought about by external forces. The point is that Carthage from its foundation was a product of discord, and Dido its focus. Further, Dido's history of familial discord presages both the breach between Trojans–Romans and Carthaginians, stemming from Aeneas' non-marital liaison with Dido, and, by contrast, the eventual concord between Trojans and Italians achieved through the marriage of Aeneas and Lavinia and sanctioned by the concord of the divine brother–husband and sister–wife, Jupiter and Juno (cf. also pp. 104f.).

There are three allusions to concord in the third book: the eventual reconciliation of Juno to the Trojans is reflected in Helenus' insistent precepts that they should worship and conciliate her (3.435–40); the 'common blood' association of concord (CI 2) appears in Aeneas' prophetic farewell to Helenus (3.500–5);[45] and finally concord is seen in the Achaemenides episode (3.588ff.). In Book 4 Juno, who is a primary source of discord throughout the *Aeneid*, offers Venus an accommodation, consisting in the marriage of Dido and Aeneas and harmonious

---

[42] The matter is disputed: cf. esp. Austin (1971) on *Aen.* 1.286ff.; but Austin (1977) on *Aen.* 6.788 *gentem* was less inclined than before to believe that *Caesar* at 1.286 is another allusion to Julius. Cf. however Horsfall (1982) 14 for a sharper insight.

[43] On Romulus and *concordia* see above, p. 97 n. 41 and Skard (1932) 205f. Since Romulus was associated with the *patres* and Remus with the *plebs* (cf. Syme (1956), the reference is probably to the concord of the *SPQR*.

[44] Cf. Weinstock (1971) 263 n. 7, and CII 2 a in general.

[45] The most plausible explanation for Aeneas' emphasis on this matter connects it with the Augustan foundation of Nicopolis – cf. Williams (1962) on *Aen.* 3.280, 505 *maneant* etc.; on the scale of Nicopolis and its significance for the regime, cf. Kienast (1982) 373f., 376f.

peace and unity between their two peoples. The invalidity of her offer and of its acceptance by Venus has already been discussed (p. 46); but the incident is thematically important since it alludes, both in outline and in some details, to the eventual harmonious solution through a marriage of that other conflict between another pair of peoples, the Trojans and Latins. The key passage is:

> quin potius pacem aeternam pactosque hymenaeos
> exercemus? habes tota quod mente petisti: 100
> ardet amans Dido traxitque per ossa furorem.
> communem hunc ergo populum paribusque regamus
> auspiciis; liceat Phrygio servire marito
> dotalisque tuae Tyrios permittere dextrae. (4.99–104)

The language and content of lines 102–4 is echoed in a similar context at 7.255–8, where the eventual marriage of Aeneas and Lavinia is in question: *paribusque in regna vocari / auspiciis* (7.256f.) corresponds with *paribusque regamus / auspiciis* (4.102f.); peace, concord and the union of two peoples are involved there too. But whereas Jupiter and destiny approve of Aeneas and Lavinia's marriage, they disapprove of Juno's proposal, as both goddesses know. Venus' stress on Juno being the wife of Jupiter (*tu coniunx*, 4.113) ironically underlines the divine couple's present lack of marital concord.[46]

This chapter opened with the familiar problem of why Virgil ends the *Aeneid* with Aeneas' killing of Turnus. But then it went on to discuss concord/discord and the manifestations of these concepts in the first six books, pointing out some resonances from the second half of the epic. The question of Turnus' death was held in abeyance. In the remainder of this chapter attention will turn to Books 7–12, where the theme of concord emerges in full force and where (particularly from Book 8 on) it becomes inextricable from the question of Turnus' death.

Immediately after the Trojan landing at Latium, Trojans and Latins both make moves towards peace and friendship (7.148ff.). But then Allecto enters the scene. Her link with discord is explicit immediately: *cui tristia bella* (i.e. civil wars) */ iraeque insidiaeque et crimina noxia cordi* (7.325f.). The next two lines, *odit et ipse pater Pluton, odere sorores / Tartareae monstrum* (7.327f.), by negating familial concord, stress that Allecto is the quintessence of discord: she is detested not just by her father, but even by her sisters, the other Furies (CI 2 a). Juno 'sharpens'

---

[46] On Virgil's Venus in contrast with the homeric Aphrodite, cf. Harrison (1981) 219–22, and above, p. 46.

this already ferocious creature and requests her to prevent the marriage of Aeneas and Lavinia, the potential source of concord between Trojans and Latins (7.331–40). Juno backs her request in sacral 'Du-Stil'[47] with a recitation of the Fury's powers, the first of which is *unanimos armare in proelia fratres* (335), a combined allusion to fraternal concord (CI 2 a) and its opposite, civil war, which illustrates well the standard ancient equivalence of familial and public harmony. Allecto agrees; significantly she first stirs up Amata to embroil Latinus' household, *quo furibunda domum* (i.e. the normal seat of concord, cf. CI 2 a, b) *monstro permisceat omnem* (348), before going on to rouse Turnus and the rest of the Italians. Pertinently, the first Italian victim is '*senior*' Galaesus: *dum paci medium se offert, iustissimus unus / qui fuit Ausoniisque olim ditissimus arvis* (7.535–7). As *iustissimus* (CII 2 c), an older man of peace and an attempted mediator between the combatants, Galaesus, apart from being a most undeserving victim of discord, resembles Latinus, and also Aeneas. The scene clearly anticipates 12.311ff., where Aeneas, unarmed, calls for peace in the midst of battle and is wounded while doing so. Finally, at 7.545 the Fury begins the report of her achievements to Juno with the words *en, perfecta tibi bello discordia tristi*.

The phrase *triste bellum* ('civil war') recurs when Aeneas returns to the forefront at the beginning of Book 8, in a scene discussed above (pp. 70f.). At 8.18–30 Aeneas is troubled, partly of course because of the powerful forces gathering against the Trojans (8.1–17 and cf. *cuncta videns*, 19), but primarily because the war is a civil one; *Aeneas, tristi turbatus pectora bello* (8.29). Aeneas the man of concord is in sharp contrast to Turnus, the energetic instigator of strife (8.1–5). In Book 8 Aeneas' anxieties about how to counter the threat of war are assuaged directly (by supportive deities – Tiber, Vulcan and Venus – and good omens, by alliance with Evander, and by prospective help from the Etruscans). But resolution of his concern about civil strife is achieved in more complex ways. Part of the answer (as was noted in Ch. 3) lies in his growing identification throughout Book 8 with Hercules. Now Hercules is a type of concord (CII 3 a), particularly in cynic thought which may, if the evidence presented in Ch. 2 is plausible, have attracted Virgil. One passage of Apuleius (*Florida* 22) is worth quoting as illustration:

Crates ille, Diogenis sectator, qui ut Lar familiaris apud homines aetatis suae Athenis cultus est; nulla domus ei umquam clausa erat,

---

[47] For discussion of prayers in the *Aeneid*, cf. most recently Jeanneret (1973), analysing (in effect) topoi and their variations.

nec erat patrisfamilias tam absconditum secretum, quin eo tempe-
stive Crates interveniret, litium omnium et iurgiorum inter pro-
pinquos disceptator atque arbiter. Quod Herculem olim poetae
memorant monstra illa immania hominum ac ferarum virtute
subegisse orbemque terrae purgasse, similiter adversum Iracun-
diam et Invidiam, Avaritiam atque Libidinem ceteraque animi
humani monstra et flagitia philosophus iste Hercules fuit.

The account of Crates the reconciler is followed immediately by the
overlapping description of Hercules the destroyer of monsters (i.e. the
vices), and the pair are identified. Apuleius is implying that Hercules
too was a 'cynic' reconciler who achieved concord by destroying the
monstrous incorporations of vice. The exemplary killing of Cacus by
Hercules described by Evander at *Aeneid* 8.185ff. (cf. 293ff.) thus
contributes to Aeneas' understanding of his own role as promoter of
concord, and reinforces the reader's awareness that the conflict between
Trojans and Latins, fuelled by discord, can only be ended by the killing
of its embodiment, Turnus. The further scenes on the shield of Aeneas
which reinforce this trend are included more perhaps for the readers'
enlightenment than for Aeneas', since they lie in his future and he is said
not to comprehend them (cf. *rerum ignarus*, 8.730). The scenes are the
reconciliation of Romulus and Tatius (8.635–41, cf. pp. 97f.), and the
battle of Actium, the solution to Rome's most recent civil war, where
Antonius is arrayed with all the forces of the East, while demons,
including *Discordia* and *Bellona*, range about (671–713).[48] The defeat of
Antonius leads to the final scene on the shield and climax of Book 8, the
triumph of Augustus (714–28). The dithyrambic genre drawn upon
here[49] and the Herculean associations of the triumph[50] tie this scene
back to the other Herculean material in Book 8, especially the killing of
Cacus.[51] The unmistakable implication is that Aeneas, like Hercules
and Augustus, must end discord by destroying its cause.

With the council of the gods at 10.1ff., which introduces the final
phase of the epic, concord comes even more prominently to the fore.
Jupiter speaks about the discord obtaining among the gods, connecting
it with the discord between Trojans and Italians. He demands peace
among gods and men and sees the future non-civil, and so licit, war
between Carthage and Rome as an acceptable substitute for the present

---

[48] On *Bellum* and *Discordia* at *Aen.* 6.279f. cf. above, pp. 95f.
[49] Cf. Versnel (1970) Index *s.vv.* Bakchos, Dionysos; Cairns (1972) 95–7; A. Hardie
(1977).
[50] Cf. Versnel (1970) 90; and esp. A. Hardie (1977) 114–20.
[51] Cf. above, p. 84 and n. 72 for the main bibliography.

illicit one (10.6–15 esp. 9: *contra vetitum discordia*). The link between divine and human kingship and the philosophical notion that the ruler of the gods maintained the harmony of the universe as a prerequisite and model for human concord (CI 3 b) have already been discussed (pp. 22-5). The prominence of these concepts at this high point of the epic, and their reappearance in a later decisive passage in *Aeneid* 12, guarantee further the importance of concord in the *Aeneid*; and Books 10-12 are in essence an account of how concord is established among gods and men through the actions of Jupiter. But at the beginning of Book 10 Juno is still opposed to Jupiter, and Jupiter admits that the time is not yet ripe for divine, and hence human, concord: *nec vestra capit discordia finem* (106). Nevertheless its establishment has begun, and this is powerfully advanced by Aeneas. The scene in which Aeneas responds to the Italians' request for a truce to bury their dead (11.108ff., cf. p. 73), combines the *gener-socer* theme with that of being first to offer peace (cf. 6.834f. and pp. 96f.) and with Aeneas' royal virtues. The two attributed to him here, bravery and justice (11.126), are also virtues strongly associated with concord (CII 2 b, c). Again the council of the Italians which follows (cf. pp. 73f.) reintroduces the *gener-socer* motif (11.440f.), but with different and dramatically ironic reference. Turnus refers to his hoped-for future relationship with Latinus, and so confirms his inevitable doom, by asserting something contrary to the fates.[52] The council restresses kingship motifs but also echoes the council of the gods in its discord, revealing in the Italian camp the internal strife which affected both Greeks and Trojans in the *Iliad*. Italian discord contrasts with the internal concord of the Trojans and their allies; for even when he loses his only son, Evander does not blame Aeneas (11.176f.) but demands that Aeneas take vengeance on Turnus (11.177–81), whereas the Italians criticise Turnus for their losses in the war (11.215–17, 360–3). Italian discord is vividly illustrated at 11.213–24, where they are divided in their views of Turnus, and again at 11.451ff. When the Latins hear of the approach of the Trojan army, there is confusion and shouting *dissensu vario* (455) and their reactions are illustrated in a simile comparing them to a flock of *rauci ... cycni* (456–8). This is a 'correction' of *Iliad* 3.2-6, where the Trojans were noisy and were compared to a flock of cranes, while the Greeks were quiet, orderly and disciplined (8f.).[53]

[52] A parallel signal is the promise made on Aeneas' behalf to Nisus and Euryalus by Ascanius of Latinus' land (*Aen.* 9.274).

[53] This interpretation appears in Schol. AT ad *Il.* 3.2 - *q.v.*, and in Schol. AbT ad *Il.* 3.5;

Aeneid 12 sees Turnus fostering discord just as the gods are about to reach concord. The truce made to allow the single combat of Aeneas and Turnus is broken, but the speech of Aeneas which fixes its terms not only anticipates the terms on which Trojans and Latins will arrive at concord, but also those on which divine concord will be achieved. The key lines are:

> non ego nec Teucris Italos parere iubebo
> nec mihi regna peto: paribus se legibus ambae 190
> invictae gentes aeterna in foedera mittant.
> sacra deosque dabo; socer arma Latinus habeto,
> imperium sollemne socer; mihi moenia Teucri
> constituent urbique dabit Lavinia nomen. (12.189–94)

The pledges of equality and freedom (CII 1 b, c) and of legality (CII 1 l),[54] the concept of 'no victors' (CII 1 i), and the prominence of marriage as the means to concord (CI 2 b), with *socer* prominently in two successive lines (192f.), all these are important associations of the theme; and all recur in the later exchange between Jupiter and Juno which will finally end discord among the gods. Juno asks:

> pro Latio obtestor, pro maiestate tuorum: 820
> cum iam conubiis pacem felicibus (esto)
> component, cum iam leges et foedera iungent,
> ne vetus indigenas nomen mutare Latinos
> neu Troas fieri iubeas Teucrosque vocari
> aut vocem mutare viros aut vertere vestem. 825
> sit Latium, sint Albani per saecula reges,
> sit Romana potens Itala virtute propago:
> occidit, occideritque sinas cum nomine Troia. (12.820–8)

and Jupiter agrees:

> es germana Iovis Saturnique altera proles, 830
> irarum tantos volvis sub pectore fluctus.
> verum age et inceptum frustra summitte furorem:
> do quod vis, et me victusque volensque remitto.
> sermonem Ausonii patrium moresque tenebunt,
> utque est nomen erit; commixti corpore tantum 835
> subsident Teucri. morem ritusque sacrorum
> adiciam faciamque omnes uno ore Latinos.

Schlunk (1974) is useful on the general principle that Virgil is influenced by the homeric scholia but does not discuss this passage.

[54] These amount to the notion of 'isopolity', current in the hellenistic and later periods: cf. Gawantka (1975) *passim* and, in connection with concord, 43 n. 9, 120 n. 64.

hinc genus Ausonio mixtum quod sanguine surget,
supra homines, supra ire deos pietate videbis,
nec gens ulla tuos aeque celebrabit honores. (12.830–40)

The stress by Jupiter on the sibling relationship between Juno and himself (12.830, cf. CI 2 a) which complements the emphasis placed by him on their conjugal state at the beginning of their discussion (12.793, cf. CI 2 b), redoubles the significance of their concord.[55] Jupiter then 'yields' to Juno even though he has defeated her, an example of the 'no victors' concept (CII 1 i); and he confirms all the concessions offered by Aeneas to the Italians at 12.189–94.[56] But while fate has thus moved forward, Turnus has remained as he was. When Juturna causes the truce to be broken, the two heroes again reveal their attitudes to strife and concord (cf. p. 75). Turnus in his last battles shows his true character repeatedly, eagerly entering the battle as soon as he sees Aeneas retire from the field (12.324ff.), and happy to slaughter Trojans indiscriminately. Thus Turnus confirms that no treaty could ever bind him to peace.

As well as shedding light on many details of the *Aeneid* and underscoring some of its underlying preoccupations, attention to the theme of concord also elucidates one feature which might otherwise seem puzzling. The *Aeneid* is the national epic of Augustan Rome, embodying the aspirations, the pride and the self-image of the rulers of the world. Yet of all the aspects of human life, it is centred most clearly on love and marriage. The three events which control its structure and narrative development most firmly are the disappearance of Creusa at the end of Book 2, Aeneas' breach with Dido in Book 4, and the prospective marriage between Aeneas and Lavinia. The disappearance of Creusa makes Aeneas an eligible widower and so allows the Dido episode to dominate the first half of the *Aeneid* and the marriage with Lavinia the second. The breach with Dido releases Aeneas for Italy and Lavinia; and his marriage with Lavinia produces the concord which makes the Roman world domination possible. Now Virgil was writing an epic and not a modern or Augustan political or historical tract; and

---

[55] On the Ptolemaic associations of the sister–wife motif cf. above, p. 98.

[56] At *Aen.* 12.192 Aeneas had said: *sacra deosque dabo*. This most naturally means: 'I shall contribute my religious rites and gods' and not: 'I shall give up my religious rites and gods'. Thus the line might seem inconsistent with Jupiter's words at *Aen.* 12.836f. But Jupiter probably means: 'I shall introduce (sc. the Trojan) religion' (cf. Tilly (1969) and Williams (1973) *ad loc.*); and *supra ire deos pietate* (12.839) compliments Aeneas' *pietas*.

erotic causation was standard within the epic tradition,[57] in the *Iliad* and *Odyssey* as well as the *Argonautica*. Again, in the Augustan period dynastic marriages were important. But it might still seem strange that the Roman national epic, written many centuries after Homer for readers of very different tastes, should depend so heavily on one man's 'widowerhood', love affair and marriage – unless of course these themes had an additional and higher significance.

Seen like this, the problem is interestingly similar to that of divine machinery in the *Aeneid*. This too is a traditional epic feature, and it is well understood that Virgil gladly used it because, in addition to its epic functions, it allowed him to introduce an extra dimension of philosophic and moral allegory.[58] The use of the traditional erotic causation of epic in the *Aeneid* serves, it may be suggested, a similar double purpose. Wheeler (1930), a paper dealing with the ancient epithalamium which is totally unconcerned with Virgil, nevertheless made some observations relevant to the *Aeneid* (p. 214). The paper speaks for itself, and the homeric origin (*Odyssey* 6.180–5) of the concept in play confirms its relevance:

> Harmonious love (*concordia*, ὁμόνοια) was an important topic of the epithalamium ... In the sixty-first poem Catullus does not use the word, but he emphasizes the idea (31–25, 100, 139–146). The rhetoricians have much to say on the subject.
>
> The wedding pair, says Dionysius, should be urged to the greatest possible harmony; the wedding orator should demonstrate its blessings and should say in fact that there is no greater blessing,
>
> ἦ ὅθ' ὁμοφρονέοντε νοήμασιν οἶκον ἔχητον
> ἀνὴρ ἠδὲ γυνή.
>
> [than when husband and wife live together concordant in mind, Μεθοδ. γαμ. 3f., cf. 5–6; Hom. *Od.* 6.183f.]
>
> Choricius praises ὁμόνοια very prettily: ἡδὺ μὲν λύρα χορδῶν συμφθεγγομένων ἀλλήλαις, ἡδὺ δὲ ζεῦγος συνωρίδος ὁμονοούσης, ἥδιστον δὲ πάντων γυνὴ ταὐτὰ φρονοῦσα τῷ συνοικοῦντι

---

[57] Antiquity had noted this feature, declaring Homer to be an erotic writer, cf. esp. Lausberg (1983) 235–7. One interesting comment (quoted by Lausberg (1983) 235 n. 102) is *Pap. Genev.* inv. 271, col.XIV.34ff.: Ἰλιὰς αὐτῶι [καὶ Ὀδύσ]σεια, τὰ μεγάλα ἔ[ρ]γα, δύο [γυ]ναικ[ῶν] ἐστιν [π]άθη, τῆς [μ]ὲν ἁρπασθείσης, τῆς δὲ βου[λο]μένης (His great works, the *Iliad* and *Odyssey*, are <love>-stories of two women, one [Helen] carried off by fate, and the other [Penelope] whose love was voluntary). Virgil's politico-moral handling of the topic may well be his 'correction' of Homer. Hor. *Ep.* 1.2.6f. (on which cf. above, pp. 85f.) alludes wittily to this concept in connection with the *Iliad*, which makes its absence from his account of the *Odyssey* all the more striking.

[58] Cf. Wlosok (1986).

[Sweet is the lyre when its strings sound harmoniously, sweet is the yoke of two horses in harmony, but the sweetest of all things is a wife of one mind with her husband, *Orat.* 6.40].

To Menander ὁμόνοια is one of the blessings of marriage, and he advises the orator, as he exhorts the wedded pair, to say that they will have dreams which will prophesy for them the birth of children, ὁμόνοια throughout life, the increase of wealth, etc. (p. 214)

It may well be that these close, and ultimately homeric, associations between marriage and concord explain Virgil's ready and heavy dependence on love and marriage. For it is in this way above all that the non-marriage of Aeneas to Dido and his subsequent real marriage with Lavinia could convey to Virgil's Augustan audience the poles of discord and concord around which the *Aeneid* moves.

The understanding of these links, which make Dido and Lavinia even more important characters in the epic than they have hitherto seemed, will stimulate further investigation of the character of Dido, not as a queen but as a woman, in Chapter 6, and analysis in Chapter 7 of that most understated and under-investigated of all Virgil's characters, Aeneas' future bride Lavinia. But one question remains: if concord is so important a theme for the *Aeneid*, why does Virgil never use the word *concordia* anywhere in it? There are a number of convergent answers. Although *concordia* is metrically suitable for the hexameter, it may have had associations which deterred Virgil from using it, associations not shared by e.g. *concors* or *discordia* or *seditio*, which Virgil does employ.[59] That Virgil was sensitive to different shadings within a group of cognates was seen (pp. 83f.) with regard to *furor* and its family, where again one of the cognates was a technical term of philosophy. But his admittance of the word *furor* into the epic makes his use of that group not entirely parallel. *TLL s.v. concordia q.v.* notes that the word is rare in poetry; it may have had too many technical and philosophical overtones to make for easy use in a variety of poetic contexts.[60] Changes of fashion may also be involved. The word (but not the concept) may have been

[59] Virgil uses *Discordia* or *discordia* at *Aen.* 6.280, 7.545, 8.702, 10.9, 10.106, 12.313, 12.583 and at *Ecl.* 1.71, *Georg.* 2.459, 2.496, 4.68, and *discors* at *Aen.* 2.423, 9.688, 10.356, *Georg.* 2.459. He also uses *dissensus* at *Aen.* 11.455, *unanimus* at *Aen.* 4.8, 7.335, 12.264, and *concors* at *Aen.* 3.542, 6.827, *Ecl.* 4.47.

[60] Even the two appearances of *concordia* in Catullus, viz *qualis adest Thetidi, qualis concordia Peleo* (64.336) and *sed magis, o nuptae, semper concordia vestras, / semper amor sedes incolat assiduus* (66.87f.), are 'technical' in the sense that they involve marriage – cf. above, p. 106.

out of vogue politically in the early Augustan decades.[61] It is a peculiarity of this period that the goddess *Concordia* seems to drop out of favour in the years 40 BC – 10 BC approximately. Julius Caesar's temple of *Concordia Nova* dates from 44 BC, while the temple of *Concordia Augusta* was begun in 7 BC, and the temple of Concordia in the Portico of Livia was dedicated in that same year. The coinage record shows a similar gap (39 BC – *c.* 10 BC) as does statuary (40 BC – 11 BC).[62] If this impression is not simply due to lack of evidence, then something about the term *concordia* may have been suspect for a time. Perhaps it was too closely associated with Julius Caesar for the 'restored Republic' to be comfortable with it. The emergence of *pax* as a key term in the official propaganda and in literature is contemporaneous with *concordia*'s eclipse.[63] In effect the vaguer term is being used as a less coloured substitute.

Virgil on the other hand, although fond of *pax*, focusses more on the concept of concord – which, with its wider philosophical dimension, gave greater scope for poetic exploitation.[64] The impressions and questions raised by Virgil's use of the ideology of kingship at pp. 5–8, 60-2 are relevant here too. As with kingship, so in his concentration on concord, he seems to have been more Caesarian than Augustus himself; perhaps, again, Virgil, an intimate of the *princeps* and aware of the reality behind the façade, was reflecting on the unofficial rather than the public policy. Neither should the possibility be overlooked that Virgil actually contributed to the foundations of Roman imperial thought; for concord, like kingship, becomes integral to imperial ideology in the succeeding centuries.

[61] Yet even here literary taste may be more significant since Julius Caesar, although much concerned with concord, never used the words *concordia* or *discordia* in his writings but instead employed *consensus, consentire, dissensio* and *dissentire*: cf. Weinstock (1971) 263.

[62] Cf. Weinstock (1971) 260-6; Hölscher (forthcoming) Katalog Nos. 1-6, 10, 70, 108-11, 116-18, 147 and Kommentar thereon. I am grateful to Prof. T. Hölscher for drawing my attention to this factor.

[63] Cf. e.g. Jal (1961), although some of his formulations may be worth questioning; Weinstock (1971) 267-9; Hellegouarc'h (1963) Index verborum latinorum *s.v.* Pax.

[64] With around 40 occurrences of *pax* and its cognates in the *Aeneid*, that term is obviously important for Virgil. But a further fundamental reason for focussing discussion on concord is the traditional 'collectivity' of the Roman state. On this, in contrast with the ethos of Greek states, and on *concordia*–ὁμόνοια as the 'positive names for this quality', cf. Griffin (1979) 73f.

5

GEOGRAPHY AND NATIONALISM

At *Aeneid* 8.10–17 a Latin embassy is sent to Diomedes to present Turnus' case against Aeneas. Trojan Aeneas has invaded Italy, declaring himself its fated king, and ready to wage a war of conquest against the native peoples. Prejudice apart, it might well be asked why the 'good king' Aeneas, with his royal duty to foster concord, has been sent by Jupiter and the fates to stir up discord by invading a foreign land. For Virgil, however, Aeneas is no foreigner. He is an Italian with a right to rule in Italy; and his destiny, far from being to stir up discord, is to establish concord within *tota Italia*. How boldly Virgil asserts this position is not always appreciated. This chapter will investigate his strategies in claiming Italian nationality for his hero and the import of that claim.

In *Aeneid* 12, just before the last battle between Aeneas and Turnus, a simile elaborates upon Aeneas' appearance and the dreadful sound he makes as he moves in his armour: *quantus Athos aut quantus Eryx aut ipse coruscis / cum fremit ilicibus quantus gaudetque nivali / vertice se attollens pater Appenninus ad auras* (12.701–3). The comparison of Aeneas, first to Mt Athos, then to Mt Eryx, and finally to the Appennines, is an allusive summary of Aeneas' journey from Troy to Italy. But the analogy with *pater Appenninus*, occupying the final two and one-third lines of this three-line simile,[1] has another function. Virgil is assimilating Aeneas to the Appennines, the most prominent feature of the landscape of central Italy – a staggeringly bold way of expressing the Italian character of Aeneas and indeed of the whole Trojan race.[2]

[1] Cf. Perutelli (1972) 43 on the third comparison, and esp. on the emphatic function of *ipse*.
[2] The description at 5.412 of Eryx as Aeneas' *germanus* adds weight to this interpretation of the simile. Various aspects of Aeneas' 'return' to Italy and related motifs are discussed by Buchheit (1963) 151–72, a seminal treatment; Wigodsky (1965); Bohn (1965); Suerbaum (1967); Schweizer (1967); Horsfall (1971); Bonjour (1975) 476–583; for brief but valuable insights into aspects of Virgil's geographical interests, cf. Hahn (1984). Perutelli (1972) 42–5 draws attention to this and two other similes of *Aen.* 12 (715–22, 749–55) where Italian geography is introduced. He rightly sees them in the wider context of the romanisation of Greek simile models through the importation of this feature (comparing also 4.441–6, 9.680, 9.710–16, 10.707–13, 11.456–8), but does not treat the implications for the italianisation of Aeneas.

The role of similes in illuminating both the details and the overall structure of Virgil's thought has been increasingly perceived in the last few decades.[3] No longer can it be assumed that any part of a Virgilian simile is accidental, unrelated to the object of comparison, ornamental or digressive. *Aeneid* 12 not only brings the epic to its climax but has the highest frequency of similes,[4] nineteen in all, as against totals ranging from one in Book 3 to sixteen in Book 10. The abundance of similes in Book 12 is a function of its climactic nature and the presence in it of decisive battle-scenes.[5] Indirect support for this view is found in two other sets of statistics. First, Books 7-12, whose subject is the war in Italy, contain seventy-one similes as against forty-two for Books 1-6, the totals being eight in 7, seven in 8, twelve in 9, sixteen in 10, nine in 11, and nineteen in 12. Secondly, the corresponding distribution of similes within Books 1-6 also shows a consistent relationship between peaks of tension and simile totals, the highest counts being in Book 5 with ten and Books 2 and 4, with nine in each. Book 6 has seven, Book 1 six, and Book 3 only one.

Certain similes of Book 12 involving Aeneas and/or Turnus have no geographical content: at 103-6 Turnus is compared to a bull before combat; at 451-5 Aeneas is like a storm; at 521-5 both are like raging fires or foaming rivers; at 908-12 Turnus is like a runner in a dream; and finally at 921-3 various aspects of Aeneas' spear-cast evoke comparisons with the effect of a siege-catapult, with a bolt of lightning, and with a whirlwind. One simile, comparing Aeneas and Turnus with two bulls in combat in Italian Sila or Taburnus (715-22), is geographically neutral, since its setting simply reflects the fact that the two heroes are doing battle in Italy. But 12.749-57 follows the same trend as the *pater Appenninus* example: Aeneas, pursuing Turnus, is likened to a *vividus Umber*, an Italian hunting hound, following a stag (with no accompanying geographical reference); and the italianisation of Aeneas is

---

[3] The most creative recent contributions in this area are West (1969); West (1970) and Perutelli (1972), which are independent of each other. Rieks (1981) offers a survey of scholarly contributions in this area which unfortunately omits them.

[4] The occasional difficulty of deciding what is and is not a simile, the insignificance of some similes, and the caution with which statistics about similes should be approached emerge from a comparison between the lists of Virgilian similes in Rieks (1981) 1093-6 and in Canali (1976) 68-71. Each contains examples not found in the other. I have in all cases adopted the highest possible totals for occurrences.

[5] Cf. Perutelli (1977) 607 n. 6, concluding, after a useful survey of previous approaches: 'si può riscontrare una generale tendenza a inserire il maggior numero di similitudini là dove più rimarcata è l'intensificazione patetica'. The iliadic background to Book 12 is of course another factor.

enhanced when the reverse process is applied to Turnus, who in three
further similes of Book 12 acquires an alien colour. The first compares
him to Mavors in the Thracian landscape of the river Hebrus, with his
attendants *Formido, Irae,* and *Insidiae*:

> qualis apud gelidi cum flumina concitus Hebri
> sanguineus Mavors clipeo increpat atque furentis
> bella movens immittit equos, illi aequore aperto
> ante Notos Zephyrumque volant, gemit ultima pulsu
> Thraca pedum circumque atrae Formidinis ora   335
> Iraeque Insidiaeque, dei comitatus, aguntur. (12.331-6)

The second likens Turnus to the Edonian (i.e. Thracian) North Wind on
the Aegean (12.365-7). The third is even more interesting, for it is the
opening simile of the book, comparing Turnus to a wounded lion raging
in the fields of Carthage:

>   Poenorum qualis in arvis
> saucius ille gravi venantum vulnere pectus   5
> tum demum movet arma leo, gaudetque comantis
> excutiens cervice toros fixumque latronis
> impavidus frangit telum et fremit ore cruento. (12.4-8)

By its initial position in the book, it sets the tone for the similes that
follow; and no comparison could have distanced Turnus from Italy
more effectively in Roman eyes than one associating him with Carthage
(*Poenorum ... in arvis*).[6] For, although in aesthetic terms the Thracian
North Wind and war-god in his homeland might seem more bleak and
alien than the tilled fields of the Carthaginians (12.4), the enormous
importance of Carthage in the *Aeneid* makes its alienating effect much
stronger. A final point: this simile recalls 4.69-73 (cf. p. 113), where
Dido is compared to a wounded doe, a link underscored by the specific
Poenorum of line 4.

To sum up: of the similes in Book 12 referring to Aeneas and/or
Turnus and involving a specific geographical reference, the two which
concern Aeneas alone contain an Italian reference, and the three which
concern Turnus alone contain a non-Italian reference; and there appear
to be no counter-trends. The homeric originals of these similes amply
confirm that the geographical references chosen by Virgil are significant.
The model for the *pater Appenninus* simile at 12.701-3, *Iliad* 13.754f.,

---

[6] This point is made by Galinsky (1968) 175. *Aen.* 12.4-6 is also reminiscent of 4.1-5
(another passage dealing with Dido); cf. esp. *saucia* (1), *vulnus* (2), *pectore* (4). The
complex unites Dido and Turnus vis-à-vis Aeneas.

GEOGRAPHY AND NATIONALISM

has no named geographical location: ἤ ῥα, καὶ ὡρμήθη ὄρεϊ νιφόεντι
ἐοικώς, / κεκληγώς (So he spoke, and set out like a snow-peaked
mountain, shouting). *Iliad* 22.189–92 is the source for *Aeneid* 12.749–57
(the *vividus Umber* simile):

> ὡς δ᾽ ὅτε νεβρὸν ὄρεσφι κύων ἐλάφοιο δίηται,
> ὄρσας ἐξ εὐνῆς, διά τ᾽ ἄγκεα καὶ διὰ βήσσας· 190
> τὸν δ᾽ εἴ πέρ τε λάθῃσι καταπτήξας ὑπὸ θάμνῳ,
> ἀλλά τ᾽ ἀνιχνεύων θέει ἔμπεδον, ὄφρα κεν εὕρῃ·

(As when a hound flushes a fawn from cover in the mountains and
pursues it through hollows and glades, and even if the fawn hides
crouching in the undergrowth, the hound nonetheless runs steadily,
tracking it down until he finds it)

Nothing parallel to the *vividus Umber* appears here or in the imitation by
Apollonius Rhodius at *Argonautica* 2.278–81.

More or less the same can be said of the similes about Turnus. His
comparison with the Thracian wind at 12.365–7 has several homeric
models,[7] but none mentions a specifically Thracian wind. The Mavors
simile of *Aeneid* 12.331–6 does have an iliadic original (13.298–303) with
a Thracian setting; but Homer's simple ἐκ Θρῄκης (301) is expanded by
Virgil, doubtless to ensure that Turnus' alienisation would not be
blunted by an erroneous presumption about the identity of Mavors.
Emphasis on Thrace establishes that Turnus is being compared, not to
the Roman and Augustan Mars, father of Romulus, divine ancestor of
the Iulii and *Ultor* along with Augustus of Julius Caesar, but to the alien
Thracian Ares. Finally, the homeric model of 12.4–8 (Turnus compared
to a wounded lion in the fields of Carthage), *Iliad* 5.136–42 (cf. *Iliad*
12.41–8), has no geographical location. That Virgil has a purpose in
placing this particular simile, with its added reference to Carthage, in
this important position is confirmed by the fact that previous similes
comparing Turnus to a lion (9.792–6, 10.454–6) resemble the homeric
model in lacking a geographical setting. So Virgil's intrusion of
geographical references into homeric contexts, or in one case his
expansion of a minor homeric geographical reference, indicates the
conceptual importance of place-names in the similes of Book 12.

Virgil's procedure here is not unparalleled: a comparable group of
geographical references in two similes of *Aeneid* 4 and one of *Aeneid* 1

[7] Cf. Knauer (1964) 428.

112

has been observed.[8] In the first simile of Book 4 Dido is compared to a wounded doe, and twice Virgil emphasises that the setting is Crete (70, 73):

> uritur infelix Dido totaque vagatur
> urbe furens, qualis coniecta cerva sagitta,
> quam procul incautam nemora inter Cresia fixit   70
> pastor agens telis liquitque volatile ferrum
> nescius: illa fuga silvas saltusque peragrat
> Dictaeos; haeret lateri letalis harundo. (4.68–73)

This simile relates to another in Book 4 (143–9), where Aeneas is compared with Apollo, and also to one from Book 1 (498–502), where Dido is compared with Diana. Both these similes introduce Mt Cynthus on Delos (4.147, 1.498); and the Aeneas–Apollo simile mentions Cretans among the worshippers of Apollo at Delos (4.145f.). The links between the archer gods Apollo and Diana, the Cretans who worship Apollo, and the Cretan *pastor* who wounds the doe, cannot be fortuitous; and it has been plausibly suggested that they underline the contribution made to Dido's story, particularly in Book 4, by the Cretan heroine Ariadne, and specifically by her characterisation in Catullus 64 (cf. also pp. 146f.).

The key 'fields of Carthage' simile at the beginning of Book 12 is immediately followed by a speech of Turnus (9–17) attacking the Trojans for cowardice, threatening Aeneas with death, calling him *desertorem Asiae* (15) and wishing that the Latins, already mentioned in line 1, may be spectators of Aeneas' death (15). Thus the opening of Book 12 refers to the three geographical locations, Carthage, Troy, and Latium, which are also conjoined in the prologue to the *Aeneid*. There Virgil names Troy and Italy in 1.1f., Latium (and Rome) in 1.6f., and Carthage in 1.13 (*Karthago Italiam contra*). The prologue confronts the reader with this conjunction, first because the epic action takes place mostly in these areas, and second, to stress that Troy and Italy in particular (linked in 1.1f.) are united by destiny, in that Rome will become the new, morally purified Troy. The recurrence of the triple geographical basis of the epic in 12.1ff. comes towards the end of a long process of persuasion: throughout the epic Virgil has contrived gradually to blur the distinction between Troy and Italy and even to suggest that Troy is Italy, or rather, since Troy cannot be refounded (cf.

---

[8] By Duclos (1970–1), on which this paragraph draws. On these and other related similes, cf. now Clausen (1987) Ch. 2.

p. 127), that Italy is Troy. By Book 12 he has prepared the reader for the alienisation of Turnus at 12.4–8, 331–6, and 365–7, and for the matching italianisation of Aeneas at 12.701–3 and 749–57.

Taken out of context, however, the concept that Italy is Troy is hardly credible. This makes it necessary to trace how the course of the epic renders it plausible. In the *Aeneid* Virgil creates, not a facile opposition between good and bad characters and causes, but complex interactions involving, on the one hand, viewpoints that are sympathetic in varying degrees (although sometimes conflicting) and, on the other, unsympathetic viewpoints.[9] Given that the *Aeneid* is the epic of Augustan Rome and that Virgil is professionally committed to the Muse (1.8), the daughter of Jupiter, who stands with the fates, the sympathetic viewpoints exclude those of characters opposed to Rome's divine destiny, however much sympathy the characters themselves may win on the human level.[10] The sympathetic viewpoints are rather those of Jupiter and the fates, of Aeneas and his followers, who eventually include his Arcadian and Etruscan allies, and of Latinus and likeminded Italians. The *Aeneid* reconciles these viewpoints and shows how that reconcilation is implemented (cf. Ch. 4). But for such a reconciliation to come about, Aeneas must first understand that his true home (*patria*) is not Troy but Italy; Latinus must realise that Aeneas, as well as being the 'foreigner' who will fulfil the prophecies and marry his daughter, is also an Italian, destined to bring greatness to Italy; and finally Juno must reach accord with Jupiter and the fates, so that Rome's destiny may be fulfilled.[11] It is the progress made towards all this by the beginning of Book 12 which allows the portrayal of Aeneas as 'Italian' and Turnus as 'alien' to seem less of a paradox.

Privy to all these viewpoints, of course, is the reader who at the beginning of the *Aeneid* is directly informed of the destiny of Aeneas and of his success in 'founding' Rome, and at 1.257–96 hears Jupiter's prophecy to Venus that Aeneas will land in Italy and be victorious in war there. Jupiter goes on to predict the foundation of Alba by Ascanius and of Rome by Romulus, and the course of Roman history up to Augustus' time. All this privileged knowledge is initially denied to Aeneas, who at first still (at least emotionally) regards Troy as home. At

---

[9] The procedure is of course homeric, and indeed involves a synthesis of the *Iliad* and *Odyssey* situations, on which, cf. Marg (1973) 13f. Bonfanti (1985) concentrates on Books 4 and 10 and her 'viewpoints' are different ones.

[10] For the opposite view, cf. e.g. Nethercut (1968) and, argued in the context of an overall interpretation of the *Aeneid*, Boyle (1972); (1986) Chs. 4f.

[11] Cf. recently Feeney (1984) and above, pp. 104f.

1.94–101, caught in the storm raised through Juno's agency, he wishes he had died at Troy (the phrase *ante ora patrum* (95) is particularly poignant). And later, trying to convince Dido that he must leave Carthage for Italy, Aeneas says that, if he had had the choice, he would have rebuilt Troy on its original site (4.340–4). So even in Book 4 Aeneas' emotional loyalty is still to the original Troy.

And yet the concept that Italy is Aeneas' true *patria* appeared much earlier: in the text it first surfaces in Aeneas' words at 1.380: *Italiam quaero patriam*. But it is found earlier than this in the chronological order of the narrative. Its earliest occurrence is in the prophecy of Creusa just after the fall of Troy:

> longa tibi exsilia et vastum maris aequor arandum,   780
> et terram Hesperiam venies, ubi Lydius arva
> inter opima virum leni fluit agmine Thybris.
> illic res laetae regnumque et regia coniunx
> parta tibi. (2.780–4)

But there is a recognised problem about this passage,[12] namely that in Book 3, subsequent in the narrative to Book 2, Aeneas and the Trojans are still ignorant of their destination. Although ready in principle to accept an alternative *patria*, they do not know where it lies. This is shown by their erroneous reaction to the oracle of Delian Apollo (3.94–8) telling them *antiquam exquirite matrem* (96). From it Anchises concludes that the Trojans should sail to Crete. Hence Creusa's words at 2.780–4 must be explained either as a slip in continuity due to the unfinished state of the epic,[13] or as an announcement by Creusa which Aeneas is not intended to understand. For how otherwise could Aeneas have stood by and allowed the Trojans to be misdirected towards Crete?[14]

The first unproblematic appearance of Italy as the *patria* of the

---

[12] For a treatment of this speech and survey of views, cf. Lundström (1977) 19–42.

[13] Cf. Williams (1962) 20; Schiebe (1983), offering a further brief survey of the history of the problem (113f.), and rightly rejecting the view that there is no inconsistency. Three points may be stressed. (1) The half line in Creusa's speech (2.787) is an indication of the uncompleted state of the text. (2) Any vagueness in Creusa's words is designed to increase the awesomeness of '*Hesperia*' rather than to conceal its identity or location from Aeneas, cf. Aeneas' own words *Ausonium, quicumque est, quaerere Thybrim* (5.83) at a point when he certainly knows that he is going to Italy, which is mentioned in the previous line. (3) If Virgil intended to be cryptic in 2.781f., this would run counter to the normal tendency of prophecies describing the sites of colonies, which are not cryptic when they give geographical directions about named places, cf. Cornell (1983) 1129–32.

[14] Aeneas moreover had already attempted an unsuccessful foundation in Thrace (3.16–68).

Trojans comes at 3.154–71, where the land indicated by Delian Apollo is now said specifically by the *penates* to be Italy (167), and not Crete. Their explanation of why this is so points to something implicit in Apollo's oracle, where (3.94) the god began by addressing the Trojans as *Dardanidae*. The *penates* remind Aeneas that Dardanus and Iasius, from whom the Trojans were descended, came originally to Troy from Italy; and this will turn out to be a key element in Virgil's italianisation of Aeneas, particularly in Book 7.[15] The correlative notion (cf. p. 121) is that Turnus was of Argive descent.

Aeneas now shares the gods' and readers' knowledge that Italy is his destination and his true *patria*. From now on, although he may sometimes waver emotionally, this knowledge remains with him and is constantly reinforced. Reminiscences of Troy do not fade entirely, especially at times of stress in Books 1 and 4; and there is a high concentration of them at 3.294–505, when Aeneas visits Andromache and Helenus at Buthrotum and sees their recreation of Troy in exile. This 'false Troy' has a nostalgic function, but is also a material warning to Aeneas that his destiny is not to recreate the old Troy, as they have done; and the visit is accompanied by repeated statements from Helenus that Aeneas' destiny lies in Italy. In telling Aeneas how to reach Italy (374ff.) Helenus speaks of *Ausonio ... portu* (3.378), names Italy at 3.381, 396, and 440, and predicts the final arrival of Aeneas in Cumae at 3.441ff. The Sibyl, Helenus says, will tell Aeneas about *Italiae populos venturaque bella* (3.458). It is in Italy, he implies, that Troy will truly be recreated, rather than in the imitation Troy which he has built: *vade age et ingentem factis fer ad aethera Troiam* (3.462).

To confirm these implications, Helenus reiterates the theme of *Ausonia* as Aeneas and his followers depart from Buthrotum (3.477 and 3.479); and Aeneas, when leaving, also specifies that his goal is *Ausonia* (3.496), and wishes Helenus and Andromache well in their *effigiem Xanthi Troiamque ... / quam vestrae fecere manus* (497f.). Finally, and to crown this emphasis, Aeneas reintroduces Dardanus and, looking

---

[15] It has often been argued that Virgil invented the Italian origin of Dardanus, cf. e.g. Buchheit (1963) 151–72 (on this point and on other passages discussed here). But Heurgon (1969) and (1969a) present epigraphic evidence which would much reduce Virgil's inventiveness; cf. also on this matter Horsfall (1973) esp. 74–9. Virgil's choice of this version does however certainly represent a deliberate rejection of the alternative – that Dardanus originated in Arcadia, on which, cf. Dion. Hal. *Ant. Rom.* 1.61, 68.3; Hill (1961) 92; Buchheit (1963) 163f.; for the Romans as Greeks, and for Latin as a Greek dialect, cf. Buchheit (1963) 166f. esp. n. 71; also Rawson (1985) 55, 68f., 111. The revelation of Delian Apollo is of course confirmed almost immediately by Celaeno (*Aen.* 3.251–4).

prophetically towards the Augustan foundation of Nicopolis,[16] speaks of the future relationship between Epirus and his own new city in terms which drastically alter the concept of 'Troy':

> si quando Thybrim vicinaque Thybridis arva   500
> intraro gentique meae data moenia cernam,
> cognatas urbes olim populosque propinquos,
> Epiro Hesperiam (quibus idem Dardanus auctor
> atque idem casus), unam faciemus utramque
> Troiam animis: maneat nostros ea cura nepotes. (3.500-5)

The Tiber and Hesperia are the objective geographical features which identify Aeneas' future city; the Troy that Rome and Epirus will in future together constitute is only a Troy of the mind: *unam ... utramque / Troiam animis* (504f.). It is no longer a geographical reality. Thus the whole incident, like the later settlement of the more faint-hearted Trojans at Segesta at 5.700-71, has a symbolic value:[17] the Trojans' abandonment of Buthrotum reiterates their abandonment of Troy at 3.8-12. It begins the de-trojanising of the Trojans: and, to signal this, the nostalgia of the Buthrotum episode is almost immediately followed by the intense excitement of their first sighting of Italy, in which the triple repetition of *Italia* in 3.523f. carries a particularly strong emotional charge:

> iamque rubescebat stellis Aurora fugatis
> cum procul obscuros collis humilemque videmus
> Italiam. Italiam primus conclamat Achates,
> Italiam laeto socii clamore salutant. (3.521-4)

Further and similar stress on Italy reappears at 1.378-80, where Aeneas answers the disguised Venus: *sum pius Aeneas, raptos qui ex hoste penates / classe veho mecum, fama super aethera notus; / Italiam quaero patriam, et genus ab Iove summo.*[18] Here the collocation *pius-patriam* is particularly telling. Again, when in Book 4 Aeneas is tarrying in Carthage, Jupiter reacts in his speech to Mercury by calling Aeneas *ducem Dardanium* (4.224), and by stressing Italy as the future home of the Trojans and seat of world domination (4.229-31), before continuing with mention of Rome in particular (4.234) and returning to Ausonia and Latium in 4.236. Again Mercury, when he carries Jupiter's commands to Aeneas (4.265-76), specifies as Ascanius' inheritance

---

[16] Cf. Williams (1962) on *Aen.* 3.280, 3.505, and esp. Buchheit (1963) 156-9.
[17] On some of the ethos of this scene, cf. G.S. West (1983) esp. 256-61.
[18] Cf. Buchheit (1963) 151f.

regnum Italiae Romanaque tellus (4.275). This divine anxiety anticipates both the revelation in Aeneas' farewell speech to Dido (4.333–61) of the powerful residual pull of the old Troy (cf. pp. 114f.), and also Aeneas' open acceptance that Italy is now his *patria*: *sed nunc Italiam magnam Gryneus Apollo, / Italiam Lyciae iussere capessere sortes; / hic amor, haec patria est* (4.345–7). These final words, echoing 1.380 (*Italiam quaero patriam*) and probably involving an etymological play on the *Roma–amor* palindrome,[19] confirm both his understanding of and assent to his destiny.

This renewed harmony between the Trojans and the fates is embodied in the games of Book 5. The naval race involves Trojan participants named as the ancestors of Roman families (5.116–23); then the *lusus Troiae* (5.553–603) glances at the Trojan descent of the Atii (568f.), the family of Augustus' mother, and foreshadows the *lusus Troiae* of the Augustan period: *hinc maxima porro / accepit Roma et patrium servavit honorem; / Troiaque nunc pueri, Troianum dicitur agmen* (5.600–2). No longer is there any tension in the Troy–Rome relationship: Rome is an established fact, Troy its superseded predecessor. Those who will stay in Sicily may, like Helenus and Andromache, require the comfort of illusions. This is the implication of *gaudet regno Troianus Acestes* (5.757) and of Juno's words of temptation to the Trojan women: *nullane iam Troiae dicentur moenia? nusquam / Hectoreos amnis, Xanthum et Simoenta, videbo?* (5.633f.). And this is why Aeneas, when laying out the town plan of Segesta, names as *Ilium* and *Troia* parts of Acestes' city (5.755–7). But he does so without emotional involvement. The process is completed in Anchises' long account of the future history of Italy at 6.756–892. By now Troy is a fading memory, mentioned only at 767 and 840 (and alluded to in 875) in the midst of abundant references to Italy, Rome and Latium.[20]

In the second half of the *Aeneid* a fresh obstacle to the destiny of

[19] Cf. Skulsky (1985) esp. 449f. On wordplay and etymology (including anagrams) in Roman poetry, cf. Cairns (1979) Ch. 4; Koster (1983) Ch. 4 (with bibliography 48 n. 6 and 49 nn. 8f.); Maltby (forthcoming) Vol. 3; McKeown (1987–) I.45–61. Ahl (1985) is excessive – cf. 264–7 on *Aen.* 12.64–72. On Virgil's use of etymology cf. above, p. 63 n. 15. In the present case the simplicity and commonness of the anagram make it unmistakable, as does its allusion to the ancient topos 'lover of his country', on which, cf. Gomme (1945–81) II.136f. (on Thuc. 2.43.1).

[20] Cf. Warwick (1975) *s.vv. Troia* etc. Adjectival forms usually serve simply to distinguish the Trojans from other groups. The noun *Troia* appears mainly either in references to the destruction of Troy or in connection with the siege of the Trojan camp in Book 10, with its resemblances to the siege of Troy. The process of reducing the importance of Troy in Book 6 had begun even earlier than Anchises' speech: at 650 the great founders of Troy are fitted into a single line.

Aeneas and Rome appears, and with it a fresh need for a rapprochement of sympathetic viewpoints. The obstacle is Turnus. He is heralded at 6.89f. (even before the final appearance of Dido in the underworld at 6.450ff.), when the Sybil speaks of 'another Achilles' arising in Latium. The new Achilles, unlike the first, will fail;[21] and the Trojans will assume the victorious role.[22] But Turnus is at least their worthy opponent; and to balance this conflict for Aeneas a new sympathetic viewpoint emerges, that of Latinus, in Book 7, and it will be shared by the Latins after Turnus' death. When Latinus is first described (7.45–9), he is provided with an impeccably Italian ancestry, beginning with Saturn and including the native gods, Picus and Faunus.[23] Next come his daughter Lavinia, her Italian suitors, and the reason why she is still unmarried (7.50ff.). At this last point the Italian emphasis seems to fade. Of the two portents which have impeded her marriage, the first was said by a *vates* to signify that an *externum ... / ... virum* (68f.) – either a 'foreigner' or a 'man from abroad' – would marry her and become master of the area. The second was said to portend fame for Lavinia but war for Latium (79f.). The oracle of Latinus' father, Faunus, again sited in impeccably Italian surroundings (7.81–91), was consulted and amplified the interpretation of the *vates* (7.96ff.), forbidding Latinus to marry his daughter to any of the Latins (96) or to Turnus (*thalamis paratis*, 97) and explaining that *externi generi* would come to continue the line (98–101).

Latinus' viewpoint and future conduct are conditioned by these events, which he interpreted to mean that he would have a foreign son-in-law. But there is an apparent obstacle: by this time Aeneas understands that Italy is his *patria*, because of his descent from the Italian Dardanus. His understanding is made explicit in his words on the banks of the Tiber, significantly addressed to the *penates* of destroyed Troy, and spoken shortly after the account of Faunus' oracle: *salve fatis mihi debita tellus / vosque ... o fidi Troiae salvete penates: / hic domus, haec patria est* (7.120–2). This reiterated espousal of Italy by Aeneas as his *domus* and *patria* may seem to stand counter to Latinus' expectation of a *vir externus–externi generi*; and the obstacle may seem to grow when Latinus comes into personal contact with the Trojan

---

[21] Cf. Wigodsky (1965) esp. 197–213. For analogies between Achilles and Aeneas, cf. Mackay (1957); West (1974). I do not share the view (cf. Wigodsky (1965) 198 n. 18) that the *alius ... Achilles* of *Aen.* 6.89 is Aeneas himself (impossible *inter alia* since he is the addressee); cf. also above, p. 68 and n. 25.

[22] Cf. Anderson (1957) for an excellent discussion of the whole topic.

[23] Cf. Buchheit (1963) 86–100, and, on Latinus in general, Balk (1968).

embassy, recognises them as Italians by descent, and mentions Dardanus, that key figure in the italianisation of the Trojans (cf. p. 116):

> atque equidem memini (fama est obscurior annis)   205
> Auruncos ita ferre senes, his ortus ut agris
> Dardanus Idaeas Phrygiae penetrarit ad urbes
> Threiciamque Samum, quae nunc Samothracia fertur. (7.205–8)

For Ilioneus confirms Latinus' statement (219ff.), adding a reference to Apollo's oracle of 3.94–6: *hinc Dardanus ortus, / huc repetit iussisque ingentibus urget Apollo / Tyrrhenum ad Thybrim et fontis vada sacra Numici* (7.240–2); and earlier in his speech Ilioneus had mentioned and described Aeneas, naming him (and the Trojans in general) specifically as descendants of Dardanus (219f.). But the potential stumbling-block is easily avoided. Latinus' ensuing recognition of Aeneas as both his predicted future son-in-law (7.268–73) and an Italian requires him to modify only slightly his interpretation of *externus vir* and *externi generi*. This he does at 7.255–7, where he shifts subtly from 'foreigner' to 'coming from abroad': *hunc illum fatis externa ab sede profectum / portendi generum paribusque in regna vocari / auspiciis*, cf. also 7.270: *generos externis adfore ab oris*. Similarly, in Latinus' initial welcome to the Trojans he first said *ne fugite hospitium* (7.202), but then, realising that they were Italians (205ff.), tactfully spoke of them not as *hospites* but as kin. It is well understood that the setting in which the Trojan embassy and Latinus meet (7.170–91) is both full of contemporary Augustan allusions,[24] and designed to reinforce the Italian and Roman ethos and ancestry of Latinus. The meeting is in the palace of Latinus' father, 'Laurentian' Picus, *horrendum silvis et religione parentum* (172), which was the Latins' *curia*, *templum* and sacred banqueting-hall (174–6), cf. *solio ... avito* (169); *templo divum patriaque ... / sede* (192f.). The building's vestibule is adorned with statues of ancestors, gods (including Saturn and Janus), kings, heroes and, prominently, Picus. Such a setting is one in which Aeneas can easily be given the benefit both of prophecy and of ancestry.

In this episode, then, the two sympathetic viewpoints of the Trojans and Latinus are quickly reconciled, in an anticipation of their further accord after the end of the *Aeneid*. Conversely the inability of Aeneas' enemies to comprehend his true nationality marks them out as hindrances to the destiny of Rome. Thus at 7.359–64, when Latinus has

---

[24] Cf. Williams (1973) on *Aen.* 7.170–91, and esp. Rosivach (1980).

already perceived that Aeneas is an Italian, Amata can still mock him as a Trojan exile and a treacherous pirate, and compare him to the *Phrygius pastor* Paris. While admittedly the Asian associations of the Trojans are not all positive (cf. pp. 125ff.), Amata's attack is for the most part counter-productive, being blatantly exaggerated and obviously biased. Similarly, her attempts to bolster Turnus' eligibility as a son-in-law unwittingly further his alienisation, already hinted at in the Achilles comparison of 6.89f. She first proffers a clearly tendentious view that, because Turnus is Rutulian and not Latin, he is *externus* (7.367–70), which, as a native-born Italian, he is patently not. Then, to strengthen her weak case, she reveals something truly damaging to Turnus, namely that he is by descent a Greek, and indeed an Argive from the fountainhead of hostility to Troy, Agamemnon's Mycenae: *et Turno, si prima domus repetatur origo, / Inachus Acrisiusque patres mediaeque Mycenae* (7.371f.). Since the Trojans are Italian in origin, this makes Turnus by implication a deadly and alien enemy to Italy.

Amata's irrational hostility is echoed in attacks by others on the Trojans as aliens and degenerate Asiatics, by Allecto (7.421–4), Turnus (9.135–9 and again at 12.11–17, 97–100), Numanus Remulus (9.598–620), and Juno (10.63–95). Some of these assaults have a basis in ancient ethnographic theory (cf. pp. 125f.). But in context they are unpersuasive, since the assailants are not content merely to state the Trojan origin of their victims, but treat it in exaggerated and thereby unconvincing ways. In contrast the friendly Etruscans, themselves of Lydian origin, when seeking to enlist Aeneas as their leader, recognise his Trojan origin in a neutral way. Interestingly they cite a prophecy concerning their conflict with Mezentius which underlines the ambivalence of the earlier *externi generi–externus vir* predictions: *nulli fas Italo tantam subiungere gentem: / externos optate duces* (8.502f.).

But even while the enemies of Aeneas spuriously declare him a degenerate foreigner, the effective alienisation of Turnus is proceeding apace. It is no accident that the roll-call of Turnus' allies in Book 7 includes a number of Greeks: Catillus and Coras (670ff.), both Argives – perhaps a significant emphasis in view of Turnus' Argive descent (cf. above); Hippolytus' son Virbius (7.761ff.); and most strikingly Halaesus (723ff.), an associate of Agamemnon[25] and specifically named as an enemy of the Trojan race (723). This description immediately follows a simile (7.718–21) comparing Turnus' Italian allies to Libyan waves or

---

[25] Cf. Williams (1973) and Fordyce (1977) on *Aen.* 7.723ff.

to ears of corn on the plain of Hermus or in the fields of Lycia, comparisons which have further alienating force. Finally Turnus' shield, which is described at 7.789–92, again recalls his Argive origin, since its device is Argive Io, with her keeper Argus and her father Inachus.

In italianising Aeneas and alienising Turnus Virgil is being neither racialist nor crudely nationalistic. Given that Roman citizenship (*civitas*) was not a racial but a legal status, and that, in antiquity, culture was more important than ethnic origins in determining nationality, such positions were in any case less possible. Virgil was, if anything, an 'internationalist'.[26] The *Aeneid* as a whole incorporates that identification of Rome with Italy which was a keynote of the Augustan age. Virgil's sympathies are even broader than this. It is true that at times he exploits a certain cultural distaste which Romans could feel for Greeks. But one of Aeneas' staunchest allies is the Arcadian Evander, although it is made perfectly clear that he is Greek, cf. *optime Graiugenum* (8.127); he is even said to be related to the Atreidae as well as to Aeneas (8.129–42).[27] By stressing the traditional hostility between Evander's Arcadians and the Latins (8.55) Virgil may in part be discounting a rival claim that Evander was the founder of Rome.[28] But Evander, Aeneas' alliance with him and the tragic death of his son Pallas, are so significant for the *Aeneid* that Virgil cannot be propounding a narrow anti-Greek view. This is confirmed by his handling of the Greek hero Diomedes, who had fought at Troy and taken part in its sack. Diomedes is now shown to have learned by experience: he refuses the Latins' request for help against the Trojans and advises them to make peace with Aeneas (11.252–95).[29] Many Greek contemporaries of Virgil were earning Roman citizenship.

Again, although Virgil alienises Turnus in many passages, Juno is allowed to prove that he is by birth (if not by ultimate descent) a native

---

[26] Cf. Grant (1963–4).

[27] Virgil of course exploits the distinction between the narrowly focussed rhetoric of characters for their own immediate needs and as characterisation (e.g. Aeneas' words here and those of Amata at *Aen.* 10.74–6), and his own narrative procedures (e.g. the similes and the construction of incidents like those of Achaemenides and Diomedes). The fact that Virgil's own procedures are not monolithic gives however a deeper and more persuasive interest to the portrayal of his characters. With Evander it must of course also be remembered that he was related to Dardanus, cf. Clausen (1987) Appendix 10.

[28] Cf. Hill (1961) 90f.; on Greek allies and anti-Greek sentiment in the *Aeneid*, cf. also Wigodsky (1965) 197–213.

[29] A further minor indication of this trend comes in the Achaemenides incident (3.588–691), cf. General Index *s.v.* and Harrison (1986).

Italian: *indignum est Italos Troiam circumdare flammis / nascentem et patria Turnum consistere terra, / cui Pilumnus avus, cui diva Venilia mater* (10.74–6).[30] An even more impressive demonstration of Turnus' deep Italian roots comes in his last battle with Aeneas. There Faunus, the very god who confirmed that a *gener externus* would marry Lavinia, answers Turnus' prayer for help (12.777–9): he causes the stump of an oleaster sacred to himself to hold fast Aeneas' spear (780–3). Part of the god's reason was that the Trojans had cut this tree down to clear the field of battle (12.766–71). But the crucial position accorded to this incident, in the run-up to Turnus' death, must indicate that Faunus is also partly motivated by his recognition that Turnus is one of his own people, a native Italian.

These counter-currents do not reverse the main tenor of Virgil's handling of Aeneas and Turnus in terms of geography and nationality. An overall impression is created throughout the *Aeneid* that Aeneas is truly an Italian, not only by descent, but also because of his concern with the welfare of Italy. Similarly Turnus, although Italian by birth, behaves like an alien Greek and, heedless of Italy's welfare, promotes there a war which ought to have ended long before at Troy. Analogies with the propaganda of the Civil Wars and their aftermath abound.[31] Consequently, although the young and warlike Turnus might seem initially designed for a role as anti-hero analogous to that of Hector in the *Iliad*, his alienisation and his incomprehension of destiny weaken his moral and heroic status.[32] Thus Aeneas and Latinus are left as the real representatives of their two peoples. In this the contrast with the *Iliad* is again striking, for Priam assumes this position only after Hector's death, while Latinus holds it throughout. It is only because of the viewpoint held by Latinus that the Latins and Trojans will be able to unite on a basis of moral as well as political equality.

That viewpoint is unable to make headway during Turnus' political and military ascendancy, but is expressed both before and during the

[30] The exact relationship of Pilumnus to Turnus seemingly varies at different points in the epic, so that at 9.3 he is Turnus' *parens*, at 10.76 his *avus*, and at 10.619 his *quartus pater*. On this and the possible reason for the variations, cf. Cartault (1926) 691 (n. 1 to p. 660).

[31] On the slogan *tota Italia*, cf. Syme (1939) Ch. 20. The facts behind it are clearest in the entry of Italians to the Senate in the reign of Augustus, cf. Wiseman (1971). On the anti-Antonian propaganda before and after Actium, cf. Scott (1929); (1933); Syme (1939) 270–7, 289f.; on the 'official' literary view of the battle of Actium and of Antonius' role in the Actian War, cf. Paladini (1958); on Antonius in Propertius (with some exaggeration), cf. Griffin (1985) Ch. 2.

[32] On the role of Hector in the *Iliad*, cf. the sensitive treatment of Macleod (1982) 8–10.

war. At 7.601–19 Latinus cannot bring himself to open the gates of war against the Trojans (cf. p. 66). The implication is that he does not view the Trojans as *hostes* but as members of the same race as the Latins. The point is made sharply: Virgil dwells on the contemporary Roman observance of the practice (7.602–15) and selects, as examples of the kind of enemies against whom war is declared, Getae, Hyrcani, Arabs, Indians and Parthians (604–6). For Latinus, declaring war against the *Aeneadae* with this ritual is a *foedum ministerium* (619) which he shuns. The gates are in this case *tristis* (617); to open them is to sanction civil war. Again Latinus takes any opportunity arising during the war to plead for peace. At 11.314–35 he offers to give to the Trojans as a site for their city Italian land owned by himself, or ships to go elsewhere, and he proposes an embassy to arrange a truce; and at 12.195–211, in the preliminaries to the final battle, Latinus matches Aeneas' eagerness for peace. Latinus will resume direction of events on the Italian side after Turnus' death; and in that respect the end of the *Aeneid* will differ from the end of the *Iliad*. There the fatal duel between Achilles and Hector leads only to a temporary respite, while the combat between Aeneas and Turnus brings lasting peace.

The viewpoint of Jupiter and the fates is impressively similar to those of Latinus and Aeneas. Jupiter declares at 10.8 his absolute opposition to the war: *abnueram bello Italiam concurrere Teucris*; and he concludes the divine council by promising, for the present, to be impartial (10.107–13). In part this is a response to the immediate situation and to pressure from Juno – on one level he is simply pretending to wash his hands of the conflict.[33] But on a deeper level Jupiter's statement signals his belief in the unity of the two peoples; and when reconciliation is at last in sight in Book 12, Aeneas will pledge himself to it in analogous terms (12.189–94) – cf. pp. 104f. He too will make no distinction between Trojans and Italians: they will become one people because for Aeneas they are already one people; and Jupiter in this latter context now ratifies Aeneas' proposal to the letter (12.834–40). All this further shows that the nationalism esteemed by Virgil is not petty or chauvinistic. Rather it is based on morality:[34] for Virgil, Turnus is alien to Italy not because of his Greek blood – for he also has Italian blood – but because he is devoted to discord and to the irrational and short-sighted continuation in Italy of old Greek feuds. Similarly, Aeneas is an

---

[33] Cf. Harrison (1980) 389f.
[34] On the political aspects however, cf. Buchheit (1963) 166–72.

Italian not just because of his racial origins, although they are important, but because he comes to Italy as the bringer of peace and concord. Nationalism in the *Aeneid* and its geographical signals are therefore aspects of the theme of *concordia* after a civil war, which is one of the major preoccupations of the *Aeneid* (cf. Ch. 4).

The arguments of the present chapter may contribute to a current debate about Virgil's racial attitudes to Troy and the Trojans: the point at issue arises from Virgil's undoubtedly positive view of the Italians, expressed *inter alia* in his characterisation of Camilla (7.803–17, 11.535–94) and in the speech of Numanus Remulus (9.598–620).[35] This speech is the main focus of controversy, since it not only praises the Italians but viciously attacks the Trojans as Asiatic degenerates living in luxury and indolence (614–20). In this it echoes the prayer of Iarbas at 4.206–18, with its almost identical charges against the Trojans and its symmetrical location in the *Aeneid*,[36] and also various remarks of Turnus and others.

As is well known, behind these attacks lies the tradition of ancient ethnography, with its theories linking the nature of a terrain and the character of its inhabitants.[37] The virtues and hardihood of the Italians were regarded as the product of the rugged and mountainous landscape of Italy; contrariwise Asiatics were conventionally seen as soft degenerates affected by the luxurious terrain of Asia. This view of Asiatics goes back to the Hippocratic Περὶ ἀέρων ὑδάτων τόπων (*Airs Waters Places*) (ed. Jones) 12, where Asia is asserted to be less wild in terrain and more temperate in climate than Europe. These 'facts' are alleged to be responsible not only for the fruitfulness of Asia and the fine physique of its inhabitants (12.40f.) but also for their lack of τὸ ... ἀνδρεῖον καὶ τὸ ταλαίπωρον καὶ τὸ ἔμπονον καὶ τὸ θυμοειδές (bravery, endurance, industry and spiritedness). Instead (12.43f.) 'pleasure' (ἡδονή) rules. In *Airs Waters Places* 16 the differences between Europeans and Asiatics

---

[35] Cf. Horsfall (1971) and Winnington-Ingram (1971–2) for penetrating analyses of Numanus Remulus' speech. Thomas (1982) Ch. 4 surveys the interpretative problems; and Dickie (1986) places it most valuably in its cultural and literary context. Pani (1975) handles the ambivalence of the *Troia resurgens* theme in the early principate.

[36] Cf. Thomas (1982) 99f.

[37] For a brief but helpful survey of the ethnographic tradition cf. Thomas (1982) 1–7. Borzsák (1971) traces the moralising side of the ethnographic tradition from (and before) 'Hippocrates' to Virgil, noting that it is influential also in the *Georgics*. Trüdinger (1918) is still fundamental in this area and his list of topoi (175) an essential guide; Rehm (1932) examines Italian material in the *Aeneid* in a mechanical but thorough way; cf. now also Dickie (1986), and, for a parallel examination of the influence of the ethnographic tradition on the *Georgics*, Ross (1987) Ch. 2.

are again emphasised: the latter (3ff.) are less warlike and more gentle in character because of the uniformity of the seasons and the absence of virulent heat and cold. They are feeble particularly (14ff.) because most of Asia is ruled by 'kings', which the treatise glosses (19) as δεσπόζονται (they are under a master) i.e. like slaves. However Asiatic races which are αὐτόνομοι (i.e ruled by laws of their own making) are said to be the most warlike of men, and are excluded from this stricture (33ff.). Because Numanus' words appear to have the backing of this ancient 'science', they have impressed some modern scholars. Commentators have also tended to think that, since Virgil is clearly endorsing Numanus' positive view of the Italians, he must also be concurring with Numanus' negative view of the Trojans.

This however does not follow. There is no reason to accept the views of Numanus uncritically and as a single package. Indeed Virgil characteristically warns against this in his introduction to Numanus' speech, when he describes him as: *digna atque indigna relatu / vociferans tumidusque novo praecordia regno* (9.595f.). What are *digna relatu* and what *indigna*? The bravery, toughness and parsimony of the Italians are qualities which emerge throughout Books 7-12, and they are portrayed as worthy opponents in the present for the Trojans, and worthy allies and kin in the future. But even here there is a jarring note: as has been pointed out,[38] Numanus' boast that the Rutulians live on rapine would hardly have endeared them to an Augustan audience. When we come to Numanus' criticisms of the Trojans, the *Aeneid* itself speaks against him: the effeminacy and degeneracy he (and others) attribute to them are hardly documented at all, particularly after the temptations of Carthaginian luxury have been overcome.[39] If anything the stigma of luxury lies with the Rutulians;[40] and although not all Trojans are praiseworthy,[41] Aeneas, Ascanius and many other prominent Trojan heroes demonstrate 'Italic' virtues.[42] These include martial valour: the prowess of Aeneas is shown both in battle and in the testimony of his former adversary Diomedes, who represents Aeneas as a greater figure in the Trojan War than the *Iliad* had allowed (11.282-92).[43]

---

[38] So Horsfall (1971) 1113.
[39] Cf. Horsfall (1971) 1113f.
[40] Cf. Winnington-Ingram (1971-2) 65.
[41] Cf. Winnington-Ingram (1971-2) 66f.
[42] Cf. Horsfall (1971) 1109.
[43] That Virgil constantly 'corrects' Homer, and some of the reasons for this, have been demonstrated by Harrison (1981). For further examples of this feature, cf. General Index *s.v.* 'correction'.

Numanus' fate after his speech further clarifies Virgil's views. As soon as he has finished speaking, he is shot down by Ascanius, after the young man has offered up a successful prayer to Jupiter. Ascanius follows his victorious shot with the words *i, verbis virtutem inlude superbis!* (9.634), characterising *virtus* as Trojan and Numanus as vainglorious. Ascanius' closing words rebut the charges of Numanus once more: *bis capti Phryges haec Rutulis responsa remittunt* (9.635). The incident belongs to a category of homeric and Virgilian episodes in which two heroes meet in battle, frequently with fatal outcome for one.[44] Numanus' words come over as boastful, and are followed by merited destruction. The truth-value of his attacks on the Trojans is slight.[45]

This does not mean that all anti-Trojan views expressed in the *Aeneid* are empty rhetoric intended to ring hollow. Asia and its people were too strongly associated with luxury and vice for these attacks to have no significance.[46] They are also linked with the ambivalent status of Troy in the Augustan age. Although the mother city of Rome, Troy was tainted with vice; at *Georgics* 1.501f. Virgil names the sin of Laomedon as the cause, or origin, of the Roman civil wars.[47] Above all the refoundation of Troy was a taboo subject[48] – although this seems to have been understood not so much as physical refoundation but rather as the political adoption by Rome of the moral bankruptcy of Troy. The clearest statement of the Augustan establishment's attitude to 'Troy' is the speech of Juno at Horace *Odes* 3.3.18–68. Horace has here acceded in full to the Virgilian view, which Virgil restates at *Aeneid* 12.824 and 828 in the pleas of Juno, *neu Troias fieri iubeas Teucrosque vocari*, and *occidit, occideritque sinas cum nomine Troia*, which Jupiter agrees to at 12.833–40.

The taint of Troy could not thus be dismissed completely by the Roman reader. He could cope with it partly by reflecting that in fact

---

[44] Krischer (1979) 147–9 discusses usefully such scenes, but not the speech of Numanus Remulus.

[45] Cf. Horsfall (1971) 1115, noting divine approval of Ascanius' shot, the vindication of Trojan youth and 'divine censure of Rutulian ideology'; also Maurach (1968) esp. 357–60.

[46] Cf. Horsfall (1971) 1116.

[47] Cf. also *Aen.* 4.541f. and most recently Feeney (1984) 192. Virgil's view 'corrects' Hor. *Epod.* 7.17–20, which makes Romulus' fratricide the cause. Doubtless Octavianus' increasingly Romulean aspirations (leading him eventually to choose the name Augustus) in part explain the correction. Harrison (1981) 213 (*q.v.*) rightly expounds a more important motive for the Virgilian version: it offered, as the other did not, hope for an end to civil war. Interestingly Romulus is pointedly named both in Virgil's version and in Horace's accession to it.

[48] Cf. Grant (1963–4) 6f.; Cairns (1971) 451f.

Troy had fallen, and that the guilt inhered primarily in the physical city – the walls built by the gods for Laomedon. But another part of the solution for the Augustan reader lay in the italianisation of Aeneas and the Trojans. For once Aeneas and the Trojans are revealed as Italian by ancestry, the taint of Asia is much diminished; and although they have spent much of their lives in Asia, they are now in Italy and have acknowledged Italy as their *patria*. Their 'return' has brought them back to the fountainhead of virtue, the Italian landscape. Ancient ethnographic theory appears to have recognised the determinant role of terrain over race. At *Airs Waters Places* 12.41–4 (cf. Jones *ad loc.*) the enfeebling effects of Asia are said to be felt by 'native' and by 'immigrants' alike . Similarly, the hardening and morally improving ambience of Italy can be presumed to have begun work on the Trojans from the moment of their arrival. So anything said by any speaker in the *Aeneid* in praise of Italy and the Italians does not exclude Aeneas and the Trojans. It will apply all the more to their descendants, who will also share the blood of the *Latini*, the autochthonous children of Italy who have never left its shores; and Jupiter himself predicts *commixti corpore tantum / subsident Teucri* (12.835f.).

6

DIDO AND THE ELEGIAC
TRADITION

Up to this point the *Aeneid* and its main characters have been examined
in the light of Augustan public concerns – political, philosophical and
moral. This approach reflected the status of epic as the most public of all
literary forms. But if the *Aeneid* related only to such spheres, it would
have found few readers. In fact personal feelings and motivations
suffuse its entire action; and for this dimension Virgil found inspiration
in a richly varied literary heritage, which included but ranged far
beyond earlier epic. Indeed, it cannot be stressed too strongly that
private and public aspects of the *Aeneid* and its epic predecessors are not
(and were not for Virgil) separable. For example, Chapter 4 highlighted
love and marriage (which, whatever else is involved, certainly call on
personal emotions) as a vector for political concord, both in antiquity in
general and in the *Aeneid*; and in doing so it also recalled hellenistic
views of Homer as an erotic writer, with his 'love stories of two women',
the *Iliad* and *Odyssey*. Now Virgil also presents, in his single epic, the
love stories of two women, Dido and Lavinia, who are crucial for
discord and concord, and who are test cases for the *Aeneid*'s interaction
not just with earlier epic but with other literary kinds. Dido, the focus
for this chapter, is more striking than any woman in Homer, and
already in antiquity her characterisation had attracted scholarly
attention.

In his *Noctes Atticae* (9.9.12) Aulus Gellius (second century AD)
mentions a criticism of Virgil made by the celebrated first-century AD
literary and textual scholar M. Valerius Probus.[1] Probus had declared
that Virgil's most infelicitous homeric borrowing was from *Odyssey* 6, a
simile applied by Homer to Nausicaa and transferred by Virgil to Dido.
The two passages are:

> οἵη δ᾽ Ἄρτεμις εἶσι κατ᾽ οὔρεος ἰοχέαιρα,
> ἢ κατὰ Τηΰγετον περιμήκετον ἢ Ἐρύμανθον,
> τερπομένη κάπροισι καὶ ὠκείῃς ἐλάφοισι·

---

[1] On Probus, cf. most recently Zetzel (1981) esp. Ch. 3; Jocelyn (1984–5); Timpanaro
(1986) Indice dei nomi e delle cose principali *s.v.* Probo, Valerio, and, on the passage
under discussion, 29 n. 18.

τῇ δέ θ᾽ ἅμα νύμφαι, κοῦραι Διὸς αἰγιόχοιο,   105
ἀγρονόμοι παίζουσι· γέγηθε δέ τε φρένα Λητώ·
πασάων δ᾽ ὑπὲρ ἥ γε κάρη ἔχει ἠδὲ μέτωπα,
ῥεῖά τ᾽ ἀριγνώτη πέλεται, καλαὶ δέ τε πᾶσαι·
ὥς ἥ γ᾽ ἀμφιπόλοισι μετέπρεπε παρθένος ἀδμής.
                                              (*Odyssey* 6.102–9)

(As archer Artemis goes along the mountains, over lofty Taygetus
or Erymanthus, taking her pleasure from (killing) the boars and
swift deer; and attendant on her, the countryside nymphs,
daughters of aegis-bearing Zeus, take their sport too – and Leto
rejoices in her heart. Artemis is a full head taller than all the
nymphs, and is clearly distinct from them, though they are all
beautiful. Even so the maiden stood out among her attendants.)

> qualis in Eurotae ripis aut per iuga Cynthi
> exercet Diana choros, quam mille secutae
> hinc atque hinc glomerantur Oreades; illa pharetram   500
> fert umero gradiensque deas supereminet omnis
> (Latonae tacitum pertemptant gaudia pectus).
>   (*Aeneid* 1.498–502)

Probus' detailed censure, which has won the approbation of some
modern scholars,[2] does not face up to the most startling element of the
simile, the link which Virgil, by transferring it, makes between Nausicaa
and Dido. It is all the more startling because Virgil uses the Nausicaa
simile to mark the first appearance in person of Dido in the *Aeneid*.
Probus is concerned with the comparisons Artemis–Nausicaa, Diana–
Dido. Using his own words, we might rather redirect our attention, and
ask why Virgil transferred the simile of the virgin Artemis and her
nymphs disporting themselves in the hunt on the mountains, used by
Homer of *virgo Nausicaa ludibunda inter familiares puellas in locis solis*,
to Dido, who is not a virgin, *in urbe media ingrediens inter Tyrios
principes cultu atque incessu serio, 'instans operi ... regnisque futuris'*
[*Aeneid* 1.504].

One approach can be eliminated. Virgil often 'corrects' homeric
aspersions on the Trojans and the deities favourable to them.[3] But
Nausicaa has nothing to do with the Trojans, and Artemis offers no
scope for 'correction', since she was friendly to the Trojans in the *Iliad*

---

[2] Pöschl (1977) 85ff. conveniently reports earlier reactions to Probus' criticism and
discusses the simile penetratingly; recently again on the topic M.K. Thornton (1985).
Probus of course missed the important Apollonian influence on it, for which, cf. Conrardy
(1904) 29–31, treating *Arg.* 3.876–84, a simile referring to Medea which itself draws on the
Nausicaa simile.
[3] Cf. esp. Harrison (1981), and cf. General Index *s.v.* 'correction'.

and, with Leto, healed Aeneas when Apollo carried him off wounded to his temple (5.445-8). There is of course some by-play between the Diana of *Aeneid* 1.498ff., whose *pharetra* (500), as Probus notes, is the only trace of her hunting, and the Venus of 1.314f., *virginis os habitumque gerens et virginis arma / Spartanae*, with bow (318) and by implication (cf. 323) *pharetra*;[4] and there may be an element of homeric correction in this new image of Venus.[5] But this by-play does not explain anything about the Dido–Nausicaa link.

If correction of Homer is not the reason for the link, could Virgil be emphasising a similarity between Nausicaa and Dido? Now Calypso, and even more Circe, might seem closer homeric analogues of Dido than Nausicaa. But Nausicaa is not without her claims. To begin with, her main role in the *Odyssey* is to meet and help the shipwrecked Odysseus, who is one of the main models for Aeneas (cf. below, pp. 184ff.). Then, like Dido (*Aeneid* 4.35-8, 198ff.),[6] Nausicaa has many suitors (*Odyssey* 6.34f.); and although Nausicaa deploys a façade of maidenly modesty, she is, like Dido, much concerned with marriage – and she is attracted by Odysseus.[7] Marriage is mentioned to Nausicaa in a dream by the disguised Athena (6.26-35) as the reason why she should go on her washing expedition, during which she will meet Odysseus. Her father Alcinous too is aware that marriage is on Nausicaa's mind (6.66f.), although she mentions to him not her own marriage, but that of her brothers. In his plea to her, Odysseus macarises her future husband (6.158f.), and a little later in the same speech hopes that she will have a husband and a happy marriage (6.180-2). Again, when Nausicaa has seen the washed, dressed and divinely beautified Odysseus, she instantly wishes she had such a man for her husband (6.244f.): αἲ γὰρ ἐμοὶ τοιόσδε πόσις κεκλημένος εἴη / ἐνθάδε ναιετάων, καί οἱ ἅδοι αὐτόθι μίμνειν (I wish I could have such a man as husband, who lived here and was content to remain here). Line 245, with its emphasis on her husband staying in Phaeacia, is a clear warning (cf. pp. 133f.) that Nausicaa is potentially a second Calypso wishing to do as Calypso did: τὸν δ᾽ οἶον, νόστου κεχρημένον ἠδὲ γυναικός, / νύμφη πότνι᾽ ἔρυκε Καλυψώ, δῖα θεάων, / ἐν σπέσσι γλαφυροῖσι, λιλαιομένη πόσιν εἶναι (only Odysseus, longing for his return and his wife, is kept shut up in her

---

[4] Cf. M.K. Thornton (1985), but already, in effect, Pöschl (1977) 92; Harrison (1972-3).

[5] Cf. Harrison (1981) 219-23 for Virgil's interest in 'correcting' Homer's Aphrodite, although this could only be a subsidiary motive here, cf. Harrison (1972-3).

[6] Also like Penelope, and Lavinia too (*Aen.* 7.54-7).

[7] Cf. Fenik (1974) 127f., and the earlier remarks of Woodhouse (1930) 54-65.

hollow cave by the divine and lovely goddess, the nymph Calypso, who desires him to be her husband) (*Odyssey* 1.13–15).

The topic of marriage with Odysseus continues in Nausicaa's further treatment of him. Instead of bringing him all the way to her father's house, she drops him off at a grove of Athena outside the city (6.321f.). Her prior explanation of why she does this consists of a long anticipation of the gossip which, she thinks, their simultaneous arrival might arouse (6.273–85). Her words reveal Homer's masterly command of psychology, opening up her hidden thoughts and showing her attempting to arouse Odysseus' interest by stimulating his jealousy and by representing herself as much sought-after. The imagined gossip revolves around the idea that Odysseus is handsome and strong, and has come from abroad, or is a god come from heaven, to be her husband, and that she is showing disdain for her many noble Phaeacian suitors (283f.) – cf. Dido's disdain of Iarbas and her other African suitors (*Aeneid* 4.35–8, 198ff.). Thus Homer is representing Nausicaa not as a modest maiden, but as rather forward.[8] She preserves the external decencies, although guilty of behaviour which she herself would censure in others (6.286–8).

The physical setting of *Odyssey* 6 is also unconventional: a young girl of noble family would not often be away from the city and her relatives without male escort. In this setting Nausicaa can associate with the foreigner Odysseus as she could not so easily have associated with a Phaeacian man. Odysseus' distressed condition as a shipwrecked sailor further reduces normal inhibitions; and the poet emphasises certain details which have sexual overtones. While all the girls are washing and anointing themselves (presumably naked, 96), and while they play ball in the same state (100), Odysseus is asleep in the bushes, so that only the poetic audience can see them. By the time Odysseus comes out of the undergrowth Nausicaa is ready to depart (110f.). Presumably the girls are now dressed, but Odysseus is naked (this is stressed at lines 135f.) and he clutches a strategically placed leafy branch (128f.). In this condition he twice, as noted, speaks of marriage to Nausicaa (158f., 180–5); and it can hardly be supposed that a man of Odysseus' experience hits on that topic by accident. Finally, when the maids are about to wash Odysseus in the river at Nausicaa's command, he asks the girls to withdraw, saying that he will wash himself, since he is ashamed to be naked among young girls (6.218–22); and the maids tell Nausicaa

---

[8] Knauer (1964) 155f. correctly emphasises the differences between Dido and Nausicaa.

what he has said (223). Such a combination of good breeding and disingenuous modesty underlines the tone of this rather risqué confrontation.[9]

Odysseus' defusing of the situation, once he has come to Alcinous' house, is a masterpiece of tact which confirms the implications of his confrontation with Nausicaa. He admits his meeting with her, and explains it, not altogether truthfully (for he attributes to himself and not to Nausicaa the device of coming separately to the house) but apparently to Alcinous' satisfaction (7.290–305). There follows a repetition of the idea that Odysseus might marry Nausicaa, this time by Alcinous, who has what she has not, the right to dispose of her in marriage. After disclaiming anger at Odysseus for having met Nausicaa on the beach, Alcinous says:

> αἲ γάρ, Ζεῦ τε πάτερ καὶ Ἀθηναίη καὶ Ἄπολλον,
> τοῖος ἐὼν οἷός ἐσσι, τά τε φρονέων ἅ τ' ἐγώ περ,
> παῖδά τ' ἐμὴν ἐχέμεν καὶ ἐμὸς γαμβρὸς καλέεσθαι
> αὖθι μένων· οἶκον δέ τ' ἐγὼ καὶ κτήματα δοίην,
> εἴ κ' ἐθέλων γε μένοις· (*Odyssey* 7.311–15)

(By father Zeus and Athene and Apollo, I wish that such a man as you, sharing my own thoughts, would take my daughter in marriage and be my son-in-law, abiding here; I would give a house and possessions, if you would agree to remain here)

Alcinous' offer begins by being politely indirect; but it ends, in μένοις, by being put specifically to Odysseus. Again, the phrase αὖθι μένων, echoing and varying ἐνθάδε ναιετάων and αὐτόθι μίμνειν from Nausicaa's speech (6.245), makes explicit the threat to Odysseus' return home – cf. also τοιόσδε (6.244) and τοῖος ... οἷος (7.312); κεκλημένος εἴη (6.244) and καλέεσθαι (7.313). Alcinous' offer has then many aspects: Odysseus could, by accepting it, make good any damage to Nausicaa's reputation which might be caused by their encounter; on the other hand, acceptance might imply guilt! But Alcinous has also given Odysseus a way of escape by specifying εἴ κ' ἐθέλων γε μένοις (7.315) and following it (7.315f.) with ἀέκοντα δέ σ' οὔ τις ἐρύξει / Φαιήκων (none of the Phaeacians will keep you against your will), an assurance which Odysseus gracefully seizes (7.331–3); and after this nothing more

[9] The moral state of the Phaeacians in ancient eyes (including presumably those of Homer) was not as admirable as has sometimes been thought; cf. Kaiser (1964) 217–220; Di Benedetto (1966) esp. 218–23; G.P. Rose (1969). De Vries (1977) is in contrast pro-Phaeacian; but see now, on the other side, Dickie (1984), (1986) 169–74. For further treatment of Phaeacia cf. below, Ch. 9.

is said about marriage between Odysseus and Nausicaa. In their later brief dialogue at *Odyssey* 8.459–68 it is accepted by both that Odysseus will indeed return home. But in *Odyssey* 6 and 7 Nausicaa was a real source of jeopardy to Odysseus' return, and all the more so since she was a human virgin and so a more dangerous rival to Penelope than the goddesses Calypso and Circe. Here, then, is at least one reason why Virgil exploited the simile comparing Nausicaa to Artemis for the entry of Dido,[10] the single female obstacle to the 'return' of Aeneas; and Virgil followed it up with other details from *Odyssey* Books 6 and 7, e.g. the Phaeacian–Carthaginian motifs of disdain for home-grown suitors and lack of hospitality to strangers.[11]

But this cannot be the full explanation of the Nausicaa–Dido link. Virgil must also have wished his readers to be aware of the differences between Nausicaa and Dido and have intended the Artemis–Diana simile to provoke reflection upon them. In general Virgil had a difficult task in constructing his female characters. There are really only two significant women in the *Aeneid*, Dido and Lavinia – in comparison, even Amata is a minor character. But Dido and Lavinia are also more important than most of Homer's women; and Virgil drew on several homeric women to depict each of them.[12] Dido in particular required complex modelling upon most of the female characters of the *Odyssey* – Calypso, Circe, Nausicaa and Penelope – while the female characters of the *Iliad* were ignored for this purpose,[13] in part because of the strongly odyssean character of *Aeneid* 1–4 (cf. pp. 177–9). The Nausicaa simile therefore, like Aeneas' landing in Africa with its *contaminatio* of Odysseus' arrivals at Aeaea and Phaeacia,[14] warns of this conflation, indicating that Dido cannot be equated with a single homeric prototype.

But Dido's importance as a character impelled Virgil to look for further sources of material. One such source has already been discussed in Chapter 2: since Dido is a queen, Virgil was able to draw on the ideology of kingship for this side of her personality. A further aspect of Dido is that she is a woman in love. Homeric antecedents for her in this

---

[10] Cf. Van Nortwick (1979).

[11] For the Phaeacians *Od.* 6.283f., 7.16f., 30–3; and for the Carthaginians *Aen.* 1.298–300, 302–4, 539–43, 4.211–14. Cf. esp. Horsfall (1973–4) and above, p. 133 n. 9; Harrison (1984) nn. 15, 16 *ad fin.* (= pp. 37f.,39).

[12] Cf. Knauer (1964) Register *s.vv.* Dido etc., Lavinia etc., Vergils Homerumformung etc.: Vereinigung mehrerer homer. Gestalten in Dido, Lavinia.; and, for a succinct treatment, Knauer (1981) 875, 881–3.

[13] The passivity of Homer's Helen made her unsuitable as a major model for Dido.

[14] On the complexities of Aeneas' arrival in Africa, cf. Knauer (1964) 152–73; Görler (1976) – treating it in relation to his landing in Latium; Krischer (1979) 144–7.

respect are not strongly evident. Helen was a victim of love rather than a lover; Penelope was a faithful wife; Nausicaa, for all her interest in marriage, was a virgin; and Calypso and Circe were immortals. This is why, as is well known, Virgil had to look for models also in fifth-century BC Attic tragedy, mainly in Euripides, where female protagonists who were active parties in a love affair could be found. The most celebrated of these were Phaedra, Medea and Stheneboea; and Apollonius' Medea, cast from the same mould and the first female erotic protagonist in epic, mediated the tradition to Virgil.[15] But this stereotype also has its limitations for the story of Dido. The circumstances in which those women fell in love and the results of their love are only partly analogous. Thus in the case of Phaedra the elements of incest, adultery (since she was married), her slanderous malice against her beloved, and suicide as merited self-punishment for the death of Hippolytus rather than an escape from love – all these were little help to Virgil in depicting Dido. Similarly, Medea's virginity before her affair–marriage with Jason, her murder of her brother Apsyrtus, her later infanticide when Jason abandoned her in Corinth, and her escape to Athens to live with Aegeus, all differentiate her strikingly from Dido. Again, Stheneboea's story involved elements of attempted adultery and slander as well as love and suicide. In any case, these characters were not well adapted to the central ethical needs of Augustan poetry. Later, in the first century AD, Phaedra and Medea could return in Senecan drama to incorporate the Stoic moral absolutes which were then in vogue. But Virgilian and Augustan morality, although firm in its principles, was not philo-sophically absolutist.[16] So although Virgil did draw on many details of Apollonius Rhodius' portrayal of Medea,[17] he needed to go further in his search for antecedents to Dido.

Another significant contributor to the character of Dido tends not infrequently to be indicated by scholars in passing,[18] and has been

[15] Cf. Monti (1981) 1-3 and nn. for a summary of earlier scholarly views.

[16] This proposition is exemplified for Virgil esp. above, in Chs. 1, 2 and 4. For a valuable exploration of Horace's parallel position in the *Epistles*, cf. Macleod (1979) esp. 23ff. Ovid's *Medea* will presumably have taken a less morally absolutist view of her than the surviving plays.

[17] Cf. Conrardy (1904) 11-25; Preshous (1964-5); Collard (1975), studying also the influence on Virgil of Euripides' *Medea*.

[18] E.g. Allen (1950) 262 n. 24; Pöschl (1970) 162; McKeown (1984) 185. Newton (1957) offers an interesting discussion (partly in these terms) of various images in *Aen*. 4. Interest in the matter in modern times was stimulated by the (albeit negative) remarks of De Witt (1907) – e.g. 78: '*Querellae* ... one of the few words in the episode which are characteristic of erotic elegy'. But the matter was probably well understood in antiquity, giving rise e.g. to Ovid's inclusion of the *Aeneid* in his reading list for lovers (*A.A.* 3.337f.) – cf. also below,

discussed in more detail by Guillemin (1931), and especially by Hübner (1968). Neither however made the case as fully as is possible,[19] nor, it seems, convincingly enough for it to be used confidently in the interpretation of Dido's character. So it is worth carrying further the argument that Virgil's depiction of Dido draws heavily on the tradition he found represented in contemporary Roman erotic elegy,[20] and that he relied particularly upon Propertius, a fellow protégé of Maecenas, and hence, although this can only be presumed, upon Propertius' master and Virgil's own friend, Cornelius Gallus.[21] This indebtedness would naturally have been eased by hellenistic perceptions of elegy as the appropriate vehicle for the private lives of both heroes and ordinary people, just as epic was for the public lives of heroic characters.[22] But in other ways it was a bold procedure,[23] since Virgil seems not just to have drawn on love elegy but to have characterised Dido specifically as an elegiac lover, with all the associations of excessiveness, anti-social behaviour and general *nequitia* attaching to that *persona*.[24]

The hypothesis cannot be substantiated simply through a one-to-one comparison of the Dido episode with Augustan love elegy, since ancient

n. 23. Servius' famous remark about Bk. 4 (on 4.1, where he speaks of the book's *paene comicus stilus* and continues *nec mirum ubi de amore tractatur* – on which, but with different conclusions, cf. Anderson (1981) – reflects awareness of the non-epic ethos of the book and is interesting given that New Comedy (and Roman Comedy) are sources for Roman elegy; cf. e.g. Day (1938) Ch. 5; and Yardley (1972).

[19] Guillemin (1931), after a statement about Virgil's use of the elegiac tradition (73), compares Dido with Delia and Cynthia (but also with Lesbia). Magic and various other commonplaces of erotic literature are noted (73–7), the role of the banquet discussed (74f.) and the link between Dido and the Ariadne of Catullus 64 examined (77–9). But elegy is not separated from other love poetry. Reference is made at various points below to the more detailed case of Hübner (1968). He again did not attempt to distinguish between elegiac and universal erotic motifs, and his treatment of Dido is part of an overall case for influence of elegy throughout the *Aeneid*, which is inevitably of varying plausibility.

[20] This formulation reflects both the continuing discussion of the problem of 'The origins of Latin love elegy' (cf. e.g. Cairns (1979) Ch. 9) and the many and varied Greek and Latin influences on Augustan elegy – on which, cf. esp. Day (1938).

[21] On Virgil and Gallus, cf. Boucher (1966) 25f., 84–101; Ross (1975) esp. Chs. 1, 2 and 5. For the link between Propertius and Gallus, cf. Ross (1975) esp. Ch. 4.

[22] The *Aetia* of Callimachus was perhaps the most influential work in this respect, with its love stories of Acontius and Cydippe (*Frr.* 67–75 Pf.) and of Phrygius and Pieria (*Frr.* 80–3 Pf.). But the trend is not universal: the *Argonautica* has its strongly erotic episodes (Hypsipyle, Medea), although neither woman is an 'elegiac lover'.

[23] The reappearance of elegiac elements in Ovid's *Metamorphoses* – cf. Tränkle (1963) – is doubtless due in part to Virgilian influence, but it is also a concomitant of Ovid's combination of traditional epic length and (elegiac) episodic composition, cf. *Met.* 1.1ff. and now Hofmann (1986).

[24] The *persona* appears most explicitly in Propertius, but also, with variations, in Tibullus and Ovid. Cf. e.g. Smith (1913) 27f.; Steidle (1962); most fully, Boucher (1965) esp. Chs. 1, 3, 4, 11, 12; McKeown (1987–) 1.12–24.

literary manifestations of love are numerous, ranging from epic to tragedy and from lyric to epigram – and we need to be sure that Dido's is a specifically elegiac love. Nor can it be assumed that, because elegy was the literature of love *par excellence* in the Augustan period, the coincidence of certain topoi and terms in the *Aeneid* and in Augustan elegy demonstrates elegiac influence upon Virgil without further ado; indeed such tacit assumptions by Guillemin (1931) and Hübner (1968) may have led them to argue their views less cogently than they might have done. Rather it must be shown first that Dido's overall situation and personality would have been seen by Virgil's contemporaries as those of a specifically elegiac lover, and then that Dido's love is also described in the specific language and topoi of elegy. Arguing these propositions will inevitably be difficult. Statistical methods are not appropriate, *inter alia* because elegy and other literary forms inevitably overlap to some extent in their treatment of love. On the other hand cumulative arguments should be effective; and the combination of elegiac setting and elegiac language and topoi should carry weight. A final complication can be anticipated: if Virgil did create Dido in an elegiac mould, he will not have stopped there but will certainly have wished to harmonise the borrowed elegiac material with his overall epic form.[25]

The case for Dido's overall situation being specifically elegiac is this. First, she is the active partner in her love affair, and so, in terms of the standard ancient distinction, she is the 'lover', not the 'beloved'. As such she has tragic analogues, but none of them is truly close (cf. p. 135). There is also one lyric analogue, Sappho; but Sappho was given to falling in love with young girls, and she differs from Dido in another way in which Dido is typically elegiac. Sappho was noted for her typically lyric multiplicity of loves[26] – cf. esp. *Fr.* 1.18–24 (L–P). Dido

---

[25] The principle that material borrowed from one literary form by another is harmonised with the conventions of the host is well understood; cf. e.g. the bucolicised Gallus of *Ecl.* 10 (on which cf. Ross (1975) Ch. 5) or the elegiacised Virgil of Prop. 2.34.67–76 (on which, and on the Gallus of the *Eclogues*, cf. D'Anna (1981)). For one such area of epic adaptation in *Aen.* 4, cf. Oksala (1962) 191–3. Virgil's use of details from Apollonius Rhodius' Medea in his portrait of Dido is of course a further aspect of this harmonisation. Interestingly some are also elegiac topoi, e.g. her sleeplessness (*Arg.* 3.751ff.), tears (*Arg.* 3.760ff.), suicide wish (*Arg.* 3.788ff.), and 'wandering about' (*Arg.* 4.45ff.)

[26] As a class ancient lyric poets were professionally 'promiscuous', e.g. (as well as Sappho) Alcaeus, Anacreon, Ibycus (cf. Cic. *Tusc. Disp.* 4.71) and Horace. Catullus might seem at first an exception, in that he is popularly thought to have concentrated on 'Lesbia'. But his major 'affair' with Iuventius (15, 21, 24, 48, 81, 99) must be kept in mind, as well as his episodes with ?Ipsithilla (32), Camerius (55), and Alfenus (30 – cf. Vessey (1971) 48–55).

however, like the elegiac lover,[27] is faithful to one beloved at a time – and she was long faithful to her first husband after his death.[28] Thus, as a sexually experienced person, free to love, and loving another sexually experienced and free individual, Dido looks, in comparison, much more like a Latin love elegist. It may be objected that the Latin elegiac lover is male. But in fact, being a woman does not bar Dido from this identification. To begin with, Dido is comparable with 'Sulpicia', who appears in minor Roman elegy as an active female elegiac lover.[29] Then, as is well known, the Roman elegiac tradition drew on earlier non-elegiac sources, and in one of them, hellenistic bucolic,[30] such women are found. In Theocritus *Idyll* 6 Galatea plays the active role, paradoxically pursuing Polyphemus; and Simaetha, in the 'urban bucolic' *Idyll* 2, both takes the initiative in approaching her lover and, like Dido, employs magic when her lover has abandoned her (cf. pp. 144–6).[31] Even in major Roman elegy, and especially in Propertius, the mistress at times adopts the role of 'lover'. There may be a slight shock effect in this, and indeed it is also a sign of the particular efficacy of the poet and his love poetry.[32] But it happens often enough to be part of the standard *Topik* of Roman elegy.[33] So e.g. in Propertius 1.3 and 2.29 the roles of Propertius and Cynthia are reversed,[34] with the mistress playing

[27] Gallus apparently wrote only about 'Lycoris'. Propertius occasionally contemplates a sexual lapse (2.23 – cf. 2.22, 4.8) but celebrates only Cynthia, with much emphasis on her uniqueness. Ovid makes fun of the elegiac principle in *Am.* 2.7 and 2.8 (his simultaneous affair with Corinna and her maid Cypassis) and *Am.* 2.10 (he is in love with two women at once, probably the same two). But for the most part he writes only of Corinna. Tibullus clearly represents another variant of the tradition: in Book 1 he writes both of Delia and Marathus, although, since the two 'affairs' do not interact, they may not be synchronous. In Book 2 he celebrates only Nemesis.

[28] *fides* (including fidelity after the beloved's death) is also professed by Propertius (cf. Boucher (1965) 88–98), although 4.7.39–48 suggests that the latter element was not observed by him.

[29] [Tib.] 3.13–18 = 4.7–12. Sulpicia was the neice of Tibullus' patron Messalla and an amateur poet; cf. *Kl. P. s.v.* Sulpicius B7.

[30] Day (1938) illustrates copiously the multiplicity of influences; his Ch. 4 deals with pastoral.

[31] Two other examples may be cited: first, the anonymous komastic lyric 'Alexandrian Erotic Fragment', first published in Grenfell (1896) 1–6 and republished with annotations in Powell (1925) 177–80, shows a female excluded lover attempting to gain entry; second, as Copley (1956) remarks (150 n. 59), Plutarch, in discussing the 'paraclausithyron' – the song of the excluded komast (*Mor.* 753B), 'speaks of the singer as a woman'.

[32] For the concept of 'Nützlichkeit' in Roman elegy, cf. esp. Stroh (1971).

[33] The possibility that it may derive specifically from hellenistic 'objective' elegy is suggested by the comparison made at Cat. 68.73ff., in the first extant collection of Roman elegies (Cat. 65–116), between the love of Catullus for Lesbia and that of Laodameia for Protesilaus – on this passage, cf. Macleod (1974) 82–8.

[34] This alternation is traditional in ancient love poetry, cf. e.g. Sapph. *Fr.* 1.21–4 (L–P); Theocr. *Id.* 6; 11.19–79.

the 'lover' while the poet plays the 'beloved'. Again, in Propertius 1.4 Cynthia is more involved in the affair than Propertius and more afraid it will end; and similarly, in 1.6 Cynthia is concerned about Propertius leaving her, while Propertius actually does leave her in 1.17. In 2.7 Cynthia is as much in love as Propertius, if not more, since it is her strong reaction, not his, to a 'law' threatening their affair which is initially reported.[35] 2.26 finds Cynthia devoted to Propertius,[36] 3.6 sees her distraught at a temporary abandonment by him, and 3.24 and 25 are his final rejection of her in the face of her guileful tears.

Because Dido possesses this elegiac *persona*, its facets can confidently be seen in elegiac terms. One important implication is that Dido, like the elegiac lover-poet, is permanently a lover.[37] In antiquity literature and moral philosophy recognised the possibility of love becoming a fixed and dominant element of character rather than an occasional aberration; and this is what gave force to the moralising reflections of Roman elegy upon the conflict between love and citizenship.[38] Virgil hints strongly that love is part of Dido's nature when she is first described in the *Aeneid*. Venus speaks to Aeneas after his shipwreck on the shores of Carthage; and there is complex and piquant irony in the fact that it is actually the love goddess, disguised as a virgin, who characterises Dido as a lover in a speech which also evokes other important themes of Roman elegy:[39]

> huic coniunx Sychaeus erat, ditissimus agri
> Phoenicum, et magno miserae dilectus amore,
> cui pater intactam dederat primisque iugarat   345
> ominibus. sed regna Tyri germanus habebat
> Pygmalion, scelere ante alios immanior omnes.
> quos inter medius venit furor. ille Sychaeum
> impius ante aras atque auri caecus amore
> clam ferro incautum superat, securus amorum   350
> germanae; factumque diu celavit et aegram
> multa malus simulans vana spe lusit amantem. (1.343–52)

The words *amore* (344), *amorum* (350) and *amantem* (352) are explicit;

---

[35] For a recent valuable suggestion about the real status of the *lex* of line 1 cf. Badian (1985).

[36] On the unity and meaning of this elegy, cf. Macleod (1976).

[37] Cf. e.g. Tib. 1.2.97f., 3.57; Prop. 1.1.33f. The condition is often expressed in the metaphor of *servitium amoris*, on which cf. esp. Murgatroyd (1981).

[38] Cf. Boucher (1965) Ch. 1, 127–33; Richard Müller (1952) 47–53, 66f.

[39] On the Diana–Venus link, cf. above, pp. 130f. and nn. 2, 4.

misera (344) too means 'lover' in love poetry, particularly in elegy.[40] As has been noted (pp. 54–7, 76), in antiquity being a lover was usually regarded as a moral fault. Married love could sometimes be regarded as praiseworthy, but in general the feelings between husband and wife were supposed to be analogous rather to the affection of kinsmen (φιλία, φιλέω) than to love (ἔρως, ἐρᾶσθαι).[41] The distinction can be seen clearly in Catullus 72.3f.: *dilexi tum te non tantum ut vulgus amicam, / sed pater ut gnatos diligit et generos.* It is noteworthy that, whereas Catullus disjoins *diligo* and *amica*, Virgil combines *dilectus* with *miserae* and *amore* at *Aeneid* 1.344, so as to stress the oddity of Dido's being 'in love' with her husband.[42] So the fact that Dido was married to her beloved Sychaeus did not really justify her being in love with him; and it should be remembered that Seneca criticised Virgil's patron Maecenas for being 'in love' with his wife Terentia,[43] a criticism which surely has an Augustan source.

In this first description, then, Dido is represented as someone whose permanent and strong characteristic is a morally faulty *amor*. As if to stress the moral aspect further, Virgil juxtaposes *auri ... amore* (349, Pygmalion's avarice for gold) and *amorum* (350, Dido's love for Sychaeus), placing the two forms of *amor* in the same metrical *sedes* in two successive lines. He thereby alludes to ancient moral theories which saw sexual love as analogous to many other vices, including avarice.[44]

[40] There are set contexts for its occurrence: cf. Pichon (1902) 202f. This example could fit several of Pichon's categories.

[41] On *amor, cupido,* ἔρως, φιλία etc., cf. esp. Fischer (1973); on the peculiar difficulty of *amor* and its cognates, i.e. that they cover a wider spectrum than any Greek term, *id.* 3ff., 30ff.; on *diligo* 40ff. – and cf. above, pp. 50, 55. *amor* is indeed used of marital love at Cat. 61.31–5 (where Griffin (1985) 119f. refers to the epithalamic context and the background of *Fescennina iocatio,* and where Greek lyric influence may also be in play), and there are a few other epithalamic traces of *amor* (cf. Griffin *loc. cit.*); *amor* also appears of married love in a number of Latin epitaphs (cf. Lattimore (1962) 277f.), but it is not invariable, and its appearances may reflect the influence of Roman elegy, cf. Lissberger (1934) 117–26. In any case it is rather the equivalent of στοργή than ἔρως. Even the elegiac approach to married love is curiously cautious. Prop. 4.3, dealing with the pseudonymous Arethusa and Lycotas, declares: *omnis amor magnus, sed aperto in coniuge maior* (49), but 4.11, a funerary elegy for Cornelia, wife of L. Aemilius Paullus Lepidus (cos. suff. 34 BC), says nothing about *amor* between them. Cf. also below, p. 161 and n. 34.

[42] Cf. also above, pp. 54–7 on love and morality in antiquity and on the implications for Dido's love of Aeneas; and, on the complexities and problems of 'love and marriage', most recently Griffin (1985) Ch. 6.

[43] Sen. *Dial.* 1.3.10: *amoribus anxio et morosae uxoris cotidiana repudia deflenti.* Mythical and historical examples of love between spouses in antiquity often end badly, e.g. in myth Evadne, and Laodameia, in 'history' Candaules (Hdt. 1.7–13), Spitamenes (Curt. Ruf. 8.3.1–15) and Otho (Tac. *Ann.* 13.45f.).

[44] Cf. Cic. *Tusc. Disp.* 4 esp. 68–81; Ringeltaube (1913) 84f.; Arnim (1903–24) VI Index verborum etc. *s.vv.* ἐράω, ἔρως, ἐρωτικός. Madness is a prominent comparison: on

Dido's intense and passionate love for Sychaeus extends beyond death, another elegiac topos.[45] The effect of this is that Dido, as far as the living are concerned, becomes, paradoxically, anti-love. Thus by falling in love again, this time with Aeneas, she is like those elegiac lovers who, initially anti-love, experience a conversion to being in love – although Dido's experience is rather more complex. Here a Propertian link is visible, since the theme is particularly marked in his Monobiblos, where he, Cynthia, Milanion, Atalanta, Gallus and Ponticus all experience this same conversion.[46]

Dido falls in love with Aeneas in a suitably elegiac context, the *convivium*.[47] The settings for falling in love in antiquity were limited and significant, the two most common ones being festivals[48] and, less frequently, banquets.[49] The *convivium* attended, possibly among others, by the lover and his mistress, is the main focus of the Roman elegiac love affair.[50] The love–banquet link was enhanced in Roman elegy by the literal meaning of the Latin word *convivium*, which was more expressive than its Greek equivalent, συμπόσιον: cf. *ut sapientius nostri quam Graeci; illi* συμπόσια *aut* σύνδειπνα, *id est compotationes aut concenationes, nos 'convivia', quod tum maxime simul vivitur* (Cicero *Epistulae ad Familiares* 9.24.3).[51] Indeed the *convivium* became so important in Roman elegy as to be almost synonymous with the love affair described in it. Thus the concept gives coherence to Propertius 2.30,[52] and is reflected in Lygdamus.[53] Virgil uses the word *convivium* only twice in the *Aeneid*, both times in the plural. The first example is at 1.638, where the fateful banquet at which Dido falls in love (1.719ff., 748ff.) is being prepared: *mediisque parant convivia tectis*. The second is in Book 4, where the lovesick Dido seeks the *convivia* of Aeneas as a solace for and means of furthering her love: *nunc eadem labente die*

literary and philosophical love-madness, cf. also Allen (1950), and on poetic love-madness Fischer (1973) 53f.

[45] On death (and love after death) as a theme of Roman elegy, cf. esp. Boucher (1965) Ch. 3 (with bibliography) and cf. below, p. 144 n. 71; also Richard Müller (1952) 38–42, 45.

[46] *Propertius, Milanion, and Atalanta*: 1.1. *Cynthia*: 1.3. *Gallus*: 1.5, 1.10, 1.13. *Ponticus*: 1.7, 1.9.

[47] Noted by Guillemin (1931) 75.

[48] Cf. Rohde (1914) 155f.; Nisbet–Hubbard (1978) 196f.; Cairns (1979) 67 n. 10.

[49] Always provided that women were present at them, cf. Rohde (1914) 510 n. 1. Roman *mores* were freer in bringing men and women together at banquets.

[50] E.g. at Prop. 3.10.20–32 a *convivium* appears to be in progress with only slaves present apart from Propertius and Cynthia.

[51] On the social functions of the Roman meal, cf. D'Arms (1984).

[52] Cf. Cairns (1971a) 205f.

[53] [Tib.] 3.6.59–61: *non ego, si fugit nostrae convivia mensae / ignotum cupiens vana puella torum / sollicitam repetam tota suspiria nocte.*

*convivia quaerit / Iliacosque iterum demens audire labores / exposcit
pendetque iterum narrantis ab ore* (4.77–9). Significantly, both at the
convivia where she falls in love with Aeneas, and at these *convivia* to
which she resorts in her love sickness, Dido asks Aeneas to relate his
adventures; with 4.77–9 cf. *multa super Priamo rogitans, super Hectore
multa; / nunc quibus Aurorae venisset filius armis, / nunc quales Diomedis
equi, nunc quantus Achilles* (1.750–2). In this first *convivium* the love god
himself, on the orders of his mother Venus, assumes the physical form
of Ascanius and breathes into Dido the hidden fire of love, deceiving her
with his *venenum* (1.685–8, 717–22). Amor in this general role is a
commonplace of all types of poetry; but the scene in *Aeneid* 1 is
particularly redolent of hellenistic epigram and Roman elegy, where the
boy Love with the poison on his arrows or his bird lime makes the victim
fall in love.[54]

Dido's falling in love is manifest in various 'symptoms of love'
standard in all kinds of love poetry,[55] but particularly common in
Roman elegy. One is the breaking off of her voice (4.76).[56] Another is
that very common symptom of love, sleeplessness (4.80–5), which
recurs later when she knows that Aeneas will abandon her (4.529–32).[57]
Once Dido has fallen in love, she also displays the symptom of
'wandering about' (4.68–73), which again is repeated when she realises
that Aeneas will leave her (4.300–3).[58] Before the affair and when
abandoned she sheds the typical lover's tears (4.30, 369f., 413, 437f.).[59]
To these topoi, which are not uniquely elegiac, may be added two more
from Book 4 which are unmistakably so, the lovers' hunt and the lovers'
open-air lovemaking. Hunting is of course a complex motif in elegiac
poetry, and not all its ramifications are relevant here.[60] The emphasis in
Aeneid 4 is simply on the fact that the lovers, Dido and Aeneas, hunt
together; and the presence of this motif in Roman elegy is documented
by Kölblinger (1971) 87ff. One example, from 'Sulpicia', combines
hunting (and erotic services) with love-making in the open air:[61]

---

[54] Cf. e.g. Hölzer (1899) 55f.; Hübner (1968) 15–19; Gow–Page (1965) II Indexes I to
Commentary B. English *s.v.* Eros etc.; Clausen (1987) 142 n. 8.
[55] Cf. e.g. Nisbet–Hubbard (1970) 169, 173f.
[56] Cf. e.g. Sapph. *Fr.* 31.9 (L–P), imitated in Cat. 51.9; Theocr. *Id.* 2.108; Plaut. *Poenul.*
260f.; Chariton 2.5.4; Hölzer (1899) 23f.
[57] Cf. Hölzer (1899) 48.
[58] Cf. Pease (1935) on *Aen.* 4.68 *vagatur*, 300 *totamque* etc.
[59] Cf. Pichon (1902) *s.vv. Flere, Lacrimae* etc., *Lacrimare*.
[60] Cf. Aymard (1951) Chs. 4–7, with Ch. 6 treating the erotic hunt.
[61] Cf. Kölblinger (1971) 123–58; specifically on 'love in the open air', cf. 89ff., and, on
[Tib.] 4.3.11–15, 87ff., 95ff.

> sed tamen, ut tecum liceat, Cerinthe, vagari
> ipsa ego per montes retia torta feram,
> ipsa ego velocis quaeram vestigia cervi
> et demam celeri ferrea vincla cani.
> tunc mihi, tunc placeant silvae, si, lux mea, tecum   15
>   arguar ante ipsas concubuisse plagas:
> tunc veniat licet ad casses, inlaesus abibit,
>   ne Veneris cupidae gaudia turbet, aper. ([Tibullus]4.3.11–18)

In some other examples of the 'love-in-the-open' motif the scene is *antra*, which brings to mind the *spelunca* of *Aeneid* 4.124 and 4.165.[62] As if to confirm the special literary significance of the hunting and open-air love-making motifs, Virgil signals their elegiac associations. Immediately after the love-making of Aeneas and Dido, he comments at 4.171f.: *nec iam furtivum Dido meditatur amorem: / coniugium vocat, hoc praetexit nomine culpam.* Now *furtivus amor* is the very stuff of elegy;[63] and *culpa* has commonly in elegy a meaning both of infidelity and of *nimia erga amorem proclivitas et indulgentia.*[64] In Dido's case her *culpa* is dual: 'infidelity' to her husband's memory, and excessive proclivity to love. Dido also displays the elegiac lover's hopeful self-deception. She regards the affair as a sort of marriage, as elegiac lovers sometimes do.[65] Thus these two lines confirm the intentionally elegiac flavour of the preceding scene.

Other areas of amatory *Topik* must be handled more cautiously. Dido's suicide, for example, is a complex problem. In one way it links her with the Euripidean 'bad woman' tradition (cf. pp. 55, 135), although not all such women killed themselves. Apollonius Rhodius' Medea, a closer analogue, thought of suicide although she did not go through with it.[66] On another front it ties Dido to the erotic komos, where the threat of suicide is common. In Theocritus *Idyll* 3 the goatherd who performs the komos threatens to hang himself (9) and to jump off a cliff (25–7), and finally he says that he will lie down and be eaten by wolves (53).[67]

---

[62] Prop. 3.13.33f.; Ov. *A.A.* 2.623, *Her.* 15.137ff. *Antrum* however is not always a synonym of *speculum* but may equally well mean *convallis* (cf. Tib. 2.3.71f.: *in umbrosa ... valle*): cf. Fedeli (1980) on Prop. 1.1.11 *Partheniis ... in antris.*

[63] Cf. Pichon (1902) *s.v. Furta*; Clausen (1987) 135 n. 44 comments usefully on *furtivus* and its appearance in the *Aeneid.*

[64] Pichon (1902) *s.v. Culpa.*

[65] Cf. Pichon (1902) *s.v. Coniungere*; and esp. Prop. 2.6.42 (to Cynthia): *semper amica mihi, semper et uxor eris.*

[66] *Arg.* 3.788–819, cf. Campbell (1983a) 50f.

[67] This (like Prop. 2.14.31f.) wittily conflates the suicide motif with that of the komastic κοίμησις ἐπὶ θύραις (sleep at the doorway), Plat. *Symp.* 183A.6.

Propertius similarly speaks of lying dead before his mistress' door in a komastic context (2.14.31f.) and in a full-blown komos (2.17) he threatens to jump off a cliff (13), take poison (14) or (by implication) stab himself to death (2).[68] Some rejected lovers in the komastic tradition actually do kill themselves. This happens in [Theocritus] *Idyll* 23, Ovid *Metamorphoses* 14.701ff., and Antoninus Liberalis 39, derived from the *Leontion* of Hermesianax.[69] Now although the komastic suicide motif is not specific to elegy, the komos is the most prominent elegiac genre, its paraphernalia (exclusion, the threshold etc.) becoming virtual synonyms for elegiac love.[70] In addition elegy is obsessed with death.[71] Hence the suicide motif has a powerfully, although not uniquely, elegiac flavour.

A further group of motifs linked with Dido is perhaps even more strongly reminiscent of contemporary Roman elegy. These involve not something Dido does, but something she falsely pretends she will do. Once she has decided to die (4.475: *decrevitque mori*) and has worked out a time and a means, she addresses her sister Anna as follows:

> inveni, germana, viam (gratare sorori)
> quae mihi reddat eum vel eo me solvat amantem.
> Oceani finem iuxta solemque cadentem   480
> ultimus Aethiopum locus est, ubi maximus Atlas
> axem umero torquet stellis ardentibus aptum:
> hinc mihi Massylae gentis monstrata sacerdos,
> Hesperidum templi custos, epulasque draconi
> quae dabat et sacros servabat in arbore ramos,   485
> spargens umida mella soporiferumque papaver.
> haec se carminibus promittit solvere mentes
> quas velit, ast aliis duras immittere curas,
> sistere aquam fluviis et vertere sidera retro,
> nocturnosque movet manis: mugire videbis   490
> sub pedibus terram et descendere montibus ornos. (4.478-91)

In this passage Dido declares that she has found a way either (a) to restore Aeneas to herself or (b) to free herself from her love for him (478f.). This will be achieved (c) through the efforts of a priestess (*sacerdos*, 483), who undertakes (b) to release the minds of men (i.e.

---

[68] Prop. 2.17.2 could have general significance only, but cf. Prop. 2.34.13f., which suggests that it has specific reference.

[69] Cf., for the fuller context, Copley (1940); Rohde (1914) 83-7.

[70] Cf. Copley (1956) esp. Ch. 5.

[71] Cf. *RE s.v.* Elegie 2263-2266 for the original associations; for Augustan elegy, cf. Boucher (1965) Ch. 3, who also stresses the contemporary Roman obsession with death.

from love) through her charms (487f.), or (a) to give them *curae*, i.e. to bind them to love (488). Dido's priestess (d) has power to stop rivers, turn back stars, arouse the shades, create earthquakes, and draw trees down from the mountains by magical means (489–91). The priestess is of course reminiscent of Apollonius' Medea.[72] But she is also similar to two figures who appear in Tibullus, and to a group which turns up in Propertius. The Tibullan counterparts are particularly worth examination:

> nec tamen huic credet coniunx tuus, ut mihi verax
> pollicita est magico saga ministerio.
> hanc ego de caelo ducentem sidera vidi,
> fluminis haec rapidi carmine vertit iter,
> haec cantu finditque solum manesque sepulcris   45
> elicit et tepido devocat ossa rogo:
> iam tenet infernas magico stridore catervas,
> iam iubet aspersas lacte referre pedem.
> cum libet, haec tristi depellit nubila caelo:
> cum libet, aestivo convocat orbe nives. (Tibullus 1.2.41–50)

Here (c) a *saga* appears, who (d) draws down stars, changes the path of streams, causes earthquakes, raises and controls the shades, and alters the weather. She claims (b) to be able to free Tibullus from love through her charms and drugs (59f.). But Tibullus is unwilling, and calls upon her to exercise another of her powers (a) and to make Delia fall in love with him too (63f.): *non ego totus abesset amor, sed mutuus esset, / orabam, nec te posse carere velim.*

In Tibullus 1.6.43–54 a priestess of Bellona (c) (*sacerdos*, 43) can bear fire and lashes and self-mutilation, and can utter prophecies. She gives precepts about lovers' 'fidelity', the inviolability of love, and the punishment of those who try to violate it. Her power to bear pain is an analogue of (d), i.e. the other two witches' control over the physical universe, and her erotic precepts allude to their practical actions in that field, i.e. (a) and (b). Similar ladies appear at Propertius 1.1.19–24. They are (c) witches, and (d) mistresses of the illusion of drawing down the moon. Propertius wants them (a) to make his beloved fall more deeply in love with him than he is with her. In this case he will believe (d) their more extravagant claims to control over streams and rivers. Thus the

---

[72] Cf. Pease (1935) on *Aen.* 4.479 *quae* etc.; Hügi (1952) 64–6, 79–99. Magic is of course a widespread theme in ancient poetry: cf. Fahz (1904) 10f.,16ff.; Tupet (1976) – bibliography: 421–6; treatment of *Aen.* 4: 232–66. There are also important homeric antecedents: cf. Kaiser (1964) 197–208.

figure of a priestess–*saga* with powers over the universe and over love is well established in contemporary Roman elegy,[73] and seems to have been influential upon *Aeneid* 4.478–91.

Another area requires greater caution. The propemptikon, like the komos, can appear in any form of literature; all propemptika can easily be characterised by expressions of affection;[74] and finally the accident of survival has preserved more elegiac than lyric propemptika. Nevertheless Dido's propemptikon to the departing Aeneas (4.305–30, 365–87)[75] does have more links in its language and topoi with elegiac propemptika than with others. In particular it is close to Propertius 1.8, which preserves motifs from a lost propemptikon by Cornelius Gallus known to have been widely influential in Augustan poetry;[76] and although the argument cannot be pressed too far, Dido's propemptikon does have a strong elegiac tone. The linguistic features which give it this tone appear in the entries of Pichon (1902) referred to below in the summary of linguistic evidence for elegiac influence upon the Dido episode; and many of the topics involved have been well enough treated by Hübner (1968).[77] But it is also worth observing that Dido's propemptikon is one means whereby Virgil reconciles the elegiac character of the Dido episode with its role in the epic. This is because Dido's propemptikon also draws prominently on two epic sources. The first is *Argonautica* 4.355–90, the speech made by Medea when she thinks Jason is going to abandon her to the Colchians. The second, which is also indebted to this same Apollonian passage, is Catullus 64.132–201, in which Ariadne, abandoned by Theseus, speaks at the edge of the sea. The Virgilian imitations of Catullus have been studied by a number of scholars,[78] and so can be summarised here briefly, viz.: C. 132f. = V. 4.305, 366f. (esp. *perfide*); C. 136f. = V. 4.308, 311 (esp. *crudeli(s)*; C. 140f., 158 = V. 4.315f.(esp. *miserae ... conubia*); C. 149–51

---

[73] The appearance of witches in Prop. 1.1 (and again in Prop. 3.24.10, within the single epilogue elegy Prop. 3.24/25, on which, cf. Fedeli (1985) 672–6) is particularly significant since Propertius carefully assembles in these programmatic poems motifs typical of elegy – cf. now also on 1.1 Fedeli (1980) 60.

[74] Cf. Menander Rhetor in *Rhetores Graeci* ed. L. Spengel (1856) 3.395.26–31.

[75] For analyses of these passages, cf. Hübner (1968) 60–77; Cairns (1972) 131–5.

[76] Cf. e.g. Boucher (1966) 97; Hübner (1968) 64; Fedeli (1980) 204f.

[77] E.g. on *Aen.* 4.307f.: *nec te noster amor ... / ... tenet?* (63–5); storms (65); wishes, good and ill (65f.); pleas (66–9); request for delay (66, 70f.)

[78] E.g. Guillemin (1931) 77–9; Oksala (1962); Hübner (1968) 60–77; other treatments are noted in Duclos (1970–1) 194 n. 6; Monti (1981) 1–3 and nn.; Németh (1981–2). Numerous other links between Cat. 64 and *Aen.* 4 are noted in these discussions, particularly in the exhaustive treatment of Oksala (1962) *q.v.*

= V. 4.373-5 (esp. *eripui–excepi*); C. 154-7 = V. 4.365-7 (esp. *genuit, leaena–tigres, sub rupe–cautibus*); C. 136-8 = V. 4.369f. (esp. *flectere–flexit, miserescere–miseratus*); C. 158-61 = V. 4.327-30 (esp. *serva–capta*); C. 188-95, 200f. = V. 4.382-6, 376 (cf. also *Argonautica* 4.383ff.).[79] By exploiting the speech of Catullus' Ariadne in these particulars Virgil helps bridge the gap between the elegiac ethos and the epic context of Dido's love affair.

Finally, the elegiac tone of the Dido episode can be confirmed in detail by assembling the linguistic and minor conceptual features of the story which underpin its elegiac flavour. No single word or group of words is decisive, but all are mutually supportive and reinforce the elegiac aspects of the narrative and *Topik* already discussed. For brevity's sake, backing is supplied whenever possible from Pichon (1902). Here again the argument is cumulative; and no pretence is made to completeness. Indeed a number of the terms documented by Hübner (1968) and not included in the present list might well be incorporated as supplementary evidence.[80]

i The term *amor* and its cognates used of Dido and her emotions. Cf. Pichon *s.vv. Amans; Amare; Amatores; Amor*

1.344	et magno miserae dilectus *amore*
1.350f.	securus *amorum* / germanae
1.352	vana spe lusit *amantem*
1.675	sed magno Aeneae mecum teneatur *amore*
1.721	et vivo temptat praevertere *amore*
1.749	infelix Dido longumque bibebat *amorem*
4.54	impenso animum flammavit *amore*
4.85	infandum si fallere possit *amorem*
4.101	ardet *amans* Dido
4.171	nec iam furtivum Dido meditatur *amorem*
4.296f.	at regina dolos (quis fallere possit *amantem*?) / praesensit
4.370	num lacrimas victus dedit aut miseratus *amantem* est?
4.531f.	rursusque resurgens / saevit *amor*
	(cf. turpique *cupidine* captos, 4.194)

[79] Other minor touches, e.g. winds in Cat. 64.142 and 164 and in *Aen.* 4.378 and 381, congruences of metrical *sedes*, and the copious use in both texts of *figurae* productive of tension and excitement (rhetorical questions, e.g. Cat. 64.180-3 and *Aen.* 4.368-70, asyndeton, and anaphora) may be noted.
[80] I.e. (page nos. of Hübner (1968)) *ars* (8-10), *furere* (10-13), *ossa* (13-15), winged love (15-19), *famae oblivisci* (44-8), jealousy (50-3), *recipere* (53f.), *repellere* (54), *dominus* (55), *rapere* (55), *potiri* (56). Similarly the discussion of the love–war equivalence and of Dido's falling in love (and death) as a 'capture' in Newton (1957) 31-7 provides further supplementary support.

ii The lover Dido as *miser–infelix*. Cf. Pichon *s.v. Miseri*

1.344	et magno *miserae* dilectus amore
1.712	praecipue *infelix*, pesti devota futurae
1.719	insidat quantus *miserae* deus
1.749	*infelix* Dido
4.68f.	uritur *infelix* Dido totaque vagatur / urbe furens
4.420f.	*miserae* hoc tamen unum / exsequere
4.437	talibus orabat, talisque *miserrima* fletus
4.450	tum vero *infelix* fatis exterrita Dido
4.529	at non *infelix* animi Phoenissa
4.596	*infelix* Dido, nunc te facta impia tangunt?

iii Love as a 'wound' etc., plus physical descriptions of love in similar terms. Cf. Pichon *s.vv. Medullas* etc.; *Ossa*; *Saucius*; *Vulnera*; Newton (1957) 37f.

4.1f.	at regina gravi iamdudum *saucia* cura
4.2	*vulnus* alit venis et caeco carpitur igni.
4.66	*est* mollis flamma *medullas*
4.67	interea et tacitum vivit sub pectore *vulnus*
4.102	ardet amans Dido traxitque *per ossa* furorem

iv Love as 'care'. Cf. Pichon *s.v. Cura*

4.1	at regina gravi iamdudum saucia *cura*

v Love as a 'fault'. Cf. Pichon *s.v. Culpa*

4.19	huic uni forsan potui succumbere *culpae*
4.172	coniugium vocat, hoc praetexit nomine *culpam*

vi Love as 'madness', 'fever' or 'heat'. Cf. Pichon *s.vv. Aestus*; *Furor*; *Insani* etc.; *Irasci*; *Vesani*

4.65f.	quid vota *furentem* / quid delubra iuvant?
4.68f.	uritur infelix Dido totaque vagatur / urbe *furens*
4.91	nec famam obstare *furori*
4.101	ardet amans Dido traxitque per ossa *furorem*
4.300f.	*saevit inops animi* totamque incensa per urbem / bacchatur
4.474	ergo ubi concepit *furias* evicta dolore
4.532	*saevit* amor *magnoque irarum fluctuat aestu*
4.595	quae mentem *insania* mutat?

vii Love and fear. Cf. Pichon *s.v. Timere*

4.9	quae me *suspensam* insomnia *terrent*
4.298	omnia tuta *timens*

viii Love and softness. Cf. Pichon *s.v. Mollis*

4.66	est *mollis* flamma medullas

ix Rejected love causes *taedium vitae*.[81] (Cf. love until death, 4.26–9.[82])

4.451f.	fatis exterrita Dido / *mortem orat; taedet caeli convexa tueri*

---

[81] Cf. Boucher (1965) Ch. 3. [82] Cf. e.g. Prop. 1.19 and Fedeli (1980) 438–53.

x Love as fire. Cf. Pichon *s.vv. Ardens*; *Ardere*; *Flammam* etc.; *Flagrare*; *Ingens*; *Urere*; Newton (1957) 39–43

1.688	occultum inspires *ignem*
1.713f.	expleri mentem nequit *ardescitque* tuendo / Phoenissa
4.2	et caeco carpitur *igni*
4.23	agnosco veteris vestigia *flammae*
4.54	impenso animum *flammavit* amore
4.66	est mollis *flamma* medullas
4.68	*uritur* infelix Dido
4.101	*ardet* amans Dido traxitque per ossa furorem

xi Love as compulsion. Cf. Pichon *s.v. Cogi*

4.412	improbe Amore, quid non mortalia pectora *cogis*
4.414	*cogitur* et supplex animos summittere amori

xii The lover as a submissive suppliant. Cf. Pichon *s.vv. Submissus*; *Supplices*

4.414	*supplex animos summittere* amori

xiii Reproaches of the beloved by the lover for perfidy, cruelty etc. Cf. Pichon *s.vv. Crudelis*; *Inprobus* (*sic*); *Perfidi*

4.305	dissimulare etiam sperasti, *perfide*
4.311	*crudelis*
4.366	*perfide*
4.386	dabis, *improbe*, poenas
4.421	*perfidus* ille

The case rests here. If Virgil indeed went to contemporary Roman elegy for material and inspiration for his portrayal of Dido, this has at least two major implications. First, it bears further on his moral assessment of Dido. The Euripidean tradition, partly mediated through Apollonius, offered Virgil examples of bad and mad women who had fallen in love and who had performed evil deeds as a result; and he did draw on this tradition. But its influence was diminished by the fact that it did not offer Virgil what he wanted. Dido is no murderess or monster; her moral faults are those of a lover only, and her violence is directed solely at herself. Virgil needed to portray Dido's love for Aeneas as wrong, and as destructive in tendency, while preserving the reader's sympathy for her emotional stress and suffering. The characterisation, topoi and language offered by elegy were close to Virgil's requirement. The elegiac lover was weak, foolish, worthless and morally culpable; but he was not treacherous or cunning or murderous. So Virgil could employ the more sympathetic stereotype of the elegiac lover as a balance and complement to the other major stereotype upon which he drew in his portrayal of

Dido, that of the bad king. The two stereotypes could thus provide the basis of Virgil's representations of Dido as a private and a public figure respectively.

The second implication is literary. In drawing on contemporary erotic elegy Virgil was not just enriching the character of Dido. His overall aim in the *Aeneid* was to be the Roman Homer and here, as everywhere, he was engaged in *aemulatio* of Homer.[83] Ancient scholarship believed that Homer had invented and generated all the literary forms.[84] In an attempt at inverse emulation of Homer, and partly following in the steps of Apollonius Rhodius,[85] Virgil was trying to reabsorb into his epic all the diverse forms of literature which had originated from the homeric epics. It is well understood that, in addition to his epic sources, Virgil has exploited and incorporated Attic tragedy in the *Aeneid*.[86] But Virgil's neglected uses of other literary forms are equally important. This chapter has argued that in the Dido episode the tradition of Roman elegy found its place in the *Aeneid* through her story and *persona*. Chapter 7 will argue that Virgil absorbed the lyric tradition through the *persona* of his other major female character, Lavinia.

[83] This was publicly recognised even before the *Aeneid* was completed (Prop. 2.34.61-6) and was understood throughout antiquity. Its best modern documentation is Knauer (1964).

[84] This notion was commonly expressed in antiquity through the image of Homer as 'Ocean', the source of all literary streams; cf. F. Williams (1978) 87-9, 98f. The ancient view that Homer was an erotic writer (cf. above, p. 106 n. 57) could have eased Virgil's reabsorption of erotic elegy into epic.

[85] Cf. Hügi (1952) 80: 'Das dritte Argonautenbuch ist stark lyrisch-elegisch befärbt'; for lyric influences, cf. below, Ch. 7.

[86] For bibliography, cf. Suerbaum (1980-1) 114, 134f., 148-51, 267f. König (1970) is fundamental. Among other recent useful treatments, cf. Stabryła (1970), Wlosok (1976), Lefèvre (1978), Muecke (1983); and, most recently, Clausen (1987) 53-8.

7

LAVINIA AND THE LYRIC
TRADITION

Lavinia is a paradox. She is indisputably a key figure in the *Aeneid*. Yet
she hardly ever appears in person and, compared with more robust
personalities, she seems insubstantial and lacking in individuality. The
following account of her is characteristic:[1]

> Lavinia is portrayed by Virgil as a gentle and dutiful princess of
> great filial devotion; she is not individualised at all. She is rarely
> mentioned in the *Aeneid*, and never speaks; she is important only as
> a part of the plot, a part of the destinies of Troy and Latium. She is
> quite remote from human passion, a distanced figure, simply a
> passive instrument of destiny in the hands of father or husband.[2]

If this assessment is correct – and it clearly contains much truth – then
Virgil has treated Lavinia as he treats no other major character; and
most modern scholars have reacted by giving Lavinia little attention.
An exception is Woodworth (1930), which assembles what Virgil says
about Lavinia in an attempt to prove her importance. Its main thesis,
that Lavinia stands for Livia,[3] is unconvincing. But in drawing together
sensitively the evidence for Lavinia's significance, Woodworth has
made a valuable contribution, and it is regrettable that her study has not
had more impact.

This chapter will attempt to investigate the sources of Virgil's
portrayal of Lavinia, in the hope that she may emerge as a more
interesting, and less anomalous, Virgilian character than she has
hitherto seemed. Its starting point is the valid scholarly perception[4] that
Lavinia's status as the unmarried daughter of king Latinus has
determined her characterisation, or lack of it. Lavinia is the only major
character in the *Aeneid* who is a young virgin of high birth intended for

[1] Williams (1973) on *Aen.* 7.52f.
[2] Cf. also Williams (1973) on *Aen.* 12.64 *Lavinia*: 'the daughter of Amata and Latinus is
not strongly characterised by Virgil: she never speaks and is merely a part of the plot'.
Essentially similar accounts are given by Boas (1938) 83–5; G.S. West (1975) Ch. 9; cf. also
Lyne (1983a) 61f., collecting a number of past assessments of Lavinia, many to the same
effect; Griffith (1985) 313.
[3] Derived from Drew (1927) 84f.
[4] Cf. above, and n. 2, and below, p. 153 and n. 11.

marriage.[5] Ancient societies, both literary and real, differed considerably in the freedom enjoyed by their women. The homeric epics appear to represent a female life-style distinct from that glimpsed in the lyrics of Sappho; Periclean Athens, the hellenistic cities, early Rome, late republican and Augustan Rome, and late imperial Rome all exhibit individual conditions. But a woman's social class played at all times a determinant role in the degree of freedom and personal development permitted to her.[6] That is why, throughout antiquity, one constant seems to have been that, whatever possibilities women in general had, the unmarried daughters of better-off citizens were more circumscribed than their married, widowed, divorced, non-citizen, or slave female contemporaries. This is not surprising, given that marriage in antiquity was, among the propertied, primarily a political and financial institution, and that the eligibility, and consequently the social and financial value, of a daughter could be affected not just by actual indiscretions, but also by scandal.[7]

Hence Virgil was not able, for example, to make extensive use of Homer's Nausicaa as a model for Lavinia; as was indicated in Chapter 6, much of the interest of Nausicaa's role in the *Odyssey* is that, although likewise a virgin of high birth, she found herself by chance able to talk freely and without the presence of a chaperone to an eligible male, Odysseus, a shipwrecked sailor in need of urgent assistance, who in any case (at least until he spoke and washed) might have been of a lower class and so ineligible.[8] Virgil was well aware of Nausicaa as a possible prototype for Lavinia,[9] but had to reject her because her overall image was inappropriate: she was too forward to provide a basis for the characterisation of the mother of the Roman race. The other available epic virgin, Apollonius' Medea, was even less suitable: not only did she

---

[5] Camilla, as a warrior and also doomed to an early death, falls into a different category; the epithets assembled by Moseley (1926) Appendix I.ix make this clear, esp. when contrasted with those used of Lavinia, cf. *ibid.* xvii. Cf. also Jax (1938) 23f.

[6] In addition to classic treatments of ancient women, e.g. Balsdon (1962) and Vatin (1970), cf. more recently Pomeroy (1975); Gardner (1986); B. Rawson (1986). As noted (above p. 9), Dido, as a queen regnant, is regarded in her public capacity as a 'king'.

[7] The clearest proof of this is Archilochus *P.Colon.* 7511.1–35 = *Fr.* 196a West (1980), which sets out to slander Neoboule and her sister. Some early commentators innocently took this account by Archilochus of a sexual conquest as a love poem; Carey (1986) 63 n. 14 corrects this view. On scandal and women, cf. also Schaps (1977) and below, pp. 161f.

[8] The gibe later made against Odysseus by Euryalus at *Od.* 8.159–64, that he is a merchant, suggests however that social mobility already existed in Homer's time.

[9] The many suitors topos (cf. above, p. 131 and n. 6) makes one clear link; for another cf. below, p. 156 n. 20. On Nausicaa as a part-prototype for Apollonius' Medea, cf. e.g. Collard (1975) 138; Campbell (1983a) 56–9.

fall in love with the stranger Jason, and keep a solitary rendezvous with him, but she betrayed her father and murdered her brother for him. So although Apollonius' Medea was in other ways analogous to Lavinia, Virgil's portrayal of Lavinia could not make any real use of Medea. In consequence Virgil was compelled to make shift without a substantial epic prototype for Lavinia. He also had to accept, in accordance with the social facts of all ancient life, that, since Lavinia was an unmarried girl, her main significance would lie not in her personality or actions, but in her potential political and social value as a marriage partner, a circumstance which dictated that she should frequently be described as, and conceived of, as *coniunx*, but be given little emotional scope and no choice, or wish for choice, in the matter of her future husband.[10] Lavinia is then, as has often been said, portrayed as the ideal Roman *filia familias* – something she would have remained, in legal terms, even after her marriage to Aeneas.[11]

But this formulation only reinforces the problem: how was Virgil not only to compensate for the lack of a major epic original for Lavinia, but, in the absence of such an original, to present her as a character who, in spite of saying nothing, and doing virtually nothing, nevertheless has a considerable impact in the epic? It was vital for Virgil to achieve this, since Lavinia's marriage with Aeneas is destined to unite the Latins and Trojans as ancestors of the Romans, and, being the basis of Jupiter's plans for the future Roman world, must reverberate throughout the epic as an event divinely fated and prophesied. Virgil's main technique was a literary device particularly at home in epic, which operates at different levels: a character's significance is shown, not directly, but indirectly through his or her effect on other characters. Some minor examples of this in Homer have recently been studied.[12] It has been shown that Homer often conveys the importance, status, influence or interest of a character, object or event not by describing that character etc. as important, influential and so forth, but by allowing the reader to observe within the narrative the reactions of other actors to him, her or

[10] The view advanced by Lyne (1983a) about Lavinia's blush (*Aen.* 12.64–70), that she is in love with Turnus, seems to me fanciful. On this, cf. also below, p. 159, and esp. Todd (1980), arguing that the cause is 'the thought of Aeneas as a husband' (29). In effect *Aen.* 12.64–70 (cf. 12.606) is a conflation and 'correction' of the various passages where Apollonius' Medea blushes: *Arg.* 3.296–8 and 3.963 (because of her love for Jason); 3.681f. (out of 'virgin shame' – but she then speaks (3.688ff.) 'guilefully' (687)); 3.725 (for joy).
[11] As the proto-patrician ancestor of the Iulii and *pontifex maximus* – cf. Rose (1948) – Aeneas, it should be assumed, would have married Lavinia by *confarreatio*, which placed the wife in her husband's *manus* and so *in loco filiae*; cf. Buckland (1963) 118f.
[12] By Krischer (1977), on the basis of earlier observations.

it. Two homeric passages will sufficiently demonstrate the principle. In *Iliad* 1.533–5 the supremacy of Zeus among the gods is indicated at their first council (this is a prudential indication since the council will be turbulent) not by honorary epithets, but by the fact that the other gods stand up in respect for him when he enters: ... θεοὶ δ' ἅμα πάντες ἀνέσταν / ἐξ ἑδέων σφοῦ πατρὸς ἐναντίον· οὐδέ τις ἔτλη / μεῖναι ἐπερχόμενον, ἀλλ' ἀντίοι ἔσταν ἅπαντες (The gods arose all together from their seats before their father, nor did any dare to keep his seat as Zeus approached, but they all stood up in his presence). Similarly the beauty of Helen is conveyed at *Iliad* 3.156–8 not by a description of it, but by the reactions of the old men on the walls of Troy.[13] They see her, and, although as old men they are less impressionable than young men, they comment that it is no wonder the Trojans and Achaeans have been fighting so long over her. Such minor examples of the device can also be found in early Greek lyric, especially in Sappho. E.g. in *Fr.* 31.5–16 (L-P)[14] Sappho catalogues her physical reactions to the presence of a girl. Their number and depth constitute cumulative proof of the girl's beauty, although this is not even mentioned.[15]

Apart from minor examples like these, large-scale use of the same device is found in epic when characters must be absent from the narrative, or must, e.g. because they are women, play a relatively unobtrusive role in the action. The poet brings the character's significance to the reader's attention by causing him or her to be constantly prominent in the words and thoughts of other characters. Thus for much of the *Iliad* (Books 2–8, 10–17) the leading actor, Achilles, whose anger is announced in its first line as the principal epic theme, is in his tent, far from the forefront of action. And yet the very absence of Achilles dominates the development of the narrative; he is named and talked of throughout;[16] and in the middle of his absence a whole book (9) is devoted to an unsuccessful attempt by the Greeks to

---

[13] Cf. Krischer (1977) 79.

[14] Roman appreciation of this poem is implied by its imitation in Cat. 51.

[15] The device is a favourite of Sappho, who often praises girls not by detailing their charms but by revealing the effects they have on others, notably herself: for some of the ramifications of this, cf. Howie (1977) and (1979). The frequent use of the device by Sappho is not irrelevant to its Virgilian application to Lavinia, since the girls she praises seem like Lavinia to have been unmarried girls of good family; cf. also below, pp. 161f.

[16] The only objective criterion of his prominence is inevitably crude, viz. a frequency count of the appearances of his name in these books: Achilles is named 83 times in *Il.* 2–8 and 10–17. This and the word counts in nn. 17f. below derive from Prendergast (1962) and Dunbar (1962). They exclude other references to the epic characters (e.g. by patronymic or pronoun) – which of course makes them even cruder.

persuade him to return to the centre of action. Similarly, but even more strikingly, the principal character of the *Odyssey*, Odysseus, whose cunning is likewise announced as its main epic theme in its first line, is absent from the action throughout Books 1–4; but in compensation these books are shot through with references and allusions to the absent Odysseus.[17] On a smaller scale Helen in the *Iliad* and Penelope in the *Odyssey* are treated in the same way. They do make appearances in the forefront of action, and these may determine the direction taken by the narrative;[18] and yet their underlying importance as motives for the epic actions is underscored more frequently by references to them and reflections upon them in their absence.

This technique is used repeatedly by Virgil to convey the importance of Lavinia. She appears in the latter books, infrequently, but determines the development of the epic action when she does appear. However for the most part she surfaces in the words of others – and, *pace* Williams (1973), she is not 'rarely mentioned' but, if all references and allusions to her are collected, is in fact a frequent theme virtually throughout the *Aeneid* and particularly at significant points. In Books 1–6 she features in three important prophecies. Before the Trojans have even left Troy Aeneas' first wife Creusa alludes to her as Aeneas' future wife, in veiled terms and without naming her: *illic res laetae regnumque et regia coniunx / parta tibi; lacrimas dilectae pelle Creusae* (2.783f.). Her marriage is then mentioned twice in Book 6, first in the prophetic words of the Sibyl, *causa mali tanti coniunx iterum hospita Teucris / externique iterum thalami* (6.93f.), where again Lavinia is not named, and secondly in the prediction of Anchises who, while showing Aeneas his posterity in the Underworld, indicates among them:

> Silvius, Albanum nomen, tua postuma proles,
> quem tibi longaevo serum Lavinia coniunx
> educet silvis regem regumque parentem,
> unde genus Longa nostrum dominabitur Alba. (6.763–6)

It is here that Lavinia is first named in the *Aeneid*. Her description

---

[17] Cf. above, p. 154 n. 16. Odysseus is named 69 times in *Od.* 1–4. Thus he seems to feature even more prominently there than does Achilles in the parts of the *Iliad* where he is absent from the action. But this is probably compensatory: whereas Achilles is prominent in *Il.* 1 (and 9), Odysseus enters the action only in *Od.* 5.

[18] Cf. above, p. 154 n. 16. Helen is named 15 times in *Il.* 3 and 24 times in the rest of the *Iliad*. Penelope is much more prominent in the action of the *Odyssey* than is Helen in the *Iliad*: she is overwhelmingly more so than Lavinia in the *Aeneid*. The last point is tellingly illustrated by the fact that, whereas Lavinia does not speak at all in the *Aeneid*, Penelope does so 28 times in the *Odyssey*. There are 55 additional mentions of her.

coniunx and her fecundity in Aeneas' old age assure the destiny of Rome. In addition to these passages, it should be remembered that whenever in Books 1–6 the city of Lavinium, Rome's predecessor named after her, is mentioned (viz. at 1.2, 258, 270; 4.236, 6.84) Lavinia is implicitly present – and it will be observed that this happens for the first time in the second line of the *Aeneid*.

Although not infrequently heralded in Books 1–6, Aeneas' marriage with Lavinia, like its related theme of concord, is better represented in Books 7–12. But, again like concord, it has narrative consequences throughout the whole epic. It necessitated Creusa's removal by Venus at the end of Book 2, and Dido's rejection by Aeneas and consequent death in Book 4, before generating in Books 7–12 the Virgilian counterpart of the Trojan war, in which Lavinia is the object of strife, as was Helen at Troy. Book 7 signals Lavinia's importance as *coniunx* in two ways, the first implicit, the second explicit. The striking invocation of Erato (7.37) in the so-called 'second prologue' of the *Aeneid* (7.37–45) has allusive ramifications which include *Venus Genetrix* as the ancestress of the Iulii and of the whole Roman race, and possibly also the *Roma–Amor* palindrome.[19] But above all it is an implicit warning of Lavinia's vital role in the remainder of the epic. This warning is then explicitly confirmed in the first major passage concerning her (7.52ff.). Virgil mentions her numerous Italian suitors,[20] of whom Turnus was most outstanding (54–7), and relates (58–70) how Latinus was deterred from this match by a number of portents, one of them interpreted by a *vates* as signifying that a 'foreign' *vir* would come to marry Lavinia and would become king in Latium.[21] Virgil then introduces a further portent which involved Lavinia, whom he now describes for the first time:

> praeterea, castis adolet dum altaria taedis,
> et iuxta genitorem astat Lavinia virgo,
> *visa* (nefas) longis comprendere *crinibus ignem*
> atque omnem ornatum *flamma* crepitante cremari,
> regalisque accensa *comas*, accensa coronam   75
> insignem gemmis; tum fumida *lumine* fulvo
> involvi ac totis Volcanum spargere tectis. (7.71–7)

---

[19] Cf. above, p. 118 and n. 19.
[20] The many suitors (or lovers) topos (on which, cf. also above, p. 152 and n. 9), e.g. Hom. *Od.* 6.34f. (about Nausicaa); Pind. *Pyth.* 9.103–25; 10.55–9; Call. *Aet. Frr.* 67.9f., 69 (Pf.), is an implicit guarantee of the individual's beauty.
[21] On this scene and its other functions, cf. above, pp. 64f.

Now in *Aeneid* 2, at the fall of Troy, Aeneas was about to return to the battle when Creusa held out to him his young son, whose first appearance this is in the chronological narrative and who is repeatedly named as Iulus (2.674, 677, 682); at this point a portent occurs:

> ecce levis summo de vertice *visus* Iuli
> fundere *lumen* apex, tactuque innoxia mollis
> lambere *flamma comas* et circum tempora pasci.
> nos pavidi trepidare metu *crinemque* flagrantem   685
> excutere et sanctos restinguere fontibus *ignis*. (2.682-6)

The parallel, both in content and language, is unmistakable, and it links the ancestor of the Iulii, and the wife-to-be of Aeneas, marking them out as uniquely important for the future of Rome;[22] and this is in part spelled out in the interpretation given of Lavinia's portent: *namque fore inlustrem fama fatisque canebant / ipsam* (7.79f.).

Throughout Books 7–12 the exceptional prominence conferred on Lavinia by this omen is confirmed, although she does not appear in person until Book 11, but instead, by means of the epic device already discussed, is kept in the forefront of attention by being constantly thought about and spoken of by others. Naturally enough, the omens concerning her are followed up by Latinus, and this process generates further references to her: the oracle of Faunus tells Latinus not to marry her to a Latin, but to a foreigner (7.96–101), advice which Latinus endeavours to follow at 7.267–73, when he offers Lavinia in marriage to Aeneas through the Trojan ambassadors.[23] More striking is the frequency with which Lavinia is mentioned by Aeneas' enemies. Their concern with her testifies to her vital role in the fated future which they wish to frustrate. Thus Juno names Lavinia at 7.314, acknowledging her as the destined wife of Aeneas (*atque immota manet fatis Lavinia coniunx*), but spitefully offers her a bloody dowry and Bellona, instead of herself, as *pronuba* (7.318f.),[24] an ill-wish which she repeats at 7.555f. Then Amata, infected by the fury Allecto, passionately urges Latinus to marry Lavinia to Turnus (7.359–72); and, perceiving that her words have no effect on Latinus, hides Lavinia in the woods to prevent her

---

[22] The Iulus *prodigium* is confirmed by the grant to Anchises (at his request) of the *auspicium maximum* at *Aen.* 2.692–8; cf. Heinze (1915) 55–7. On such phenomena in Roman legend, cf. Ogilvie (1965) on Liv. 1.39.1.

[23] This early offer of Lavinia's hand to Aeneas is another feature derived from Homer's Nausicaa, who is offered, remarkably quickly, to Odysseus at *Od.* 7.311–16, cf. above, pp. 133f.

[24] Contrastingly Juno was indeed *pronuba* at the pseudo-marriage of Aeneas and Dido (*Aen.* 4.166) with its ill-omened background – cf. above, pp. 46–9.

union with Aeneas (7.385–405). Again the disguised Allecto, when trying to incite Turnus to violence (7.421–34), advances as one argument the prospect of his losing Lavinia (7.423f.).

One recurrent motif of Books 7–12 (cf. also pp. 209f.) is the attack on Aeneas as a second Paris who is attempting to steal Turnus' 'wife', Lavinia. This motif again has the constant effect of stressing Lavinia's importance, both in her own terms and as an analogue of the iliadic Helen. Juno initiates it when speaking about Aeneas at 7.319–22: *nec face tantum / Cisseis praegnas ignis enixa iugalis; / quin idem Veneri partus suus et Paris alter, / funestaeque iterum recidiva in Pergama taedae;* and it appears with greater or lesser explicitness in the mouths of Amata (7.363f.), Turnus (9.136–9), Numanus (9.600), and Juno again (10.79). The motif is partly reversed, with powerful irony, at 11.215–17, where the Latin women curse Turnus' 'marriage', and at 11.368–73, where Drances alleges that the Latins are dying *ut Turno contingat regia coniunx* (371). The words *regia coniunx* echo *Aeneid* 2.783, and they reveal Turnus' design as unequivocally contrary to destiny; and the echo strengthens Drances' earlier recommendation that Lavinia should be married to Aeneas (11.352–6). These references to Lavinia maintain her prominence, although she has as yet figured only in the account of the fire omen. When she appears in person in the narrative, she is retiring and does not speak. There are three such occasions: at 11.477–85 she accompanies her mother Amata and the other Latin matrons to the temple of Pallas, where they pray for Latin success in the war against the Trojans. Her appearance at this point stresses that a crisis has been reached in the war and that Latinus' city is under immediate threat.[25] Lavinia is again as in 6.93 (cf. what is said of Helen at *Iliad* 22.116) pointedly called *causa mali tanti* in this very passage (480), so that the crisis, identification of her as its cause, and her appearance in the action all coincide. The incident thus signals that the end of the war is near. But she herself says nothing and is seen only fleetingly.

Lavinia's next appearance comes near the beginning of Book 12, at the point where Turnus' fate is being sealed and where simultaneously the means of ending the war is being found. Since his allies will no longer continue the war on his behalf, Turnus must undertake single combat with Aeneas. This he accepts at 11–17, and he concedes that, if he loses, Aeneas will marry Lavinia: *cedat Lavinia coniunx* (17). The royal family

[25] Cf. Hom. *Il.* 6.286–311 and Knauer (1964) 286–9; cf. below, p. 175.

try to dissuade him – first Latinus (19–45), and then Amata, who even threatens suicide if he dies in battle (56–63). At this point Lavinia, who is now revealed to be present, weeps at her mother's words, and blushes (64–9), either at the thought of marriage with Aeneas, or at Turnus' manifestation of love for her, or just out of embarrassment at being the object of attention. The effect on Turnus is compelling:[26] *illum turbat amor figitque in virgine vultus; / ardet in arma magis* (70f.). He is revealed as a lover (cf. p 76); his eagerness for battle is rekindled; and his death becomes a certainty. At this crucial point the beauty of Lavinia has been the deciding factor. As the climax of his speech telling Amata that he is resolved to do battle, Turnus invokes Lavinia and marriage in the impressively spondaic line *illo quaeratur coniunx Lavinia campo* (80). Lavinia is seen a third time, again very fleetingly, when she mourns the suicide of Amata (12.605f.). She is also mentioned at two other key points in Book 12: Aeneas ends his oath during his abortive attempt to fix terms for peace by swearing *mihi moenia Teucri / constituent urbique dabit Lavinia nomen* (193f.); and almost at the end of the *Aeneid*, Turnus renounces Lavinia, surrendering her to Aeneas as part of his unavailing plea for life: *tua est Lavinia coniunx* (937).[27]

Virgil has then employed a thoroughly epic device,[28] which Homer also used for female characters, to stress Lavinia's importance without detracting from her portrayal as a chaste virgin fit to be the wife of the first Roman. There are however two differences between all the homeric characters mentioned and Lavinia. First, the homeric characters, when they are in the forefront, assume in person the status given to them in their absence; this does not happen with Lavinia, who remains personally unobtrusive throughout. Second, Virgil's direct descriptions of Lavinia do not find adequate parallels in Homer (cf. also pp. 175f.). These differences raise the possibility that Virgil drew also on non-homeric material for his portrait of Lavinia. If he did so, then of course he may have had sources now lost to us, e.g. in the *praetexta*. But if the search is confined to preserved texts, then a plausible candidate for Virgil's inspiration (although it has not, to my knowledge, been proposed hitherto by Virgilian scholarship) is the lyric tradition,

[26] On 'Lavinia's blush', cf. above, p. 153 n. 10 and below, pp. 162f.

[27] This phrase, with which Turnus formally concedes 'ownership' of Lavinia, is based on standard Roman law usage, especially in *mancipatio* and *legis actio per sacramentum*. Cf. Buckland (1963) 235f., 610f.

[28] But it is also found outside epic: for its presence in lyric cf. above, p. 154 and n. 15, and Tib. 2.1, where it is employed prominently in honour of Tibullus' patron Messalla – *absentis* (32).

represented for us, and probably also for Virgil, most prominently by the early Greek lyric poets.[29] Early Greek lyric offered copious material for the portrayal of young virgins, especially in the works written for performance by, and largely about, such girls, the so-called partheneia.[30] It did so for a number of convergent reasons. Much ceremonial poetry was performed by girls of that age-group on behalf of the whole archaic community; again, women's cults, and the hymnic and other lyric poetry associated with them, were a prominent feature of early Greek society; and thirdly, epithalamic and other marriage-related poetry appears to have played an important social role in early Greek aristocratic circles.[31] Virgil could have moved easily from his overall homeric inspiration into the world of early Greek lyric, since Homer and the archaic lyric poets were constantly associated in the literary consciousness of later antiquity, and since Homer was a major source for them;[32] and it may have been the high profile of epithalamic poetry in archaic Greece which interacted with Virgil's need to emphasise marriage in the latter half of the *Aeneid*, and initially turned his attention to early Greek lyric as a potential source for his portrait of Lavinia.

Against the background of early Greek lyric, Virgil's lack of precision and detail in his descriptions of Lavinia, her thoughts and her actions, can be understood not just as dictated by Roman social custom but as enriched by a literary provenance. For in early Greek lyric analogous descriptions can be found, characterised specifically by lack of precision and detail – although, as will be seen, not lacking in meaning and resonance. The reasons why early Greek lyric poets avoided indivi-dualisation in this area are various. At its most basic level, archaic

---

[29] So little hellenistic lyric survives that it is an unknown quantity in such discussions. It has become clear however of late – cf. esp. Nisbet–Hubbard (1970) and (1978) – that early Greek lyric is indeed, as Horace himself claims (esp. *O.* 1.1.35), the main source for his *Odes*, so that the tendency of Pasquali (1920) to see in them a preponderance of hellenistic influence (epigrammatic rather than lyric) no longer commands assent.

[30] For discussion of the term and possible examples of partheneia see below, p. 164 n. 44. Had further works, and more substantial portions of works, like Call. *Aet. Fr.* 67–75 (Pf.) – the story of Acontius and Cydippe – or 80–3 (Pf.) – that of Phrygius and Pieria – survived, then a more complex literary ancestry for the portrait of Lavinia might have been sketchable. But there is no reason to think that it would be fundamentally different, given the heavy dependence of hellenistic poets on early Greek lyric, on which, cf. below, pp. 173f., 217f.

[31] For the cults and performances of women (and especially girls) cf. Brelich (1969) and Calame (1977) *passim*. On marriage and early Greek lyric, cf. Page (1955) 119–26; Brelich (1969) Indice degli argomenti *s.v.* matrimonio etc.; Calame (1977) I and II, Indices analytiques *s.vv.* épithalame, mariage.

[32] Cf. e.g. Treu (1955); Weber (1955).

Greek virgins will in truth have had few distinguishing characteristics, since they were married off very young. In addition many early Greek lyrics seem to have been written with multiple performance in mind; and those not containing a proper name (except perhaps the poet's) were possibly intended to be sung by and of any number of people,[33] making precision inappropriate. A final and pressing consideration for early Greek lyric poets was prudence. Given the vulnerability of unmarried girls to scandal, and given the sensible assumption that much laudatory lyric describing unmarried girls was written by commission to celebrate the merits and the marriages, or forthcoming marriages, of young members of noble families, there was obviously a paramount need to praise the girls without creating openings for malicious interpretations and gossip.[34]

A number of solutions were found to this problem, and they were often employed in combination.[35] One was to place the praise of a girl in the mouth of a female poet or chorus,[36] as Virgil puts praise of Lavinia into the mouth of her mother, Amata (7.389f.). Another was to use the epic-derived technique described earlier of praise through description of others' appreciative reactions to the encomiand. Although a less direct method of encomium, it was safer, especially in the case of vulnerable girls, since a person unwittingly arousing strong emotional reactions in others clearly cannot necessarily be held morally responsible for those reactions. Indeed the poet may claim, with more or less sincerity, to disapprove of such feelings, even when experiencing them personally and simultaneously advancing them as proof of the good qualities of their subject. Virgil uses this technique obliquely when he introduces the subject of Lavinia's future marriage to Aeneas: the excessive and unpleasant ways in which Juno, Amata, Turnus, and

[33] I am indebted here to discussions with Mr J.G. Howie on the significance of proper names in early Greek poetry.

[34] Cf. e.g. Nausicaa's fear of scandal (above, p. 132) and Archilochus' blackening of Neoboule (above, p. 152 n. 7). On marriage poetry, cf. above, p. 160 n. 31 and Cairns (1977a) 146f., where the general principle is modified: in order to interest their audience in commissioned wedding poems, archaic poets may sometimes have flirted with danger in this area by suggesting that young people about to get married had been in love before the event. This may e.g. explain Alcaeus *Fr.* 10b (L–P), where an apparently respectable girl admits openly to being in love.

[35] Presumably the reputations of young men were guarded in parallel ways: e.g. male homosexual praise may have been a covert denial of heterosexual immorality. Praise by women of men seems to be restricted to girls wishing for husbands or women for sons (sons-in-law?), e.g. Nausicaa; Alcman *Fr.* 81 (PMG); Pind. *Pyth.* 9.97–103; and cf. Cairns (1977a) 146f.

[36] In the latter case the poem is choric 'Weibliche Rollenlyrik'; a certain monodic example is Alcaeus *Fr.* 10b (L–P).

Numanus react to it guarantee Lavinia's attractiveness but cast no slur upon her or the marriage. The principal solution however found by the lyric poets was to idealise and generalise their descriptions of young girls, so that nothing individual was said about any one girl. These catch-all descriptions are composed from a fairly limited repertoire of highly colourful concepts and terms, all of them chosen both for their virtually universal applicability and for their ability to create an atmosphere of encomiastic excitement and to suggest the girls' radiant beauty and the beholders' excited response to it. At the same time, since nothing is being said which relates uniquely to any particular girl, no scandal or gossip can result.

This last technique is closest to Virgil's treatment of Lavinia. To demonstrate how close the resemblance is, a schematic analysis of his account is offered, which will then be compared in detail, first with the early Greek partheneia, and then with a broader selection of archaic lyric poetry. Fragments of Sappho and Alcaeus are cited below in the numbering of Lobel–Page (1955), and those of the 'melic' poets in that of Page (1962).

(1) Lavinia's most frequently noted characteristic is her long, and (in the MSS reading at 12,605) golden, hair.[37] Her hair is mentioned twice in the omen scene where she is first described: *visa, nefas, longis comprendere crinibus ignem* (7.73); and *regalisque accensa comas* (7.75). It reappears in Amata's pretext for hiding her away in the woods: *sacrum tibi pascere crinem* (7.391); and it is emphasised yet again in the final glimpse of her: *flavos Lavinia crines* (12.605).

(2) Lavinia's face and cheeks and their colour – white and red – are mentioned twice. The first occasion is heightened through two comparisons, with ivory and purple dyes, and with lilies and roses:

> accepit vocem lacrimis Lavinia matris
> flagrantes perfusa genas, cui plurimus ignem   65
> subiecit rubor et calefacta per ora cucurrit.
> Indum sanguineo veluti violaverit ostro
> si quis ebur, aut mixta rubent ubi lilia multa
> alba rosa, talis virgo dabat ore colores. (12.64–9)

At this point Lavinia's beauty, enhanced by her blush which brought her complexion into line with the ancient ideal of white and red, was decisive in strengthening Turnus' resolve to do single combat for her with Aeneas. The second reference to Lavinia's cheeks and their colour

---

[37] On the textual problem in *Aen.* 12.605 see below, p. 164 and n. 45.

is fleeting: *et roseas laniata genas* (12.606), where she tears her cheeks and her hair as a sign of mourning for her mother.

(3) The third physical feature of Lavinia described is her eyes: *oculos deiecta decoros* (11.480) – lovely, but modestly downcast.

(4) A general impression is given by (1)–(3) of Lavinia's beauty; it is given further indirect praise in Amata's boast that Lavinia is worthy of a god,[38] in her case Bacchus: *euhoe Bacche fremens, solum te virgine dignum* (7.389).

(5) Lavinia's apparel is mentioned only at 7.73–6, in the fire-omen context. She has on her head *ornatus* (7.74), which must be at least partly coterminous with her *coronam / insignem gemmis* (7.75f.),[39] her jewelled (presumably gold) hair-band.

(6) Virgil emphasises frequently that Lavinia is *virgo* (7.72, 318, 362, 389; 11.479; 12.69, 70); and at one point he expatiates on her being of marriageable age and having many suitors: *iam matura viro, iam plenis nubilis annis. / multi illam magno Latio totaque petebant / Ausonia* (7.53–5). Her role as disputed future *coniunx* of Aeneas is of course omnipresent (cf. pp. 155ff.). At 7.71 the two themes of virginity and marriage are united in *castis ... taedis*; the torches she holds here are being implicitly contrasted with those of marriage.

(7) Lavinia's actions are few and negative. She is obedient, home-loving and an only daughter (7.50ff.). She is passive when abducted by her mother (7.385ff.). Presumably Amata's report that she dances in honour of Bacchus (7.390f.) is to be believed. She accompanies her mother and the other *matres* on the procession to the temple of Pallas to intercede for the city (11.477ff.). She blushes at 12.64ff. and mourns for her dead mother at 12.604ff.

Naturally a number of these features, particularly (1)–(3), could be paralleled in descriptions of women from many types of ancient literature. Long golden hair,[40] a white and red complexion,[41] and lovely eyes are commonplaces of female beauty throughout virtually all antiquity.[42] But if the descriptions of Lavinia are compared with those of virgins in early Greek lyric poetry in particular, especially in the

---

[38] On the topos, cf. e.g. Hölzer (1899) 22f., for related topoi *id.* 19–22.

[39] This is suggested by the antithetic structure of *Aen.* 7.73–6, viz.: A *crinibus*, 73; B *ornatum*, 74; A *comas*, 75; B *coronam*, 75.

[40] Cf. Jax (1933) 10–12, 70–4, 125, 142, 166; (1938) 26–8, 39f.; Pease (1935) on *Aen.* 4.590.

[41] Cf. Jax (1933) 46f., 76, 126f., 142, 147–50, 168f.; (1936) 47–50; (1938) 16, 20, 25, 29f., 32f.

[42] Cf. Jax (1933) 12f., 44f., 74f., 126, 142, 167; (1938) 28f.

partheneia, there is a significant correspondence both in what is mentioned and, perhaps more importantly, in what is not. The portraits of Lavinia and of the lyric virgins together stand in contrast with descriptions of beautiful women in other literary forms, where there is a more complete coverage of all possible aspects of female beauty.[43] The best-preserved partheneion is Alcman *Fr.* 1.[44] Given the differences in date and function between it and Virgil's descriptions of Lavinia, the similarities are indeed striking. The most frequently mentioned physical feature of the girls who appear and speak in Alcman *Fr.* 1 is their hair (1). Hagesichora's hair blooms like pure gold (51–4); a little later the girls refer to 'the hair of Nanno' (70); and yet again, near the end of the preserved portion of the partheneion, one of the girls has 'lovely yellow hair' (101). The repeated emphasis in this and in other lyric texts (cf. pp. 168, 170) on girls having golden hair may be an additional argument on the side of the MSS reading *flavos* at *Aeneid* 12.605 against the Danieline scholion's *floros*.[45] At Alcman *Fr.* 1.40f. the chorus speaks of Agido's

---

[43] Jax (1933), (1936), and (1938) offer a fairly thorough survey of the material. Particular features may be, if not characteristic of one literary area only, then at least non-characteristic of one, or some. E.g. tallness is specifically an epic, and epic-derived, aspect of female beauty, and specifically not a lyric one: cf. Jax (1933) 8f., 42, 68f., 124, 146, 183. This may be one reason why Dido is indirectly described as tall (cf. above, p. 41), while Lavinia is not.

[44] Calame (1977) esp. II.149–76 rightly regards this term as not designating a genre of content. He points out the dubiety of its pre-Alexandrian existence as a class of poem, and highlights (II.156ff.) its classification in Proclus among poems addressed to the gods but also containing praise of men. Finally he is again rightly sceptical about scholarly attributions to the class partheneion. He defines the class as follows: 'Le parthénée se définit donc, dans la tradition de la critique littéraire postalexandrine, comme un poème lyrique écrit pour un choeur de jeunes filles, chanté par des jeunes filles, en l'honneur de jeunes filles' (II.155). In these terms the class partheneion is useful for interpreting Virgil, whose understanding of it would have been similar. Calame's study is based mainly on Alcman *Frr.* 1 and 3, which he rightly regards on internal grounds as fulfilling the Alexandrian criteria; with other alleged partheneia he is more sceptical. Puelma (1977), which is independent of Calame (1977), includes a survey of the recent abundant secondary literature on Alcman *Fr.* 1. Griffiths (1972) deserves close attention for its important insights into the epithalamic links of *Fr.* 1.

[45] The variant is derived from Probus: cf. *TLL s.v. florus*; but, cf. also Jocelyn (1984–5) esp. (1985) 472: 'Whether, however, *tempore* at *Aen.* 1.44 and *floros* at 12.605 occurred in the text chosen by Probus as his base... or were corrections made to that text on the basis of collation with others or were pure conjectures, entered and marked as such, we cannot tell.' Some earlier editors of Virgil were tempted by the variant, but not e.g. Mynors (1969). Goold (1970) esp. 134–40 is a methodologically valuable paper for this type of problem. Most recently Timpanaro (1986) 99–112, 211f., surveys the history of the *flavos/floros* controversy and argues sensitively and ingeniously for *floros*. *flavos* is perhaps further supported by the links between Lavinia's golden hair and the *ignis*, *flamma* and *lumen* of the omen scene, which also have parthenaic associations (cf. Alcman *Fr.* 1.39–41, mentioning the 'light of Agido' and comparing her to the sun), and by the complex assonance of *Aen.* 12.605: *filia prima manu* **flavos Lavinia** *crines*.

'light' and compares her to the sun. This must allude in part to her hair; but it is also curiously reminiscent of the real *ignis, flamma* and *lumen* which, in the omen of *Aeneid* 7.71ff., surround the head of Lavinia. Finally gold, not golden hair but a piece of jewellery, probably a bracelet, turns up at Alcman *Fr.* 1.64f. Its proximity to the 'Lydian headband' (μίτρα Λυδία) of 67f. suggests that this headband too may be of gold – cf. (5).

Further facial description of the girls is very limited in Alcman *Fr.* 1. But other aspects of the face of Virgil's Lavinia are paralleled. Hagesichora has a silvery (i.e. a white) face (2) at line 55. Facial redness is not attributed to any girl in Alcman *Fr.* 1, although at 64f. 'purple' (in antiquity a brilliant reddish colour), meaning probably an article of purple clothing,[46] is one item in a catalogue of beautiful things which includes gold, the Lydian mitra, the hair of Nanno and so forth (64–76). Then again, at 68f. the young girls are ἰανογλεφάροι, a word of disputed meaning – 'violet-eyed' or 'violet-eyelidded' (i.e. 'dark-eyed') (3) (cf. ἐρογλεφάροι 'with eyes looking love' – of the Charites at line 21); and the glance of one of the girls, Philylla, is mentioned at line 75 (cf. *Aeneid* 11.480). Throughout, the girls are constantly represented in terms which characterise them as beautiful and desirable (4). None is said to be worthy of marriage with a god; but the disapproval of such marriages shown in lines 16–19 is an oblique glance at the topos, and one of the girls, Areta, is said to be godlike (71). The clothing of the girls is not detailed, but one of the items in the catalogue of beautiful things is a 'Lydian headband' (67f.). As noted, it may be a golden headband, as doubtless Lavinia's was, cf. (5).[47]

The girls speak frequently of themselves as young virgins (6), viz: παρσένος (86), νεανίδων (68), νεάνιδες (90), παίδων (99). Their interest in their own beauty and ornaments in itself shows them to be of marriageable age, and the fragment begins with a discussion of marriage (cf. esp. 16ff.). Lines 85–9, although somewhat obscure, seem also to be linked with marriage; and indeed it has been well argued that the partheneion as a whole is epithalamic.[48] In Alcman *Fr.* 1 the girls are taking part in a choric dance and song performance at a festival (7)

---

[46] Cf. Calame (1977) II.98.

[47] Diadems and funerary headbands made wholly or partly of beaten gold sheet were in use in Greece from the early Helladic period, cf. Higgins (1961) General Index *s.vv.* bands, funerary; diadems etc. For island diadems 800–600 BC, cf. *id* 105f., and, on the shortage of gold in Greece 600–475 BC, 118f.

[48] Cf. esp. Griffiths (1972); above, p. 161 n. 34; and p. 163 and n. 38 – on Lavinia as a fit bride for Bacchus (*Aen.* 7.389f.) and Alcman *Fr.* 1.16–21.

(41–4, 60–3, 81–5, 99), with which may be compared Lavinia's probable participation in the dance honouring Bacchus (*Aeneid* 7.390f.). Alcman's girls are also in some sense carrying an offering to a goddess (60–3), although there is scholarly dispute about whether or not it is a robe.[49] This at least invites comparison with Lavinia's participation in the Latin women's procession to the temple of Pallas (7), when they carry to the goddess *dona* (*Aeneid* 11.479), probably a robe (11.477–85).[50]

There are of course items in Alcman's descriptions of the girls which are absent from Virgil's descriptions of Lavinia. But these relate also to the performance of Alcman *Fr.* 1 by the girls. Thus the chariot-riding and sailing imagery of 92–5, and some of the animal imagery (horse, 45–52; owl, 85–7; swan, 100f.) refer to the literary, musical, and dance aspects of the performance as well as to the girls themselves. Similarly the one piece of physical description in Alcman *Fr.* 1 which is not paralleled in Virgil's Lavinia – i.e. the epithet 'fair-ankled' (καλλίσφυρος, 78) applied to Hagesichora – refers at least in part to her dancing. Apart from these items, the only other description of the girls in Alcman *Fr.* 1 amounts to a few general adjectives, viz. 'lovely' (ἐρατά, 76); 'desirable' (ἐπιμέρῳ, 101), and 'godlike' (σιειδής, 71) – cf. (4).

A final point is worth making: at Alcman *Fr.* 1.43–5 the chorus of maidens says (paradoxically) that the chorus-leader does not permit them to praise or blame Agido. In this polar expression they display an ancient attitude towards respectable women which recurs in the famous words given by Thucydides to Pericles in his funeral speech.[51] It is particularly interesting for Virgil's treatment of Lavinia to find this view advanced both in a partheneion, and at the beginning of a passage in which the girls will in fact indulge in a great deal of mutual praise, including praise of Agido. It is an indication that, even where girls are praising other girls, and are doing so in a loosely epithalamic and therefore to some extent licensed context, a formal profession of caution was desirable if not mandatory. Both the generalised nature of Alcman's descriptions and the items selected for praise are similarly precautionary. They are also, in practical terms, of wide applicability, since any healthy young girl is likely to have pleasant hair and eyes and a youthful skin, even if, for example, she is short or fat, and any girl of the propertied classes will have an attractive (probably golden) headband.

---

[49] Cf. e.g. Puelma (1977) 20 n. 49; Calame (1977) II.128–30, concluding that it is a robe.
[50] This is guaranteed by the main homeric antecedent (*Il.* 6.288ff. esp. 289, 293, and 302f.).
[51] For discussion cf. esp. Schaps (1977).

Various other items of praise are, as noted, functional in the choric context, for example a good voice and nimble feet. The eulogy is thus harmlessly vague throughout: no personality is attributed to the girls, so that nothing can give offence or be made the foundation for scandal. Alcman *Fr.* 1 consists of one hundred and one short lines, equal in length to around fifty hexameters. All the descriptive material extracted above (except places where the chorus simply call themselves 'maidens') derives from four short passages, adding up to twenty-one lines, the equal of ten hexameters, and amounting to one-fifth of the fragment. This concentration of relevant descriptive material makes it worth quoting the passages so as to underpin the argument that the girls' self-portrait and Virgil's account of Lavinia overlap positively to a considerable extent.

(i)
     ἐγὼν δ᾽ ἀείδω
Ἀγιδῶς τὸ φῶς· ὁρῶ   40
F᾽ ὥτ᾽ ἄλιον, ὅνπερ ἀμιν
Ἀγιδὼ μαρτύρεται
φαίνην· ἐμὲ δ᾽ οὔτ᾽ ἐπαινῆν
οὔτε μωμήσθαι νιν ἁ κλεννὰ χοραγὸς
οὐδ᾽ ἀμῶς ἐῆ· (39–45)   45

(I sing of Agido's light. I see her like the sun that Agido calls to shine as witness on us. But our noble chorus-leader forbids me to praise or blame her in the least).

(ii)
      ἁ δὲ χαίτα
τᾶς ἐμᾶς ἀνεψιᾶς
Ἁγησιχόρας ἐπανθεῖ
χρυσὸς [ὣ]ς ἀκήρατος·
τό τ᾽ ἀργύριον πρόσωπον,   55
διαφάδαν τί τοι λέγω; (51–6)

(My cousin Hagesichora's hair blooms like gold unalloyed; and her silvery face – what can I say of it openly?)

(iii)
     οὔτε γάρ τι πορφύρας
τόσσος κόρος ὥστ᾽ ἀμύναι,   65
οὔτε ποικίλος δράκων
παγχρύσιος, οὐδὲ μίτρα
Λυδία, νεανίδων
ἰανογ[λ]εφάρων ἄγαλμα,
οὐδὲ ταὶ Ναννῶς κόμαι (64–70)   70

(We have not abundance enough of purple to withstand <them>, nor can our writhing all-gold snake, nor our Lydian headband, glory of violet-eyed young girls, nor even the hair of Nanno)

(iv)   ἀ δ' ἐπιμέρῳ ξανθᾷ κομίσκᾳ (101)
                    (and she with her desirable yellow hair)

Negative control must be sought partly in the standard works on feminine beauty in antiquity, which reveal how extensive the field of possible description was;[52] and partly through examination of other early Greek lyrics. The absence from Alcman *Fr.* 1 and from Virgil's treatment of Lavinia of many additional possible descriptive topics is further proof of a meaningful relationship between the two texts.

But this relationship is unlikely to be direct imitation of the one text by the other. Given Roman and hellenistic interest in early Greek lyric,[53] Virgil may well have known Alcman *Fr.* 1; but it would be a remarkable coincidence if he was influenced by the very partheneion of which the largest portion has survived by accident. It is more likely that he knew a wide range of partheneia and had a topical perception of their conventions. For whether or not there really was an archaic lyric genre partheneion, the classification had been created in the hellenistic period.[54] That the poems so classified by antiquity did have certain standardised contents can be demonstrated even from the scrappy fragments of the other poem which can be classed fairly securely as a partheneion, Alcman *Fr.* 3: these echo a number of those descriptive elements of Alcman *Fr.* 1 which were extracted above for comparison with the portrait of Lavinia. They are supplemented by a few further extracts (marked *) from other possible parthenaic fragments. The largest of these, Pindar *Fr.* 94b, is cited from Snell–Maehler II (1975).

(1) *(Fair) hair:* κόμ[αν ξ]ανθὰν τινάξω – 'I shall shake my yellow hair' (Alcman *Fr.* 3.9); νοτία Κινύρα χ[άρ]ις / ἐπὶ π]αρσενικᾶν χαίταισιν ἴσδει – 'the moist grace of Cinyras sits upon the hair of young girls' (Alcman *Fr.* 3.71f.); for gold linked with hair cf. (5).

(3) *Eyes – the glance:* ὕπνον ἀ]πὸ γλεφάρων σκεδ[α]σεῖ γλυκύν – 'she will scatter sweet sleep from her eyelids' (Alcman *Fr.* 3.7); τακερώτερα / δ' ὕπνω καὶ σανάτω ποτιδέρκεται – 'her glance is more melting than the look of sleep or death' (Alcman *Fr.* 3.61f.).

(4) *Generalised attribution of beauty: passim.*

(5) *Hairband–wreath:* ἀλλὰ τὸ]ν πυλεῶν' ἔχοισα – 'but having the garland' (Alcman *Fr.* 3.65);[55] ἢ χρύσιον ἔρνος ἢ ἁπαλὸ[ν ψίλ]ον – 'either a golden ?wreath or a soft feather' (Alcman *Fr.* 3.68); στεφάνοισι

---

[52] Cf. above, p. 164 n. 43.
[54] Cf. Calame (1977) II.149–76.

[53] Cf. below pp. 173f., 217f. and n. 68.
[55] I.e. 'crown', cf. Calame (1977) II.107–9.

θάλ- / λοισα παρθένιον κάρα – 'my maiden head flourishing with crowns' (*Pindar Fr. 94b.11f.). Robes and laurel branches: *Pindar Fr. 94b.6–8.

(6) Emphasis on virginity–marriage: ἐπὶ π]αρσενικᾶν χαίταισιν – 'on the hair of maidens' (Alcman Fr. 3.72); παίδα – 'girl' (Alcman Fr. 3.82); ἁ παίς – 'the girl' (Alcman Fr. 3.84); παι[δῶν] ἀρίσταν – 'the finest of the girls' (*Alcman Fr. 5.2 col.1.14); παρσενικαὶ μελιγάρυες ἱαρόφωνοι – 'honey-voiced, holy-tongued maidens' (*Alcman Fr. 26); παρθένιον κάρα – 'maiden head' (*Pindar Fr. 94b.12); ἐμὲ δὲ πρέπει / παρθενήϊα μὲν φρονεῖν / γλῶσσᾳ τε λέγεσθαι – 'it behoves me to think maidenly thoughts and choose only such for my tongue' (*Pindar Fr. 94b.33–5). *Alcman Fr. 81 introduces the only explicit reference to marriage in his work outside Alcman Fr. 1:

> αἰ γὰρ ἐμοὶ — ἐνθάδε ναιετάων· ἄμφω μὲν ἀθετεῖ Ἀρίσταρχος. διστάζει δὲ περὶ τοῦ πρώτου, ἐπεὶ καὶ Ἀλκμὰν αὐτὸν μετέβαλε παρθένους λεγούσας εἰσάγων 'Ζεῦ πάτερ, αἰ γὰρ ἐμὸς πόσις εἴη' (Schol. Hom. Od. 6.244, i 314 Di.)
>
> ('I wish ... living here.' Aristarchus athetizes both lines. But he is not sure about the first, because Alcman imitated it, introducing maidens who say 'Father Zeus, I wish he were my husband'.)

The line of Alcman quoted is, as we are told, part of a song sung by maidens; it is particularly interesting for the present discussion that it survives in a scholion to Odyssey 6.244, where Nausicaa, seeing Odysseus' newly revealed good looks, says to her attendants: αἲ γὰρ ἐμοὶ τοιόσδε πόσις κεκλημένος εἴη – 'I wish such a man could be my husband'. The precise context of Alcman's line cannot however be recovered.[56]

(7) Dancing (sometimes alluded to in descriptions of feet): ἀπ]αλοὶ πόδες – 'tender feet' (Alcman Fr. 3.10), cf. πεδ' ἀγῶν' ἵμεν – 'to go to the contest' (Alcman Fr. 3.8); διέβα ταναοῖς πο[σί] – 'she crossed on slender feet' (Alcman Fr. 3.70); ἤλυθον ἐς χορόν – 'I went to the dance' (*Pindar Fr. 94b.39). Singing: *Pindar Fr. 94b.11–15, 31–7. Procession: ?κατὰ στρατόν – 'down through the people' (Alcman Fr. 3.73) – although this may just refer to Astymeloisa's fame among the people; *Pindar Fr. 94b.66–70.

---

[56] It may derive from a context like Pind. Pyth. 9.97–103 or 10.55–9 (cf. Theocr. Id. 2.76–82) where girls are attracted to athletes, with (in the Pindaric cases) marriage in mind. The usual sexual interest expressed in partheneia is homosexual – cf. Calame (1977) I and II Indices analytiques s.v homosexualité (féminine).

There is virtually no further material describing girls in Alcman *Fr.* 3 (or in the other possible parthenaic fragments), and hence nothing to contradict the hypothesis proposed above on the basis of Alcman *Fr.* 1.[57] One further item in Pindar *Fr.* 94b is reminiscent of the familial settings in which Lavinia is shown. At lines 66–75 the daughter of the encomiand Pagondas (who is addressed at line 66 as 'son of Damaina', i.e. of his mother) is associated with the procession led by him; and she is said to have been trained by her own mother, Andaesistrota , in mental and physical accomplishments.

The hypothesis proposed might however be thought intrinsically too narrow, inasmuch as early Greek lyric poetry in general could seem *a priori* a more plausible source for Virgil's description of Lavinia than the narrower compass of the parthenia. Quotation and citation of the relevant evidence from the broader sphere of all archaic lyric is perhaps the easiest way to reveal what backing this view might have. First, the elements of other early lyric descriptions of young girls and their activities which overlap with those of the parthenia may be assembled – naturally without any claim to completeness; and more could be assembled if the Pindaric and Bacchylidean epinicia were laid under contribution.

(1) *(Fair) hair:*[58] ξάνθα δ᾽ Ἑλένα σ᾽ ἐίσ[κ]ην – 'I liken you to fair-haired Helen' (Sappho *Fr.* 23.5); ἀλλὰ ξανθοτέρα<ι>ς ἔχη[/ τα<ι>ς κόμα<ι>ς δάιδος – 'but with your fair hair, ?brighter? than a torch' (Sappho *Fr.* 98a.6f.); ξανθὰ Μεγαλοστράτα – 'fair-haired Megalostrata' (Alcman *Fr.* 59b.3); ξα]νθᾶς Ἑλένας περὶ εἴδει – 'over the beauty of fair-haired Helen' (Ibycus *Fr.* 282.5); ἐρασιπλόκαμον Πριάμοιο κόραν – 'the lovely-haired daughter of Priam' (Ibycus *Fr.* 303a.2); καὶ κ[όμη]ς, ἤ τοι κατ᾽ ἁβρὸν / ἐσκία[ζ]εν αὐχένα – 'and the hair that shaded your tender neck' (Anacreon *Fr.* 347.1.1f.); ξανθῇ δ᾽ Εὐρυπύλῃ – 'fair-haired Eurypyle' (Anacreon *Fr.* 372.1); ἀπέκειρας δ᾽ ἁπαλῆς κόμης ἄμωμον ἄνθος – 'you cut the perfection of your young hair' (of a boy) (Anacreon *Fr.* 414); εὐέθειρα χρυσόπεπλε κούρα – 'fine-haired, gold-robed, girl' (Anacreon *Fr.* 418). *Dark hair:* ἰόπλοκ᾽ ἄγνα

---

[57] Alcman *Fr.* 3.80 has one girl wishing that another should ἀπαλᾶς χηρὸς λάβοι (take my tender hand). This clearly has an erotic aspect (cf. now Davies (1986)) but could also involve dancing with linked hands, cf. e.g. Hom. *Il.* 18.594, *Hymn* 3.196. For the controversies about the relationships of the individuals named in Pind. *Fr.* 94b, cf. Calame (1977) I.119–21.

[58] Fair hair is also frequently an attribute of men, particularly heroes, in early Greek poetry, e.g. Achilles, Odysseus, Menelaus, Meleager and Rhadamanthus in Homer, cf. Dunbar (1962) and Prendergast (1962) *s.vv..*; and e.g. Alcman *Fr.* 5.2col.1.18; Pind. *Nem.* 3.43, 7.28. On 'the blond type', cf. the long note of Pease (1935) on *Aen.* 4.590.

μελλιχόμειδε Σάπφοι – 'Violet-tressed, holy, sweet-smiling Sappho' (Alcaeus *Fr.* 384); ἔτικτε δ᾽ Ἄτλας ἑπτὰ ἰοπλοκάμων φιλᾶν θυγατρῶν / τάνδ᾽ ἔξοχον εἶδος – 'Atlas begot her as the most beautiful of his seven violet-tressed daughters' (Simonides *Fr.* 555.3f.).

(2) *Face and cheeks and their colour*: κἀμάρυχμα λάμπρον ἴδην προσώπω – 'and to see the shining glitter of your forehead' (Sappho *Fr.* 16.18); μαλ]οπάραυε – 'apple-cheeked' (Alcaeus *Fr.* 261b.5); οὐκ ἀδιάντοισι παρειαῖς – 'with cheeks not unwetted by tears' (Simonides *Fr.* 543.5).

(3) *Eyes*: ἑλικώπιδα / ... / ἄβραν Ἀνδρομάχαν – 'glancing-eyed, tender Andromache' (Sappho *Fr.* 44.5–7); γλαυκώπιδα Κασσάνδραν – 'bright-eyed Cassandra' (Ibycus *Fr.* 303a.1); ἑλικοβλεφάρου – 'with glancing eyes' (Simonides *Fr.* 555.2).

(4) *General beauty (and godlike appearance)*: *passim*, cf. esp. Sappho *Fr.* 96.21ff.; and (indirectly) Sappho *Fr.* 31.

(5) *Hairband of purple or gold*: ἐπ᾽ ἀλικίας μεγ[/ κ]όσμον αἴ τις ἔχη<ι> φόβα [/ πορφύρῳ κατελιξαμέ[ν ... / ἔμμεναι μάλα τοῦτο – 'that in her youth it was great adornment to bind your hair in a purple headband' (Sappho *Fr.* 98a.2–5); μ]ιτράναν δ᾽ ἀρτίως κλ[/ ποικίλαν ἀπὺ Σαρδίω[ν – 'of late an ornate headband from Sardis' (Sappho *Fr.* 98a.10f.); σοὶ δ᾽ ἔγω Κλέι ποικίλαν [/ οὐκ ἔχω πόθεν ἔσσεται [/ μιτράν<αν> – 'I have no source to provide you an ornate headband, Cleis' (Sappho *Fr.* 98b.1–3).

(6) *Emphasis on eligibility, virginity and marriage*: μάκαιρα παρσένων – 'blessed among maidens' (Alcman *Fr.* 59b.2); Sappho *passim*, cf. Page (1955) 119–26; κόραν – 'girl' (Ibycus *Fr.* 303a.2); κοῦρα – 'girl' (Anacreon *Fr.* 418); παρθένος – 'maiden' (Simonides *Fr.* 585).

(7) *Dancing*: universal in choric lyric. *Procession*: Sappho *Fr.* 44.15. *Going to temple*: Sappho *Fr.* 94.24–7.

It may be added that two of the items found in Alcman *Fr.* 1 but not present in Virgil's portrait of Lavinia, viz. animal comparisons and beautiful ankles, do recur in non-parthenaic lyric descriptions of girls. But there they are probably entirely erotic rather than also performance-linked. The examples are:

(a) *Animal comparisons*: ἐλάφω δὲ] βρόμος ἐν σ[τήθεσι φυίει φοβέροισιν – 'The fearful cry of the hind springs up in my timid heart' (Alcaeus *Fr.* 10b.5); λῦσαν δ᾽ ἄπρακτα νεάνιδες ὤ- / τ᾽ ὄρνις ϝιέρακος ὑπερπταμένω – 'the girls ?panicked fruitlessly, like birds when a hawk flies overhead' (Alcman *Fr.* 82).

(b) *Beautiful ankles (step)* : τᾶ]ς <κ>ε βολλοίμαν ἐρατόν τε βᾶμα – 'I

could wish <to see> her lovely step' (Sappho *Fr.* 16.17); γυναίκων
τ᾽ ἄμα παρθενίκα[ν] τ. .[. .].σφύρων – 'of women and maidens ...
of their ankles' (Sappho *Fr.* 44.15).[59]

There is then, not surprisingly, a fair amount of common ground in
the description of girls between the partheneia and other archaic lyric.
But there are also some counter-indications to the notion that early
Greek lyric in general is the primary influence upon Virgil's description
of Lavinia, rather than the limited class of partheneia. The aspects of
female (not necessarily virginal) beauty and activity treated throughout
archaic lyric are much broader than those found in the partheneia; and
these additional descriptive elements cannot be seen as referring even in
part to the singing and dancing of a chorus of virgins. The relevant
material, again assembled without claim to completeness, is:

(a) *Sweet smile*: μελλιχόμειδε Σάπφοι – 'sweet-smiling Sappho'
    (Alcaeus *Fr.* 384).

(b) *Sweet speech and desirable laughter*: ἆδυ φωνεί- / σας ὐπακούει /
    καὶ γελαίσας ἰμέροεν – '<the man who> listens to your sweet
    words and desirable laughter' (Sappho *Fr.* 31.3–5).

(c) *Purple mouth*: πορφυρέου ἀπὸ στόματος / ἰεῖσα φωνὰν παρθένος
    – 'A girl speaking from purple mouth' (Simonides *Fr.* 585).

(d) *Nudity and semi-nudity*: καί σε πόλλαι παρθένικαι πέ.[/ . . . .]λων
    μήρων ἀπάλαισι χέρ[σι /. . .]α· θέλγονται τὸ[σον] ὡς ἄλει[ππα /
    θή[ϊο]ν ὕδωρ – 'and many maidens come down to you, bathing
    their ?beautiful thighs with tender hands, soothed by your divine
    water like oil' (Alcaeus *Fr.* 45.5–8). Here the poet describes the
    virgins of Aenus, a Lesbian colony in Thrace, washing in the river
    Hebrus. Presumably this was a ritual, and possibly a pre-marriage
    custom: but the poet visualises it erotically and lingers on the girls'
    thighs, a physical feature of particular sexual fascination to the
    Greeks.[60] Again Ibycus *Fr.* 339 refers to the most notorious
    example of Greek female nudity, the naked gymnastics of Spartan
    girls (once more emphasizing their thighs), as does Anacreon *Fr.*
    399: ἐκδῦσα κιθῶνα δωριάζειν – 'stripping off her tunic to be
    Dorian naked'.

(e) *Attendance at banquets and drinking parties*: Sappho *Fr.* 2.13–16;
    Sappho *Fr.* 94.10–23; Alcaeus *Fr.* 376.

[59] Similarly the white arm which the girl stretches out to young men at Bacch. *Fr.* 17
(Sn.–Mae.) *q.v.* is erotic.
[60] Because of the strong homosexual bent of Greek male society, cf. Dover (1978) esp.
70, 98f., 197. On Roman interest in nudity, cf. now Griffin (1985) Index *s.v.* nakedness.

(f) *Physical love-making*: Archilochus P.Colon. 7511.1–35; Sappho
Fr. 94.21–3.

The overall impression is that early Greek lyric poetry could use a
broader range of material to describe young girls than could the
partheneia, which restricted themselves to items appropriate for virgins
anticipating marriage. Later, other literary forms drew on and elabo-
rated these conventions of lyric.[61] So Virgil's apparent return to the very
limited range of descriptions found in lyric partheneia implies a
deliberate choice of model, designating Lavinia, like the girls in the
partheneia, as a young eligible virgin destined for marriage. It may also
give the details of her portrait independent value in characterising her as
beautiful and desirable because they have this function also in the
partheneia. In discussing Alcman *Frr.* 1 and 3, Calame (1977) demonstrated that various standard topics of the partheneia – purple, gold,
hairbands and so forth – have intrinsic erotic and encomiastic
associations. Thus purple is especially connected with Aphrodite in
early Greek literature and life.[62] The Lydian mitra has strong sexual
overtones and special associations with the onset of puberty,[63] and with
it is linked closely the sexual symbolism of the girls' long hair and that of
gold signifying the highest physical beauty.[64] The crown has similar
links;[65] and another metal symbol associated with beauty is silver.[66]
Finally perfume, described periphrastically as 'the soft χάρις (grace) of
Cinyras' (a mythical king of Cyprus), is said to 'sit upon' the hair of
maidens in Alcman *Fr.* 3.71f. It is no accident that the periphrasis
introduces the term χάρις, since it too has a role in the erotic complex
generated in the partheneia.[67] If, then, Virgil is drawing on the
parthenaic tradition, he will be aiming at a paradoxical result. On the
one hand the representational conventions derived from the partheneia
might make Lavinia seem insipid; but on the other, the parthenaic terms
used to describe her physical appearance and dress carry associations
which confer on her a greater vividness and substance.

From the viewpoint of literary history it would by no means be
strange if the Augustan Virgil conceived Lavinia in early Greek
parthenaic terms. There was intense hellenistic Greek interest, scholarly

---

[61] Notably hellenistic epic (see e.g. below, p. 174 n. 74), elegy, and epigram. But also
Theocritus, esp. *Id.* 18.
[62] Cf. Calame (1977) II.98f. and, for the whole complex, 86–109.
[63] Cf. Calame (1977) II.99–101.   [64] Cf. Calame (1977) II.101–3.
[65] Cf. Calame (1977) II.107–9.   [66] Cf. Calame (1977) II.102.
[67] Cf. Calame (1977) II.63f., 99, 103, 106. For the wider associations of χάρις and
beauty, cf. Jax (1933) 40–2, 66f., 80f., 123, 146, 161, 166, 170; (1936) 48; (1938) 15f., 19.

173

and poetic, in archaic lyric;[68] and the late Roman republic and the Augustan age were no less involved in the imitation of early Greek lyric, first by Catullus and the other 'neoterics', and then by Horace in his *Odes* and *Epodes*.[69] We cannot, given the difficulty of defining the genre, be certain that specific Roman lyrics were written as partheneia. But Horace's *Carmen Saeculare* was certainly composed for performance by a chorus of *pueri* and *puellae*, as seemingly was *Odes* 4.6, which may well have been another saecular hymn.[70] The *Carmen Saeculare* was performed, and *Odes* 4.6 published, after the death of Virgil. We know, however, that saecular interest had been lively throughout the twenties BC;[71] and the hymn for the occasion, as well as its Greek models, must have been a matter of interest to Roman poets throughout the period. Moreover other 'parthenaic' hymns were being written, and performed, at this time: Horace himself composed in the late thirties or early twenties BC, in imitation of Catullus 34, a choric hymn (*Odes* 1.21) also at least purporting to be sung by girls and boys;[72] and in Asia such hymns were performed by choirs from the Augustan period on in honour of Rome and Augustus.[73] Finally some elements of Apollonius Rhodius' treatment of Medea[74] would have offered Virgil a part-precedent in epic for his borrowings from early Greek lyric; and it has now been shown (if further proof were needed of his direct interest in early Greek lyric) that in his *Georgics* he is indebted to epinician material mediated through Callimachus.[75]

Virgil's 'lyric' and 'parthenaic' treatment of Lavinia seems to extend also to the overall impact of some of the scenes in which she appears: of

[68] Cf. Fraser (1972) Chs. 8, 10, 11, and General Index under the names of the lyric poets.
[69] The notorious influence of hellenistic poetry upon the '*cantores Euphorionis*' is consistent with the simultaneous influence, both direct and indirect, of earlier literature, cf. e.g. Cat. 34, 51.
[70] Cf. Cairns (1971) 443f.
[71] Cf. Syme (1939) Index *s.v. Ludi Saeculares*; and esp. *Aen.* 6.792–4.
[72] Cf. Cairns (1971) 440–4. On Cat. 34, cf. most recently Wiseman (1985) 92–107, reviewing earlier approaches and suggesting a new place and occasion of performance.
[73] Cf. Price (1984) Index *s.v.* choirs honouring emperor etc.
[74] E.g. some of the Apollonian Medea's frequent 'symptoms of love' (e.g. *Arg.* 3.284–98, 751ff., 961–5, 998–1024, 1130) may be lyric in origin, cf. esp. Sappho *Fr.* 31 (L–P), although there are generic forces at work here too, cf. Cairns (1972) General index *s.v.* 'symptoms of love'. The overall picture of Medea at *Arg.* 3.828ff. also has a lyric flavour: she is παρθενική at 3.829, and there is stress on her ὁμηλικίη at 3.814, her maids at 3.838ff., who are ἥλικες (840), and her singing with them at 3.897f. (cf. 949f.) – but see Campbell (1983a) 56–9 on the Nausicaa/Medea comparisons and contrasts. Other lyric elements are her fear (she is compared to a fawn) at 4.11–13 – cf. Alcaeus *Fr.* 10b (L–P), and what she says about halcyons at 4.362–4 – cf. Alcman *Fr.* 26.
[75] Cf. below, p. 217 and Thomas (1983).

the five, three have no substantial surviving epic antecedent. The first involves the fire omen of 7.71ff. No homeric parallels are offered by Knauer (1964) for this scene. There may well have been a lost Ennian model, given that this sort of portent is frequent in Roman religion. But even so, the lyric flavour of the light and of the fire playing around Lavinia's long golden hair with its *ornatus* of a jewelled crown should not be undervalued.[76] The second scene is when Lavinia is hidden in the woods (7.385ff.). The homeric parallels are so minor as to be negligible;[77] but line 393, *idem omnis simul ardor agit nova quaerere tecta*, with its unusual word-patterns – all but one word is disyllabic – and weak third-foot caesura, gives a strong hint of the galliambic metre. That hint would not only underscore the moral dubiety of Amata's thiasos, but would point to orgiastic Greek lyric poetry written in galliambics. The third scene in which Lavinia appears, 12.64ff., contains only a one-line homeric reminiscence;[78] in both Virgil and Homer the respective lines introduce a simile and are not part of the main narrative: *Indum sanguineo veluti violaverit ostro (Aeneid* 12.67) = ὡς δ' ὅτε τίς τ' ἐλέφαντα γυνὴ φοίνικι μιήνῃ – 'as when a woman dyes ivory with purple' (*Iliad* 4.141). Epic material does of course return in Turnus' speech, especially when he reiterates the view that the war can only be resolved by single combat (*Aeneid* 12.78–80 = *Iliad* 3.88–93). But even here the homeric reminiscence is conceptual rather then verbal.

This is not to say however that Virgil has flagged in his integration of Lavinia's lyric aspects into their epic matrix – already demonstrated in his use of epic-derived techniques of indirect presentation (cf. pp. 153ff.). The other two episodes in which Lavinia appears are without doubt primarily of epic inspiration and are intended to be viewed as such. The first is the procession to the temple of Athena (11.477ff.); although such processions also have lyric antecedents,[79] this scene echoes in detail *Iliad* 6.286ff. (cf. also *Iliad* 6.86–101, 269–79), the procession of Trojan women led by Hecuba in a vain attempt to save Troy by prayer. In the *Aeneid* analogue, the end of the war is much nearer than it was in the *Iliad*, and this makes the scene even more dramatically prominent. The last appearance of Lavinia – more low-

---

[76] The scene described at Eur. *Med.* 1156ff., where Glauke dons the poisoned gold crown and robes just before her marriage and is burnt up by them, is presumably a macabre variant upon lyric descriptions of young girls so attired and with marriage in prospect.

[77] Cf. Knauer (1964) 400; see also above, p. 153 n. 10, p. 174 n. 74.

[78] Cf. Knauer (1964) 426; see above, p. 153 n. 10.

[79] Cf. Brelich (1969) Indice degli argomenti *s.v.* processioni.

key, but again undeniably epic – is at the mourning for Amata (*Aeneid* 12.604ff.). This episode draws on the mourning of women for Patroclus (*Iliad* 19.282ff.), and for Hector (*Iliad* 24.710ff.).[80] Although the verbal reminiscences are not close, the links are sure. Hence, as with his elegiac sources for Dido, Virgil does blend his lyric inspiration for Lavinia fully into the epic structure.

A speculative suggestion concerning Augustan literary history ends this chapter. It is that Virgil's forays into elegy and lyric may each represent a debt and indirect tribute to another poet from the circle of Maecenas. I have already noted (p. 136) that Propertius' own literary *persona* is the closest parallel among the elegists to the elegiac Dido of the *Aeneid*. If Virgil consciously drew on Propertius for his portrayal of Dido, then it is perhaps even more likely that by depicting Lavinia in lyric terms he was gracefully alluding to Horace, whose ambition to rival the nine lyric poets of early Greece paralleled Virgil's own emulation of Homer. For in *Odes* 1.3, published in 23 BC, Horace – if a view currently proposed is correct[81] – had paid a lyric poet's tribute to his friend Virgil's *Aeneid*, then in process of composition, with the standard image of a dangerous sea-voyage representing the writing of the epic. It may be that Virgil reciprocated in his own fashion, by modelling his most significant heroine, the mother of the Roman race, on some of those same Greek lyric predecessors who inspired Horace in his *Odes*.

[80] Cf. Knauer (1964) 429.
[81] Cf. esp. Lockyer (1967–8); Santirocco (1986) 27–30; the hypothesis has recently been challenged by J.S. Campbell (1986–7) 314f. n. 3, without substantive arguments.

8

THE *AENEID* AS *ODYSSEY*

In Chapters 6 and 7 Virgil's borrowings from contemporary Roman elegy and archaic Greek lyric have been examined. But of course the principal model for all ancient epic poets up to and including Virgil was Homer. Modern scholarship has explored extensively Virgil's indebtedness to Homer. Chapters 8 and 9 nevertheless tackle it again, in part to reveal once more those Virgilian concerns seen earlier, in part to arrive at a new formulation of Virgil's *homerica imitatio*. The traditional formulation, i.e. that the first six books are modelled on the *Odyssey*, the second six on the *Iliad*, is expressed succinctly at Servius *ad Aen.* 7.1: *primi sex ad imaginem Odyssiae ..., hi autem sex ad imaginem Iliados dicti sunt.* This 'dichotomic' approach was standard in late Roman scholarship on Virgil (cf. also Macrobius *Saturnalia* 5.2.6 and Servius *ad Aen.* 1.1);[1] and it may well go back to the Augustan age. As an initial viewpoint it has much to commend it: the voyages of Aeneas in *Aeneid* 1–6 are clear analogues of Odysseus' voyages in the *Odyssey*; and Aeneas' battles in Books 7–12 obviously reflect those of the *Iliad*. Knauer's fundamental work shows how much detailed imitation and reminiscence underlie this bipartite view; and, in the hands of scholars like Heinze, Pöschl, and particularly Knauer, who is most aware of its limitations, it becomes a powerful tool for the understanding of the *Aeneid*.[2]

This chapter and the next move, along lines already adumbrated by other scholars,[3] away from this traditional view. Its shortcomings have long been recognised, notably the presence in the Virgilian *Odyssey* and *Iliad* of features from the 'wrong' homeric epic. But the scale of displacement is not always appreciated: major elements of Aeneas'

---

[1] The words at Donatus *Vit. Verg.* 75f. (Hardie), *argumentum varium ac multiplex et quasi amborum Homeri carminum instar*, might at first appear to embody a more complex judgement, but in fact probably reflect the same view.

[2] I.e. Heinze (1915); Pöschl (1977); Knauer (1964); (1981).

[3] There are a few hints in Williams (1963), but the main impetus comes from Knauer (1964), where much of what is developed in this chapter is at least foreshadowed, and (1981); cf. also Schmidt (1983), who advances his own formulation, and Lausberg (1983), who summarises and applies that of Knauer.

arrival and initial experiences in Italy in *Aeneid* 7–8 derive from Odysseus' and Telemachus' arrivals in the *Odyssey*.[4] Conversely, although games are not out of place in the odyssean half of the *Aeneid*, given that *Odyssey* 8 contains the Phaeacian games (cf. Ch. 9), those of *Aeneid* 5 derive their material largely from the funeral games for Patroclus in *Iliad* 23. Similarly the account of the wooden horse and the fall of Troy (*Aeneid* 2) lies within the odyssean half, and these themes, although not strictly speaking iliadic (since they come from the *Little Iliad* of Lesches and the *Sack of Troy* of Arctinus),[5] are more akin to the subject matter of the *Iliad* than to that of the *Odyssey*. Again the 'suitor motif' of the *Odyssey* is prominent throughout the iliadic half, while the odyssean *Aeneid* 1 has many iliadic aspects. Numerous details could be added, such as the odyssean monster Cacus in *Aeneid* 8,[6] or the modelling of the *signum Veneris* (*Aeneid* 8.520–40) on *Odyssey* 15.160–81.[7] It is however the cumulative impact of Knauer's 'Listen der Homerzitate in der Aeneis'[8] which most undermines the bipartite view: for if trivial and merely verbal items are left aside, it leads to the conclusion that sustained iliadic influence begins only in *Aeneid* 8, and odyssean influence declines only in *Aeneid* 9.

All this suggests that a more accurate description of the *Aeneid* in terms of the two homeric epics is needed. For the *Odyssey* retains the structural and thematic importance it had in Books 1–6 well into, and indeed throughout, the 'iliadic' Books 7–12, while iliadic or quasi-iliadic episodes surface also in the 'odyssean' *Aeneid* 1–6. This makes the *Aeneid*, not a bipartite work divided by subject matter (i.e. voyages or battles), but a unitary *Odyssey* with significant iliadic episodes. Nothing could be more natural, since both *Odyssey* and *Aeneid* are 'Returns',[9] and the outline structures of both are similar. The odyssean inspiration for Aeneas' travels and stay at Carthage (Books 1–4) is well recognised; subsequently the games of *Aeneid* 5 balance the Phaeacian games of

[4] Cf. Knauer (1964) 241–59. On some of the non-odyssean elements of *Aen.* 1–6, cf. also Williams (1963) 266f.

[5] Cf. Severyns (1938–63) IV.89f., 91–3, and, for a survey of the *Aeneid*'s relationship with the cyclic epics, Kopff (1981).

[6] *Aen.* 8.193–275, cf. esp. the cave-dwelling monster Cyclops of *Od.* 9.152–542.

[7] Cf. Knauer (1964) 257–9 and (1981) 884f., pointing out that the two portents accompanying a gift are understood only by the daughter/son of the god responsible for them. The effect is to exemplify once more the principle discussed below (pp. 194ff.), since the ultimate source of the rearming of Aeneas is the rearming of Achilles in *Il.* 18–19. On a similar piquant point, *Il.* 24.679ff. as a model for *Aen.* 4.556ff., cf. Harrison (1984) 14f., 32f.

[8] Knauer (1964) 371–527.

[9] On the *Aeneid* as a Νόστος, cf. above, Ch. 5.

Odyssey 8, although (as noted) they draw more heavily for material on *Iliad* 23; and they are followed by the descent to the Underworld (*Aeneid* 6 = *Odyssey* 11) and then the 'homecoming' of Aeneas at *Aeneid* 7.25ff. (cf. that of Odysseus at *Odyssey* 13.96ff.). The heroes are only 'recognised' at first by virtuous and privileged persons – Evander and Latinus, Eumaeus and Telemachus[10] – who understand that they have 'returned' to claim their rights, which include and are symbolised by their 'wives'. Both fight against rival suitors for their 'wives' and kill them, so obtaining their rights. These plot summaries are gross oversimplifications. But no parallel iliadic account of the *Aeneid* could be offered; and this above all guarantees the conceptual dominance in it of the *Odyssey*. External confirmation comes in Virgil's ready acceptance of additional influence on his characters, motifs, and emotional tone from Apollonius Rhodius' *Argonautica*, which is in important respects[11] a hyper-odyssean epic, choosing, in accord with hellenistic taste, to stress and enhance those episodic and folkloristic features which distinguish the *Odyssey* from the *Iliad*.

The notion that Virgil used the *Odyssey* as his chief structural and conceptual model might initially seem strange, given the prevalent impression that it is more 'lightweight' than the *Iliad*. The modern commentators responsible for this attitude have ancient scholiastic precedent when they stress the high seriousness of the *Iliad*, its noble and heroic characters and sentiments, and its profound and complex concern with honour, personal achievement and death,[12] while representing the *Odyssey* as a compound of folk-tales and everyday life. Popular judgement too in the hellenistic and Roman periods, or perhaps rather the needs of schoolmasters, also favoured the *Iliad*, which is the most frequently attested papyrus literary text, with the *Odyssey* some way behind.[13] But it may be wrong to impose on all antiquity the view that the *Odyssey* is less significant than the *Iliad*;

---

[10] On Eumaeus and Evander as analogues, cf. Knauer (1964) 252–4; (1981) 884.

[11] From which however the character of Jason is excluded, cf. below, p. 185, and Klein (1983) for recent discussion of it.

[12] Some ancient thinking is reflected by e.g. 'Longinus', and by Eustathius on the *Iliad* prooemium (4.44f.): ἀνδρώδης μὲν ἡ Ἰλιὰς καὶ σεμνοτέρα καὶ ὕψος ἔχουσα, ἐπεὶ καὶ ἡρωϊκωτέρα. ἠθικὴ δὲ ἡ Ὀδύσσεια (the *Iliad* is manly, more solemn, and sublime, since it is also more heroic, while the *Odyssey* is full of character-interest). In modern times the main impulse in this direction came from nineteenth- and early twentieth-century 'pre-oral' commentators, but such an evaluation (at least of the *Iliad*) has been revived in different ways by Griffin (1980) and Macleod (1982).

[13] Cf. Luce (1975) 180; the material is from hellenistic Egypt, but there is no reason to think it untypical.

another reading of it – less as a light-hearted tale about a professional trickster with a happy ending, and more as a heroic story in which the enemies of the royal house (and thus the state) of Ithaca were triumphantly defeated by its courageous, shrewd, virtuous and pious king, with the sustained and effective support of the goddess Athena – is just as valid.

The homeric critics working from the third century BC on up to and beyond Virgil's time[14] throw some (limited) light on the problem. One strand of their work confirms that a lower evaluation of the *Odyssey* was current also among some contemporary intellectuals. The epics were discussed primarily in terms of priority of composition, and the majority of critics believed that the *Iliad* was composed first, since they rightly saw the *Iliad* narrative as central to the epic cycle, with the *Odyssey* sweeping up incidents omitted from it, and treating the iliadic heroes as familiar figures. The most eloquent exponent of this view is the second-century AD writer 'Longinus' (9.11–15),[15] who shows the close link between the theory that the *Odyssey* was completed second and the judgement that the *Odyssey* is inferior:

δείκνυσι δ' ὅμως διὰ τῆς Ὀδυσσείας ... ὅτι μεγάλης φύσεως ὑποφερομένης ἤδη ἴδιόν ἐστιν ἐν γήρᾳ τὸ φιλόμυθον. δῆλος γὰρ ἐκ πολλῶν τε ἄλλων συντεθεικὼς ταύτην δευτέραν τὴν ὑπόθεσιν, ἀτὰρ δὴ κἀκ τοῦ λείψανα τῶν Ἰλιακῶν παθημάτων διὰ τῆς Ὀδυσσείας ὡς ἐπεισόδιά τινα [τοῦ Τρωικοῦ πολέμου] προσεπεισφέρειν, καὶ νὴ Δί' ἐκ τοῦ τὰς ὀλοφύρσεις καὶ τοὺς οἴκτους ὡς πάλαι που προεγνωσμένους τοῖς ἥρωσιν ἐνταῦθα προσαποδιδόναι. οὐ γὰρ ἀλλ' ἢ τῆς Ἰλιάδος ἐπίλογός ἐστιν ἡ Ὀδύσσεια·

[14] On the dating of the exegetical scholia, cf. e.g. Richardson (1980) 265; Lausberg (1983) 210 n. 28; Wlosok (1986) esp. 78, 83 nn. 19–22.

[15] Cf. also, on these questions (including defence of the MS reading προεγνωσμένους), Bühler (1964) 55f., and Russell (1964) *ad loc.*, citing as parallels Schol. bT on *Il.* 24.804a, which reports the view of Aristarchus' pupil, Menecrates of Nysa, and speaks of Homer reserving τὰ λοιπὰ ... τῶν διηγημάτων [ζητημάτων MS] (the rest of the stories) for the *Odyssey*, and of the *Odyssey* as containing the λείψανα (left-overs) of the *Iliad*, Eustath. on *Od.* 3.108, and the *Certamen* 275f. (Allen); cf. also Erbse (1969–) on Schol. *Il.* 24.804; Bühler (1964) 46f.; Barchiesi (1984) 93f.; Eustath. 4.38f. (on the *Iliad* prooemium). For further statements that the *Odyssey* contains the 'left-overs' of the *Iliad*, cf. e.g. Schol. HQ on *Od.* 1.284; Schol. E on *Od.* 4.69; and, most fully, Eustath. 1380.6ff. (on the *Odyssey* prooemium); cf. also below, p. 197 nn. 73f. Wender (1978) 39f., treats this feature usefully in connection with the Νέκυια (i.e. the Underworld Scene) of both *Od.* 11 and 24, noting that the living Nestor and Menelaus also appear in the narrative of the second Νέκυια, that the odyssean description of the funeral of Achilles parallels the iliadic funeral of Patroclus, and that the second *Odyssey* Νέκυια permits many of the other great iliadic heroes to make their final farewell. For the complementary phenomenon of 'anticipation' by Homer of the *Odyssey* in the *Iliad*, cf. the scholia cited at Richardson (1980) 269; Borthwick (1983).

... ἀπὸ δὲ τῆς αὐτῆς αἰτίας, οἶμαι, τῆς μὲν Ἰλιάδος γραφομένης ἐν
ἀκμῇ πνεύματος ὅλον τὸ σωμάτιον δραματικὸν ὑπεστήσατο καὶ
ἐναγώνιον, τῆς δὲ Ὀδυσσείας τὸ πλέον διηγηματικόν, ὅπερ ἴδιον
γήρως. ('Longinus' 9.11–13)

(In the *Odyssey* he shows ... that when a great mind is in decline, its
characteristic in old age is a love of telling stories. There are many
other indications that it was his second work, including the fact
that he inserted as episodes the left-overs of the action at Troy, and
from the way that he laments and shows pity for the heroes of the
Iliad as though this was something preplanned long before. For the
Odyssey is nothing more than the epilogue to the *Iliad* ... For this
reason too, I believe, the *Iliad* which is composed when he was at
the flower of his age is in its entirety dramatic and exciting, whereas
most of the *Odyssey* is narrative – that characteristic of old age.)

The logic is that the decline of a 'great spirit' in old age leads to a
preference for narrative, and this is why the dramatic and exciting *Iliad*
is followed by the 'narrative' *Odyssey*. The next lines speak of the
tension, sublimity, passions and so forth of the *Iliad*; the *Odyssey* on the
other hand is like the ebb tide of Ocean (9.13). 'Longinus' ends with
standard criticisms of details of the *Odyssey*, and by noting that πάθος
in the *Iliad* becomes ἦθος in the *Odyssey*, so that e.g the description of
Odysseus' household κωμῳδία τίς ἐστιν ἠθολογουμένη: 'forms a kind
of comedy of manners' (9.15).[16]

There is also evidence of the view that the *Odyssey* was written first –
cf. Lucian *Verae Historiae* 2.20 and the 'Herodotean' *Vita Homeri* 26–8;
and the controversy was presumably alive in Virgil's day, since it is later
mentioned as current in Seneca *De Brevitate Vitae* 13.2.[17] But it cannot
be assumed that those who regarded the *Odyssey* as Homer's first epic
also argued for its superiority: they could have judged it an inferior
practice piece. In any case this was obviously a minority view, perhaps
even an eccentric one; and it cannot be argued that Virgil shared it, or
was untouched by the general trend of hellenistic literary criticism of
Homer. On the contrary it has repeatedly been shown that Virgil made
wide use of the Homer scholia, which discussed these matters, and
which generally upheld the priority of the *Iliad*.[18] Indeed Virgil

[16] Translation by Russell–Winterbottom (1972) 471. Cf. also Russell (1964) on 'Longinus' 9.15. On the celebrated Servian view of *Aen.* 4 as *comoedia*, cf. above, p. 136 n. 18.

[17] Seneca treats the controversy as one of the useless problems discussed by *grammatici*, and Slater (1982) 348 n. 61 accepts this assessment; but the dispute could have serious interpretative implications.

[18] Cf. esp. Schlunk (1974); Lausberg (1983) 210 and n. 28; and most recently Wlosok (1986).

probably knew the theory that Homer was supplementing the *Iliad* in the *Odyssey* – which of course presupposes the prior composition of the *Iliad* – and used it as a licence for his own supplementation of both homeric epics.[19]

Other factors give clearer guidance to Virgil's esteem for each of the homeric epics. One is the assessments offered by hellenistic philosophers, particularly stoics and cynics, of the two epic protagonists. There was some adverse philosophical criticism of the homeric Odysseus;[20] but the overwhelming tendency was to defend him as a 'wise man', with the cynic Antisthenes contributing notably.[21] In contrast, the iliadic heroes, although sometimes defended by the philosophers, on the whole are treated less favourably (cf. pp. 185f.).[22] The moral status of the heroes affected that of the epics, the relative standing of which is summed up in Horace *Epistles* 1.2 (cf. pp. 85ff., 209). In these terms the *Odyssey* could easily have possessed, for Virgil and his contemporaries, sufficient intellectual and moral importance to function as the primary model for the *Aeneid*.[23]

The second indication of the *Odyssey*'s probable status in Virgil's eyes is its standing among his contemporary writers. It had been the first Greek work translated into Latin (verse) for use in Roman schools – by Livius Andronicus in the third century BC. Even then perhaps Romans were more attracted by the moral calibre of the *Odyssey*'s hero than by the tragic ethos of the *Iliad*; and even then the *Iliad* may

---

[19] E.g. the account at *Aen.* 11.225-95 (cf. 8.9-17) of the latter days of Diomedes, now settled in his distant Italian exile and chastened by his earlier experiences in battle with Aeneas before the walls of Troy, supplements (and 'corrects') the *Iliad*, as does the merciful rescue by the Trojans of Achaemenides from the Cyclops' island (*Aen.* 3.588-691) (cf. General Index *s.v.* Achaemenides).

[20] Cf. esp. Kaiser (1964) 212f., 215ff.; Kindstrand (1973) 137. For criticisms in terms of etiquette, cf. Stanford (1968) 120f.

[21] Cf. Di Benedetto (1966); Kindstrand (1973) 181-4, 210f. Stanford (1968) 121-7 discusses the 'stoic' view of Odysseus, but admits cynic influence. The epicureans also claimed Odysseus as their own, cf. Kaiser (1964) 220f.; Gigante (1984) 294-8.

[22] Cf. the evidence assembled by Richardson (1980) 272-4.

[23] This is not to say that they will have regarded it as perfect: Virgil's 'corrections' of the *Odyssey*, as well as showing his interest in homeric scholarship, also reveal a desire to avoid in his own work the celebrated ἀπίθανα (implausibilities) of the *Odyssey*. Thus Virgil reduced the ten days of drifting in the sea without food by Odysseus (*Odyssey* 12.447, a feature criticised in antiquity as improbable) to a similar experience of just over three days for Palinurus (*Aeneid* 6.355f.), in essence by conflating two odyssean experiences and by adopting the time-scale of the other (*Odyssey* 5.313-463, cf. esp. 388-90). Likewise he reduced the numerous suitors of Penelope, whose very numbers caused Homer to be attacked on the ground that Odysseus could not possibly have killed all of them with so few helpers, to the single figure of Turnus. On these ἀπίθανα, cf. 'Longinus' 9.14 and Russell (1964) *ad loc.*.

have seemed an anti-Roman epic because of its anti-Trojan slant.[24] Augustan poets did not favour the *Iliad* more. Apart from the *Aeneid* and parts of Ovid *Metamorphoses* 12–14, no extensive surviving Augustan poetry is based on Homer. The *Metamorphoses* is even-handed in its use of *Iliad* and *Odyssey* – and *Aeneid*. The minor references to Homer in Augustan poetry which involve brief mytho-logical exempla may owe more to hellenistic handbooks than to their ultimate sources;[25] in any case they seem to be fairly evenly distributed. The minor but more substantial examples of homeric influence are again not decisive: Ovid's *Heroides* contain both the odyssean '*Penelope Ulixi*' (1) and the iliadic '*Briseis Achilli*' (3). Two other epistles, '*Oenone Paridi*' (5) and '*Laodamia Protesilao*' (13) have the Epic Cycle rather than Homer as their ultimate source, with Catullus 68 also a factor in the latter. As for Propertius, 2.8 makes much use of the iliadic Achilles–Briseis theme; 3.12 contains a major *Odyssey* summary with some interesting variations;[26] 2.9 employs the *personae* of both Penelope and Briseis; 3.1 refers substantially to the *Iliad*; and in Book 4, 7 appears to have an iliadic base, while that of 8 is odyssean.[27] All in all Propertius, if anything, leans towards the *Odyssey*; and this is echoed in Tibullus, since he admits no major iliadic influence, whereas in 1.3 he assumes the *persona* of Odysseus, like himself 'shipwrecked' in Phaeacia, and like him in danger and longing to return home to his 'wife'.[28] Horace also favours the *Odyssey*. In *Epistles* 1.2 (cf. pp. 85ff.) both epics are summarised, and Horace, in philosophic mood, is more appreciative of the *Odyssey* and its hero than of the *Iliad* and its protagonists. *Epistles* 1.7.40–3 is again odyssean, as is *Satires* 2.5 with its extended dialogue between Odysseus and Tiresias. Thus an *Aeneid* based primarily on the *Odyssey* would not be out of keeping with Augustan literary taste: it may indeed have had a bias towards the *Odyssey* because of its greater concern with private life,[29] although

[24] Cf. Harrison (1981) esp. 212–23.

[25] Parthenius' Ἐρωτικὰ Παθήματα (Tales of the Sufferings of Love) and ps.-Hyginus (cf. Rose (1933)) give, on their different levels, an impression of what these handbooks may have looked like. Fraser (1972) Ch. 8 discusses valuably *inter alia* Alexandrian compilations. For a pertinent analogous case involving pictorial illustrations, cf. Horsfall (1979) esp. 43f.

[26] On all these Propertian elegies, cf. now Benediktson (1985), with *inter alia* pointers to simultaneous hellenistic influence on Propertian imitations of Homer.

[27] Cf. Dalzell (1980), usefully assembling the material, and esp. 33f. on Prop. 4.7 and 4.8; Benediktson (1985) esp. 21f., with further bibliography.

[28] Cf. Bright (1971).

[29] Cf. Cairns (1979) 29–35.

Roman poets tended to counter this type of concern by reasserting the predominant importance of public life.

But none of this in itself explains Virgil's choice of the *Odyssey* as primary model. The reasons lie in Virgil's main preoccupations, literary, cultural, philosophical, and political, as will emerge in different connections throughout this chapter and Chapter 9. One obvious advantage of the *Odyssey* is that it climaxes in a 'civil war', i.e. between Odysseus and the suitors, parallel to that fought by Aeneas. Another is the *Odyssey*'s theme of 'returning home'; the *Iliad* exemplifies the diametrically opposed tendency, in that Achilles, who could have returned home with propriety after Agamemnon's insult in Book 1, remained at Troy sulking by his ships, although he knew this would lead to his death. Achilles perceived his decision in these terms, speaking of νόστος (return) and κλέος (fame) in summing up his alternatives:

εἰ μέν κ᾽ αὖθι μένων Τρώων πόλιν ἀμφιμάχωμαι,
ὤλετο μέν μοι νόστος, ἀτὰρ κλέος ἄφθιτον ἔσται·
εἰ δέ κεν οἴκαδ᾽ ἵκωμι φίλην ἐς πατρίδα γαῖαν,
ὤλετό μοι κλέος ἐσθλόν ... (*Iliad* 9.412–15)

(If I stay here and fight over the city of Troy, then my return is lost, though my fame will be everlasting. But if I return home to my dear native land, then my fair fame is lost ...)

Thus Achilles contrasts with Odysseus νόστου κεχρημένον, 'longing for his return' (*Odyssey* 1.13) – and Odysseus achieved both fame and his return home. Given that the *Aeneid* relates a charter-myth, a Κτίσις (Foundation) disguised as a Νόστος (Return) (cf. Ch. 5), the *Odyssey* is in this respect the obvious, indeed the mandatory, model.

When it comes to the protagonists, the *Odyssey*'s suitability as a model becomes even more apparent. The *Aeneid* is dominated by a single hero, not surprisingly for the Augustan age. Other major figures appear in it: Anchises, Ascanius, Acestes, Evander and Latinus on Aeneas' side, and Dido, Turnus, Mezentius and Camilla among his opponents. But Aeneas' opponents come and go, and his allies are clearly subordinate to him. Virgil found this same situation in the *Odyssey*,[30] where Odysseus stands head and shoulders above all others

---

[30] On the *Odyssey* as not only bearing Odysseus' name, but also being unified by him, cf. e.g. Eustath. 1380.40f. (on the *Odyssey* prooemium); and also 5.5–7 (on the *Iliad* prooemium): ὅθεν ἐκεῖνο μὲν τὸ βιβλίον ἀπὸ ἑνὸς προσώπου τοῦ Ὀδυσσέως ὠνόμασεν ὑποδηλῶν τὸ ὀλίγον τῆς τοῦ γράφειν ὕλης, ὡς μόνα δῆθεν λέξων τὰ κατὰ τὸν Ὀδυσσέα κτλ. (So he named that work after a single man, Odysseus, indicating the limited scope of his material, since he was only going to tell the story of Odysseus). On the link with the

THE *AENEID* AS *ODYSSEY*

throughout; even in the *Telemacheia*, where for a long stretch he makes no personal appearance, Odysseus is constantly present in the minds, conversations and actions of others, as well as in the ironies and implications of the poet (cf. p. 155). The *Iliad* is less clear-cut: Achilles is indeed designated the protagonist in the initial line; but his opponent Hector to some extent shares this prominence, and, particularly during Achilles' absence from the war, other great men on the Greek side come to the fore. Many of these others take part in the whole action of the *Iliad*; they are usually of equal age and status to Achilles; they are at least potentially comparable with him in martial valour and each has his own episode of military glory (ἀριστεία); and some possess greater status (Agamemnon) or greater age (Nestor). While all this does not cancel Achilles' predominance,[31] it nevertheless creates the impression of a group of protagonists. The *Argonautica*, far from competing with the *Odyssey* to provide a model for Aeneas, has in Jason an unsuitable prototype, at any rate for the mature Aeneas of the later books, since Jason is an 'inverse' Odysseus, often a pawn of events rather than πολύτροπος (of many devices).[32]

A second factor in Virgil's choice of Odysseus as model for Aeneas has already been touched on (p. 182): the evaluation of the homeric heroes up to Virgil's day. Many of the most prominent iliadic figures were subjected to criticism on moral grounds:[33] thus Agamemnon's qualities as a king and a leader were in doubt, Locrian Ajax lacked self-control, Paris was cowardly, effeminate and unpopular, and Hector allegedly lacked judgement and self-awareness. As for Achilles, although his primary role in the *Iliad* was recognised, he was accused of cruelty, irrationality, ruthlessness and brutality. Defences of the heroes were offered, and the iliadic Odysseus sometimes (but by no means always) got off relatively lightly, probably because of his stature in the *Odyssey*.[34] But Achilles, although not without admirers, had a difficult

---

Aeneid, cf. also Schmidt (1983) 27; and, on Virgil's enhancement of Aeneas as a warrior and its consequences, cf. Horsfall (1987).

[31] On the homeric technique of concentrating attention on the absent hero, cf. above, pp. 154f.; the scholia were well aware both of the technique and of Achilles' preeminence, cf. Richardson (1980) 273.

[32] Cf. Klein (1983) for a stimulating account of Jason's character; also Collard (1975) 136f., with the bibliography in n. 13.

[33] Cf. Richardson (1980) 272–4, who also notes the exceptions, esp. Telamonian Ajax, Patroclus, and Menelaus.

[34] Cf. Richardson (1980) 273. On Odysseus–Ulysses in all periods, cf. esp. Stanford (1968), of which Chs. 7–9 handle his post-homeric and pre-Virgilian image, and Ch. 10 Virgil's treatment of him.

passage, particularly since Homer himself seemed to have disapproved of some of his conduct.[35] On the other hand the Odysseus of the *Odyssey* had by the hellenistic period come to represent something quite different. There was of course a 'wily Ulysses', as reflected e.g. in Horace *Satires* 2.5; but there was also an Odysseus idealised by popular philosophy, whose actions were regarded as *exempla* of virtue.[36] This Odysseus is by no means an absurd misreading of Homer. In modern eyes Odysseus' habit of lying may seem a fault, but antiquity was not so clear on this;[37] again Odysseus' travels and acquaintance with the 'minds of many men' (*Odyssey* 1.3) can truly be seen both as experiences open only to a hero more flexible and adaptable than Achilles, and as being educative.[38] Finally Odysseus' successful homecoming, gained not just through courage, a virtue shared by Achilles and other iliadic heroes, but also through justice, knowledge and self-control, which some of them lacked, may have impressed Homer's audience (as it did the hellenistic critics) more than the achievements of Achilles and his fellows. Indeed Homer's own conclusions may appear in the underworld confrontation between the living Odysseus and the dead Achilles (*Odyssey* 11.467ff.). Achilles, who died pursuing honour, now no longer desires honour (cf. 484–6) but longs for life on virtually any terms (489–91).[39] Homer and Virgil were not trying to portray in their heroes perfect men: but both Odysseus and Aeneas are good men and good

[35] Cf. Richardson (1980) 273. Wender (1978) 4, 42–4, 74f. notes that the *Odyssey* appears to be deliberately criticising the values of the *Iliad* and its heroes, Odysseus being contrasted in particular with Achilles and Agamemnon. The admiration of Alexander the Great for Achilles exemplifies (and reinforced) powerfully the positive view of Achilles.

[36] Cf. Di Benedetto (1966) 215–28; Kindstrand (1973) 181–5, 210f.; Höistad (1948) 94–102. Philosophical criticism of Odysseus must however also be borne in mind, cf. above, p. 182 n. 20.

[37] Cf. e.g. Hoffmann (1914) 23–6, 109, 136f.; Luther (1935) 87–9. Homeric 'lies' may of course have broader ramifications, cf. e.g. Richardson (1984) esp. 227–9, on Odysseus' lies to Laertes in *Od.* 24, and, on a number of aspects of Odysseus' untruthfulness, Maronitis (1981); (1983) 280–3. Du Boulay (1974) Index *s.v.* Lies has worthwhile information on 'modern' Greek practice. Recently Rutherford (1986), a brilliant reassessment of the *Odyssey* in the light of later views of it, offers valuable comments on many aspects of Odysseus' personality; on his lies, cf. 145f.

[38] On Odysseus' experiences as educative in ancient eyes, cf. e.g. Kaiser (1964) 110; Kindstrand (1973) 184. Borthwick (1983) 6–16 offers an acute and detailed demonstration of Homer's positive appraisal of the bulk of Odysseus' actions and character. Cf. also Rutherford (1986) 146 on the educative aspects of Odysseus' experiences (and on his status as a good king), and 147 and 150ff. on his character development.

[39] Cf. Wender (1978) 41–4; Macleod (1983) 2. The fact that there was cynic criticism of Odysseus for his love of home (cf. e.g. Kindstrand (1973) 137) demonstrates ancient consciousness of the topic; and given the thematic importance of the 'Return' in the *Aeneid*, Virgil must have regarded Odysseus' love of home as a further virtue.

kings, capable of moral progress (cf. pp. 35ff., 51). Most facets of Aeneas' character are based, then, on Odysseus, with only minor touches lifted from other homeric antecedents.[40] This contrasts with the way Turnus is constructed: for him Virgil draws principally on Hector, a sympathetic figure of some moral stature.[41] But to stop Turnus attracting too much sympathy, Virgil had to introduce elements of Achilles and of the odyssean suitors,[42] transferring to Dido (cf. *Aeneid* 4.327–30) certain of Hector's more winning aspects, e.g. commitment to community and family spirit. This complexity may be one reason why it is so difficult to assess Turnus justly.

A curious and ambivalent advantage for Virgil of using Odysseus, rather than Achilles, as the main model for Aeneas is that Aeneas (but in only one of the two versions used by Virgil!) can thus enjoy longevity and (possibly) an easy death. Although Achilles survives the *Iliad*, the shortness of his life is a dominant theme; and he is then killed in battle. But Odysseus has long life and an easy death ἐξ ἁλός, 'from the sea',[43] predicted for him by Teiresias (*Odyssey* 11.134–6). The prediction, as Odysseus notes, derives from divine will (11.139) and is emphasised through Odysseus' repetition of it to Penelope (23.281–3) – and cf. Penelope's comment 'since the gods have granted you a happier old age', 286. Virgil seems to have conflated, not without some unclarity, two different versions of Aeneas' death. At *Aeneid* 1.259f. (and 12.794f.) Jupiter prophesies that Aeneas will be deified, and that he will live only three years after defeating the Rutulans (265f.), although this latter point is not certain. Dido's curse too appears to reflect a version in which Aeneas dies prematurely (4.620). On the other hand Anchises, speaking, like Teiresias, in the Underworld (6.760–6), predicts that Aeneas' *postuma proles* by Lavinia, Silvius, will be conceived late in Aeneas' life (*longaevo serum*, 764). It looks as though Virgil had not made up his mind whether to make the 'founder' of Rome a man of brief and doom-laden life, or whether to exploit the longevity of Odysseus

---

[40] Cf. e.g. Knauer (1964) 343f., 354; (1981) 875. The remark of Rutherford (1986) 150, discussing the structure of the *Odyssey*, that its point is 'to introduce us to the hero at the very nadir of his fortunes' is of course equally true of the *Aeneid*. In this dimension too, then, the one epic echoes the other.

[41] On the scholia's assessments of Achilles and (exaggerated) views of the faults of Hector, cf. Richardson (1980) 273f.

[42] Cf. Knauer (1964) 343f., 291 (for Paris elements); Schenk (1984) Register *s.v.* Turnus: Homerische Vorbilder.

[43] The meaning of the phrase is controversial, cf. Heubeck–Privitera (1983) *ad loc.* Virgil may (cf. below, p. 188 and n. 44) have understood it as referring to a 'death by water', and so may have been offering an allusive interpretation.

and make Aeneas too live long. Another area of unclarity is the manner of Aeneas' death. Other sources reveal that, like Odysseus' death, it was linked with water, in Aeneas' case the river Numicus.[44] Virgil says nothing about this, although he may have presumed it; but he contrives to set Aeneas above Odysseus in death, in that, whereas Odysseus rejected immortality (*Odyssey* 5.206–24), Jupiter (as noted) predicts twice that the dead Aeneas will become an immortal.

Another important thematic advantage of the *Odyssey* over the *Iliad* as model for the *Aeneid* involves 'concord' (and 'discord') (cf. Ch. 4). Here the *Iliad* offered little, except as a model for *oppositio*. As noted (pp. 85–7), both the hellenistic scholia and Virgil's contemporaries regarded it as an epic of discord. It may be that, to differentiate the two epics and to laud Odysseus, the hellenistic critics exaggerated this discord, since there is a reconciliation between Achilles and Agamemnon, at least in *Iliad* 23 (cf. pp. 236f.). But it is stressful: their first accord, in *Iliad* 19, was grudging, patched-up, and more to do with the needs of the two leaders – Agamemnon's for protection, and Achilles' for revenge – than with a meeting of minds. Achilles had no great love for Agamemnon, only a greater anger against Hector. In *Iliad* 23, when Achilles has achieved his revenge, his courtesies towards Agamemnon are warmer and more genuine; but they still have an element of the political and public (p. 237). Similarly the coming together of Achilles and Priam in *Iliad* 24, although moving in human terms, especially when Priam expresses (486–92) and Achilles acknowledges (534–42) the analogies between Priam's plight and that of Achilles' father Peleus, is only a temporary interruption in the war. After the burial of Hector war will resume, with further casualties including Achilles himself, and will continue until Troy is destroyed. Even after the fall of Troy, neither Greeks nor Trojans will have peace, but only their perilous and in some cases fatal 'returns'. The *Odyssey* too has elements of 'discord': Odysseus' various battles during his return voyage, the quarrel among the Greeks (with some overtones of *Iliad* 1) narrated by Nestor (3.133ff.), the dispute between Odysseus and Achilles described by Demodocus (8.73–82, cf. p. 198), and, more serious, the enmity of Poseidon for Odysseus throughout, and the conflict awaiting Odysseus in his own house and kingdom. But concord does eventually prevail in the *Odyssey*, which ends with a genuine reconciliation between Odysseus and his family on the one side, and the families of the dead

---

[44] Cf. Tib. 2.5.43f., and Smith (1913) *ad loc.*

suitors on the other.[45] This is achieved through the intervention of Athena, who has obtained the consent of Zeus for her action. She asked whether it was Zeus' will to create 'evil war and dread battle' (πόλεμόν τε κακὸν καὶ φύλοπιν αἰνήν, 24.475) or 'friendship' (φιλότητα, 24.476) between the parties, and Zeus, knowing that she too desired the latter, first told her to do what she liked (24.481), and then (explaining what was fitting) decreed that the suitors' families should 'forget' the killings of their sons and brothers, and that both sides should have concord, peace and prosperity – under the kingship of Odysseus (24.483-6). The subsequent muster of both groups *inter alia* allows Laertes to make a final appearance in arms and to kill Antinous' father Eupeithes, now the chief agitator against Odysseus, just as his son, when alive, was chief suitor. This source of discord removed, Athena speaks to both sides briefly, addressing them as 'men of Ithaca', and telling them to stop fighting (24.531f.), before directing a further soothing speech to Odysseus alone (24.542-4). Athena then binds both sides to peace by oaths (24.546-8), at which point the epic ends.

Meanwhile that other source of discord, Poseidon's enmity for Odysseus, had petered out by the time Odysseus reached Ithaca. The poet indicates this limit to its scope right at the start (1.20f.), and Zeus confirms the same outcome – a safe return for Odysseus linked with the ending of Poseidon's anger (1.76-9). Indeed, although Poseidon brings to bear upon Odysseus the full weight of his anger as the hero approaches Scherie (5.282ff.), once Odysseus has returned to Ithaca Poseidon complies with Zeus' wishes, contenting himself with a final display of spleen against the Phaeacians for helping home safely the booty-laden wanderer (13.128ff.). The final act of reconciliation on Odysseus' side, his sacrifice to Poseidon, was predicted as early as 11.119-37 by Teiresias in the underworld, and this prediction was repeated by Odysseus to Penelope (23.266-84). Achievement of concord with Poseidon was, for Odysseus, perhaps even more significant than his concord with the families of the suitors, since Poseidon's wrath was the cause of his long wanderings; and the prophecy of peace with Poseidon implies also the solution of Odysseus' domestic problems in Ithaca. The prophecy's significance is underlined not just by its repetition at two key points, but also by its association with Odysseus'

---

[45] On all this, cf. Knauer (1964) 322-7: 'pax und εἰρήνη am Schluss der *Aeneis* und der *Odyssee*'. The 'problem of the end of the *Odyssey*' – on which, cf. esp. Wender (1978) *passim* – is irrelevant to this discussion, given that Virgil obviously regarded *Od.* 24 as genuine.

prophesied long and prosperous life as king of Ithaca and enigmatic easy death.[46] The achievement of concord in the *Odyssey* was thus Virgil's source for the concord agreed, although abortively, between Latinus and Aeneas, ratified by the agreement between Jupiter and Juno in *Aeneid* 12, and established firmly through Turnus' death; and the divine confirmation of human concord in *Odyssey* 24 stands behind that of *Aeneid* 12. It should also be remembered that, as well as achieving concord for himself, Homer's Odysseus was a reconciler of others. He took part in the embassy to Troy described at *Iliad* 3.205–24, which attempted to end the war by negotiation, and in that sent to Achilles in Book 9 in the hope of reconciling the estranged hero with Agamemnon. Odysseus also summed up at *Iliad* 19.215–37, when the two had actually become reconciled. In view of Odysseus' role in cynic theories of kingship, and his importance as a cynic ideal man (cf. pp. 35–6), it may be significant that cynics regarded reconciliation as one function of the philosopher.[47]

Comparison of the prologues of the *Odyssey* and *Aeneid*, which are both, apart from Virgilian 'corrections' of Homer, equally applicable to both protagonists, underlines Virgil's primary commitment to the *Odyssey* as model for the whole *Aeneid*, as well as revealing some further thematic implications. This comparison has indirect ancient precedent in the homeric scholia, which compared the *Iliad* and *Odyssey* prologues;[48] and Virgil in fact concentrates his *imitatio* of the *Odyssey* prologue on some of the very aspects discussed by the scholia.

ἄνδρα μοι ἔννεπε, Μοῦσα, πολύτροπον, ὃς μάλα πολλὰ
πλάγχθη, ἐπεὶ Τροίης ἱερὸν πτολίεθρον ἔπερσε·
πολλῶν δ' ἀνθρώπων ἴδεν ἄστεα καὶ νόον ἔγνω,
πολλὰ δ' ὅ γ' ἐν πόντῳ πάθεν ἄλγεα ὃν κατὰ θυμόν,
ἀρνύμενος ἥν τε ψυχὴν καὶ νόστον ἑταίρων.   5
ἀλλ' οὐδ' ὣς ἑτάρους ἐρρύσατο, ἱέμενός περ·
αὐτῶν γὰρ σφετέρῃσιν ἀτασθαλίῃσιν ὄλοντο,
νήπιοι, οἳ κατὰ βοῦς Ὑπερίονος Ἠελίοιο
ἤσθιον· αὐτὰρ ὁ τοῖσιν ἀφείλετο νόστιμον ἦμαρ.
                                                    (*Odyssey* 1.1–9)

[46] Cf. above, pp. 187f. and nn. 43f.

[47] Cf. Höistad (1948) Indices I *s.v.* reconciler; and above, p. 35 n. 20, pp. 101f.

[48] Cf. Eustath. 1380.30–1381.28, 1382.17–27, 1383.36–50, esp. 1380.44f.: ὁμοιοσχήμων μὲν ἥ τε τῆς Ἰλιάδος εἰσβολὴ καὶ ἡ τῆς Ὀδυσσείας κτλ. (the beginnings of the *Iliad* and *Odyssey* are similar in form etc.). For further testimony to Augustan interest in the prologues, cf. Hor. *Ep.* 1.2 esp. 19–22 (on which cf. above, pp. 85-9) and *Ars Poet.* 140–52, with Brink (1971) on 140–52 for ancient discussions of them; for commentary on their relationship to *Aen.* 1.1ff., cf. Buchheit (1963) 13–22.

(Tell me, Muse, of the man of many wiles, who had very many wanderings, when he had sacked the sacred city of Troy. Many were the peoples whose cities he saw and whose minds he knew, many the pains he suffered in his heart on the sea, seeking to safeguard his own life and the return of his comrades. But he could not save his companions, much though he tried; for they perished through their own folly, eating the cattle of the high Sungod, who deprived them of the day of their return.)

> arma virumque cano, Troiae qui primus ab oris
> Italiam fato profugus Lavinaque venit
> litora, multum ille et terris iactatus et alto
> vi superum, saevae memorem Iunonis ob iram,
> multa quoque et bello passus, dum conderet urbem   5
> inferretque deos Latio; genus unde Latinum
> Albanique patres atque altae moenia Romae.
> Musa, mihi causas memora, quo numine laeso
> quidve dolens regina deum tot volvere casus
> insignem pietate virum, tot adire labores   10
> impulerit. tantaene animis caelestibus irae?
>
> (*Aeneid* 1.1–11)

ἄνδρα (*Odyssey* 1.1) is echoed by the sound of *arma*, although of course in sense it equals *virum* (hero) (*Aeneid* 1.1);[49] and indeed the homeric scholia link ἄνδρα with ἀνδρεῖος (brave).[50] Aeneas is not named until line 92, a deliberate postponement[51] amplifying the same feature in the *Odyssey*: there Odysseus is not named until line 21, and Eustathius regarded this as an intentional contrast with the *Iliad*, where Achilles is named in the first line.[52] The adjective used of Odysseus in *Odyssey* 1.1, πολύτροπος, was controversial in antiquity;[53] indeed it was a cynic ἀπορία,[54] and although flattering meanings were given for it by most commentators,[55] Virgil preferred to 'correct' it to *fato profugus* (*Aeneid* 1.2), thus alluding to the scholiastic observation that πολύτροπος was also found in the *Posthomerica* in the phrase αἶσα πολύτροπος (cf. also

[49] Cf. Lausberg (1983) 211. The phenomenon, as found elsewhere in Virgil, is discussed by Clausen (1987) 21. 'Multiple translation' is also involved here, cf. Cic. *De Fin.* 3.15; Cat. 31.12.
[50] Schol. HMQR and EQ on *Od.* 1.1; Eustath. 1381.4f. (on *Od.* 1.1).
[51] On delayed naming in ancient literature and its significance cf. Dornseiff (1921) 107f.; Fraenkel (1950) on Aesch. *Ag.* 156f.
[52] Cf. Eustath. 1381.20–8.
[53] Eustath. 1381.36–52.
[54] Cf. Di Benedetto (1966) 213; Schol. HMQR on *Od.* 1.1.
[55] Cf. Eustath. 1381.36ff., denying for example that Odysseus is being described as chameleon-like or deceitful.

p. 194).[56] Aeneas, like Odysseus, was a fated wanderer – *fato profugus* (2) and *iactatus* (3), cf. πλάγχθη (2) – after the destruction of Troy, although not, like Odysseus, after having destroyed it;[57] Aeneas, like Odysseus, 'saw the cities and knew the minds of many men' and endured 'many sufferings in his heart on the sea' (*Odyssey* 1.3f.). Like Odysseus, Aeneas wandered 'much' (*multum*, 3) and suffered 'much' (*multa*, 5). This 'multiplicity' is a deliberate emphasis, and looks to the four appearances of the concept in the first four lines of the *Odyssey* prologue (πολύτροπον and μάλα πολλά, 1; πολλῶν, 3; πολλά, 4).[58]

Odyssey 1.4 is thematically important for the whole *Aeneid* because it incorporates the 'suffering king' motif (cf. pp. 31–8). Virgil repeatedly emphasises the sense of πάθεν: in *profugus*, 2, *iactatus* (3), *vi* (4), esp. *passus* (5), *casus* (9) and *labores* (10). In this he is sensitive to the scholiasts' distinction between the 'active' hero of the *Iliad* and the more 'passive' hero of the *Odyssey*,[59] as well as being aware that in the *Iliad* Aeneas was portrayed by Poseidon (!) as suffering undeservedly (*Iliad* 20.293–9). Aeneas resembles Odysseus in having sought to preserve his own life and those of his companions (*Odyssey* 1.5) but, another significant difference, whereas Odysseus preserved only himself (*Odyssey* 1.6–9), Aeneas succeeded in saving his comrades too – and he even saved one abandoned comrade of Ulysses (cf. p. 193).[60] Various details in the rest of the *Odyssey* prologue also fit Aeneas well. His arrival 'home', i.e. in Italy, came later than the returns of most of the other heroes of the Trojan War. Thus Aeneas found Helenus and Andromache already domiciled in Buthrotum (*Aeneid* 3.294ff.); Venus notes that Antenor had already settled at Patavium while Aeneas was still on the seas (1.242–9); and when Aeneas reached Italy, Diomedes was already founding Argyripa (*Aeneid* 11.246f.). Although the overall chronological relationship between the wanderings of Aeneas and Odysseus is not clearly indicated by Virgil, Aeneas' arrival among the

[56] Eustath. 1381.43f. On *fato profugus* (below), cf. esp. Bliss (1964).

[57] For such 'reversals', cf. Knauer (1964) Register *s.v.* Vergils Homerverständnis: Umkehrung etc.

[58] On these, cf. Eustath. 1382.20ff. The *Iliad* prologue also has μυρί' 'innumerable' (2) and πολλάς 'many' (3).

[59] Eustath. 1380.57f.: ἡ μὲν γὰρ μῆνις ἐκεῖ δραστική, ἔθηκε γὰρ μυρία ἄλγεα, ὧδε δέ, ὁ ἀνὴρ πολλὰ ἔπαθεν ἄλγεα (For the wrath there is active, since it caused many woes, but here the hero suffered many woes). The distinction in terms of ἦθος and πάθος between the two homeric epics made by 'Longinus' (on which cf. above, pp. 179f. and nn. 12 and 15, and Bühler (1964) 39ff., 44ff., 47) is also relevant here. The *Aeneid* and its hero were probably intended as the perfect blend of both characters.

[60] In the *Argonautica* Jason is implicitly protected from such a charge, cf. below, p. 206.

Cyclopes is pointedly placed after the departure thence of Odysseus (*Aeneid* 3.613–18).[61] All this hints that Aeneas, not Odysseus, is really 'the only man who, when all the others who survived, escaping war and sea, had returned home, was kept far away' (*Odyssey* 1.11–13), so that the most extended suffering is attributed to a Trojan not a Greek. Again Aeneas, like Odysseus, longed for his 'return' (*Odyssey* 1.13) 'home', in his case to Italy (cf. Ch. 5), and like Odysseus, Aeneas was 'destined by divine decree' eventually to reach it: τῷ οἱ ἐπεκλώσαντο θεοὶ οἶκόνδε νέεσθαι, (*Odyssey* 1.17). This explicit mention of fate in the *Odyssey* prologue is noteworthy, given the importance of the theme in the *Aeneid*,[62] signalled at *Aeneid* 1.2–7, where Aeneas' wanderings, and their end, are attributed to fate and the gods (*fato profugus*, 2, cf. *vi superum*, 4). Further similarities between the two prologues are that Aeneas also found himself 'not yet free of toils, even when he had reached home and was among his own people' (*Odyssey* 1.18f.), and that, like Odysseus (19–21), Aeneas had the sympathy of the gods – except for one powerful divine enemy. In Odysseus' case Poseidon was implacably hostile to him 'until he reached his own land' (*Odyssey* 1.20f.). Aeneas' trials were greater, since even after his arrival in Italy, Juno continued to pursue him with her hostility.

The prologue to the *Aeneid* is thus *inter alia* a claim that the *Aeneid* is an improved *Odyssey*, Aeneas a superior Odysseus. Virgil's comments on 'Ulysses' in the body of his epic do not conflict with this view, but tend to show Aeneas as the genuinely virtuous man that Homer and others falsely claimed Odysseus was. Ulysses is described by Aeneas as *durus* (*Aeneid* 2.7), *dirus* (2.261, 2.762) and *saevus* (3.273); and Sinon attacks Ulysses (*invidia ... pellacis Ulixi*, 2.90, cf. 97–9), although this is double-edged, since Sinon himself is a treacherous liar. Again, Ulysses' cruelty in his treatment of Deiphobus features at 6.528f., and his negligence of his comrade Achaemenides at 3.590–654, although, as is dramatically apt, the latter excuses his leader's faults (3.613, 617f., 628f.). Elsewhere Ulysses is said by Aeneas to be wily (2.44) and a

[61] Cf. also *Aen.* 5.864–6 with Williams (1960) *ad loc.* A general interest in relative mythical chronology is essentially hellenistic – cf. e.g. Call. *Hymn* 6.74–9; but in ktistic contexts, of which this is one, concern to antedate goes back at least to Pind. *Pyth.* 4, and is similarly shown in Tibullus' 'Foundation of Rome' (i.e. 2.5). On this topic cf. Cairns (1979) 74f. It is noteworthy that, although Virgil here gives Aeneas the distinction of being the latest to arrive, he also insists (*Aen.* 1.1: *primus*) that Aeneas was the first Trojan to arrive in Italy (although at *Aen.* 1.240–9 Antenor's prior arrival at Patavium appears for another purpose): cf. esp. Galinsky (1969a), rightly pointing out that there is also an implicit denial of claimed links between Odysseus and the foundation of Rome.

[62] On fate in the *Aeneid*, cf. esp. Otis (1963) General Index *s.v.* Fate (*fatum*).

master criminal (2.164), and Numanus Remulus calls him *fandi fictor* (9.602).[63] These pointers to Ulysses' bad characteristics remind us that Aeneas is free of them.

So far it has been argued that the *Odyssey* is the primary model for the whole *Aeneid*. Yet it would be foolish to underestimate the influence of the *Iliad* – even though the dichotomic view of the *Aeneid* as half-and-half *Odyssey* and *Iliad* is obviously simplistic. A more complex formulation is needed to account for the *Aeneid*'s reflection of both homeric epics simultaneously on different levels throughout.[64] Now, something close to such a formulation does survive from antiquity, in the context of comedy and satire rather than epic. A second-century AD scholion on Persius 5.161[65] comments as follows on 161ff., the imagined speech of Chaerestratus to Davus:

> hunc locum de Menandri Eunucho traxit, in quo Davum servum Chaerestratus adulescens alloquitur tamquam amore Chrysidis meretricis derelicto, idemque tamen ab ea revocatus ad illam redit. apud Terentium personae inmutatae sunt. quod exemplum inducit ad similitudinem vitiorum, a quibus recedere non possumus. hoc et Horatius [*Sat.* 2.3.259] et Terentius similiter in Eunucho cum dicit [46] 'quid igitur faciam? non eam? ne nunc quidem cum arcessor ultro?'

This describes a complex process of *imitatio*: the ultimate model is Menander; but Terence's imitation of Menander is also before Persius' eyes, and so is Horace's imitation of Terence. The scholion however does not say that Persius treated all his predecessors as being on a level, or that he practised '*contaminatio*'. Rather Persius is implied to have 'looked through' Horace to Terence, and through Terence to Menander: 'The scholiast notes that Persius inserts the name Davus from the Menandrian original into Horace's imitation of Terence *Eunuchus*'.[66]

---

[63] *fandi fictor* (*Aen.* 9.602) may repr̄ꞏt πολύτροπος in one of its adverse interpretations, cf. above, p. 191 and nn. 53–5. The picture of Ulysses in the *Aeneid* is however not unrelieved. Galinsky (1968) 163f. notes that Achaemenides' account of Ulysses' valiant acts (*Aen.* 3.626–38) associates him, Aeneas, and Hercules, as destroyers of monsters, and that Aeneas in this context calls Ulysses *infelix* (3.691). Aeneas, too, in his narrative of the fall of Troy, will hardly be unbiased.

[64] I.e. along the lines of the works cited above, p. 177 n. 3.

[65] The early date of this scholion is guaranteed by its first-hand knowledge of Menander's *Eunuchus*. The scholion's implications and the existence of this ancient technique of *imitatio* were first pointed out by DuQuesnay (1977) 55 and n. 213, 99 (Addendum to n. 213).

[66] So DuQuesnay (1977) 99 (where 'The scholiast is aware that Persius inserted' might cover the case more precisely); further on the scholion, cf. Coffey (1976) 115, 240 n. 96.

Recent scholarship has shown that this device, whereby a writer shows his awareness of his model's model by introducing something from that ultimate model not present in the more immediate model into his own imitation of his nearer predecessor, is standard Roman practice: it has recently been demonstrated *in extenso* for Ovid,[67] and for Virgil himself in his *Georgics* and *Aeneid*.[68] Roman poets, faced with the influence of two distinct (and in themselves multi-generationed) periods of Greek culture, the archaic–classical and the hellenistic, the latter itself heavily indebted to the former, showed in this way their control of the literary-historical continuum in which they worked.

The background of the *Aeneid* is just as complex as that of Persius 5.161ff., since, in addition to the homeric epics, it contains (notably) Apollonius' *Argonautica*.[69] Apollonius himself had subtly harmonised many homeric features with the changed taste of hellenistic and later readers. This allowed Virgil paradoxically to 'improve' on Apollonius by 'looking through' him to Homer, thereby giving his reminiscences of Apollonian events and characters a homeric ethos. The adventures of Aeneas, an *alter Odysseus* seen through the prism of Jason, himself modelled by inversion on Odysseus, exemplify the process well: Aeneas has a quest (to found his city) just as Jason sought the golden fleece, and Aeneas has a 'home-coming' like both Jason and Odysseus; but Jason's quest is separate from his home-coming, whereas Aeneas' quest is identical with it (cf. Ch. 5). Thus Virgil has looked through Jason to Odysseus and combined quest and home-coming. The love-life of Aeneas is handled similarly: Jason has two 'love affairs' en route, with Hypsipyle on Lemnos (Book 1) and with Medea (Books 3–4), while Odysseus on his travels was involved in different ways with three women – Circe, Calypso and Nausicaa. The Dido episode is modelled primarily on Jason's second and more significant affair, with Medea. But Virgil looks through Apollonius to the latter's source, the three 'affairs' of Odysseus.[70] For Aeneas' other and prospective relationship – with Lavinia – Virgil also draws on the marital aspects of the Jason–Medea episode, but once more looks through it to Odysseus'

---

[67] Cf. McKeown (1987–) I.37–45.

[68] Cf. Thomas (1986); Clausen (1987) 20f., 61-9. For the technique in general, cf. Cairns (1979) Ch. 2.

[69] Earlier Roman epic also naturally played a role in the transmission of material; but the entire area is fraught with difficulties: cf. e.g. Jocelyn (1964–5); Wigodsky (1972); Luck (1983). On Apollonian influence in the portrayal of Dido cf. above, pp. 47ff. and Ch. 6; and for the whole topic of Virgil's use of the *Argonautica*, cf. most recently Clausen (1987) *passim*.

[70] Cf. Knauer (1964) 177–80, 183, 214–18, 343f.; (1981) 875.

marital link with Penelope – and to his flirtation with Nausicaa, which was one of the *Argonautica*'s sources for Jason and Medea.[71] The moral implications need no spelling out:[72] Jason leaves home and bachelordom to have a minor affair with Hypsipyle, and a major affair and marriage with Medea, both abroad, after which he returns home with Medea as his wife; Odysseus goes away from home, and from marriage with Penelope, to three 'affairs' abroad, and then returns home to the same wife; Aeneas leaves home and wife, Creusa (but he goes as a widower); he has a major affair abroad (but no other); and then he comes 'home' to his (second) 'wife', Lavinia.

Virgil uses the same technique for characterisation. Jason (cf. p. 185) is a man of doubt and hesitations, in contrast with his model, Odysseus 'of many wiles'. The Aeneas of *Aeneid* 1–4, as yet imperfectly aware of his destiny, shares some of Jason's traits. But as Aeneas' knowledge of fate grows, his moral stature and determination increase in parallel. In Books 5–12 he develops steadily towards a personality more like that of Odysseus, particularly in 7–12, where, like Odysseus in the latter half of the *Odyssey*, Aeneas has reached 'home' and must fight to possess it. For Dido, as is well known, Virgil drew heavily on Apollonius' Medea. But Dido is an altogether grander and more admirable figure – a queen regnant, not a sorceress–princess, and a woman prepared to die for love. The enhanced grandeur is achieved in part by Virgil's emphasis on her kingship (cf. Ch. 2). But by looking through Medea to her three homeric antecedents, two goddesses and an archaic princess untainted by sorcery, Virgil also gives Dido attributes of all three – and he even mixes in elements of Penelope. His intentions are manifest in one significant 'correction': whereas Medea suggested, and collaborated in, the treacherous murder of her own brother Apsyrtus (4.450ff.), Dido is guilty of no such crime; rather the incident is 'reversed' in the murder of Dido's husband by her brother, Pygmalion (*Aeneid* 1.343ff.) – and her own innocence of such crimes is pertinently stressed at 4.600–2: *non potui abreptum divellere corpus et undis / spargere? non socios, non ipsum absumere ferro / Ascanium patriisque epulandum ponere mensis?*

But since this chapter's main concern is with Virgil and Homer, attention now turns primarily to the relevance of this technique

---

[71] On some of the details, cf. Knauer (1964) 155; Campbell (1983a) 56–60.

[72] It involves in particular an ancient commonplace, the 'Near and the Far'; for this topos in Greek poetry cf. esp. Young (1968) 35–68, 116–20; also Howie (1977) 214–18. Its archetypes are clearly provided by Paris and Helen in the *Iliad* and (reversed) by Odysseus in the *Odyssey*.

(looking through a source to its source) for Virgil's handling of the *Odyssey* and *Iliad*. A prerequisite to examination of the *Aeneid* in these terms is that Homer himself was (or could be argued to have been) practising self-imitation, i.e. that the *Iliad* is in certain senses the 'source' for the *Odyssey*. Now, such an understanding is consistent with the majority view of ancient commentators already mentioned (p. 180), that the *Odyssey* was written after the *Iliad*. It is consistent too with scholiastic conceptions of the *Odyssey* as containing the 'left-overs' of the *Iliad*.[73] This latter approach was worked out in detail (for example, Eustathius (1380.7-11) notes the deaths of Achilles and the two Ajaxes, the ἀριστεία of Neoptolemus, Odysseus' ruse when he entered Troy, and the story of the wooden horse as such incidents),[74] and it assumes at least negative *imitatio* of the *Iliad* by the *Odyssey*.[75] But no ancient account of 'homeric self-imitation' in general survives. So before this concept can be used to interpret Virgil, it must be established as an intrinsically plausible way of looking at Homer.

Crucial in establishing it is the continuity between the two homeric epics provided by the figure of Odysseus. Odysseus' high odyssean status, emphasised at *Odyssey* 1.2, 'sacker of Troy',[76] accords with his iliadic importance. There he belongs to the first rank of heroes: he takes Briseis home at 1.308ff. and 430ff.; and in Book 2, at Athena's command, he stops the flight of the Greeks (169ff.), deals with Thersites (244ff.), and makes a speech telling the Greeks to stay at Troy until it falls (278ff.). He is pointed out by Helen at 3.191ff., and his embassy to Troy narrated at 3.203ff. Again, Odysseus is prominent at 4.329ff., where he is first reproached and then mollified by Agamemnon, as the

---

[73] Cf. above, p. 180 and n. 15; also e.g. Schol. E on *Od.* 3.248 and Q on *Od.* 4.187. A cookery metaphor is involved in at least some manifestations of the concept, since Eustath. 1380.10f. in discussing the matter also refers to a καρύκευμα – a 'savoury sauce(?)'.

[74] Cf. also Schol. E on *Od.* 4.497.

[75] There are also many positive similarities between the two epics (on which, cf. below, pp. 200-2). Some modern scholars might attribute these to a common stock of epic characters and incidents; but ancient readers would more easily have thought them due to imitation of the *Iliad* by the *Odyssey*. On Virgil's recognition of parallelisms in the two homeric epics, cf. Knauer (1964) Register *s.v.* Vergils Homerverständnis: Parallelisierung von Il. u. Od.; (1981) 884, 887f. Among modern approaches, cf. e.g. Macleod (1983) 3: 'If, then, the *Odyssey* is the same sort of poem as the *Iliad*, and if it refashions and reconsiders the central theme of the *Iliad*...'; Maronitis (1983) 279f. (with bibliography n. 2); Harrison (1984) 15f.; Pucci (1987).

[76] The point is stressed at Eustath. 1382.57f.: ὅτι δὲ αὐτὸς εἷλε τὴν Τροίαν διὰ τῆς τοῦ δουρείου ἵππου μηχανῆς, δῆλον. ἐρεῖ γὰρ ὁ ποιητής· σῇ δ' ἥλω βουλῇ πόλις Πριάμοιο (that he captured Troy with the device of the wooden horse is clear, since the poet will say 'the city of Priam was taken though your plan'). Cf. also Schol. AT on *Il.* 2.278.

battle lines are joined; and his prowess is described later in the same book (4.491ff.). In Book 5 Odysseus is present in battle at 669ff., and in Book 9 he takes a major part in the embassy to Achilles (169ff.). In Book 10 he and Diomedes are protagonists in the *Doloneia*, while in Book 11 he is in the forefront of battle (310ff.), and long carries the brunt of the fighting (396ff.). In Book 14 Odysseus resists Agamemnon's motion that the Greeks should leave Troy (82ff.); and at 19.154ff. he gives advice about eating before fighting, and then cements the reconciliation between Agamemnon and Achilles (215ff.). Finally, Odysseus wrestles on equal terms with Ajax, son of Telamon (23.708ff.), and wins the foot-race in the funeral games for Patroclus (23.754ff.). The *Odyssey* is fully conscious of Odysseus' iliadic importance; it is implied in Phemius' song and the subsequent discussion at *Odyssey* 1.325ff., in Helen's tale of how Odysseus entered Troy in disguise (*Odyssey* 4.240ff.) and in Menelaus' account of the wooden horse episode (4.266ff.). Later, the bard Demodocus awakens memories of the strife of Odysseus and Achilles (*Odyssey* 8.73–82); the strife tale enhances Odysseus by making him protagonist in a 'wrath' scene analogous to the iliadic 'wrath',[77] certain details being selected to echo those of *Iliad* 1:[78] the best of the Greeks are involved; Agamemnon, although not a protagonist, is a malevolent presence; the quarrel initiates troubles for Greeks (and Trojans); and the plan of Zeus is fulfilled. Demodocus also tells, at Odysseus' request, of the wooden horse (8.487–520). Here Odysseus is represented as leader in the enterprise (494, 502), and his slaying of Deiphobus is heroic (519f.). Other iliadic characters are also important in the early books of the *Odyssey*, in particular Nestor, Menelaus and Helen; and the tales told of Nestor and Menelaus in *Odyssey* 3–4 carefully fill in the events of the interval between *Iliad* and *Odyssey*,[79] thus marking the latter as a sequel, as well as anticipating Odysseus' safe return home.

Certain real or apparent parallels in structure between the two homeric epics would also have made them resemble model and imitation. The *Iliad* has a recognised ring-compositional form, with the ties between Books 1 and 24 being particularly clear.[80] For example, in

[77] Cf. Macleod (1983) 4, who highlights in this context the terms κλέα (*Od.* 8.73) and κλέος (*Od.* 8.74), noting also *Od.* 9.19f. and *Il.* 9.189.

[78] Here, as in the similar quarrel which begins the Greeks' disastrous return from Troy (*Od.* 3.132–61), specific iliadic influence is surely at work rather than epic commonplace. The details are worked out by Macleod (1983) 9.

[79] Cf. above, p. 180 n. 15, p. 197 nn. 73f.

[80] Cf. e.g. Macleod (1982) 16–35, discussing the place of Book 24 in the structure of the

198

Iliad 1 Agamemnon refuses to ransom old Chryses' living daughter, thereby bringing immediate plague on the Greeks through the intervention of a god, and precipitating further destructive 'wrath'; in contrast, in Book 24 Achilles agrees to ransom old Priam's dead son when Priam has already received assistance from a god. Similarly, there is an angry confrontation in *Iliad* 1 between Achilles and Agamemnon, with Nestor attempting unsuccessfully to mediate, while in *Iliad* 23 Agamemnon's brother, Menelaus, clashes in like fashion with Nestor's son, Antilochus, and Achilles succeeds in making peace between them (cf. p. 237). Yet again, both *Iliad* 1 and 24 involve consultations between Achilles and Thetis. In Book 1 Thetis subsequently intercedes with Zeus, and obtains his pledge that the Trojans will be granted victory until the Greeks give due honour to Achilles, this decree being promulgated in an assembly of the gods. In Book 24 the order of events is reversed, as are the circumstances; a divine assembly takes place in which Zeus decrees that Achilles shall return the body of Hector, and Thetis is then sent by Zeus to inform Achilles of this decision.

The *Odyssey* is sometimes said to lack such symmetry as a whole, although certain sections are acknowledged to contain ring-structures. But an ancient reader who had seen the *Iliad* in terms of ring-composition could easily have applied a similar analysis to the *Odyssey*. The fact that the landing of Odysseus on Ithaca takes place in Book 13 could have called attention to a symmetry in the arrangement of his narrations to his hosts – his preceding true tales in Alcinous' palace and his subsequent mendacious tales in Eumaeus' hut, and later to Penelope in his own palace. Again, the early and last books of the *Odyssey* have enough in common to seem parallel: Book 1 has a divine council (26ff.) as does Book 24 (472ff.) Both the beginning and the end of the epic have as their main locus the palace of Odysseus. In Book 1 Telemachus' guest there is the disguised Athena, from Book 17 on the disguised Odysseus. Telemachus clashes with the suitors unsuccessfully in Book 1 at home, in Book 2 in the Ithacan assembly. In Books 22–23 (along with Odysseus) he clashes successfully with the suitors, and in Book 24 with their Ithacan families. The first books see Telemachus go on his travels, the last the final homecoming of Odysseus. Virgil might well have thought that Homer, in his second epic, was employing the same

---

Iliad; 32–4 treat in greater detail the links between Books 1 and 24. For a more detailed piece of homeric self-imitation, cf. Colaclidès (1981). On homeric structures in general, cf. esp. Whitman (1958) Chs. 5, 11; Moulton (1977) Ch. 2. Whitman (1958) Ch. 12 is more sceptical about the *Odyssey*.

technique of ring-composition as he used in the *Iliad*, with greater subtlety.

Such features would have pointed the way to a comparison of the two epics, where in any case balances of characters, settings and events are independently patent. For example the iliadic Priam and the odyssean Laertes are in certain terms equivalents, as is shown in the final books of the epics. In *Iliad* 24 the aged Priam comes to the tent of Achilles to ransom his dead son Hector, and on the way is met by Hermes, who tells him various lies (352ff.). Priam finds Achilles in his tent, apart from his men and with only two companions (471ff.); he begs Achilles to remember his own father Peleus, old and perhaps surrounded by enemies, just as Priam himself now is, and with no one to defend him (486–9).[81] Peleus however, so Priam says in *Iliad* 24, at least hopes for the return of a living son (490–2), whereas many of his own sons, including Hector, are dead (493ff.). Priam and Achilles then weep together (507ff.), and Achilles raises Priam up (515). All this is paralleled, with variation, in *Odyssey* 24: there Odysseus comes to the farm where his old father Laertes lives on his own, except for Dolios[82] and other slaves, far away from the city (202). Odysseus separates himself from his companions, finds Laertes completely alone in his garden, and weeps (226ff.); then he tells Laertes various lies (244ff.).[83] When he subsequently reveals himself to his father, and is acknowledged by him, Laertes is in a fainting state, and is supported by Odysseus (348). The ways in which the *Odyssey* subtly echoes in this scene not just the main outline of the *Iliad* 24 narrative, but also the hints given by Priam to Achilles about Peleus, are noteworthy, as is the contrasting outcome of the *Odyssey* scene. Whereas in the *Iliad* Achilles has killed the son (Hector) of his older living enemy (Priam), in the *Odyssey* the elderly father of Odysseus (Laertes) will kill the old father (Eupeithes) of the younger enemy (Antinous) whom his son Odysseus has already killed.

A more complex equivalence involves the character of Odysseus

---

[81] This concern was already alluded to by Achilles at *Il.* 19.321–37, and significantly it still torments the dead Achilles in Hades in *Od.* 11.494–503. Cf. Macleod (1983) 2. Rutherford (1986) 162 n. 87 reports acute observations on these scenes by Mr E.L. Bowie.

[82] Dolios had been sent to Laertes by Penelope (*Od.* 4.735 – cf. Wender (1978) 54–6). As Wender notes, this dispatch has a function in the plot, since it adds Dolios and his sons to Odysseus' forces in the field. Laertes' state varies at different points (cf. Wender (1978) 52–4, 58f.): he was even more solitary at *Od.* 1.188–93, where he had only one old woman with him.

[83] On this scene, cf. most recently Richardson (1984) esp. 227–9.

himself: the *Odyssey* has perceived that the good qualities of the iliadic Achilles and Hector are complementary,[84] and it unites them in Odysseus: like Achilles, Odysseus is a great warrior; like Hector he is a devoted family man, with a wife and son and a stake in his community. Less central, but still *en masse* significant, equivalences are numerous. For instance, the two quarrels narrated in the *Odyssey* have already been noted (pp. 188, 198) as analogues of the iliadic 'wrath'. The shield of Achilles in *Iliad* 18 is echoed in the landscape and atmosphere of Alcinous' Phaeacia. The hut of Eumaeus is a bucolic version of the Achaean encampment at Troy, and more particularly of the tent of Achilles in *Iliad* 9. The palaces of Menelaus, Alcinous, and Odysseus in the *Odyssey* are equivalents to Priam's palace in the *Iliad*. The battle between Odysseus and his helpers on one side and the suitors on the other (22), and his later confrontation with the suitors' relatives (24.495ff.), reflect the great iliadic battles, and the games of *Iliad* 23 have as their analogue the Phaeacian games of *Odyssey* 8 (cf. Ch. 9). Resonances are found in smaller details also. In the *Iliad* the doomed Hector despises omens (12.200ff.), while in the *Odyssey* the suitors do so (2.146ff.), and laugh at the prophecy of Theoclymenos (20.350ff.). The exiled Phoenix was given refuge by Peleus, and so became the faithful companion of his son Achilles (*Iliad* 9.434ff.): the kidnapped Eumaeus was bought by Laertes, and thus became the faithful slave of his son Odysseus and grandson Telemachus (*Odyssey* 15.390ff.). In *Iliad* 1 Achilles withdraws from the assembly of the Greeks and goes apart to live in his tent. The *Odyssey* offers two partial parallels: Telemachus in *Odyssey* 1 goes off from the Ithacan assembly to journey in search of Odysseus; later Odysseus, during his first days in Ithaca, lives apart from the city in the hut of Eumaeus. Telemachus' withdrawal is also parallel in other terms to the withdrawal of Chryses in *Iliad* 1 after his repulse by Agamemnon. At *Iliad* 1.442ff., Odysseus participates in the first sacrifice of the epic, made to Apollo, arch-enemy of the Greeks, far away from the Greek encampment at Chryse. The first sacrifice in the *Odyssey* also happens away from the epic's main setting on Ithaca – at Pylos; and it is made to Poseidon, arch-enemy of Odysseus, with Telemachus, son of Odysseus, taking part (*Odyssey* 3.4ff., 43ff.). Finally

---

[84] One important feature of Achilles' character borrowed by Virgil for Aeneas is Achilles' major and obvious capacity for moral self-improvement, as seen in his 'reconciliations' with Agamemnon and Priam. Odysseus may seem in contrast a relatively static character in moral terms, but Rutherford (1986) argues well that he too 'learns and develops through suffering' (147).

the funeral of Achilles described at *Odyssey* 24.36–94 is parallel to the funeral of his dearest friend Patroclus in *Iliad* 23.[85]

Examples could be multiplied; but enough have been given to show a possible reading of the *Odyssey* as *imitatio cum variatione* of the *Iliad*,[86] which would have allowed Virgil to look through the *Odyssey* to the *Iliad*. This approach offers useful insights into Virgil's poetic, moral and political intentions. One application of it – to the games found in all three epics – will be reserved for Chapter 9.[87] The remainder of this chapter will apply it to various incidents, characters, and themes of the *Aeneid* derived from Homer, some of them discussed earlier, but without benefit of this viewpoint. The last will be a topic already treated in Chapter 3, the end of the *Aeneid*, and in particular the death of Turnus. To begin at the beginnings: the relationship of the *Aeneid* and *Odyssey* prologues was analysed above (pp. 190–3); but what of the *Aeneid* prologue's well-recognised iliadic features and their further implications for its odyssean features?[88] First, there is the anger of Juno: on a straightforward level the assonance between *memorem ... iram* (*Aeneid* 1.4, cf. *memora*, 8) and μῆνιν (*Iliad* 1.1) links it with the anger of Achilles.[89] Virgil thus stresses his hero's superiority: whereas Achilles was angry, Aeneas is the victim of Juno's anger. But, when the odyssean background too is considered, the picture becomes more complex: Juno's wrath and its effects are indebted to two parts of the *Odyssey* prologue, the obstacle placed in the way of Odysseus' return by Calypso (1.13–15) and the anger of Poseidon (1.20f.). Virgil has looked through these passages, not just to the wrath of Achilles (*Iliad* 1.1ff.), but also to the anger of Apollo against Agamemnon (1.9ff.), echoed obliquely too in *Odyssey* 1.7–9, describing the hostility of Helios to the companions of Odysseus. The result is a resonant evocation of the importance of Juno

[85] Wender (1978) 37–9.

[86] The potential value of the notion for the interpretation of Homer is well indicated by Macleod (1983), and (indirectly) by Rutherford (1986); cf. also most recently Pucci (1987).

[87] The discussion in this chapter is not intended to be exhaustive. More examples readily occur, e.g. the links between Latinus, Laertes and Priam. Priam in *Il.* 24 is echoed by Laertes in *Od.* 24. For the parallel figure in *Aen.* 12, Latinus, Virgil looks first to the widower Laertes, who unknown to himself has a surviving son. This element Virgil retains both in Latinus' living daughter and in his living future son-in-law Aeneas; and he assimilates Latinus more closely to Laertes by making Amata commit suicide in *Aen.* 12. But Laertes emerges victorious; and so Virgil also looks through Laertes to Priam. For although Priam's son is dead (as Turnus will die!), and his wife is still alive, Priam is, and will remain, a defeated king, as Latinus too (in a modified sense) will remain a defeated ruler.

[88] On this question, cf. also Buchheit (1963) 13–22.

[89] Cf. Lausberg (1983) 211 and n. 31.

in Roman cult and history. Her anger is unjust and destructive; but its setting within a group of divine wraths, which range from the just to the peevish but are all capable of being appeased, emphasises that in the long term the goddess herself has a positive role to play in the workings of fate.[90] Another complex interaction involves the implicit contrast between Aeneas, who brought his people to Italy (*Aeneid* 1.5ff.), and Achilles, whose anger sent many strong souls of heroes to Hades (*Iliad* 1.3f.). On one level (for another see pp. 206f.) Virgil looks through the well-intentioned but unsuccessful Odysseus, who tried but failed to save his comrades, to the destructive Achilles, thereby enhancing Aeneas in two dimensions simultaneously.

Again, the first sacrifices of the *Iliad* and *Odyssey* were featured above (p. 201) as, apparently, model and imitation. The expected analogue in the *Aeneid* would be a first sacrifice to Juno. But this is not what happens. Virgil first mentions sacrifice at 1.48f., not however in the context of a sacrifice to Juno, but in a speech of Juno complaining that, if Aeneas escapes unscathed, she will have no sacrifices: *et quisquam numen Iunonis adorat / praeterea aut supplex aris imponet honorem?* If these words raise the reader's expectation of a sacrifice to Juno, it will be disappointed. The first meal in the *Aeneid* begins at 1.210ff., but, because the Trojans are shipwrecked and their meat is deer already killed by Aeneas' bow, no sacrifice to Juno (or any other god) is possible; and there is rough justice in this, since the shipwreck was Juno's responsibility. The first true opportunity for worship of Juno comes at 1.723ff., at Dido's welcoming banquet for the Trojans. Here libations are poured, and Juno is indeed honoured in them, briefly (*bona Iuno*, 734). But Jupiter and Bacchus precede her at greater length as the honorands of the first two of the three libations (731–4). Ancient social custom is influential here,[91] but Juno's touchiness on the subject of sacrifice will hardly have been mollified – and the reader should be aware of this. Worship of Juno in the *Aeneid* is neither peripheral to the plot nor personal to the hero, as was sacrifice to the hostile god in the *Iliad* and the *Odyssey* respectively. Thus in the *Iliad*, although Odysseus' placation of Apollo does have public importance, contributing to ending the plague Apollo inflicted on the Greeks, it does not alter Apollo's overall hostile view of the Greeks. In the *Odyssey* the participation of Telemachus in the sacrifice to Poseidon is thematically

---

[90] Cf. esp. Feeney (1984). [91] Cf. e.g. Fraenkel (1950) on Aesch. *Ag.* 245.

more significant, since it anticipates the detailed means of Odysseus' reconciliation with Poseidon set out in *Odyssey* 11 and 23 (p. 189); but Odysseus' reconciliation is personal. In the *Aeneid* Juno's worship will be a central part of the compact between her and the Roman people (12.840: *nec gens ulla tuos aeque celebrabit honores*). To stress this, Virgil abstains from making worship of her the first religious event in the epic, just as he abstains from making it the first sacrifice of the Trojans after they have left Troy. Instead he chooses another significant time and place for it, and he prefaces it with the precepts of Helenus at Buthrotum:

> unum illud tibi, nate dea, proque omnibus unum   435
> praedicam et repetens iterumque iterumque monebo,
> Iunonis magnae primum prece numen adora,
> Iunoni cane vota libens dominamque potentem
> supplicibus supera donis: sic denique victor
> Trinacria finis Italos mittere relicta. (*Aeneid* 3.435–40)

Helenus' instruction links worship of Juno with successful occupation of Italy. It is therefore no surprise that, when the Trojans first land on the heel of Italy, they sacrifice to her. Juno is worshipped in combination with another goddess who opposed the Trojans at Troy, Pallas (541f.), and the pretext for giving Pallas prominence is that her temple is at hand (3.531: *templumque apparet in arce Minervae*). But Juno receives greater emphasis, and the command of Helenus is recalled: *praeceptisque Heleni, dederat quae maxima, rite / Iunoni Argivae iussos adolemus honores* (3.546f.). Thus Virgil has looked through the first sacrifice of the *Odyssey*, with its anticipation of a personal permanent reconciliation with a god, to the first sacrifice of the *Iliad*, with its public, but temporary, one. The fusion results in a sacrifice to Juno, on the Trojans' first arrival in Italy, which anticipates a permanent and public reconciliation between her and the Trojans–Romans.

Yet another incident in the *Aeneid* for which Virgil looks through the *Odyssey* to the *Iliad* is the love-making of Dido and Aeneas (4.165–72). The ultimate model is *Iliad* 14.153–351, the 'beguiling of Zeus', in which Venus and Juno also collaborated to bring about a 'seduction'. But the love-making of Zeus and Hera is conjugal; and that was not the desired ethos for the first union of Aeneas and Dido. Another (illicit) iliadic love-making is that of Paris and Helen (3.424–48); but its circumstances are too different for it to make a useful model. Virgil solved his problem by looking through the odyssean divine union of Ares and Aphrodite (8.266–366) to the 'beguiling of Zeus' of *Iliad* 14.[92] The love-making of Ares and Aphrodite was already linked in Homer with the 'beguiling of Zeus', in that Hephaestus, the wronged husband of *Odyssey* 8, had built for Hera the chamber on Olympus in which she prepared herself for the seduction of Zeus (*Iliad* 14.166–8).[93] So the Ares–Aphrodite affair contributes to the Dido–Aeneas relationship those elements of illicitness and public disapproval (voiced by the female deities at least at *Odyssey* 8.324, cf. *Fama* at *Aeneid* 4.173ff.) which are absent from the 'beguiling of Zeus', while *Iliad* 14 with its aura of stability and cosmic significance adds an element of bitter irony.

Another episode similarly treated is Latinus' initial offer to Aeneas of marriage with his daughter Lavinia – and his dispatch of gifts to Aeneas, together with Aeneas' response to them (7.268ff.). This incident draws on king Alcinous' parallel offer to Odysseus of marriage with his daughter Nausicaa and of gifts (*Odyssey* 7.311ff.). Thus the Phaeacian episode contributes doubly to the *Aeneid*,[94] serving as part-model for Aeneas' arrivals both in Carthage and in Italy. But there are differences from the odyssean scenario in *Aeneid* 7. Odysseus, because of his commitment to return home, evaded Alcinous' offer of marriage to Nausicaa, although he did eventually take (different) gifts from Alcinous. Aeneas wants to accept Latinus' offer of marriage, so both Lavinia and Latinus' gifts are congenial to him, and the gifts are accepted on the spot. Like Odysseus, he makes no formal reply about the marriage, but only because he is prevented by the war stirred up by Juno and Allecto. Another difference is that Latinus' gifts are preceded and matched by rich gifts sent to him by Aeneas (7.243–8), which partly demonstrates that Aeneas is free from greed, as did his earlier refusal of Carthage and its wealth, and partly stresses Aeneas' equality with Latinus as another Italian king. The overall *imitatio cum variatione* of the episode results from Virgil having looked through his odyssean model to its analogue in *Iliad* 9. When Agamemnon wishes to be reconciled with Achilles, he offers him gifts, the return of Briseis, and, when they both get back to Greece, one of his own daughters in marriage, with a dowry but without payment of bride-price (121–57, 260–99). Achilles at this point (308–427) refuses all Agamemnon's

[92] The *Argonautica* also plays a role in the transmission, cf. e.g. Lausberg (1983) 235.
[93] Cf. Braswell (1982); Macleod (1983) 9f.
[94] For the phenomenon in general, cf. Knauer (1964) Register *s.v.* Vergils Homerum-formung: dédoublement etc.

offers, including his daughter (388–400). Eventually, after Patroclus' death, Achilles accept gifts from Agamemnon (19.277ff.). But there is no further reference to the marriage, which is thus evaded by Achilles. Virgil has inverted the ultimate model in *Iliad* 9, where everything is refused, partly by combining it with *Iliad* 19, where gifts are taken, and partly by looking at it 'through' *Odyssey* 7, itself probably a shrewd imitation of the same iliadic passages, where Odysseus is evasive about marriage but hopes to take gifts later. The effect is to point up the difference between the grudging reconciliation of Achilles and Agamemnon in the *Iliad* and the true future concord of the Trojans and Latins, and between Odysseus' evasiveness about marriage and Aeneas' open willingness.

Virgil's combination in Aeneas of the good qualities of Achilles and Odysseus, and the *Aeneid* prologue's emphasis on this, have already been discussed (pp. 190–3). As noted, Aeneas saves his companions whereas Odysseus did not. Even the *Odyssey* was slightly uneasy about Odysseus' failure: 1.5f. states that he tried to save them and failed, and 1.7–9 lays the blame squarely on the men's stupidity and wickedness. But the loss of his companions was no credit to Odysseus, and in *Odyssey* 24 Eupeithes, when stirring up the relations of the dead suitors against Odysseus, begins with criticism of Odysseus' failure to bring back his men:

> ὦ φίλοι, ἦ μέγα ἔργον ἀνὴρ ὅδε μήσατ' Ἀχαιούς·
> τοὺς μὲν σὺν νήεσσιν ἄγων πολέας τε καὶ ἐσθλοὺς
> ὤλεσε μὲν νῆας γλαφυράς, ἀπὸ δ' ὤλεσε λαούς,
> τοὺς δ' ἐλθὼν ἔκτεινε Κεφαλλήνων ὄχ' ἀρίστους. (426–9)

> (My friends, this fellow has really done a lot for the Greeks! He took some of them – many and brave they were – off with him in his ships, and lost both the hollow ships and the men; others, when he came back here, he killed – Cephallenia's best.)

That the point rankled in later discussion is shown by the beginning of the *Argonautica*: when initiating the quest, Pelias hoped to deprive Jason of his return (1.17); but in fact Jason brought back both the Golden Fleece and his companions; and 1.1 recognises this by referring to the plural 'men of old' whose κλέα are being sung of, just as the last line of the epic (4.1781) addresses the returned heroes in the plural. In making Aeneas too bring his companions safely 'home', Virgil is following Apollonius; but he looks through Jason to Odysseus, and through him to Achilles. For (cf. p. 203) although Achilles is, *qua* manslayer (*Iliad* 1.3–5), the direct antithesis of Aeneas, on another level Achilles did save his Myrmidons who went to war with him, since they later returned home under his son, Neoptolemus.[95] A further Virgilian 'correction' in this area is the contrast between Aeneas' loss of Pallas and Achilles' loss of Patroclus. Through morally unjustifiable absence from battle Achilles was indirectly to blame for the death of Patroclus; but Aeneas is guiltless of Pallas' death, since his absence was for good and compelling reasons. This correction functions within the overall portrait of an Aeneas who, like Odysseus, tries to save his men, and who, like Achilles for the most part, succeeds; and the moral superiority of Aeneas over both Achilles and Odysseus is thus further established.

The achievement of concord among men in both the *Aeneid* and the *Odyssey* was discussed in Chapter 4, where the *Iliad* was seen predominantly as an epic of discord, with only a partial and unsatisfactory achievement of concord in its final books. The parallel manifestations of concord and discord among the gods in the three epics deserve further brief treatment here in the light of Virgil looking through the *Odyssey* to the *Iliad*. In *Iliad* 1 there is a council of the gods, but it produces no solution to their discord: the war must take its course, with Zeus withdrawing help from the Greeks as a favour to Thetis. In *Iliad* 24, although a truce and the burial of Hector is decreed by Zeus, the gods reach no final agreement about peace between Greeks and Trojans. Thus the continuing human conflict is mirrored at the divine level. *Odyssey* 1 and *Odyssey* 24 also contain divine 'councils', in imitation of those of *Iliad* 1 and *Iliad* 24. Both these odyssean councils however achieve harmony and agreement, and a peaceful course of action is agreed upon and forwarded. But both councils, more particularly the second (24.472–88) in which only Zeus and Athena participate (still however, I suggest, qualifying as a 'council' because of the supreme god's participation), but also the first, a full council except for Poseidon (1.22–95), lack the grandeur of the divine councils of the *Iliad*. Virgil looks through the concordant divine councils of the *Odyssey* to their grander but discordant counterparts in the *Iliad*. His first divine 'council', between Jupiter and Venus (*Aeneid* 1.227ff.), arrives at no immediate solution, and in this it resembles both the iliadic examples. But like the odyssean councils it is concordant; and like that of *Odyssey* 24 it involves only two gods. The second divine council of the *Aeneid* (10.1ff.) reaches only a partial and interim solution, and in this it

---

[95] This is stated explicitly by Menelaus at *Od.* 3.188f., cf. Heubeck–West–Privitera (1981) *ad loc.* Cf. also (on related lines) Pind. *Isthm.* 8.51–6.

resembles more the iliadic councils. But the third council, (12.791ff.), although again it involves only two gods, Jupiter and Juno, is decisive: since they are the greatest gods and also the divine antagonists of the *Aeneid*, it signals the achievement on a cosmic scale of that concord among gods and men which is foreshadowed in minor terms in *Odyssey* 24.[96]

Virgil's handling of kingship as an institution may be examined in the same light. The homeric epics, and the *Iliad* in particular, are, as noted (pp. 3f.), full of kings; but homeric kingship is unstable.[97] The *Iliad* is, in one sense, about this, since the dispute between Achilles and Aga-memnon, which is the cause of the 'wrath', concerns the relative claims of royal rank and fighting qualities. Their reconciliation involves Agamemnon's superior kingship being acknowledged by Achilles and due honour being given to Achilles for his superiority in battle. But this compromise in fact simply polarises the two conflicting principles, and is hardly productive of stability in the institution of kingship. The same instability is seen in the *Odyssey*: Odysseus, as king of Ithaca, and his son and heir Telemachus, are being challenged in Odysseus' absence by the suitors. The suitors' real goal is explicitly declared by Eurymachus to have been replacing Odysseus as king of Ithaca.[98] But in the *Odyssey* Odysseus reestablishes his dynasty convincingly: he kills all his rivals; his father kills the father of one of them; and his son takes part in the battles. Royal status and military might are thereby shown to belong to the same house; and the three generations of warrior-kings underline the hereditary principle.[99] Virgil has negated one feature shared by both homeric epics: in terms of royalty the dynasty Anchises, Aeneas, Iulus is unchallenged within the Trojan community.[100] They have external enemies, but Aeneas (and Iulus) are better warriors than all their adversaries. Virgil has thus given Aeneas both the military primacy of Odysseus (and Achilles) and the royal primacy of Agamemnon; and this makes king Aeneas the superior of all the kings of the homeric epics.

Some ethical and cultural aspects of the epic tale of the *Aeneid* merit

[96] Knauer (1981) 875 may represent the *communis opinio* in stating that there is only one divine council in the *Aeneid*, while there are many in the *Iliad* (i.e. Books 4, 8, 20 etc.). What was the divine quorum? I have proposed just above that in ancient epic the colloquy of two gods (if one is the supreme god) can have the status of a *concilium deorum*.

[97] Cf. Qviller (1981).

[98] Cf. esp. *Od.* 22.52f.; also 1.384–404.

[99] On the 'family' as a central concern in the *Odyssey*, cf. Wender (1978) esp. 68.

[100] Cf. Harrison (1981) 213f., contrasting the less clear situation of the royal house of Troy in the *Iliad* (i.e. the conflict between *Priamidae* and *Anchisiadae*, of which Virgil was aware, and which he resolved at *Aen.* 2.270–97).

brief attention here. The moral defects of the *Iliad* narrative in the eyes of Virgil's contemporaries have been noted (pp. 85ff.), on the basis of Horace *Epistles* 1.2.6ff.: it stems from *amor* (6),[101] and involves *stultorum ... aestus* (8), madness (14), discord, treachery, crime, lust, and anger on both sides (15f.). This moralising view is partial and distorted: Augustan readers would also have regarded the siege and sack of Troy as an heroic enterprise, with great armies joined in battle over the life or death of a powerful city. But in moral mood they would have agreed with Horace that the chief characters, and the conduct of affairs by both Greeks and Trojans, were frequently vitiated by personal and communal faults. Moreover the aim of the enterprise would have condemned it in Roman eyes, since although Romans would have conceded that the gods willed the destruction of Troy for its faults,[102] they would not have seen its destruction as *ipso facto* a good thing. Hence for a Roman reader the *Iliad* narrative was inevitably flawed. From Horace's viewpoint the *Odyssey* does not merit similar censure. It has an ideally virtuous hero who, by sedulous avoidance of the vices symbolised by Sirens, Circe and Phaeacia, reaches home and recovers wife and kingdom (*Epistles* 2.1.8ff.). But on the other hand the adventures of Odysseus are episodic and, with the exception of his battle with the suitors, lack the grandeur of the *Iliad*; and the tenor of hellenistic and Roman *Odyssey* criticism, as exemplified in 'Longinus' 9.11ff.,[103] would suggest that Romans also perceived this. Virgil therefore models the *Aeneid* narrative primarily on the morally positive *Odyssey* story, as he models Aeneas primarily on Odysseus. But looking through it to the *Iliad* involves a reversal: the *Aeneid* anticipates the foundation of Rome, the second and eternal Troy, whereas the *Iliad* anticipated the destruction of the first Troy. On another level it involves attributing to Aeneas the mighty deeds and devotion to public affairs of the iliadic heroes, as well as Odysseus' conspicuous rejections of vice.

Another area of application is the war between the Trojans and the Italians which occupies a substantial part of the 'iliadic' half of the *Aeneid*. The Italians, and Turnus in particular, see this war as a second

---

[101] Usually for Romans a vice, cf. above, pp. 54–7.

[102] Cf. esp. Hor. *O.* 3.3.18–68, and above, p. 127.

[103] This point is made specifically by Eustath. 1380.40f.: ἡ δὲ Ὀδύσσεια, φανερῶς ἐξ ὡρισμένου προσώπου τοῦ Ὀδυσσέως δηλαδή, ἐπιγέγραπται, ὃς μόνος ἐνταῦθα τὴν ὅλην ποίησιν συνιστᾷ (the *Odyssey* is clearly composed on the limited basis of the character of Odysseus, who in this respect alone gives unity to the poem); cf. also Schol. bT on *Il.* 24.804: μικρὰ γὰρ ἦν ἡ ὑπόθεσις περὶ τῆς οἰκίας Ὀδυσσέως μόνον (for otherwise [i.e. if he had not kept the 'left-overs' of the *Iliad* for the *Odyssey*] the subject of the *Odyssey* would have been small-scale, namely the household of Odysseus alone).

'siege of Troy': for them the Trojans are once more on the defensive, beleaguered in a stronghold; and once more a Trojan 'Paris', i.e. Aeneas, is stealing a foreign 'Helen', i.e. Lavinia, who is properly the bride of a 'Menelaus', i.e. Turnus.[104] In these terms the assembled Italian allies listed in *Aeneid* 7.641ff. are equivalent to the massed Greeks at Troy in *Iliad* 2, and the moral advantage lies with Turnus and the Italians, as it once lay with the Greeks. This assessment appears to be strengthened by the genuinely heavy influence of the *Iliad* on the final books of the *Aeneid*, which is not limited to the battle-scenes. Thus Hera–Juno opposes the Trojans, while Aphrodite–Venus supports them; the *Iliad* contributes to Aeneas' concession of a truce for the burial of the dead in Book 11 – cf. Achilles at *Iliad* 24.668–70; and the truce and duel between Aeneas and Turnus draw both on the duel between Paris and Menelaus in *Iliad* 3 and on that between Hector and Ajax in *Iliad* 7, with the motifs of the truce-breaking and the annulment of the duel borrowed from *Iliad* 4.

But, as Chapter 5 argued, Virgil makes it clear that, even in iliadic terms, the Italian case is weak: the roles and moral status of Turnus and Aeneas, and of the Italians and Trojans, can all too easily be reversed, so that the Trojans are seen to have right on their side, as did the Greeks in the *Iliad*. On this basis it is the Trojans who have come to 'Troy', i.e. Italy, to claim for 'Menelaus', i.e. Aeneas, the wife whom 'Paris', i.e. Turnus, is unjustly keeping from him; and Virgil repeatedly shows the anti-Trojan view to be implausible, above all by putting it in the mouths of biased characters (cf. pp. 87, 121). But when the conflict of *Aeneid* 7–12 is also seen through the prism of the *Odyssey*, the position of Turnus and the Italians becomes doubly untenable. Most significantly the ending of the *Aeneid* in anticipated reconciliation derives from the *Odyssey*'s linked themes of Odysseus' predicted concord with Poseidon and his accord with the families of the suitors (cf. pp. 188–90); and the reconciliations of the Romans with Juno, and of the Romans with the Italians, are motifs which run throughout the *Aeneid* – as do their analogues in the *Odyssey*. They start in the speech of Jupiter to Venus in Book 1 (279–85); the theme is picked up again at 10.6ff.; and it receives its final expression at *Aeneid* 12.793–842, where Jupiter gives his decisive authorisation for concord among men. But instead of introducing the reconciliation with Juno into Anchises' prophecies, or having Aeneas repeat those prophecies to another mortal which would have paralleled

---

[104] On Lavinia and Helen, cf. Knauer (1964) Register *s.v.* Lavinia wie Helena; (1981) 882f.

exactly what happens in the *Odyssey*, Virgil places all such predictions in the mouth of Jupiter so as to render them more impressive. Virgil also combines their final expression in Book 12, analogous to Odysseus' repetition of the prophecy of Teiresias, with further information about Aeneas' personal future as one of the *di indigetes*, and with further emphasis on the future prosperity of the Roman race. This context, namely Jupiter's great prophecy of concord and peace, thus also incorporates Zeus' prophecy of concord, wealth, and peace for the Ithacans at *Odyssey* 24.483-6. Furthermore, as early as Book 7 Virgil had pointed to the odyssean aspect of the last books. The clue is his emphasis on Turnus being the suitor of Lavinia most favoured by her mother among the many who have sought her in marriage:

> multi illam magno e Latio totaque petebant
> Ausonia; petit ante alios pulcherrimus omnes   55
> Turnus, avis atavisque potens, quem regia coniunx
> adiungi generum miro properabat amore. (7.54-7)

By designating Turnus as the most prominent and handsome within a band of suitors, Virgil equates him with Antinous, the chief among the suitors of Penelope,[105] and is inviting us at this early stage of the Trojan arrival in Italy to recall the final books of the *Odyssey*. From this standpoint the wars of *Aeneid* 7-12 are an analogue of Odysseus' conflict with and destruction of the suitors of Penelope, and of the succeeding skirmish with their relatives; and this is the reason why the reconciliation of the Trojans with the Italians matches Odysseus' reconciliation with his people of Ithaca in *Odyssey* 24. Virgil has looked through the last books of the *Odyssey* to their model in the *Iliad*, and has combined elements from both, taking in particular from the *Iliad* the major battles, duels etc. which were miniaturised in the *Odyssey*.

Finally, the killing of Turnus (on which cf. Chs. 3 and 4) is also illuminated by the approach developed in this chapter, although so many strands of *imitatio* are involved that this exposition cannot hope to do justice to them. It is well known that the iliadic equivalent of Aeneas' killing of Turnus is Achilles' killing of Hector, and Turnus' rejected pleas to Aeneas before his death (*Aeneid* 12.931-8) equate with those of Hector to Achilles (*Iliad* 22.338-43). However there is a crucial

---

[105] Antinous fulfils this role throughout the *Odyssey*, although for local reasons Euryalus sometimes steps into the limelight, e.g. in Athena's words at *Od.* 15.16-18 (on which, cf. Fenik (1974) 236-40). On Antinous' good looks, cf. *Od.* 17.454, where his wits are said not to match his beauty; 17.381, where his speech is compared unfavourably with his appearance; and the epithet 'of godly form' applied to him at 21.277.

difference between these appeals. Hector asked only for the return of his corpse to Troy for burial, not for his life, and Achilles (initially) refused (345–54). Turnus however asks either for life or for the return of his corpse to his people, i.e. for burial (12.935f.); Aeneas will, it must be presumed, allow his victim burial; but he kills the helpless Turnus, despite his pleas. Now in the *Iliad* battlefield appeals for mercy are always rejected, and those killed in battle can expect no burial.[106] So when Virgil modifies Achilles' behaviour by not making Aeneas refuse Turnus burial, he is looking through the end of the *Odyssey*, where there is no question of the dead suitors being denied burial. That would be inconsistent with the reconciliation envisaged between Odysseus and the suitors' families. The unspoken assumption of the *Odyssey* that the suitors will be buried had ramifications earlier in the *Aeneid* too. For although the circumstances of Turnus' killing of Pallas were particularly unpleasant, especially when Turnus wished that Pallas' father Evander were present to witness his son's death (10.443),[107] on the other hand Turnus willingly granted Pallas burial (10.492–4), whereas Hector intended to deny Patroclus burial.[108] Thus Virgil attributes the less barbarous odyssean attitude concerning the burial of enemies also to the Italians. But Turnus' credit is not thereby much strengthened: whereas Hector killed in Patroclus a man of equal age and strength, Turnus killed in Pallas a much younger and weaker man (*Aeneid* 10.459).[109]

The death of Turnus echoes three particular killings in *Odyssey* 22–4, those of Eurymachus (22.44–88), Leiodes (22.310–29), and Eupeithes (24.513–25). The first happens when Odysseus has just shot down Antinous, chief of the suitors and chief culprit. At this point Eurymachus, the second most important suitor, begs Odysseus not to kill the others. He blames Antinous for everything, saying that Antinous wanted to be king of Ithaca and that he had planned to ambush and kill Telemachus (22.52f.). Odysseus refuses (22.61–7); Eurymachus then calls on the rest of the suitors to resist Odysseus (70–8), and is shot down by him (81ff.). Presumably Eurymachus' tactless reference to the plot of

---

[106] So Macleod (1983) 14.

[107] Cf. the behaviour of Neoptolemus at *Aen.* 2.526–58.

[108] Hector's intention (*Il.* 17.125–7) of cutting off Patroclus' head and giving his body to the dogs was regarded by the homeric scholia as a justification of Achilles' barbaric handling of Hector's corpse, even though it is not mentioned in that context, cf. Richardson (1980) 269. It is noteworthy that Virgil does not make Turnus treat Pallas as Hector intended to treat Patroclus, but that Virgil does advance the death of Pallas as justification for Aeneas' killing of Turnus at the very moment of killing him.

[109] Cf. Horsfall (1987) esp. 53.

the suitors (led by Antinous but acting as a group) to kill Telemachus, influenced Odysseus' refusal. In the second killing too (22.310–29), a suitor, the seer Leiodes, begs Odysseus for mercy and is refused. Odysseus' reason is interestingly reminiscent, not just of his own motivation in refusing Eurymachus' pleas, but also of both Achilles' reason for killing Hector and Aeneas' immediate motive for killing Turnus. Achilles and Aeneas refused mercy because of another death which their victims had been responsible for. In Hector's case this was the death of Patroclus, in Turnus' that of Pallas. Odysseus refuses Leiodes his life because, he says, as a seer Leiodes must often have prayed for Odysseus' own death, and that he himself possess his wife (22.321–5). It is because of these two odyssean episodes that one detail of Virgil's adaptation of the iliadic killing of Hector is as it is. The armour taken by Hector from Patroclus is mentioned in the last encounter of Achilles and Hector (*Iliad* 22.322f.), but only to underline the irony of Achilles' spear passing through a gap in it into Hector's body. In *Aeneid* 12.940–4 however the stripped armour of Pallas is an important motivation: Aeneas' impulse to be merciful to Turnus is checked (945ff.) when he sees that Turnus is wearing the baldric *Pallantis pueri* (941), whom Turnus had killed.

The final odyssean killing contributing to the scene of Turnus' death is Laertes' slaying in battle of Antinous' father, Eupeithes (*Odyssey* 24.513–25). This carefully placed incident has several functions, some discussed earlier (pp. 189, 200). Its importance is underlined by Athena's specific instruction to Laertes to kill Eupeithes (24.517–19), which also signals that the citizens of Ithaca, who have come in arms against their king, are, although provoked by the slaughter of their sons, absolutely in the wrong. Again, the killing of the chief suitor's father by the father of Odysseus reenacts, and so reinforces the implications of, the earlier killing of Antinous by Odysseus. The slain father and son, we are told, share a lack of piety: like his son, Eupeithes has no care for the gods, in that he ignored the warnings of Medon (24.443–9) that an immortal god was fighting on the side of Odysseus. There is more: Homer is indicating that, for concord, peace, and prosperity to prevail on Ithaca (24.483–6), Eupeithes, a man of discord 'good at persuading' others – for that is the meaning of his name[110] – must die. So the end of the *Odyssey* has the same implication as the end of the *Aeneid*; and Virgil

[110] For Homeric etymologies, notably of proper names, cf. esp. Rank (1951), and e.g. Werner (1963); Haywood (1984). Richardson (1980) 283 assembles evidence of the scholiasts' awareness of this feature.

introduces an oblique reminiscence of the last lines of the *Odyssey*. There three generations of Odysseus' family stand together in battle. This is not directly paralleled at the end of the *Aeneid*, but Virgil refers there to Pallas, a (dead) young man of Iulus' age, who has a father, Evander, coeval with the (dead) Anchises. The effect of Virgil having looked through several episodes from the end of the *Odyssey* to the killing of Hector in the *Iliad* is therefore to strengthen the moral case for the destruction of Turnus: for the odyssean material transforms the killing of an enemy (Hector) into the killing of a man of discord (Turnus), who, like Eupeithes, revived strife when the gods willed that it cease. In the *Odyssey* the death of Eupeithes is immediately followed by the achievement of concord. Virgil chose to end the *Aeneid* with the death of Turnus, and to leave the implementation of concord for the future. For the Roman poet, concord belonged to a larger time-scale: it was a goal initially achieved in the union of Trojan and Latin, but ultimately and finally only in Virgil's own life-time.

9

THE GAMES IN HOMER
AND VIRGIL

Why did Virgil include athletic games in the *Aeneid*; and why did he place them in Book 5? The first of these two frequently asked questions[1] is usually answered mainly in terms of Virgil's imitation of Homer: because Homer devoted a book of the *Iliad* (23) to the funeral games for Patroclus, Virgil also gave a book to those for Anchises.[2] A subsidiary reason sometimes offered is the Augustan revival of interest in athletics, forwarded by Augustus himself.[3] For Virgil, however, homeric imitation was not an end in itself, and no feature of the *Aeneid* is ever sufficiently explained by describing it as such without further clarification. This is particularly so when that feature, like the games, is virtually absent from the *Argonautica*,[4] and so cannot be deemed an essential ingredient of an ancient epic.

The subsidiary reason requires cautious handling. The advent of the Augustan regime, with its guarantee of peace and prosperity, certainly did contribute to a general expansion of Greek agonistic activity;[5] and Augustus favoured this trend, with, for example, the Actian Games, which he himself instituted.[6] But Greek games had been familiar at Rome from the third century BC on and were to continue throughout the empire.[7] Again, Augustus' personal interest in athletics is attested, and two aspects of it emphasised by Suetonius (*Augustus* 45.2) may indeed, as is often said, have inspired Virgil, namely the *princeps'* fancy for boxing matches, including those in which he matched a Greek and a Roman (cf. *Aeneid* 5.362ff.), and his habit of rewarding all competitors

---

[1] E.g. Williams (1960) ix–xiii.

[2] E.g. Williams (1960) ix–xiii; the whole tradition of epic games is studied valuably by Willis (1941).

[3] Williams (1960) ix–xi; Harris (1968–9) 17–19.

[4] The sole 'event' is the non-agonistic boxing match between Polydeuces and Amycus at *Arg.* 2.1–97; on its links with and differences from the Virgilian boxing match, cf. Briggs (1981) 976f.

[5] Cf. Harris (1968–9) 18f.; Arnold (1960) 246; Mähl (1974) 33–5.

[6] Cf. e.g. Williams (1960) xf.; the probable inclusion of a naval race in these games is especially noteworthy, on which cf. Willis (1941) 404f.; Kraggerud (1968) 128.

[7] Cf. Harris (1968–9) 15–19; Mähl (1974) 29–39; Crowther (1983).

in Greek-style games (cf. pp. 241–3).[8] But on the other hand there is a great cultural gap between Homer and Virgil with respect to games. The identity of and relations between performers and audience in archaic Greece were different from those of Virgil's time. The difference in the performers is not simply that between amateurs and professionals, since in some senses early Greek athletes were just as professional as later ones.[9] It is rather that there was a greater bias towards upper-class performers in early Greece, although this is not absolute, and a lesser tendency, although again there are exceptions, for early Greek athletes to be life-long career professionals.[10] Moreover the cultural echelon in which early epinician poetry is set, and the difficulties and costs of travel in the period, suggest that, at least at the major games, a mainly aristocratic audience watched mainly aristocratic athletes. By the Augustan period the ethos had changed: the growth in the fourth and third centuries BC of the associations of 'Artists of Dionysus' had turned all performing arts into established careers,[11] so that athletes were now entirely professional; and, whatever their original social status, they were not, as performers, socially identified with any one group among the spectators. More serious than this, there is little evidence from the late republic and early empire of a substantial increase in the popularity among Romans of athletics, as opposed to beast shows and similar exhibitions. Indeed there is reason to think that the 'emphasis on entertainment and the spectacular rather than on individual competition

[8] Cf. also Mähl (1974) 33; RE s.v. P. Vergilius Maro. Anhang: Die Leichenspiele etc. 1487f. (Mehl). The uneven combat between a Macedonian and a Greek in the camp of Alexander the Great (with its tragic, and for Alexander, discreditable aftermath) reported at Diod. Sic. 17.100f.and Quint. Curt. 9.29 will hardly explain Augustus' interest in matching different nationalities. It is worth noting however in view of Maecenas' patronage of Virgil that boxing had great importance in Etruscan culture, cf. Thuillier (1985) esp. 181f.; but the presence of boxing in the legendary games instituted by Romulus in honour of Iuppiter Feretrius (as recorded by Ennius Ann. 1 Fr. li (Skutsch)) is probably more significant. The rewarding of all (or almost all) competitors in games was an epic convention (cf. below, pp. 241–5 on Achilles in the Iliad and Willis (1941) 410f.), so that Augustus' behaviour may be life imitating literature.
[9] Cf. Young (1984) 107–76, vigorously contesting traditional views that all early Greek athletes were amateurs.
[10] Cf. Young (1984) 107–74, simultaneously undermining older beliefs that early Greek performers and audience were exclusively upper-class. Young's two theses are mutually supportive; and at least a thorough review of standard assumptions is necessary. But a completely classless games circuit in the sixth and fifth centuries BC does not square with the cultural, especially the literary, evidence; cf. also, on the aristocratic ethos of the odyssean games, Dickie (1984) esp. 247–52.
[11] Cf. RE s.v. Technitai (V A2.2473–558) (Poland); and, for the poetic dimension, A. Hardie (1983) Ch. 2 esp. 24–30.

which distinguished the Roman from the Greek games'[12] continued unabated.

As for the second question, why Virgil positioned his games in *Aeneid* 5, when the *Iliad* games appear in its penultimate book, it has been said that Virgil's games 'serve to diminish the tension after the powerful and moving tragedy of the fourth book, and to give relief and variation before the majestic unfolding of Book VI.'[13] Although the games of Book 5 do have this function, such an explanation is insufficient, since Virgil could have relieved tension at this point in a number of other ways. A subsidiary reason offered, namely that the honouring of Anchises in the games links them and Book 5 to the rest of the *Aeneid* via the theme of *pietas*, is again clearly true, but again is hardly the last word. Doubtless further solutions along similar lines could be advanced: for example, Anchises dies in Book 3 and his funeral games occur in Book 5, so that Book 4, where Aeneas deviates from the path of fate, is thereby bracketed and hence, as it were, excluded from the mainstream of the epic.

But this chapter will begin by taking a completely different approach to the two questions. It will in the first place direct attention to the Augustan revival of interest in epinician poetry, its subject matter and its ideals, an interest mediated to the Augustans mainly by Callimachus.[14] This revival is seen elsewhere prominently in certain Horatian odes; and its important influence on the beginning of Virgil's own third *Georgic* has recently been demonstrated.[15] Such a trend exemplifies the Augustan attraction towards archaic–classical and early hellenistic, as opposed to later hellenistic, Greek culture, an attraction evidenced equally by the Augustan taste for archaic–classical, early hellenistic and archaising sculpture.[16] In literature of course the movement is reinforced by the overall concern of early hellenistic Greece with the poetry of its own past.[17] Thus in this respect Augustan

---

[12] Crowther (1983) 272.

[13] Williams (1960) xi. This approach may derive in part from Mandra (1934) 60–2, who rightly notes that the emphasis on *pietas* in Book 5 would be out of place until the affair with Dido was over. Heinze (1915) 145f. has further useful considerations.

[14] Cf. Newman (1967) 45–52; (1985); Thomas (1983).

[15] By Thomas (1983) esp. 92–101 (*q.v.*). For Pindaric influence on Horace (probably more direct), cf. e.g. Fraenkel (1957) 276–85, 291–7, 426–40. Other Augustan writers too fall under at least indirect Pindaric influence, e.g. Propertius – cf. now Thomas (1983) 101–3.

[16] Cf. e.g. Lawrence (1972) Ch. 11; Strong (1976) 79–107.

[17] Cf. e.g. Wimmel (1960) Stichwortindex *s.v.* Hesiodfigur; Reinsch-Werner (1976); Pfeiffer (1968) I.177, 220, General Index *s. vv.* Apollonius Rhodius, Archilochus, Alcaeus,

writers and readers were recreating the cultural world of Callimachus, and so were sharing the mentality of a poet who, in his elegiac epinicia, had achieved the tour de force of reproducing the ethos and language of the choric odes of Pindar and Bacchylides within a more restricted metrical compass.[18] The fact that Callimachus and his contemporaries had, like their archaic–classical models, frequently addressed their works to the most prominent men of their time gave them a further relevance for the Augustans.

The suggestion that an Augustan revival of interest in the choric lyric epinicia of sixth- and fifth-century BC Greece (and in their hellenistic successors) stimulated Virgil to imitate in epic hexameters the still earlier homeric games which had been treated in the same metre, involves no anachronism. It has been shown that the athletic values later found expressed in the lyric epinicia of Pindar and Bacchylides are already present fully-fledged in the Phaeacian games of *Odyssey* 8,[19] as in the funeral games of *Iliad* 23;[20] and this is part and parcel of an overwhelming general influence by Homer on lyric poetry. Hence the ideals of and ideas about athletic games which are propagated in their most explicit form by Pindar and Bacchylides are in truth homeric,[21] and it is this which makes it possible that those lyric expressions of them motivated Virgil to introduce homeric-style athletic games into the *Aeneid*, and to place them in *Aeneid* 5. It should be stressed however that not all the athletic values found in lyric reappear in Virgil. Rather Virgil has selected a subset in accordance with his different purposes, period, and literary form. But those he does select add up to a major literary debt, as can be seen by listing the concepts and studying their immanence in Book 5.

(1) For both Greeks and Romans, games were primarily a religious

---

Alcman, Anacreon, Bacchylides, Callimachus, Homer, Ibycus, Pindar, Sappho, Simonides, Stesichorus, etc.; Index of passages discussed *s.v.* Archilochus; Fraser (1972) III General Index under the same headings.

[18] Cf. esp. Parsons (1977), on which cf. Hollis (1986); Thomas (1983) 92–101.

[19] Cf. Dickie (1984).

[20] Cf. Dickie (1984a).

[21] Criticism of athletes and athletics is also found in antiquity, but not in Virgil's sources: cf. e.g. Bowra (1964) 185–8 on the Greek, and Mähl (1974) 40–54 on the Roman evidence. Bowra (1964) is flawed in its account of the nature and functions of Pindar's poetry because of its failure to come to grips with Bundy (1962); however Bowra (1964) Ch. 4 contains convenient and citable discussions of Pindar's ostensible attitudes. I am grateful to Dr Bonnie MacLachlan for advice about the overlap and non-overlap between epinician values and those of *Aen.* 5, with reference in particular to the epinician concepts of φθόνος (envy) and of alternation in the victor's fortunes, both of which are absent from the *Aeneid*.

activity, pleasing to the gods and to the dead – whose funerals they might accompany and honour – and under the protection of the gods.[22] The sacral nature of Greek athletic games is reflected in their being held during a god's festival and in a sacred enclosure; and other places where athletics were practised or performances given, e.g. gymnasia, stadia, and wrestling schools, were also holy, dedicated to tutelary deities, and often associated with temples. Games may have had even greater religious significance for the Romans.[23]

(2) Games were associated with the heroic past: according to Pindar the great games were founded by heroes of the pre-Trojan war period, Heracles, Pelops, Pylades and Orestes, Adrastus, (?)Sisyphus.[24] This made all competitors, and especially victors, the successors and equals of these heroes; and a number of them, e.g. Milo and Philippus of Croton, Euthymus of Locri, and Cleomedes of Astypalaea, claimed or were awarded, after death or even in life, the status of demigods.[25]

(3) Victory in the games conferred on the victor κλέος (glory), τιμά (honour), and δόξα (fame), characteristics which made him outstanding among his fellow men.[26]

(4) The Greeks did not believe that victory and its rewards were achieved by accident, or purely through the advantages of wealth and birth.[27] Heredity and innate qualities were indeed important,[28] but so was ἀρετά (virtue) in general,[29] as well as a nobility of soul which did not shrink from generous expenditure (δαπάνα), and which thus justified morally the victor's possession of wealth.[30] More however was called for: the victor had to be willing to show τόλμα (boldness)[31] and to confront κίνδυνος (danger) on his path to victory;[32] and, both in actual competition and in the preceding training, he must be ready to embrace

[22] Cf. e.g. Bowra (1964) 162f. On games and the dead, cf. Meuli (1968); Willcock (1973) 2.

[23] Roman use of deliberate procedural errors to allow the iteration of games etc. reflects however both religious scrupulosity and a lack of spirituality.

[24] Cf. Bowra (1964) 162–5.

[25] Cf. Bowra (1964) 188–91; Young (1971) 40f.

[26] Cf. Bowra (1964) 177f., Index II s.v. Glory; Slater (1969) s.vv. κλέος, τιμά, δόξα; Dickie (1984) 247–51.

[27] Wealth properly employed was however deemed a positive attribute and could in itself be an object of praise: cf. e.g. Pind. Pyth. 2.56–61, 5.1–9 (where 'virtue' and 'repute' also feature).

[28] Cf. Bowra (1964) 170–2; Slater (1969) s.v. φυά.

[29] Cf. Slater (1969) s.v. ἀρετά; and for praise of victors' 'virtues' etc., cf. Thummer (1968–9) I.38–48.

[30] Cf. Slater (1969) s.v. δαπάνα; Colace (1978); Szastyńska–Siemion (1981).

[31] Cf. Slater (1969) s.v. τόλμα.

[32] Cf. Slater (1969) s.v. κίνδυνος, and esp. Pind. Ol. 6.9–11.

the necessity of πόνος (toil).[33] The upshot was that the victor's 'fame' etc. was not mere casual celebrity, but was the product and guarantee of his genuine moral worth.[34]

(5) As well as intrinsic personal qualities, the victor required the external help of a god. In Pindar this view is standard;[35] and indeed victory was regarded as a proof of divine favour. In Homer these notions can be seen operating both explicitly and implicitly. Diomedes wins the chariot race with the aid of Athena (*Iliad* 23.388ff.), as Antilochus recognises (*Iliad* 23.404–6); and Odysseus wins the foot race in the same way (*Iliad* 23.768ff.), while Meriones is implied to have won the archery competition through the help of Apollo (*Iliad* 23.872f.). Conversely it may be suggested that the failure in *Iliad* 23 of Telamonian Ajax (otherwise a doughty hero) in no less than three competitions is due to lack of divine aid.[36] The motif of divine assistance is a further reminder of the religious ethos of games, but also represents one ancient view of achievement in life in general.

(6) The fame achieved by a victor was not merely personal; it extended to his family, including his ancestors, and to his city. The family of the victor is frequently praised in the epinicia,[37] as is his city, to which, like Psaumis of Camarina in *Olympian* 4, he gives a share of his own 'glory'.[38]

(7) Games were associated with peace.[39] The four Panhellenic meetings (Olympian, Pythian, Nemean and Isthmian) were accompanied by a general truce.[40] Similarly victory in the games conferred ἡσυχία (quiet) and εἰρήνα (peace) on the victor – not of course in the actual toil of the games, but afterwards, and indeed for the rest of his life. Pindar repeatedly makes this explicit, associating the victor's 'peace' and 'quiet' with a number of other virtues and blessings. So, for example, in *Nemean* 1.69–72 Heracles, as paradeigmatic victor in the battle of the gods and giants, will enjoy 'peace', 'quiet' and ὄλβος (happiness and plenty):

[33] Cf. Bowra (1964) 172f., 176; Slater (1969) *s.vv.* βία, πόνος; Dickie (1984) 237–40.
[34] Cf. Bowra (1964) 177–82.
[35] Cf. Bowra (1964) 173–8; Thummer (1968–9) I.33–5 (praise of divine help).
[36] This was an ancient view, cf. Willcock (1973) 4f. Ajax's failures in the games may also anticipate his premature and tragic death.
[37] Cf. e.g Thummer (1968–9) I.47, 49–54.
[38] Pind. *Ol.* 4.10–12; for praise of the city in epinicia, cf. Bowra (1964) 177f.; Thummer (1968–9) 47, 55–65; Bernardini (1983) 35–7.
[39] Cf. Bowra (1964) 176f., Index II *s.v.* Quiet; Burton (1962) 174–80; Slater (1969) *s.vv.* εἰρήνα, ἡσυχία.
[40] Cf. Ebert *et al.* (1980) 14–18 for discussion of the controversial details.

... αὐτὸν μὰν ἐν εἰρή-
 νᾳ τὸν ἄπαντα χρόνον <ἐν> σχερῷ
ἡσυχίαν καμάτων μεγάλων   70
ποινὰν λαχόντ᾽ ἐξαίρετον
ὀλβίοις ἐν δώμασι, δεξάμενον
θαλερὰν Ἥβαν ἄκοιτιν καὶ γάμον
δαίσαντα πὰρ Δὶ Κρονίδᾳ,
σεμνὸν αἰνήσειν νόμον.

(... but, having been allotted quiet as a special reward for his great
labours, will spend eternity in peace in the blessed halls, and,
having received Hebe as his lovely wedded wife and celebrated his
marriage in the house of Zeus, son of Cronos, he will praise
[Zeus's] holy law.)

Again, in *Olympian* 13.1ff. the victor's house is 'kindly to citizens and
hospitable to strangers' (1–3), his city, Corinth, is 'blessed with plenty'
(ὄλβιος) and in it live the children of Themis, 'Good government'
(Εὐνομία), Justice (Δίκα), and 'Peace (Εἰρήνα) the dispenser of wealth
among men' (6–8). In *Olympian* 4 the victor Psaumis is hospitable to
strangers (15) and, with his 'pure mind' (καθαρὰ γνώμα), he is disposed
to ἡσυχία φιλόπολις ('city-loving quiet') (16). The real victor of *Pythian*
4, Damophilus, a political exile from Cyrene who has given his victory
to its ruler, Archesilas, wants to return home to take part in symposia[41]
and to enjoy 'quiet' (ἡσυχία), harming and receiving harm from no one
(293–7); and in *Fr.* 109 (Sn.–Mae.) ἡσυχία is linked with 'good weather'
(εὐδία) i.e. tranquillity, and with the absence of strife, while in *Olympian*
1.97–9 Olympic victors are said to have honey-sweet εὐδία for the rest of
their lives. Perhaps the most interesting Pindaric passage in this
connection, however, is *Pythian* 1.70, where Hieron, as victor, is to
bring about the collective 'harmonious quiet' (σύμφωνος ἡσυχία) of his
people. This phrase is clearly the archaic Greek equivalent of *pax et
concordia*.[42]

(8) Love and erotic language, mainly homosexual, played a large role
in the ethos of the games and of epinician poetry. Victors were, like their
achievements, 'beautiful', and they were deemed to inspire love in all
who saw them – and the spectators at the games were male.[43] The
homosexual erotic flavour of the games is unsurprising in the overall

---

[41] On the symposium as the focus for this conceptual complex, cf. esp. Slater (1981).
[42] For the question of the archaic Greek equivalents of '*concordia*', cf. above, pp. 89f.
[43] Cf. Bowra (1964) 167–70 and Index II *s.v.* Love; Burton (1962) Subject Index *s.v.*
erotic language; Young (1971) 18f., 40. The victor's attractions could also be felt by
females, cf. Cairns (1977a) 142–7.

context of Greek society;[44] and, given the agonistic importance of peace and concord (7), it is further eased in all its dimensions by the ancient overlap among familial, erotic, and political 'concord' (cf. Ch. 4).

(9) In opposition to (7) and (8) stands another important association of games: they were equated with war in epinician poetry (cf. e.g. *Pythian* 2.1–8 and *Isthmian* 1.50f.),[45] and they were generally regarded by the Greeks as a training for war. It has been shown that athletics and war have in common 'toil' (πόνος), that they require the same virtues, and create the same type of product. Examples of the association have been detected not just in philosophical but in historical circumstances, and a particularly good one (Xenophon *Agesilaus* 1.25f., *Hellenica* 3.4.16f.) has been analysed.[46] There Xenophon's Agesilaus established games and prizes among the army which he had gathered at Ephesus. The prize for the hoplites was given for good general physical condition, i.e. εὐεξία – exactly what athletics were designed to produce; and there were also prizes for the cavalrymen, the peltasts and the archers. The association of athletics and war of course goes back to Homer. The games of *Iliad* 23 prepare the Greeks for their eventual sack of Troy; and in the *Odyssey* Odysseus' discus throw at 8.186–98 (with its accompanying boast (202–33) – see pp. 233f.) anticipates his battle with the suitors, as does his later boxing match with Irus (18.64–107) and his competitive bow-shot (21.404–11) just before the battle. In the same way the suitors are 'prepared' by their two sets of exercises (*Odyssey* 4.625–7, 17.167–9).[47]

These ideas and ideals, it is suggested, help explain both Virgil's extended imitation of the homeric games, and the location of the Virgilian games in Book 5; and this suggestion will now be explored in the light of each of the topics listed above.

(1) The *Aeneid* is above all a religious poem, in that it narrates the fulfilment of a divinely inspired mission. In Book 4 Aeneas successfully overcame an obstacle which could have prevented this, but considerable divine intervention was needed to keep him on the right path. It is therefore appropriate that he should now engage in a major religious act reconfirming the right relations of the Trojans with the gods. All Roman games, and the *Ludi Saeculares* in particular, had such a

[44] For all aspects of this topic, cf. esp. Dover (1978).
[45] Cf. also e.g. Bowra (1964) 183f.; Young (1971) 39–42.
[46] Cf. Bowra (1964) 183f.; and, for a better treatment including a discussion of the Xenophon example, Dickie (1984) esp. 237–43.
[47] On the odyssean implications, cf. Dickie (1984) esp. 238–43. It is well known that the Phaeacians and the suitors of Penelope are alike in a number of ways.

reestablishment of divine relations as their main ostensible function.[48] It is no barrier to this view that the Virgilian games honour the dead Anchises, since after death he becomes a primary spokesman for the divine will underlying Aeneas' mission. So at the turning point of the *Aeneid* which Book 5 is, and just before the Trojan landing in Italy, such a significant religious event is fully in place. The religious ethos of the games of Book 5 is introduced plainly at lines 42–103, where Aeneas sets the scene for them by appearing primarily in the roles of *paterfamilias* and priest.

(2) and (3) The heroisation of, and conferment of fame, glory, and honour upon, the Trojan competitors, and especially the victors among them, are concepts explicitly acknowledged in Book 5 – cf. *optatum ... honorem* (201), *hi proprium decus et partum indignantur honorem / ni teneant, vitamque volunt pro laude pacisci* (229f.) and *non laudis amor nec gloria cessit* (394). The process is reinforced by the archaic associations of certain prizes given in the games, which look to the Trojan heroic past, e.g those given to the individual ship-captains (250–67) with their memories of Troy and of the Trojan war: the *Amazonia pharetra* full of Thracian arrows and the *Argolica galea* of 311–16; the shield of 359–61 also with Trojan provenance and history; and the *crater* once given by Cisseus to Anchises (535–8). Archaic flavour derives too from Entellus, associated as he is with Eryx (391, 401–20, 483f.), and from reminiscences excited by the *lusus Troiae* – the young Priamus who is reviving his grandfather's name and riding a Thracian horse, and Iulus' Punic horse, a gift of Dido (563–7, 570–2). The heroisation of various Trojans is both required and best achieved in Book 5. Most of the great Trojan heroes of the *Iliad* and the Epic Cycle perished at Troy, and indeed Aeneas was the only major Trojan warrior to survive.[49] Between the Trojans' departure from Troy and landing in Italy no fighting, except for an abortive brush with the Harpies (3.234–44), took place, so that none of

---

[48] Cf. *Kl. P. s.v.* Saeculum; Pighi (1941). The point is well illustrated earlier in the *Aeneid* by the Trojans' celebration of games at Actium after the Harpies episode (3.278–88). The relevance of the games having Anchises as their honorand is reinforced when later in Book 5 (722ff.) the ghost of Anchises arranges for that very meeting in the underworld in Book 6 at which Aeneas will learn of the destiny of Rome.

[49] On the question of the heroising of Trojans, cf. Wimmel (1973) 25; and most recently Horsfall (1987), who discusses various individuals and their subsequent fortunes in the *Aeneid* in terms partially parallel to those in which they are discussed below. As emerges from his discussion, there is (as always in Virgil) an exception to the rule – Serestus, who is not even a competitor in the games (although he is mentioned during them at 5.487, where his ship's mast is used in the archery competition) but whose later profile is similar to that of several victors and major competitors in them.

them had an opportunity for great deeds. But the games give a number of Trojans the possibility of gaining heroic status, and their location in Book 5 is again apt in these terms, since it enables the Trojans to arrive in Italy with several established major heroes, some of whom reappear later. Significantly Aeneas, already an iliadic hero and hence not in need of the glory of agonistic victory, does not compete. In this of course he resembles Achilles in *Iliad* 23, but the reasons are different.

Of those who do participate in the games, Nisus and Euryalus are the longest on stage later (9.176–449); and their prominence in Book 9 certainly motivated in part (cf. also (8)) the foreshadowing of their fate in Book 5 and their acquisition of heroic grandeur there.[50] Hence they are the best examples of the principle that games confer heroic status. With the other competitors in Virgil's games heroisation is combined with another major, and partly contradictory, function inherited from the iliadic games, that of reminding the reader of 'the great figures who have been out of sight in recent books';[51] and the iliadic games are further influential on those of *Aeneid* 5 in that, as in *Iliad* 23, the winners there are not always the greatest heroes. All this is well exemplified in the naval race, the most important event in the Virgilian games,[52] which is won by Cloanthus. He had appeared three times in Book 1 (222, 510, 612), but does not reappear after Book 5, so that his participation, and his victory despite not being the most important competitor, are iliadic in inspiration. The runner-up, Mnestheus, is outstanding throughout the *Aeneid*, since he had appeared once in Book 4 (288), but is named five times in Book 9 (171, 306, 779, 781, 812), once in 10 (143) and six times in the final book (127, 384, 443, 459, 549, 561). With Mnestheus the heroising function of agonistic competition is in play; and it is no accident that Virgil makes him the only competitor to take part in two events, and awards him the distinction of cutting the bird's string in the archery contest (5.510f.), which equates him with the celebrated, and to Romans sympathetic,[53] Teucer of *Iliad* 23.865–7. Virgil's wish to enhance Mnestheus may also be seen in his reference to him as *modo victor* (strictly speaking inaccurate since Cloanthus won) in the naval race (5.493), an appellation which develops the homeric idea of

---

[50] Cf. e.g. Kraggerud (1968) 195–211. Horsfall (1987) 51f. remarks on the characterisation of Aeneas' companions, (52): 'Perhaps only Ilioneus, Achates, and Mnestheus acquire any substance in our memory.' This may seem pessimistic.

[51] Cf. Willcock (1973) 3.

[52] On the ship race, cf. Kraggerud (1968) 126–79.

[53] Perhaps in part because his mother Hesione was Trojan (daughter of Laomedon). Cf. also Hor. *O.* 1.7 and Cairns (1972) 211–16.

avoiding defeat as a modified form of victory.[54] The other competitors in the ship race, Sergestus and Gyas, had both appeared in book 1 (Gyas along with Cloanthus at 222 and at 612, Sergestus with Cloanthus at 510). Sergestus then featured at 4.288 with Mnestheus. Thus to some extent their roles in Book 5 remind us of them in iliadic fashion. But Gyas subsequently turns up again in the battles of book 12, striking down Italians in the company of Mnestheus (459f.); and Sergestus will reappear at 12.561, along with Mnestheus as at 4.288. These two men then are, like Mnestheus, heroised by the games, but on a lesser scale. The association at later points of these competitors in the most important race is a significant reminder of the concordant nature of Virgil's games (cf. pp. 227f., 236ff.).

Apart from Nisus, Euryalus and Mnestheus, the participants in the foot race and in the archery competition are not in general as prominent later in the *Aeneid* as those of the ship race. Of the runners only Diores reappears, to be killed by Turnus at 12.509–12. Of the archers Acestes is indeed an important figure, mentioned four times in Book 1, although he does not appear there in person; but he is Sicilian and will remain in Sicily, so that his prominence throughout the games is iliadic, in that he makes his final appearance in Book 5, and is named later only twice in reminiscences (9.218, 286). Of the boxers, Dares (a Trojan) is killed by Turnus at 12.363. The winner Entellus (a Sican) naturally appears nowhere else in the *Aeneid*; but Virgil is also contriving in the latter feature to echo the fact that Epeius, the victorious boxer of *Iliad* 23, is unknown elsewhere in the *Iliad*. In addition to the heroisation of the Trojans, the games confer heroic status on their descendants, Virgil's contemporary Romans as a group. The initially puzzling fact that most of the competitors have no links with known Roman *gentes*, and those who do are not, apart from Iulus, linked with the *gentes* most prominent in Virgil's day,[55] has two disparate consequences. It enhances the status

[54] The model is Antilochus at *Il.* 23.401ff., and the ethos of concord in *Aen.* 5 (on which cf. below, pp. 227f., 236ff.) encourages a more generous interpretation of victory. Servius *ad Aen.* 5.493 among other views reports that Urbanus (third century AD) understood *modo* as *propemodum, paene*. Cf. also Kraggerud (1968) 144–7 for the notions that Mnestheus' appellation *victor* is linked with Aeneas' gift to him of the *lorica* which he himself had acquired as *victor* (5.261) – a reversal of Achilles' gift to Eumelus at *Il.* 23.560–3 – and that 'victory' is 'not coming last' (cf. *Aen.* 5.196, 210, and also Servius on 5.493). Mnestheus' 'victory' is further enhanced by the other reversal of Homer implicit in Aeneas' gift to him of a Trojan war trophy, since Diomedes, victor in the (equivalent) chariot race of *Il.* 23, drove in it horses which he had taken in battle from Aeneas (291f.).

[55] Cf. e.g. Williams (1960) on *Aen.* 5.117 – Mnestheus = Memmii, Sergestus = Sergii, Cloanthus = Cluentii, Gyas = Geganii(!). The parallel association of Atys (568f.) with the *gens Atia* – and his/its link with the Iulii – suggests however that Virgil may not have been

of the Iulii, since they are presiding (Aeneas) and performing (Iulus) at the games; and it spreads the effect of heroisation more widely among Augustan Romans by making the heroised athletes more generally representative of the race as a whole. The *lusus Troiae* at the end of the games is an especially strong focus for this trend in both its dimensions – and its non-competitive nature enhances this function.

(4) The sufferings and toils of Aeneas are frequently in the forefront in the *Aeneid*. The games however allow the Trojan people in general, and a number of Trojan heroes other than Aeneas, to display 'virtue', 'boldness',[56] and 'toil' parallel to those of Aeneas. There is constant emphasis on these concepts: *viribus audax* (67), *vires / ... animos* (191f.), *nec quisquam ... / audet* (378f.), the effort of Mnestheus' rowers (197–200) heaving *certamine summo* (197), *summis enixus viribus urget* (of Mnestheus, 226), *animos* (292), *virtus animusque* (363), *vastis cum viribus* (of Dares, 368), *acrior ad pugnam redit ac vim suscitat ira; / tum pudor incendit vires et conscia virtus* (of Entellus, not a Trojan but an ally, 454f.), *vires* (475), *laborem* (499), and *validis ... viribus* (500). This heavy stress on the Trojans' efforts in the games partly compensates for their sufferings being somewhat played down elsewhere so as to highlight those of Aeneas, the suffering hero par excellence. Another motive is to emphasise that the virtues Rome derived from her Trojan strand came from the parallel qualities of the whole Trojan people, which are first displayed prominently in the games. The communal 'virtue' of the Trojans is matched by the *Aeneid*'s later descriptions of Italian life, particularly in the speech of Numanus Remulus (esp. 9.603–13) and the account of Camilla's early life at 11.539–86, which show that the traits of hardihood essential for true virtue descend to the Romans also from their Italian ancestors.[57]

(5) The theme of divine assistance for the victor is announced almost programmatically near the beginning of the games, when Mnestheus

completely out of sympathy with the writers of *De familiis Troianis*, although he doubtless shared Messalla's scepticism about many claims. But the crucial point is that Virgil is writing within a patronage context, so that the epic concentrates mainly on the Iulii, with (here as elsewhere) some emphasis on allied houses like the Atii – the Claudii and Marcelli appear in other contexts. It is interesting that the lack of stress in the games on old Roman families still flourishing in the Augustan period (on which cf. also Wiseman (1974) 153f.) is paralleled by what happens in Horace *Odes* 1–3: cf. Syme (1986) 392: 'Apart from Messalla Corvinus and the augur Murena, no aristocrat is certified in the three books.' *Odes* 4 (13 BC) contrasts, cf. *id.* 396ff.

[56] It is notable that the Trojan group left behind in Sicily is described as *invalidum metuensque pericli* (716), and (cf. (3)) *animos nil magnae laudis egentis* (751).

[57] Cf. esp. Horsfall (1971); Dickie (1986).

says of the naval race: *superent quibus hoc, Neptune, dedisti* (195). It is
then exemplified twice, first in Cloanthus' prayer to the sea-gods and
Portunus' help for him in the same event (233–43), and second in
Aeneas' call to Dares to recognise that Entellus has divine aid (466f.).
But the theme has implications beyond the bounds of Book 5. Aeneas
stands apart from the heroes of the homeric epics, and from Apollonius'
Jason, because he (and the Trojans) have a divinely ordained and
assisted mission. Moreover Aeneas has the backing not of a single god
or group of gods like a homeric hero, but of fate, which is equated with
the collective will of the gods, headed by Jupiter. The eventual victory of
Aeneas over Turnus and his allies will also accord with the ancient view
of victory as involving both personal qualities and divine help; and in
this sense the games foreshadow the successful completion of Aeneas'
mission.

(6) Some of the lines noted above under (2) and (3) as giving the
Trojans a flavour of archaic heroism during their games introduced the
ancestors and ancestral city of the Trojans. These lines also suggest the
sharing of the glory of victory throughout the victors' community. It is
notable that, apart from the Sicans, who, as *comites* of Acestes with his
Trojan mother, become honorary Trojans, and apart from the two
Greeks, Salius and Patron,[58] sent with Aeneas by Helenus, who are now
'naturalised' Trojans, all the named competitors belong to the single
Trojan community. The unitary 'racial' identity of Virgil's competitors
both signals their concord (cf. also (7)), and allows the glory of victory
to remain within the same 'community'; and even in a context where
Trojans and Sicans are thought of as a single people, in fact there is only
one Sican victor, Entellus. He may well be a deliberately significant
exception, especially if Virgil altered tradition by making him a Sican –
the notice of Servius on *Aeneid* 5.389 states that according to Hyginus
Entellus was a Trojan. A number of factors are in play here besides the
homeric precedent noted: one is Rome's link with Sicily (especially with
Segesta and Eryx) – for Entellus was the eponym of Sicilian Entella and
also the pupil of Aeneas' 'brother' Eryx;[59] doubtless another is
Augustus' taste for mixed-race boxing matches (cf. p. 215). But the most
important factor is moral. Dares the defeated Trojan competitor spoke
boastfully before the match (5.383–5). In a reversal of Homer's

---

[58] On these, cf. Williams (1960) on *Aen.* 5.297f.; Horsfall (1981) 144f.
[59] Cf. Williams (1960) Index Rerum et Verborum *s. vv.* Eryx, Segesta; Kraggerud (1968)
215–21; and for the overall importance of Sicily in the *Aeneid* esp. Galinsky (1968) and
(1969).

treatment of the boastful boxer, Epeius (cf. *Iliad* 23.664ff.),[60] who won his match (cf. also pp. 239–41), Virgil makes Dares lose to the more modest Entellus. Since the Trojans' wanderings are accompanied by moral purification and progress, the Trojan champion who displays homeric boastfulness must be defeated, albeit by a Sican, since Virgil rejects elements of behaviour which fall below the standard of his ideal Trojan community. Similarly, at the end of the games a moral lapse by some Trojan women leads to their exclusion from the future Roman race, when they are left behind in Sicily against their will (5.767–71).

(7) Because of the long-standing associations of games and victory with peace and concord, the games of *Aeneid* 5 and the victories won in them are indicative of the concord of the Trojans. The various emphases adopted by Virgil to enhance this theme – having only one single combat event which is in any case broken off, the prizes for all or many competitors, and the ending of the games in the non-competitive *lusus Troiae* (545–603) – will be discussed in more detail below. All reinforce the associations of Virgil's games with peace and concord. Virgil wished to display conspicuously the unity of the Trojans at this turning point in the epic, particularly since Book 5 follows the troubled period at Carthage,[61] and since Trojan concord and peaceful intentions will contrast so sharply with Italian internal discord and disunity (and external aggressiveness) in *Aeneid* 7–12. Simultaneously the concord of this single community (which however incorporates outsiders, the Sicans) as it engages in its games anticipates the concord of the Trojans and Italians after the end of the epic.

(8) The most emotionally charged episode in Virgil's games is the self-sacrifice of Nisus for Euryalus in the foot race. Here Virgil is exploiting the homoerotic aspects of the epinicia. Running is the only event reserved for swift, and hence young, competitors; and Virgil, as he introduces the pair, is true to the epinician ethos in stressing the beauty of the beloved, the 'boy' Euryalus, and the high moral status of his lover Nisus' passion: *Euryalus forma insignis viridique iuventa, / Nisus amore pio pueri* (295f.). The erotic flavour continues in language and concepts

---

[60] Willcock (1973) 9 n. 3 protests with some justification against the 'strange opinion ... that Homer finds the boxing distasteful, and characterizes Epeius as a vulgar boaster'. But Virgil's 'reversal' may suggest that in fact he too found the victory of Epeius problematic in this respect. Epeius was later to be the builder of the wooden horse, which may further explain the Virgilian reversal. There can of course be no question of Entellus wishing to humiliate the Trojans, cf. Stégen (1971), or of the episode being anti-Augustan, cf. Poliakoff (1985).

[61] Cf. Kraggerud (1968) 129.

familiar from the Latin love-poets: Nisus falls *infelix* (329),[62] but is *non tamen Euryali, non ille oblitus amorum* (334).[63] When Euryalus wins with his lover's help, the crowd responds like Pindar's spectators: *tutatur favor Euryalum lacrimaeque decorae, / gratior et pulchro veniens in corpore virtus* (343f.).[64]

(9) Once the Trojans land in Italy they will, despite their peaceful intentions, find themselves engaged in a savage war which will recreate for them the siege of Troy. The military training which they undergo in Sicily in their athletic games is thus absolutely in place;[65] and it is interestingly reminiscent of Agesilaus' tactics at Ephesus. It is (*inter alia*) to make this implication of the games unmistakable that Virgil ends them with the *lusus Troiae*, in which the Roman youths practise military manoeuvres: Iulus leads an *agmen* and *turmae* (549f.), he (and the others, cf. 585) appear *in armis* (550, cf. 557f.), and they enact mock *fugae* and *proelia* (593, cf. 585).[66]

This approach to the two questions set out at the beginning of this chapter might appear to give precedence to epinician literary influence over the contemporary 'real-life' background in explaining the presence and location of the games of *Aeneid* 5. That appearance would be delusory. Literature and the literary influences current at a particular time are part of contemporary life. Hence the contributions made to the *Aeneid* by Roman elegy (Ch. 6), or by early Greek lyric poetry and its hellenistic successors (Chs. 7 and 9), or by the homeric epics as mediated through their hellenistic interpreters (Chs. 8 and 9), are all just as 'Augustan' as the contributions made by the contemporary vision of *tota Italia* (Ch. 5) or by currently relevant ideas such as the ancient stereotype of the ideal king (Chs. 1–3) or the politico-philosophical concept of concord (Ch. 4) – or indeed by the personal tastes and interests of Augustus. Another possible misapprehension too needs to be avoided: because the agonistic ideals found in the homeric epics were first amplified and made fully explicit by the Greek epinician poets, and were transmitted to Virgil by them and by their hellenistic successors, the importance of the homeric background for the games of Book 5 is

---

[62] Cf. Pichon (1902) *s.vv. Infelix, Miseri*.

[63] Lovers in ancient literature are greatly concerned that they should be kept in the beloved's mind: cf. esp. the *memor sis* topos of the propemptikon, on which Cairns (1972) 199f.

[64] Cf. Bowra (1964) 167–70.

[65] Cf. Kraggerud (1968) 130; Wimmel (1973) 26.

[66] Since Aeneas himself orders the holding of the *lusus*, it anticipates the emergence of Aeneas as *imperator*, on which theme (although not this point) cf. Nisbet (1978–80).

not thereby diminished. On the contrary, the homeric games are as all-important as they are omnipresent in *Aeneid* 5; and no answers to the questions asked at the beginning of this chapter would be adequate which did not take account of them. The rest of the chapter will do this.

Scholarly discussions of the homeric background to *Aeneid* 5 tend to focus strongly on *Iliad* 23. This is to a large extent justified, since a high proportion of the content of Virgil's games derives from that source. But there are four firm pointers to additional influence on the games of *Aeneid* 5 from the Phaeacian games of *Odyssey* 8. The first is simply the placement of Virgil's games – in Book 5, just before Aeneas' descent into the underworld in Book 6, rather than near the end of the epic, as in the *Iliad*. This location recalls that of the games of *Odyssey* 8, also positioned before the centre of that epic, and before Odysseus' descent into the underworld in Book 11. Furthermore the Phaeacian games come chronologically at the penultimate stage of Odysseus' wanderings, immediately before his arrival home in Ithaca, as those of *Aeneid* 5 come just before the Trojans' journey ends in their 'return' home to Italy. And it is perhaps also relevant that Phaeacia and Sicily are both fertile islands. The second pointer is Virgil's allusions to three proper names from the games of *Odyssey* 8. The name of the defeated runner Salius of *Aeneid* 5 (as well as alluding to the aetiology of the dancing priests – *Salii*) is the Latin equivalent of Ἅλιος, an unsuccessful competitor but an excellent dancer in *Odyssey* 8 (119, 370).[67] Again, the Virgilian Euryalus is homonymous not only with the defeated boxer of *Iliad* 23.677–99, but also with the victorious wrestler of *Odyssey* 8.127. Finally the name Nautes which occurs at *Aeneid* 5.704 (outside the games however) is a near homonym of the Ναυτεύς of *Odyssey* 8.112, an otherwise unremarkable competitor. The third pointer is the overall layout of the games in the three epics:

Aeneid 5	*Iliad* 23	*Odyssey* 8
Naval race	Chariot race	Running (nautical names)
Running	Boxing	Wrestling
Boxing	Wrestling	Jumping
Archery	Running	Discus
	Duel in armour	Boxing
	Weight-throwing	
	Archery	
[Acestes' shot]	[Javelin]	[Odysseus' discus throw]
(*lusus Troiae*)		(Dancing and Singing)

[67] The link Salius–Ἅλιος would involve either the derivation *sal* = ἅλς or *salio* =

230

There are of course some resemblances between the layouts of the games of *Aeneid* 5 and *Iliad* 23. But, as this table shows, in the number of competitive events (*Aeneid*: 4, *Odyssey*: 5; *Iliad*: 7), in the incident of a single 'competitor' shooting or throwing outside the strict framework of an event (*Aeneid*: Acestes, *Odyssey*: Odysseus; *Iliad*: no one, but cf. the javelin cancellation), and most of all in having a non-competitive 'event' at the end (absent from the *Iliad*), the games of *Aeneid* 5 and *Odyssey* 8 are significantly closer to one another than either is to the games of *Iliad* 23.

The fourth and last pointer to odyssean influence on the games of *Aeneid* 5 is the overall pattern of competitors, entries, supernumeraries, and prizes in the three sets of games. In *Aeneid* 5, excluding the unnamed *multi ..., quos fama obscura recondit* (302), 16 named individuals compete, and of these Mnestheus alone competes twice, so that there are 17 entries in all. Of the 16 competitors Acestes is given the archery prize even though he has no chance to shoot at the target, since Eurytion has already shot it down. Now in *Iliad* 23, 13 individuals in all actually compete, and one more (Agamemnon) tries to do so. Of those who do succeed in competing, 4 enter two events (Odysseus, Antilochus, Diomedes, and Epeius), 1 (Ajax son of Telamon) competes three times, and 1 (Meriones) competes twice and tries to enter a third event. This means that there are 20 actual entries and 2 additional attempted entries. Nestor is given a prize although he does not even attempt to compete; and Agamemnon and Meriones are given prizes even though Achilles has called off the javelin throw. In the games of *Odyssey* 8 the situation is simpler, and closer to *Aeneid* 5: there are 16 named competitors in the five events. All seem to take part in all events, since none are said to be eliminated through injury in the second event, wrestling: thus there will have been 80 entries. Odysseus is a supernumerary: he takes no part in the five regular events, but subsequently, after the competition is over, responds to a challenge by throwing an even heavier discus, and by exceeding the other contestants' performance. It would be a bold interpreter who undertook to explain all these statistics, particularly since there is an apparent indication that Virgil may have diverged from an earlier plan, or may have intended further

---

ἄλλομαι (cf. Isid. *Etym.* 16.2.3 associating *sal* and *exilire*!); Virgil may be making an implied comment on the theory of the origin of Latin in Greek by making Salius a Greek (and from Arcadia, not Aeolis!). On Salius, the Salii, and Euryalus, cf. further Kraggerud (1968) 185–7; Williams (1960) on *Aen.* 5.297f. On names in *Aen.* 5, cf. esp. Morland (1957) (concerned mainly however with iliadic influence) – also Morland (1956); Knauer (1964) 156f. n. 3.

revision in this area. This is Aeneas' outline of his projected games at 5.66–9, where an extra event which did not take place (javelin-throwing) is seemingly inserted (68), and where the order of events is different. But it is at least clear that Virgil was conscious of the number of events and competitors in Homer's games and his own, and that he went some way towards assimilating his games in these terms to those of Phaeacia. Virgil chose, for example, to have 16 competitors, exactly the same figure as in the *Odyssey*, 'correcting' Homer by making Acestes, one of the 16, the 'anomaly' in place of Odysseus, who in *Odyssey* 8 is additional to the 16 competitors. Similarly Virgil preferred on the whole not to have one individual compete in a number of events, Mnestheus being exceptional (for reasons discussed, pp. 224f.). Although in reality this makes his games more like those of *Iliad* 23, since in the *Odyssey* all 16 competitors take part in everything, paradoxically it creates an illusion of odyssean simplicity in this area, simply because the same individuals are not repeatedly brought to the reader's attention as competitors.

These arguments for odyssean influence on the games of *Aeneid* 5 have been set out at some length because the hypothesis of such influence could seem intrinsically implausible. For the formal gymnastic section of the Phaeacian games is brief (21 lines, *Odyssey* 8.110–30); and even when extended by the challenge to and performance of Odysseus (131–234) and the non-competitive dancing and singing (235–384), they come to less than half the length of the games of *Iliad* 23 (600 lines, 257–897). And the iliadic games do indubitably provide copious material for Virgil's games. The table of events (p. 230) shows this as clearly as it shows influence from the *Odyssey*. Every Virgilian competitive event has its direct antecedent in the *Iliad*. The long naval race of *Aeneid* 5.114–285 is a close analogue of the long chariot race of *Iliad* 23.262–650.[68] The next Virgilian event (running, 286–361) amplifies the foot race of *Iliad* 23 (740–97); the boxing match of *Aeneid* 5.362–484 extends that of *Iliad* 23.653–99, with Apollonian influence en route (*Argonautica* 2.1–97); and the archery contest which closes the competitive part of Virgil's games (485–544) expands that of *Iliad* 23.850–83. Moreover the greater length and detail of the last two Virgilian events is due in part to their reflecting a conflation of a greater number of parallel iliadic events,[69] viz: *Iliad* 23's boxing + wrestling +

[68] The precise details are listed at Knauer (1964) 389–93.
[69] For the Virgilian technique in general, cf. Knauer (1964) Register *s.v.* Vergils Homerumformung etc.: 'Kontaminationen', Konzentrierung etc.

duel (i.e. single combat events) = *Aeneid* 5's boxing; and *Iliad* 23's archery + javelin + weight-throwing (i.e. projectile events) = *Aeneid* 5's archery.

But this indubitable iliadic influence does not in fact diminish the plausibility of odyssean contributions. It has already been argued (pp. 197ff.) that Virgil would have seen many features of the *Odyssey* as written with an eye to their iliadic analogues, and this naturally applies to the games of the two epics. One example is the boasts and retractions of Alcinous, and the counter-boasts of Odysseus in *Odyssey* 8. At 102f. Alcinous claims that the Phaeacians are preeminent in boxing, wrestling, jumping and foot-racing; and then, at 8.246–53, he retracts what he said about boxing and wrestling, but continues to claim preeminence in foot-racing, sailing, dancing and singing.[70] Alcinous' change of ground is both courteous and realistic, given that in the interval Odysseus has bested the Phaeacians at discus-throwing, before challenging them precisely at boxing, wrestling and running (206), claiming skill in archery (215–28) and (an appendage) in javelin-throwing (229), and finally modifying his boast about running by admitting that his legs have been weakened by shipwreck (230–33). But the episode also has a complex relationship with the games of *Iliad* 23. There Odysseus (just after the boxing match) competed in wrestling with Ajax son of Telamon and drew (700–39). But Ajax, at a point after the end of the *Iliad*, lost to Odysseus in the contest for the arms of Achilles; and Odysseus' boast about wrestling in *Odyssey* 8 is therefore an updated allusion to his iliadic match. Similarly Odysseus' claim to skill at running, and his subsequent modification of it, gain their piquancy from the fact that in *Iliad* 23 Odysseus won the foot race outright against better competitors (778f.). Thus Odysseus' boasts in *Odyssey* 8 about his skills in heavy events (boxing and wrestling) and a light event (running), are equally based on his competence as proved in the *Iliad*. His further lengthy boast about his skill in archery (*Odyssey* 8.215–28) looks of course mainly in the opposite direction, anticipating his future prowess in the archery competition of *Odyssey* 21. In this it resembles his boast about boxing, which anticipates his victory over Irus in *Odyssey* 18. But Odysseus went on in *Odyssey* 22 to shoot down the suitors in battle: so in *Odyssey* 8 Homer has him claim that his skill as an archer lies specifically in using his bow in battle. This detail also

---

[70] For a stimulating account of Alcinous' boasts and retractions and Odysseus' reactions to them, cf. Dickie (1984) 245–55. On Odysseus' boasts about archery and boxing, cf. now Krischer (1985) 15–18.

explains why Odysseus did not compete at archery in *Iliad* 23, where the contest was peaceful. Again Homer is careful to have Odysseus concede (*Odyssey* 8.219f.) that among mortal men only Philoctetes excelled him in warlike archery. The mention of Philoctetes, whose achievements at Troy took place after the end of the *Iliad*, updates Odysseus' status as an archer, and this again compensates for his non-participation in the earlier archery of *Iliad* 23. Odysseus' appended boast about javelin-throwing is *inter alia* an allusion to the abortive competition at *Iliad* 23.884–97 working along partly parallel lines.[71]

The matter of layout and numbers of competitors and events has already been raised (pp. 230–3); and in this area too it could be urged that the *Odyssey* is looking back at the *Iliad*. The 16 competitors of *Odyssey* 8 look like an enhancement of the 13 actual competitors of *Iliad* 23 plus the one would-be competitor not allowed to compete (Agamemnon), plus the one non-competitor given a prize (Nestor) – hence 13 + 1 + 1 = 15. Further odyssean emulation of the *Iliad* would appear in the fact that Odysseus, given presents and honour by the Phaeacians *inter alia* because of his discus throw (*Odyssey* 8.387–418), becomes a seventeenth 'competitor', making two more than the 'maximum' (in all senses) number found in the *Iliad*. In these terms the Virgilian pattern (16 competitors, 1 unable to compete), which falls between that of the *Odyssey* and the *Iliad*, would revise the odyssean layout by 'correcting' it in the direction of the *Odyssey*'s iliadic model.[72] Again, the complex presented by the *Odyssey* – the supernumerary discus throw of Odysseus, followed by his unmet challenges (*Odyssey* 8.202–33), and by gifts and honour for Odysseus, together with non-competitive dancing and singing – may emulate the final cancelled contest (javelin-throwing) of *Iliad* 23.884–97, where the two would-be competitors get gifts and one of them, Agamemnon, is conspicuously honoured by Achilles. Yet again, the five contests of the *Odyssey* could have been arrived at by the exclusion of the three warlike contests of the *Iliad*, viz. duel in armour, archery and javelin-throwing. Odysseus' stress on the bellicose significance of archery (*Odyssey* 8.215–28), and his appending javelin-throwing to it (229), may (in addition to their other functions, cf. pp. 233, 236) note and compensate for these exclusions. Finally, the first item in the *Odyssey* list might have been arrived at by the substitution of

---

[71] There Agamemnon is given the prize without competing. The *Odyssey* line may imply that Odysseus has replaced the now-dead Agamemnon as 'king of men'.

[72] Virgil may also be seeking to include a more rationally explicable non-competitor as a 'correction' of homeric 'implausibility'.

running, a peaceful and inexpensive event, for the expensive and warlike chariot race, an event in any case not suited to the Phaeacians.

On another level, the games of *Odyssey* 8 could be thought to be reversing the status of those of *Iliad* 23. The iliadic games have the flavour of a panhellenic meeting like the four great competitions of the Greek world: they involve many events and competitors from many cities; only specialists take part in their own specialist contests; and the prizes competed for are valuable. But the odyssean games are much more like the epichoric games of a single city, or the 'friendly' matches of ephebes in the gymnasia of later epochs. They are a simple set of five games (a variant pentathlon?) for competitors from a single city; all the competitors take part in all events; and the prizes are not specified (131), presumably because they are not valuable. The inclusion of non-competitive dancing and singing further differentiates the Phaeacian games from those of *Iliad* 23. But for all this the Phaeacian games still make a further curious indirect bow to the main event of the iliadic games. Alcinous twice stresses Phaeacian skill with ships (247, 253); and although there is no specific hint of a naval race in them, the almost exclusively nautical names of the sixteen Phaeacian pentathletes (Acroneos, Ocyalus, Elatreus, Nauteus, Prymneus, Anchialus, Eretmeus, Ponteus, Proreus, Thoon, Anabesineos, Amphialus, Euryalus, Laodamas, Halius, Clutoneus)[73] (8.111–19) may do more than simply point to Phaeacian links with the sea. It is almost as though Homer remembers the chariot race of *Iliad* 23, and reflects that the Phaeacian equivalent (impossible of course for a number of reasons) would have been a naval race.[74] If so, Virgil took the hint.

These links or apparent links between *Iliad* 23 and *Odyssey* 8, which must have eased Virgil's use of both in *Aeneid* 5, suggest that the canon developed in Chapter 8 for understanding Virgil's homeric imitation will once again be useful here. This chapter continues with a more detailed examination of *Iliad* 23 as the ultimate source for *Aeneid* 5 and of some ways in which Virgil looks through the games of *Odyssey* 8 to

---

[73] The exception is Laodamas. The nautical names, like some others in Homer, are clearly *ad hoc* inventions by the poet rather than traditional. I am not aware of an onomasticon of this type from later Greece, although the later –ιππος names of Eretria provide a chariot-based(!) analogue, cf. Bechtel (1900). On Naubolides (*Od.* 8.116) as a patronymic, not a name, cf. Stanford (1959) *ad loc.*

[74] Cf. Willis (1941) 401. The main reasons are that Odysseus has no ship and is weary from his shipwreck; and in any case Phaeacian excellence in sailing must at least be reserved to them. Virgil would of course have picked up the hint all the more easily if there was a naval race at the Actian games, cf. above, p. 215 n. 6.

this ultimate source; in the process it will elaborate on some of the agonistic concepts already revealed as important for *Aeneid* 5. Much of this investigation will focus more or less sharply around the theme of concord, and the role played by *Odyssey* 8 in helping Virgil to embody it in the games of *Aeneid* 5. Before embarking on this study, however, it may be worth pointing out that the first and longest event in Virgil's games, the naval race, is almost an explicit acknowledgement of the vital role played in them by the Phaeacian games.[75] Of course it would have been absurd for Virgil to make the sea-travelled Trojans hold a chariot race on arrival in Sicily; and his sensitivity to such matters is shown in his specification that the horses on which most Trojan youths rode in the *lusus Troiae* (another part-substitute for the iliadic chariot race) were borrowed from Acestes (*Aeneid* 5.573f.). Again it might be said that the substitution in *Aeneid* 5 of a ship race for the iliadic chariot race involves the very easy and common ancient equivalence between ships and chariots.[76] But nevertheless the 'programmatic' presence of the naval race at the beginning of Virgil's games seems to evoke the maritime setting of Phaeacia (emphasised in the nautical nomenclature of its athletes). And other touches, e.g. the priority Virgil gives to running over the 'heavy' event, boxing,[77] and the prominence in *Aeneid* 5 of archery, confirm this, particularly since the archery is linked with Odysseus' long and pregnant boast of his skill in it on Phaeacia (cf. pp. 233f.).[78]

Concord has been noted (7) as a motif associated with games in general; and the games of *Iliad* 23 have as one of their major functions to signal, confirm, and make as public as possible, the renewal of concord which had taken place between Achilles and Agamemnon in Book 19. The stress on concord is most obvious in the final episode of the games, when Achilles makes an honorific address to Agamemnon (*Iliad*

---

[75] Cf. also above, p. 215 n. 6, and above, p. 235 n. 74 on the Actian games and the *Iliad–Odyssey* interaction.

[76] In the Phaeacian episode it occurs explicitly at Hom. *Od.* 13.81–5; the point is also made by the simile at *Aen.* 5.144–7, comparing the ships in the race to chariots in a chariot race, cf. Williams (1960) *ad loc.* and Skutsch (1985) 623f. On the ancient metaphorical ship–chariot equivalence, cf. also e.g. Hom. *Od.* 4.708f.; Aesch. *Suppl.* 32, *PV* 468; Soph. *Trach.* 656, *Elect.* 730; Eur. *Med.* 1122f., *IT* 410f.; Plat. *Hipp. Maj.* 295D; [Dem.] *Or.* 61.29; Cat. 64.9.

[77] On the significance of the order in which Virgil presents his borrowings from Homer, cf. esp. Krischer (1979).

[78] The discus-throwing of *Odyssey* 8, analogous to the javelin- and weight-throwing which precede and follow the archery contest of *Iliad* 23, gives the ambience of Odysseus' boasts a greater resemblance to the iliadic sequence.

23.890–4), and awards him the better prize in the cancelled javelin-throwing contest. But the theme of Achilles' concord with Agamemnon is also manifest at various earlier points in *Iliad* 23, particularly in Achilles' consistently respectful behaviour towards his former adversary (43–53, 155–60, 236–48, 272);[79] and these public demonstrations also, in another dimension, anticipate the private 'concord' which Achilles will establish with Priam in Book 24. Both these accords are of course flawed (cf. p. 188), the first being practical rather than heartfelt and leading eventually to the death of Achilles, while the second is a temporary truce which will not prevent the destruction of Troy. But the motif has a prominence in *Iliad* 23 which goes well beyond the concord of Achilles and Agamemnon. For example, Achilles steps in promptly to stop an incipient quarrel between Idomeneus and Ajax son of Oileus (490–8); then, after the chariot race he awards Eumelos a prize more honorific than his place in it merits (536–8); and finally he gives way with good grace to Antilochus, who protested that he had been deprived of his rightful reward (555–62). Similarly although Menelaus is at first angry with Antilochus (566ff.), Antilochus behaves in a conciliatory fashion (586ff.) and Menelaus responds with courtesy, so that the episode ends by summing up their relationship in the epic.[80] Then Antilochus, who has come last in the foot race, gracefully compliments the winner Odysseus as well as Achilles (787–92). Again Achilles stops the hung wrestling match between Odysseus and Ajax son of Telamon, declaring it a draw (733–7); and likewise the Achaeans as a group stop the duel between Diomedes and Ajax son of Telamon, fearing for Ajax's safety, although this event too is then honorifically declared a draw (822f.). Finally the 'great-hearted' winner in the boxing match, Epeius, sets the loser back on his feet (694f.). It was then this concentration in *Iliad* 23 on the motif of concord which suggested its development in *Aeneid* 5.

But although Virgil's underlining of harmony and peace in the games of *Aeneid* 5 imitates these iliadic incidents in numerous detailed ways, his imitations usually also involve *aemulatio*. In overall terms his games celebrate not a warrior killed in battle, like those of *Iliad* 23, but an old man who died peacefully and who will become spokesman for the divine impulse towards concord. In keeping with this Virgil seeks in general to to bring out the public-spiritedness of the Trojans' actions, in contrast

---

[79] Many of the ways in which Books 23 and 24 echo Books 1 and 2 are discussed by Macleod (1982) 16–35; cf. also, on the Achilles–Agamemnon material, Dickie (1984a).

[80] Cf. esp. Willcock (1973) and (1983).

to the Greeks of the *Iliad*, who were motivated in essence by selfish individual pride and self-interest: he wishes, that is, to contrast implicitly Trojan φιλανθρωπία ('philanthropy' i.e. love of one's fellow-men) with homeric Greeks' φιλοτιμία (love of one's own honour) – drawing doubtless on the posthomeric view of the Phaeacians as outstanding for φιλανθρωπία[81] (cf. also pp. 239f.). Thus Aeneas at the end of the ship race behaves like Achilles after the chariot race, but with an additional element. Although both give prizes to all competitors, when Aeneas gives one to Sergestus, who came in last after an accident, he does so for a non-iliadic reason: *servatam ob navem laetus sociosque reductos* (283)[82] – a line which images in brief Aeneas' own concern with saving his comrades in the wider context of the epic. When in the foot race another accident occurs, Virgil is conflating an incident from the chariot race of *Iliad* 23 (Antilochus impedes Menelaus, 417ff.) and its outcome (Menelaus' anger and appeasement by Antilochus, 566ff.), with the accident in the foot race at *Iliad* 23.773ff. (Ajax son of Oileus slips and falls because of Athena's intervention), and with Ajax's subsequent protests and their result (778ff.). The circumstances are different and more complex in the *Aeneid*: whereas Antilochus impeded Menelaus so as to come before him in the race, and Athena caused Ajax to slip, fall, and come second, in contrast Nisus slipped by sheer chance, but then voluntarily fouled Salius, thus giving victory to his beloved Euryalus. Hence when Aeneas both satisfies Salius and compensates Nisus for coming last in the race through his accident, he is acting differently from Achilles at *Iliad* 23.586ff. (after the chariot race) and at 23.785ff. (after the foot race). The difference is that Achilles in the first incident simply compensates for misfortune, whereas Aeneas is also rewarding Nisus' action on behalf of another; and this contrast is enhanced by parallel divergences in the second iliadic incident, where Ajax gets his second prize, which he has won, but is laughed at for his protests, while it is the third runner, Antilochus, who receives an extra reward – and that for his flattery of Achilles! In the boxing match of *Aeneid* 5 Virgil is less polemical: when Aeneas intervenes to save the vanquished Dares, his motive is not that of the Greeks in *Iliad* 23 in the duel between Ajax and Diomedes, fear of losing a great warrior; but his compassion does find a closer parallel in Achilles' intervention in the wrestling match at *Iliad* 23.735–7.

[81] The evidence is noted at Dickie (1984) 271 n. 19.

[82] Cf. also Virgil's own contrasting verdict on Gyas stated in the same set of terms: *oblitus decorisque sui sociumque salutis* (5.174).

Phaeacian ethos also provides the games of *Aeneid* 5 with the concept that all (or most) of the competitors belong to a single community, which has glory, honour and fame conferred on it by their athletic achievements – cf. (3). The games of *Aeneid* 5 do this more efficiently than those of the Phaeacians, whose self-esteem and boasted prowess are reduced when the stranger Odysseus beats them all at the discus, and professes himself able to do so at most other sports. The Virgilian event closest to the community spirit of the Phaeacian 'pentathlon' with its 16 competitors is the foot race, which has 7 named competitors, 5 of them obscure in the rest of the epic, as well as other unnamed entrants, and most of these competitors will be non-specialists. In these terms Virgil's foot race contrasts markedly with that of *Iliad* 23, which has 3 competitors only, all of them well-known, and all specialists. Here, in the very event where the Phaeacian ethos of 'philanthropy' is in any case most potent because of Nisus' action on Euryalus' behalf, Virgil has chosen also to stress most openly the epichoric 'Phaeacian' nature of his games.

The Phaeacian combination of 'philanthropy' and community spirit creates in *Aeneid* 5 an overall ambience of concord; and it is through this essentially odyssean prism that Virgil looks when drawing further upon the concordant spirit of *Iliad* 23. Aeneas replaces the Achilles of *Iliad* 23 as the discreet and genial president of his games. Characteristically however, whereas the philotimous Achilles needed to explain why he was not participating in the games of *Iliad* 23, and winning the chariot race (!) (274–84),[83] the more philanthropic Aeneas says nothing about his own possible participation. Virgil here has recast Achilles via the attitude (or would-be attitude) of Odysseus at the Phaeacian games. Two other Virgilian omissions also enhance the spirit of unanimity: those of the iliadic spear-fight (23.798–825) and wrestling (23.700–39). An armed duel would have been discordant, whether two Trojans, or a Trojan and a Sicilian ally, had fought. Wrestling would have been a virtual doublet of boxing, and the duplication of such an event might again have suggested discord. In literary terms the boxing match is (cf. pp. 240f.) Virgil's bow not only to *Iliad* 23.653–99, but to the *Argonautica*, where it is the unique (non-agonistic) 'event' (2.1–97); but Virgil's alterations of his models constantly clarify his moral and political concerns.[84] He

[83] According to Antilochus, he would also have won the foot race (791f.). Some aspects of Aeneas' behaviour in *Aen.* 5 derive from the simultaneous influence of Agamemnon as portrayed in *Il.* 23, cf. Kraggerud (1968) 225ff.

[84] Having only one single-pair combat allows the motifs of all three iliadic combats to be combined, on which technique, cf. above, p. 232 n. 69.

balances Dares' arrogance at the beginning of the contest (383–5) with Entellus' justified vaunt at its end (474–6); and he supplements the iliadic boxing match, which once begun goes through to its end without further speech from anyone, by drawing on words from the other two duels of *Iliad* 23. Both of these were stopped, the first by Achilles (*Iliad* 23.735–7), the second by the Achaeans (822f.), in each case with a declaration that neither fighter had won, and Virgil looks to these speeches for Aeneas' intervention to end the boxing with firm but kindly words to the defeated Dares (5.465–7).

The greater length of the Virgilian boxing match also allows a further, and exclusively odyssean, motif to enter it – the stimulus given to a competitor to take part in an event. In *Iliad* 23 the only trace of this motif is the challenge uttered by Epeius before the boxing match, and this is not addressed to any one individual (23.667–75). Otherwise in *Iliad* 23 competitors need no encouragement to participate. But in *Odyssey* 8 Odysseus is subjected both to the pleasant and discreet invitation to compete of Laodamas (145–51), and to the unpleasant and discourteous incitement of Euryalus (159–64). Virgil reproduces in part the general challenge of Epeius in Dares' words before the boxing match (*Aeneid* 5.383–5), although significantly Dares avoids Epeius' blood-thirsty threats. Virgil then looks through Odysseus' experiences on Phaeacia to the iliadic boxing match, and, preserving the concordant ethos of his own games by leaving out the rudeness of the odyssean Euryalus, instead he makes Acestes *gravis ... dictis* (389) – *gravitas* being a moral category unknown to Greek thought – invite Entellus to take up Dares' challenge (389–93). Acestes uses courteous language which looks in part to that of Laodamas in *Odyssey* 8 (cf. κλέος, 147). He appeals to Entellus' heroic status and (implicitly) to his courage, as well as mentioning his protector 'god', Eryx, his fame and his prizes (*Aeneid* 5.389–93) – all standard agonistic concepts, cf. (2), (3), (4), (5). Entellus then insists that his love of praise and glory (394f.) – cf. (3) – has not diminished through fear (i.e. that he preserves his courage) – cf. (4); he blames his not having come forward on old age (395–8), thus picking up the excuse made by Odysseus at *Odyssey* 8.181 – but contrast 136f.; and finally, in accepting the challenge, he shows his 'virtue' – cf. (4) – by rejecting greed as a motive (399f.). All this enhances the moral aspect of Entellus' victory, which is further augmented by his agreement that the boxing gloves shall be lighter than first suggested and of equal weight (415–25). This topic, which at first sight is absent from the *Iliad* (and *Odyssey*), in part reverses the scenario of *Argonautica* 2.51–9; there the servant of Amycus, king of the Bebrykes, sets out matched (fearsome) gloves for the combat, and Amycus' subsequent speech, giving Polydeuces the choice of them, reveals the motive for this action as the king's contempt for Polydeuces. In contrast, in *Aeneid* 5 the production of equal, but less terrifying, gloves stresses the fairness, and minimises the discord of the combat, as well as reducing its danger, while still conveying Entellus' contempt for his boastful opponent. But there may in fact also be an iliadic reminiscence here; the matched boxing gloves may incorporate a 'solution' to a homeric problem. At *Iliad* 23.807–9 Achilles seems to be offering as prizes in the spear duel a sword to the victor (807f.), and arms (presumably Sarpedon's, cf. 798–800), to be 'held in common' by both victor and loser (809). The spear duel appears, as modern commentators have noted, somewhat implausible in this and other respects.[85] It may be suggested that Virgil (or a previous commentator), encouraged by τεύχεα ἑσσαμένω (arming themselves) in line 803, took the offending line τεύχεα δ' ἀμφότεροι ξυνήϊα ταῦτα φερέσθων (809) to mean not 'let them take these (i.e. Sarpedon's) arms as a jointly owned prize' but 'let them don the same (i.e. equal) arms <for the fight>', i.e. interpreting ταῦτα as ταὐτά, = τὰ αὐτά. On this hypothesis *Iliad* 23.809 would indeed be the source of the equal arms motif of *Aeneid* 5.400–25.

The stress on concord in *Iliad* 23 involved the extremely generous giving of prizes by Achilles to the competitors in his games. Thus all the participants in the chariot race received them, as did all the boxers, wrestlers, runners, duellists, archers, and javelin throwers. Only in the weight throwing was the loser unrewarded, presumably because the weight of iron to be thrown was itself the prize (826–35). Virgil imitates this feature of *Iliad* 23, but with one modification which unites odyssean and iliadic influence and greater realism. His ship-captains, boxers, and archers are all rewarded; but in the most Phaeacian of all his events, the

---

[85] It must be stressed however that neither the scholia nor Eustathius show concern about *Il.* 23.809. The suggestion made below does not of course explain the apparent discrepancy between 23.798–800 and 23.807f. To do this would require the assumption that victory in the duel would not necessarily require the shedding of blood, but could be won 'on points', and that Achilles is offering one prize for victory and another, extra, prize for blood-letting. On this assumption the prizes are then divided, with Ajax getting the lesser prize, the armour, while Diomedes gets the better (extra) prize, the sword of Asteropaeus (823–5). Curiously this scenario would then parallel that found later in the aborted javelin-contest, where prizes are also split, with the better one (the cauldron) going to Agamemnon (884–6, 892f.). The suggestion which follows may find support in Virgil's translation elsewhere of an Apollonian variant reading in the Homer text, cf. Clausen (1987) 21.

foot race with its many entrants, only the first three runners, plus Salius and Nisus, receive prizes. This means that Patron and Panopes (*Aeneid* 5.298, 300), along with the 'unknowns' (302), get nothing. It might be argued that the two named and unrewarded competitors stand for the three unprized losers of the iliadic weight-throwing, Leonteus, Ajax son of Telamon, and Epeius – although the last wins the boxing match and is rewarded for that, while Ajax draws the wrestling match and duel in armour and gets prizes in both, so that these two at least have some consolation. However Virgil must also be conscious in this respect of the Phaeacian games, where only the winners get prizes. If Aeneas' failure to reward all the runners might seem to diminish the ethos of concord, there is the proximate counterweight of Euryalus' victory, its cause and its sources. The name Euryalus is (cf. p. 230) both iliadic (the defeated boxer of 23.664ff.), and odyssean (the victorious Phaeacian wrestler of 8.127, who later taunted Odysseus with such dramatic results at 158ff.). Virgil bows to both sources: the Euryalus of the *Aeneid* wins, like his odyssean counterpart, but, unlike him, he gives vent to no unseemly remarks. Something of the ethical and erotic importance of this scene and of the pair, Nisus and Euryalus, has already been signalled (pp. 228f.); and it goes further. These are not any two Trojans or lovers: their love is a major tragic theme of *Aeneid* 9 which balances the love of Dido and Aeneas in *Aeneid* 4;[86] and the iliadic loser Euryalus emerges again implicitly in the fateful scene of *Aeneid* 9.422ff., where Nisus again disadvantages himself for Euryalus, but this time sacrifices not a race but his life, and is unable to help Euryalus, who is killed too.

Further Virgilian 'corrections' by omission in the area of prize-giving are worthy of remark. The iliadic chariot race causes a great deal of contention: as noted (pp. 237f.), one competitor (Menelaus) bickers with another (Antilochus) during it (23.425–41), and two spectators (Idomeneus and Ajax son of Oileus) then quarrel about who they think is winning (23.450–89). Then after the chariot race there are disputes among winning and losing competitors (23.540–85); and there is a final minor dissension when Ajax protests about Athena's help to Odysseus in the foot race (23.782f.). But contention among competitors is absent from the parallel naval race and its aftermath in *Aeneid* 5. The one touch of irritation in the race, when Gyas throws his own over-timid steersman into the sea (172–5), creates a comic incident (cf. 180–2), although Virgil disapproves of Gyas' action. But interestingly Virgil did

[86] Cf. most recently on the tragic aspects of Nisus and Euryalus, Pavlock (1985).

feel the need to retain elsewhere the iliadic motif of contention between competitors, perhaps because the presence of a parallel confrontation between Euryalus and Odysseus in *Odyssey* 8 made the topos canonical. Virgil decided to follow the *Odyssey* by associating contention with his own Euryalus, but not to involve Euryalus directly, and to place the dispute (like Ajax's protests) after the foot race, but only after setting up a love-interest which would mask it. Hence it is Salius, significantly not a Trojan, who complains of his loss of first place in the foot race (340–2); then Diores, for selfish reasons, in effect supports Euryalus (345–7), and later Nisus bewails his mishap (353–6). All the while however Euryalus says nothing; like his odyssean counterpart, he is good-looking (*Odyssey* 8.176; *Aeneid* 5.344), but, unlike him, he does not talk stupidly (*Odyssey* 8.166–85). These small notes of discord are countered fully by Aeneas' immediate and generous gifts to all the complainants. His actions are of course modelled on Achilles' behaviour towards Eumelus, Antilochus, and Nestor at *Iliad* 23.534ff., towards Antilochus at 795–7, towards Ajax and Diomedes at 822–5 (where Achilles is the ἥρως of line 824), and towards Agamemnon and Meriones at the end of the games (890–4).[87] But they are in no sense prudential, as Achilles' open-handedness was, nor is there serious risk of Aeneas' generosity creating further disharmony. Rather it is unselfish and compelling towards harmony.

Virgil's archery contest (5.485–544) also furthers the motif of concord. Like his boxing match, it is longer than its iliadic prototype (60 lines against 33), and there are twice as many competitors in the *Aeneid* (4 against 2). These features do not simply compensate for the smaller number of Virgilian events; and it should be observed that although longer, the *Aeneid* contest is the more sophisticated in that it takes more for granted. The iliadic archery contest turns, like the foot race of *Iliad* 23, on whether a contestant has or has not prayed to a god (23.863f., 872f.). Virgil's contest turns on more and larger issues, and Aeneas, unlike Achilles, does not even explain the gradations of success to be achieved by the competitors, so that Virgil is assuming his readers' knowledge of the parallel event in *Iliad* 23. The first and second competitors in *Aeneid* 5 miss (502–11), the second (Mnestheus) cutting the string attaching the target to the mast, while the third, Eurytion, hits the flying bird (515f.). Virgil's point here is partly to rehabilitate Eurytion's dead brother, Pandarus. In Greek tradition Pandarus was

---

[87] Antilochus' courtesies and generosity make other important contributions to this theme, cf. above, pp. 237f., and Willcock (1973) and (1983).

stigmatised as a truce-breaker,[88] and at *Iliad* 4.86ff. he had been persuaded by Athena disguised as Laodokus to shoot an arrow at Menelaus, thus ending the truce between Greeks and Trojans. Pandarus was described there (104) as ἄφρων (senseless) for being so persuaded. Virgil in contrast speaking *propria persona* apostrophises Pandarus as *clarissime* (5.495), and continues: *qui quondam, iussus confundere foedus / in medios telum torsisti primus Achivos* (496f.), implying that, because he acted 'under orders' in breaking the truce, Pandarus should not be reproached. Eurytion then (5.514) calls upon his dead brother for help with his shot, so that his success in it elevates Pandarus to the status of deified hero.

This rewriting of 'history' i.e. of *Iliad* 4.86ff., is followed by a different sort of 'correction', which involves the archery contest of *Iliad* 23. When at *Aeneid* 5.519ff. Acestes is left as the remaining competitor, but lacks a target to shoot at, he nevertheless shoots his arrow into the air; it catches fire, and blazes like a comet. Aeneas welcomes this as an omen of Acestes' future greatness, gives him a valuable gift, a cup once owned by Anchises, crowns him with bay, and hails him as victor over all the others. The entire passage caused problems in antiquity.[89] But one obvious aspect of it is Virgil's emulation of (in the main) Achilles' gifts to Nestor and Agamemnon at *Iliad* 23.615–23 and 890–5. Nestor, who did not compete in the chariot race, was given the fifth prize purely as a mark of honour; and in giving it to him Achilles remarked that Nestor would not take part in the boxing or wrestling matches, or in the javelin-throwing or foot race because of his old age (23.621–3). Agamemnon is given the more valuable javelin prize (and the other would-be competitor Meriones is given the less valuable prize) when Achilles vetoes the match as an honour to Agamemnon. In one dimension then Virgil is 'correcting' Homer by offering a more rational account of how a non-earned prize can be given: Acestes is one of the competitors in the archery contest, which does take place; but he has no target to shoot at, so that (even leaving aside the omen which follows his shot) he has a greater claim to a prize than a non-competitor like Nestor or an exempted competitor like Agamemnon. Another function of the episode is to equate Acestes with Nestor, an older figure of great authority in both *Iliad* and *Odyssey*, and also with the 'king of men' Agamemnon. But most of all Virgil is constructing a context in which to display conspicuously yet again the concord of the Trojans: for far from

---

[88] Cf. for this and other vices of Pandarus *RE s.v.* Pandaros (van der Kolf).

[89] Cf. Williams (1960) 140–5.

protesting, the real victor Eurytion, whom Virgil here calls *bonus* (541) to underline his point, is neither offended nor envious when Aeneas hails Acestes as victor (541f.).

It is worth noting too that in this episode Virgil again looked through the prism of *Odyssey* 8 to the iliadic games. Acestes is throughout portrayed as an older man (*senior*, 5.301 573), and the emphasis is maintained in the archery contest: *ausus et ipse manu iuvenum temptare laborem* (499) – cf. *pater* (521, 533). The analogy set up between Acestes and Nestor through their supernumerary prizes underlines the motif further. But the odyssean use of the 'older competitor' topos deserves close attention: in the aftermath of the five competitive events of *Odyssey* 8, when Odysseus is being incited to show his agonistic skill, his more mature age is stressed directly or indirectly several times (8.136f., 181f., cf. also ξεῖνε πάτερ, 8.145). This emphasis is itself derived from *Iliad* 23: when Odysseus wins the foot race there, he is explicitly and emphatically said by Antilochus to belong to an older generation (789–92). This is a high compliment, and an enhancement of his victory, since running is in essence a young man's sport. It may be that Virgil is giving an aural[90] signal of his indebtedness to the presence of the motif in *Odyssey* 8 when he makes Aeneas address Acestes with the words *sume, pater* (*Aeneid* 5.333), just as Laodamas addressed Odysseus as ξεῖνε πάτερ (145).[91] At all events Virgil seems to have been further influenced within this complex of analogies by *Odyssey* 8.202–33 where Odysseus' boasts, significantly to the Phaeacian νέοι (young men) about his skills at various events, including running, allude (cf. pp. 233f.) to his prowess in the iliadic games. This passage will have struck Virgil all the more forcibly since it itself echoes Nestor's boasts in *Iliad* 23 of his former skills as a boxer, wrestler, runner, javelin thrower and charioteer (626–45).[92] The older man Acestes then, when he appears as a competitor in the archery contest, is the iliadic Nestor seen through the glass of the Odysseus of *Odyssey* 8. The recurrence of the older

---

[90] For this technique cf. *Aen.* 1.1ff. where *arma* (1) echoes ἄνδρα (*Od.* 1.1) and *memorem* (4) μῆνιν (*Il.* 1.1), and above, pp. 191, 202.

[91] *sume, pater* is found only here in the *Aeneid*. ξεῖνε πάτερ (which is absent from the *Iliad*) is addressed to Odysseus at *Od.* 7.28 and 7.48 by Athena disguised as a Phaeacian girl, and by Laodamas at 8.146. The variant πάτερ ὦ ξεῖνε is addressed, again to Odysseus, by the loyal Philoetius (20.199) and by the comparatively decent suitor Amphinomus (18.122). The honorific aspect, the link with Odysseus, and the Phaeacian context are thus all established.

[92] This is another 'variant pentathlon' (cf. above, p. 235), although only three of the events overlap with the standard pentathlon, which consisted of discus, jumping, javelin, running and wrestling, cf. *Kl. P. s.v.* Pentathlon.

competitor motif in Virgil's boxing match, where the victor Entellus is also an older man, reflects the same set of influences, and relies in particular on the Odysseus of *Odyssey* 8 being, like Entellus, a 'victor' challenged and provoked to take part in the games against his will (cf. p. 240). Here too stress on present age and former youth is strong, and honorific: *sed enim gelidus tardante senecta / sanguis hebet, frigentque effetae in corpore vires. / si mihi quae quondam fuerat quaque improbus iste / exsultat fidens, si nunc foret illa iuventas* (395–8, cf. 389, 409, 415f., 430–2, 474f.).[93]

The final event in Virgil's games, the *lusus Troiae*, reveals further major influence from *Odyssey* 8. The non-competitive singing and dancing there are just as integral to the Phaeacian games as the *lusus* is to those of *Aeneid* 5 (*nondum certamine misso*, 545).[94] Alcinous institutes a display of dancing and singing (236ff.), after repeated boasts about Phaeacian skills – at sailing and running – and after expatiating on the Phaeacians' love of the doings of peace – drinking, dancing, singing, lyre-playing, fresh clothes, warm baths and 'beds'. Although the singing and dancing are put on to impress Odysseus, not to allow individual Phaeacians to win prizes, the circumstances show that the Phaeacians were well aware of contests in these areas. The youths dance on a floor laid out by the public officers whose duty it was to supervise 'contests' – ἀγῶνες (258–60). Then Demodocus sings, and there is more virtuoso dancing,[95] before Odysseus closes the proceedings diplomatically by acknowledging the Phaeacians' superiority in dancing (382–4). The continuity of the proceedings in *Odyssey* 8 allows Virgil to make the *lusus Troiae* the crowning point of his games; and certain of its functions, e.g. to hold the balance between reminiscences of the past greatness of Troy (563–7, cf. p. 223) and anticipations of the future greatness of Rome (esp. 568f.), and to introduce a hellenistic aetiological and historical account of its own history (596–603), are analogues to the purpose of the latter events on Phaeacia, i.e. communal self-glorification. The *lusus* has another important function which takes a hint from its

[93] In addition to the various moral emphases imported by Virgil, a realistic 'correction' may be in play here, since in ancient boxing strength rather than speed was significant. On the distinction between heavy and light events, cf. Dickie (1984) 272 n. 32.

[94] According to Williams (1960) *ad loc. q.v.* this line means that Aeneas set about arranging the *lusus* before the archery competition was over, i.e that the *certamen* is the archery competition, and not the games as a whole. He compares *hoc ... misso certamine* (5.286). But whereas *hoc* in that line certainly does show that a single event is there in question, the absence of *hoc* here shows that the games as a whole are meant.

[95] On these performances cf. esp. Braswell (1982) and Dickie (1984) esp. 253–7, 267–70.

odyssean model, but in part reverses it: the *lusus* underlines the martial significance of the Sicilian games (cf. (9)) by substituting military manoeuvres for the Phaeacian dancing etc., activities antithetic to fighting.[96] The substitution is hinted at slyly in the word *choris* (5.581).[97]

But the *lusus* also, through its non-competitive nature, plays a consummate role in that portrayal of concord which is a primary purpose of Virgil's games throughout; and in this connection, Virgil's reversal of his odyssean model is matched by his echoing of it. The Phaeacians in one tradition of later antiquity became (mainly on account of Homer's descriptions of them)[98] a byword for luxury, so that Virgil's choice of the military exercises of the Trojan–Roman youth to replace the Phaeacian songs and dances must on one level be moralising and pointed. But on the other hand Homer's archaic Greek audience, especially the Ionians, had a lively interest in and appreciation of luxury, and they expressed it in their literature, their art, and their dress.[99] So Homer's account of the Phaeacians as a people given up to the joys of feasting, dance, and song must in part represent a sympathetic appreciation of the enjoyments of peace and prosperity. This aspect of *Odyssey* 8, particularly as it is incorporated in the final, non-competitive events in the Phaeacian games, will not have escaped Augustan readers, especially in view of the connotations of εἰρήνη and εὐφροσύνη possessed by symposia throughout antiquity.[100] The Augustans would have found these associated concepts powerfully relevant to Virgil's picture of the Trojans watching Ascanius leading his squadrons in the *lusus Troiae* to honour his grandfather, and joyfully seeing in the boys' faces the features of their Trojan ancestors. Moreover Virgil's contemporaries would have regarded his description as no mere academic reconstruction, given the major political and social importance of 'peace and concord' in the twenties BC, the period down to which Virgil traces the continuity of the *lusus* (5.596–603). It is in this context that the deliberate multiple ambivalence of the concluding line

---

[96] Cf. esp. Dickie (1984). I believe, with Stanford (1959) *ad loc.*, that the first bout of Phaeacian dancing (*Od.* 8.262–5) is not synchronous with Demodocus' song, and also (in the hope of dealing with the question more fully elsewhere) that it may not be as peaceful a display as their second bout (370–80).

[97] It might appear imprudent to place so much stress on this single word. However the word (and concept) appear elsewhere to function as an expected signal of the choric nature of a hymn, cf. Cairns (1984) 142.

[98] Cf. esp. Dickie (1984).

[99] Cf. e.g. Gomme (1945–81) I.101–6.

[100] Cf. Slater (1981); Dentzer (1982) 451f.

of the *lusus* description comes into its own: the *sanctus pater* of *hac celebrata tenus sancto certamina patri* (5.603) becomes at once Anchises, Aeneas, and, in foreshadowing, Augustus.

LIST OF MODERN WORKS CITED

To avoid anachronism, works are generally listed here and cited in the body of the work with their original date of publication. Second and subsequent editions are taken account of only where there has been significant change. Sometimes information about a reprint is given where this might be helpful. In text and footnotes citations are by surname of author, date, (volume), and page number(s) only. Where more than one author has the same surname, the author(s) cited less frequently retain their initial(s) or first name in citations. Such abbreviations of journal or series titles as are used generally follow the conventions of *L'Année Philologique*.

Aalders, G.J.D. (1975). *Political thought in Hellenistic times*. Amsterdam
Adam, T. (1970). *Clementia principis: der Einfluss hellenistischer Fürstenspiegel auf den Versuch einer rechtlichen Fundierung des Principats durch Seneca* (Kieler Historische Studien 2). Stuttgart
Ahl, F. (1985). *Metaformations: soundplay and wordplay in Ovid and other Classical poets*. Ithaca–London
Allen, A.W. (1950). 'Elegy and the classical attitude toward love: Propertius I, 1', *YClS* 11.255–77
Anderson, W.S. (1957). 'Vergil's second *Iliad*', *TAPA* 88.17–30
—— (1981). 'Servius and the comic style of *Aeneid* 4', *Arethusa* 14.115–25
André, J.-M. (1966). *L'otium dans la vie morale et intellectuelle romaine: des origines à l'époque augustéenne*. Diss. Paris
Arnim, H. von (1903–24). *Stoicorum Veterum Fragmenta*. Vols 1–4. Leipzig
Arnold, I.R. (1960). 'Agonistic festivals in Italy and Sicily', *AJA* 64.245–51
Austin, R.G. (1971). *Publi Vergili Maronis Aeneidos liber primus: with a commentary*. Oxford
—— (1977). *P. Vergili Maronis Aeneidos Liber Sextus: with a commentary*. Oxford
Aymard, J. (1951). *Essai sur les chasses romaines: des origines à la fin du siècle des Antonins (Cynegetica)* (Bibliothèque des Ecoles françaises d'Athènes et de Rome 171). Paris

Badian, E. (1985). 'A phantom marriage law', *Philol.* 129.82–98
Baker, R. (1980). 'Regius puer: Ascanius in the Aeneid' in *Vindex Humanitatis: essays in honour of John Huntly Bishop* (ed. B. Marshall), 129–45. Armidale NSW
Balk, C. (1968). *Die Gestalt des Latinus in Vergils Aeneis*. Diss. Heidelberg
Balsdon, J.P.V.D. (1962). *Roman women: their history and habits*. London

249

Barchiesi, A. (1984). *La traccia del modello: effetti omerici nella narrazione virgiliana* (Biblioteca di *MD* 1). Pisa

Barker, E. (1956). *From Alexander to Constantine: passages and documents illustrating the history of social and political ideas 336 B.C.–A.D. 337.* Oxford

Barner, G. (1889). *Comparantur inter se Graeci de regentium hominum virtutibus auctores.* Diss. Marburg

Barrett, W.S. (1964). *Euripides Hippolytos: edited with introduction and commentary.* Oxford

Bartelink, G.J.M. (1965). *Etymologiseering bij Vergilius* (Mededelingen d. Koningkl. Nederland. Akadem. v. Wetensch. Afd. Letterkunde 28.3). Amsterdam

Basson, W.P. (1984). 'Vergil's Mezentius: a pivotal personality', *Acta Classica* 27.57–70

Bechtel, F. (1900). 'Das Wort ΙΠΠΟΣ in den eretrischen Personennamen', *Hermes* 35.326–31

Benediktson, D.T. (1985). 'Propertius' "elegiacization" of Homer', *Maia* 1.17–26

Bernardini, P.A. (1983). *Mito e attualità nelle odi di Pindaro: la Nemea 4, l'Olimpica 9, l'Olimpica 7* (Filologia e Critica 47). Rome

Bieler, L. (1935). ΘΕΙΟΣ ΑΝΗΡ: *das Bild des 'göttlichen Menschen' in Spätantike und Frühchristentum.* Vienna (repr. Darmstadt 1967)

Billerbeck, M. (1982). 'La réception du cynisme à Rome', *Ant. Class.* 51.151–73

Binder, G. (1971). *Aeneas und Augustus: Interpretationen zum 8. Buch der Aeneis* (Beiträge zur klassischen Philologie 38). Meisenheim am Glan

Bliss, F.R. (1964). *'Fato profugus'* in *Classical, Mediaeval and Renaissance studies in honor of Berthold Louis Ullman* (ed. Charles Henderson Jr.), 1.99–105. Rome

Boas, H. (1938). *Aeneas' arrival in Latium: observations on legends, history, religion, topography and related subjects in Vergil Aeneid VII, 1–135.* Diss. Amsterdam

Bohn, R. (1965). *Untersuchungen über das Motiv des 'Gelobten Landes' in Vergils Aeneis und im Alten Testament.* Diss. Freiburg im Breisgau

Bonds, W.S. (1978). *Joy and desire in the 'Aeneid': Stoicism in Vergil's treatment of emotion.* Diss. Pennsylvania

Bonfanti, M. (1985). *Punto di vista e modi della narrazione nell'Eneide* (Biblioteca di *MD* 3). Pisa

Bonitz, H. (1870). *Index Aristotelicus.* Berlin

Bonjour, M. (1975). *Terre natale: études sur une composante affective du patriotisme romain.* Paris

Born, L.K. (1934). 'The perfect prince according to the Latin panegyrists', *AJPh* 55.20–35

Borthwick, E.K. (1983). 'Odyssean elements in the Iliad', *Inaugural Lecture.* Edinburgh

Borzsák, I. (1971). 'Von Hippokrates bis Vergil' in *Vergiliana: recherches sur Virgile* (edd. H. Bardon and R. Verdière) (Roma Aeterna 3), 41–55. Leiden

Boucher, J.-P. (1965). *Etudes sur Properce: problèmes d'inspiration et d'art* (Bibliothèque des Ecoles françaises d'Athènes et de Rome 204). Paris

(1966). *Caius Cornélius Gallus* (Bibliothèque de la Faculté des Lettres de Lyon 11). Paris

Bowra, C.M. (1933-4). 'Aeneas and the Stoic ideal', *GR* 3.8-21

(1964). *Pindar.* Oxford

Boyancé P. (1955). 'Sur la théologie de Varron', *REA* 57.57-84

Boyle, A.J. (1972). 'The meaning of the Aeneid: a critical inquiry', *Ramus* 1.63-90, 113-52

(1986). *The Chaonian dove: studies in the Eclogues, Georgics, and Aeneid of Virgil* (*Mnem.* Suppl. 94). Leiden

Braswell, B.K. (1982). 'The song of Ares and Aphrodite: theme and relevance to Odyssey 8', *Hermes* 110.129-37

Brelich, A. (1969). *Paides e parthenoi* (Incunabula Graeca 36). Vol. 1. Rome

Briggs, W.W. Jr. (1981). 'Virgil and the Hellenistic epic', *ANRW* 2.31.2.948-84

Bright, D.F. (1971). 'A Tibullan Odyssey', *Arethusa* 4.197-214

Brink, C.O. (1971). *Horace on poetry 2: the 'Ars Poetica'.* Cambridge

(1982). *Horace on poetry 3: Epistles Book II: the letters to Augustus and Florus.* Cambridge

Brunt, P.A. (1975). 'Stoicism and the principate', *PBSR* 43.7-35

Buchheit, V. (1963). *Vergil über die Sendung Roms: Untersuchungen zum Bellum Poenicum und zur Aeneis* (*Gymnas.* Beihefte 3). Heidelberg

Buckland, W.W. (1963). *A text-book of Roman law from Augustus to Justinian* (3rd edn rev. P. Stein). Cambridge

Bücheler, F. (1904). *Petronii Saturae et Liber Priapeorum* (4th edn). Berlin

Bühler, W. (1964). *Beiträge zur Erklärung der Schrift vom Erhabenen.* Göttingen

Bundy, E.L. (1962). *Studia Pindarica. I The eleventh Olympian ode. II The first Isthmian ode* (Univ. Calif. Publ. Class. Philol. 18.1-2). Berkeley-Los Angeles

Burkert, W. (1972). 'Zur geistesgeschichtlichen Einordnung einiger Pseudo-pythagorica', *Fondation Hardt, Entretiens sur l'antiquité classique* 18.23-55. Vandoeuvres-Geneva

Burton, R.W.B. (1962). *Pindar's Pythian odes: essays in interpretation.* Oxford

Cairns, F. (1971). 'Five "religious" odes of Horace (I,10: I,21 and IV,6: I,30: I,15)', *AJPh* 92.433-52

(1971a). 'Propertius, 2.30 A and B', *CQ* 21.204-13

(1972). *Generic composition in Greek and Roman poetry.* Edinburgh

(1977). 'Geography and nationalism in the *Aeneid*', *LCM* 2.109-16

(1977a). 'Horace on other people's love affairs (*Odes* I 27; II 4; I 8; III 12)', *QUCC* 24.121-47

(1979). *Tibullus: a Hellenistic poet at Rome.* Cambridge

(1984). 'Propertius and the Battle of Actium (4.6)' in Woodman-West (1984), 129-68, 229-36. Cambridge

(1985). 'Concord in the *Aeneid* of Virgil', *Klio* 67.210-15

Calame, C. (1977). *Les choeurs de jeunes filles en Grèce archaïque* (Filologia e critica 20-1). Vols. 1-2. Rome

Campbell, J.S. (1986-7). '*Animae Dimidium Meae*: Horace's tribute to Vergil', *CJ* 82.314-18

Campbell, M. (1983). *Index verborum in Apollonium Rhodium* (Alpha-Omega A.62). Hildesheim-Zurich-New York

(1983a). *Studies in the third book of Apollonius Rhodius' Argonautica* (Altertumswissenschaftliche Texte und Studien 9). Hildesheim-Zurich-New York

Camps, W.A. (1969). *An Introduction to Virgil's Aeneid*. Oxford

Canali, L. (1976). *L'Eros freddo: studi sull'Eneide* (Filologia e Critica 16). Rome

Carey, C. (1986). 'Archilochus and Lycambes', *CQ* 36.60-7

Cartault, A. (1926). *L'art de Virgile dans l'Enéide* (Université de Paris: Bibliothèque de la Faculté des Lettres. 2.4-5). Vols. 1-2. Paris

Chesnut, G. F. (1978). 'The ruler and the logos in Neopythagorean, Middle Platonic, and Late Stoic political philosophy', *ANRW* 2.16.2.1310-32

Classen, C.J. (1962). 'Romulus in der römischen Republik', *Philol.* 106.174-204

(1965). 'Die Königszeit im Spiegel der Literatur der römischen Republik (Ein Beitrag zum Selbstverständnis der Römer)', *Historia* 14.385-403

Clausen, W. (1987). *Virgil's Aeneid and the tradition of hellenistic poetry* (Sather Classical Lectures 51). Berkeley-Los Angeles

Coffey, M. (1976). *Roman Satire*. London-New York

Colace, P.R. (1978). 'Considerazioni sul concetto di "πλοῦτος" in Pindaro' in *Studi in onore di Anthos Ardizzoni* (edd. E. Livrea and G.A. Privitera) (Filologia e critica 25), 2.735-45. Rome

Colaclidès, P. (1981). 'Créativité dans un vers d'Homère (*Il.* 22.490)', *SO* 56.7-11

Collard, C. (1975). 'Medea and Dido', *Prometheus* 1.131-51

Conrardy, C. (1904). *De Vergilio Apollonii Rhodii imitatore: commentatio philologa*. Diss. Freiburg in der Schweiz

Copley, F.O. (1940). 'The suicide-paraclausithyron: a study of ps.-Theocritus, Idyll XXIII', *TAPA* 71.52-61

(1956). *Exclusus amator: a study in Latin love poetry* (American Philological Association: Philological Monographs 17). New York

Cornell, T.J. (1983). 'Gründer' in *Reallexikon für Antike und Christentum* 12.1107-71. Stuttgart

Crowther, N.B. (1983). 'Greek games in republican Rome', *Ant. Class.* 52.268-73

D'Anna, G. (1981). 'Cornelio Gallo, Virgilio e Properzio', *Athenaeum* 59.284-98

D'Arms, J.H. (1984). 'Control, companionship and *clientela*: some social functions of the Roman communal meal', *Echos du Monde Classique / Classical News and Views* 28.327-48

Dahlmann, H. (1954). 'Der Bienenstaat in Vergils Georgica', *Akad. d. Wiss. und der Lit. in Mainz. Abh. der Geistes- und Sozialwiss. Kl.* 10.547-62. Wiesbaden

Dalzell, A. (1980). 'Homeric themes in Propertius', *Hermathena* 129.29–36

Davies, M. (1986). 'Alcman and the lover as suppliant', *ZPE* 64.13f.

Day, A.A. (1938). *The origins of Latin love-elegy*. Oxford

De Grummond, W.W. (1967). 'Virgil's Diomedes', *Phoenix* 21.40–3

De Romilly, J. (1972). 'Vocabulaire et propagande ou les premiers emplois du mot ὁμόνοια' in *Mélanges de linguistique et de philologie grecques offerts à Pierre Chantraine* (Etudes et commentaires 79), 199–209. Paris.

De Vries, G.J. (1977). 'Phaeacian manners', *Mnem.* 30.113–21

De Witt, N.W. (1907). *The Dido episode in the Aeneid of Virgil*. Diss. Chicago

Dearing, B. (1952). 'Gavin Douglas' *Eneados*: a reinterpretation', *PMLA* 67.845–62

Delatte, L. (1942). *Les traités de la royauté d'Ecphante, Diotogène et Sthénidas* (Bibliothèque de la Faculté de Philosophie et Lettres de l'Université de Liège 97). Liège–Paris

Dentzer, J.-M. (1982). *Le motif du banquet couché dans le proche-orient et le monde grec du VIIe au IVe siècle avant J.-C.* (Bibliothèque des Ecoles françaises d'Athènes et de Rome 246). Rome

Di Benedetto, V. (1966). 'Tracce di Antistene in alcuni scoli all' "Odissea"', *SIFC* 38.208–28

Di Cesare, M.A. (1974). *The altar and the city: a reading of Vergil's Aeneid*. New York–London

Dickie, M. (1984). 'Phaeacian athletes', *Papers of the Liverpool Latin Seminar* 4.237–76.

(1984a). 'Fair and foul play in the funeral games in the *Iliad*', *Journal of Sport History* 11.8–17

(1986). 'The speech of Numanus Remulus (*Aeneid* 9,598–620)', *Papers of the Liverpool Latin Seminar* 5.165–221

Dillon, J. (1977). *The middle Platonists: a study of Platonism 80 B.C. to A.D. 220.* London

Dorandi, T. (1982). *Filodemo: il buon re secondo Omero: edizione, traduzione e commento* (Istituto italiano per gli studi filosofici: la scuola di Epicuro 3). Naples

Dornseiff, F. (1921). *Pindars Stil.* Berlin

Dover, K.J. (1978). *Greek homosexuality*. London

Drew, D.L. (1927). *The allegory of the Aeneid*. Oxford

Du Boulay, J. (1974). *Portrait of a Greek mountain village*. Oxford

Duclos, G.S. (1970–1). 'Nemora inter Cresia', *CJ* 66.193–5

Dudley, D.R. (1937). *A history of Cynicism: from Diogenes to the 6th century A.D.* London

Due, O.S. (1973). 'Zur Etymologisierung in der Aeneis' in *Classica et Mediaevalia Francisco Blatt septuagenario dedicata*, 270–9. Copenhagen

Dunbar, H. (1962). *A complete concordance to the Odyssey of Homer* (2nd edn rev. B. Marzullo). Hildesheim

DuQuesnay, I.M.Le M. (1977). 'Vergil's fourth *Eclogue*', *Papers of the Liverpool Latin Seminar* 1.25–99

Dvornik, F. (1966). *Early Christian and Byzantine political philosophy: origins and background* (Dumbarton Oaks Studies 9). Vols. 1–2. Washington D.C.

Dyck, A.R. (1983). 'Sychaeus', *Phoenix* 37.239–44

Ebert, J. *et al.* (1980). *Olympia von den Anfängen bis zu Coubertin.* Leipzig

Erbse, H. ed. (1969–). *Scholia Graeca in Homeri Iliadem (Scholia vetera).* Vols 1–6. Berlin

Erffa, C.E. von (1937). ΑΙΔΩΣ *und verwandte Begriffe in ihrer Entwicklung von Homer bis Demokrit* (*Philol.* Suppl. 30.2). Leipzig

Fahz, L. (1904). *De poetarum Romanorum doctrina magica: quaestiones selectae* (Religionsgeschichtliche Versuche und Vorarbeiten 2.3). Giessen

Farber, J.J. (1979). 'The *Cyropaedia* and Hellenistic kingship', *AJPh.* 100. 497–514

Farron, S. (1981). 'The death of Turnus viewed in the perspective of its historical background', *Acta Classica* 24.97–106

(1982). 'The abruptness of the end of the *Aeneid*', *Acta Classica* 25.136–41

(1985). 'Aeneas' human sacrifice', *Acta Classica* 28.21–33

Fears, J.R. (1977). *Princeps a diis electus: the divine election of the emperor as a political concept at Rome* (Papers and Monographs of the American Academy in Rome 26). Rome.

(1981). 'The cult of virtues and Roman imperial ideology', *ANRW* 2.17.2. 827–948

Fedeli, P. (1980). *Sesto Properzio: il primo libro delle elegie: introduzione, testo critico e commento* (Accademia Toscana di Scienze e Lettere La Colombaria: Studi 53). Florence

(1985). *Properzio: il libro terzo delle elegie: introduzione testo e commento* (Studi e commenti 3). Bari

Feeney, D. (1983). 'The taciturnity of Aeneas', *CQ* 33.204–19

(1984). 'The reconciliations of Juno', *CQ* 34.179–94

(1986). 'History and revelation in Vergil's underworld', *PCPS* 212.1–24

(1986a). 'Following after Hercules, in Virgil and Apollonius', *PVS* 18.47–85

Fenik, B. (1974). *Studies in the Odyssey* (*Hermes* Einzelschr. 30). Wiesbaden

Fischer, E. (1973). *Amor und Eros: eine Untersuchung des Wortfeldes 'Liebe' im Lateinischen und Griechischen.* Hildesheim

Flory, M.B. (1984). 'Sic exempla parantur: Livia's shrine to Concordia and the Porticus Liviae', *Historia* 33.309–30

Fontenrose, J. (1968). 'The gods invoked in epic oaths: *Aeneid*, XII, 175–215', *AJPh* 89.20–38

Fordyce, C.J. (1977). *P. Vergili Maronis Aeneidos libri VII–VIII: with a commentary.* Oxford

Fraenkel, E. (1950). *Aeschylus Agamemnon: edited with a commentary.* Vols. 1–3. Oxford

(1957). *Horace.* Oxford

Fraser, P.M. (1972). *Ptolemaic Alexandria.* Vols 1–3. Oxford

Fraustadt, G. (1909). *Encomiorum in litteris Graecis, usque ad Romanam aetatem historia*. Diss. Leipzig

Frère, H. and Izaac, H.J. (1961). *Stace: Silves*. Vols. 1–2 (2nd edn). Paris

Fuchs, H. (1926). *Augustin und der antike Friedensgedanke: Untersuchungen zum neunzehnten Buch der Civitas Dei* (Neue Philologische Untersuchungen 3). Berlin

Funke, P. (1980). *Homónia und Arché: Athen und die griechische Staatenwelt vom Ende des peloponnesischen Kriegs bis zum Königsfrieden (404/3–387/6 v. Chr.)* (*Historia* Einzelschr. 37). Wiesbaden

Galinsky, G.K. (1966). 'The Hercules–Cacus episode in *Aeneid* VIII', *AJPh* 87.18–51

(1968). '*Aeneid* V and the *Aeneid*', *AJPh* 89.157–85

(1969). *Aeneas, Sicily, and Rome* (Princeton Monographs in Art and Archaeology 40). Princeton N.J.

(1969a). '*Troiae qui primus ab oris* ... (*Aen.* I, 1)', *Latomus* 28.3–18

(1972). *The Herakles theme: the adaptations of the hero in literature from Homer to the twentieth century*. Oxford

(1981). 'Vergil's Romanitas and his adaptation of Greek heroes', *ANRW* 2.31.2.985–1010

Gardner, J.F. (1986). *Women in Roman law and society*. London–Sydney

Gardthausen, V. (1891–1906). *Augustus und seine Zeit*. Vols 1–2. Leipzig (repr. Aalen 1965)

Gawantka, W. (1975). *Isopolitie: ein Beitrag zur Geschichte der zwischenstaatlichen Beziehungen in der griechischen Antike* (Vestigia 22). Munich

Getty, R.J. (1950). 'Romulus, Roma, and Augustus in the sixth book of the *Aeneid*', *CP* 45.1–12

Giangrande, G. (1967). '"Arte allusiva" and Alexandrian epic poetry', *CQ* 17.85–97

Gigante, M. (1984). 'Per l'interpretazione del libro di Filodemo *Del buon re secondo Omero*', *La Parola del Passato* 217.285–98

Gilbert, A.H. (1938). *Machiavelli's Prince and its forerunners: The Prince as a typical book de Regimine Principum*. Durham N.C.

Gillis, D. (1984). 'The heroism of Anchises', *La Parola del Passato* 218.321–41

Glenn, J. (1981). 'Odyssean echoes in *Aen.* 10.880–82', *AJPh* 102.43–9

Godman, P. (1987). *Poets and emperors: Frankish politics and Carolingian poetry*. Oxford

Görler, W. (1976). 'Aeneas' Ankunft in Latium: Beobachtungen zu Vergils epischer Technik', *Würzburger Jahrbücher für die Altertumswissenschaft* 2.165–79

Gomme, A.W. (et al.) (1945–81). *A historical commentary on Thucydides*. Vols. 1–5. Oxford

Goodenough, E.R. (1928). 'The political philosophy of Hellenistic kingship', *YCIS* 1.55–102

(1938). *The politics of Philo Judaeus: practice and theory*. New Haven (repr. Hildesheim 1967)

Goold, G.P. (1970). 'Servius and the Helen episode', *HSCPh* 74.101–68

Gotoff, H.C. (1984). 'The transformation of Mezentius', *TAPA* 114.191–218

Gow, A.S.F. and Page, D.L. (1965). *The Greek Anthology 1: Hellenistic epigrams*. Vols. 1–2. Cambridge

(1968). *The Greek Anthology 2: The Garland of Philip and some contemporary epigrams*. Vols 1–2. Cambridge

Grant, M. (1963–4). 'Virgil the European', *PVS* 3.1–11

Grenfell, B.P. (1896). *An Alexandrian erotic fragment and other Greek papyri chiefly Ptolemaic*. Oxford

Griffin, J. (1976). 'Homeric pathos and objectivity', *CQ* 26.161–87

(1979). 'The fourth *Georgic*, Virgil, and Rome', *GR* 26.61–80

(1980). *Homer on life and death*. Oxford

(1985). *Latin poets and Roman life*. London.

Griffin, M.T. (1976). *Seneca: a philosopher in politics*. Oxford

Griffith, M. (1985). 'What does Aeneas look like?', *CP* 80.309–19

Griffiths, A. (1972). 'Alcman's Partheneion: the morning after the night before', *QUCC* 14.7–30

Grimal, P. (1966). 'Le "bon roi" de Philodème et la royauté de César', *REL* 44.254–85

(1986). 'Les éléments philosophiques dans l'idée de monarchie à Rome à la fin de la République', *Fondation Hardt, Entretiens sur l'antiquité classique* 32.233–73. Vandoeuvres–Geneva

Guillemin, A.-M. (1931). *L'Originalité de Virgile: étude sur la méthode littéraire antique* (Collection d'études latines 7). Paris

Hahn, I. (1984). 'Trojanitas, Latinitas, Tuscitas, Graecitas in der Aeneis' in *Symposium Vergilianum* (ed. I. Tar) (Acta Universitatis de Attila József nominatae: Antiqua et Archaeologica 25: Minora opera 21), 43–74. Szeged

Hardie, A. (1977). 'Horace *Odes* 1,37 and Pindar *Dithyramb* 2', *Papers of the Liverpool Latin Seminar* 1.113–40

(1983). *Statius and the Silvae: poets, patrons and epideixis in the Graeco-Roman world* (Arca 9). Liverpool

Hardie, P.R. (1983). 'Some themes from gigantomachy in the 'Aeneid'', *Hermes* 11.311–26

(1986). *Virgil's Aeneid: Cosmos and Imperium*. Oxford

(1986a). 'Cosmological patterns in the *Aeneid*', *Papers of the Liverpool Latin Seminar* 5.85–97

Hare, R.M. (1952). *The language of morals*. Oxford

Harris, H.A. (1968–9). 'The games in Aeneid V', *PVS* 8.14–26

Harrison, E.L. (1960). 'Notes on Homeric psychology', *Phoenix* 14.63–80

(1972–3). 'Why did Venus wear boots? – some reflections on Aeneid 1.314f.', *PVS* 12.10–25

(1977–8). 'Metempsychosis in Aeneid six', *CJ* 73.193–7

(1979). 'Snakes and buskins', *Eranos* 77.51–6

(1980). 'The structure of the Aeneid: observations on the links between the books', *ANRW* 2.31.1.359–93

(1981). 'Vergil and the Homeric tradition', *Papers of the Liverpool Latin Seminar* 3.209–25

(1984). 'Vergil's Mercury' in *Vergilian Bimillenary Lectures 1982* (ed. A.G. McKay) (*Vergilius* Supplementary Volume 2), 1–47. Vancouver

(1984a). 'The *Aeneid* and Carthage' in Woodman–West (1984), 95–115, 214–25

(1986). 'Achaemenides' unfinished account: Vergil *Aeneid* 3. 588–691', *CP* 81.146f.

Harrison, S. (1986). 'Vergilian similes: some connections', *Papers of the Liverpool Latin Seminar* 5.99–107

Haywood, M.S. (1984). 'Word play between θέω/θοός and θεός in Homer', *Papers of the Liverpool Latin Seminar* 4.215–18

Heinze, R. (1915). *Virgils epische Technik*. Leipzig–Berlin (repr. Stuttgart 1965)

Hellegouarc'h, J. (1963). *Le vocabulaire latin des relations et des partis politiques sous la République* (Publications de la Faculté des Lettres et Sciences Humaines de l'Université de Lille 11). Paris.

Henrichs, A. (1981). 'Human sacrifice in Greek religion: three case studies', *Fondation Hardt, Entretiens sur l'antiquité classique* 27.3–55. Vandoeuvres–Geneva

(1984). 'The sophists and Hellenistic religion: Prodicus as the spiritual father of the Isis aretalogies', *HSCPh* 88.139–58

Heubeck, A., West, S. and Privitera, G.A. (1981). *Omero Odissea volume I (libri I–IV)*. Milan

Heubeck, A. and Privitera, G.A. (1983). *Omero Odissea volume III (libri IX–XII)*. Milan

Heurgon, J. (1969). 'Les Dardaniens en Afrique', *REL* 47.284–94

(1969a). 'Inscriptions étrusques de Tunisie', *Académie des Inscriptions et Belles-lettres: Comptes rendus 1969* 526–51

Higgins, R.A. (1961). *Greek and Roman jewellery*. London

Hill, H. (1961). 'Dionysius of Halicarnassus and the origins of Rome', *JRS* 51.88–93

Höistad, R. (1948). *Cynic hero and Cynic king: studies in the Cynic conception of man*. Uppsala

Hölscher, T. (forthcoming). 'Homonoia/Concordia' in *Lexicon Iconographicum Mythologiae Classicae*. Zurich–Munich

Hölzer, V. (1899). *De poesi amatoria a comicis atticis exculta, ab elegiacis imitatione expressa: pars prior*. Diss. Marburg

Hoffmann, M. (1914). *Die ethische Terminologie bei Homer, Hesiod und den alten Elegikern und Jambographen*. Tübingen

Hofmann, H. (1986). 'Ovid's *Metamorphoses*: carmen perpetuum, carmen deductum', *Papers of the Liverpool Latin Seminar* 5.223–41

Hollis, A. (1986). 'The composition of Callimachus' *Aetia* in the light of *P. Oxy.* 2258', *CQ* 36.467–71

Horsfall, N.M. (1971). 'Numanus Remulus: ethnography and propaganda in *Aen.*, ix, 598f.', *Latomus* 30.1108–16

(1973). 'Corythus: the return of Aeneas in Virgil and his sources', *JRS* 63.68–79

(1973–4). 'Dido in the light of history', *PVS* 13.1–13

(1976). 'Virgil, history and the Roman tradition', *Prudentia* 8.73–89

(1979). 'Stesichorus at Bovillae?', *JHS* 99.26–48 and plates II–IIIc

(1981). 'Virgil and the conquest of chaos', *Antichthon* 15.141–50

(1982). 'The structure and purpose of Vergil's parade of heroes', *Ancient Society* 12.12–18

(1985). 'Enea – la leggenda di Enea' in *Enciclopedia Virgiliana* 2.221–9

(1987) '*Non viribus aequis*: some problems in Virgil's battle-scenes', *GR* 34.48–55

Hošek, R. (1967). 'Die Auffassung der Concordia bei den Dichtern des Prinzipats', *Sbornik Prací Filosofické Fakulty Brnenské University E* 12.153–62

How, W.W. and Wells, J. (1912). *A Commentary on Herodotus: with introduction and appendixes*. Vols. 1–2. Oxford

Howie, J.G. (1977). 'Sappho *Fr.* 16 (LP): self-consolation and encomium', *Papers of the Liverpool Latin Seminar* 1.207–35

(1979). 'Sappho *Fr.* 94 (LP): farewell, consolation and help in a new life', *Papers of the Liverpool Latin Seminar* 2.299–342

Hübner, U. (1968). *Elegisches in der Aeneis*. Diss. Giessen

Hügi, M. (1952). *Vergils Aeneis und die hellenistische Dichtung* (Noctes Romanae 4). Bern–Stuttgart

Jal, P. (1961). '"Pax Civilis"–"Concordia"', *REL* 39.210–31

Jax, K. (1933). *Die weibliche Schönheit in der griechischen Dichtung*. Innsbruck

(1936). 'Τόποι', *WS* 54.43–51

(1938). *Der Frauentypus der römischen Dichtung*. Innsbruck–Leipzig

Jeanneret, R. (1973). *Recherches sur l'hymne et la prière chez Virgile: essai d'application de la méthode tagménique à des textes de l'antiquité*. Brussels

Jocelyn, H.D. (1964–5). 'Ancient scholarship and Virgil's use of republican Latin poetry', *CQ* 14.280–95, 15.126–44

(1984–5). 'The annotations of M. Valerius Probus', *CQ* 34.464–72, 35.149–61, 466–74

Kahn, C.H. (1983). 'Arius as a Doxographer', in *On Stoic and Peripatetic ethics: the work of Arius Didymus* (ed. W.W. Fortenbaugh) (Rutgers University Studies in Classical Humanities 1), 3–13. New Brunswick–London

Kaibel, G. (1878). *Epigrammata Graeca ex lapidibus conlecta*. Berlin

Kaiser, E. (1964). 'Odyssee-Szenen als Topoi', *MH* 21.109–36, 197–224

Kennedy, G. (1963). *The Art of Persuasion in Greece*. London–Princeton N.J.

Kienast, D. (1982). *Augustus: Prinzeps und Monarch*. Darmstadt

Kindstrand, J. F. (1973). *Homer in der Zweiten Sophistik* (Acta Universitatis Upsaliensis: Studia Graeca Upsaliensia 7). Uppsala

Klein, T.M. (1983). 'Apollonius' Jason: hero and scoundrel', *QUCC* 42.115–26

Kleinschmidt, E. (1974). *Herrscherdarstellung. Zur Disposition mittelalterlichen Aussageverhaltens, untersucht an Texten über Rudolf I. von Habsburg* (Bibliotheca Germanica 17). Berne–Munich

Kloft, H. (1979). *Ideologie und Herrschaft in der Antike* (Wege der Forschung 528). Darmstadt

Knauer, G.N. (1964). *Die Aeneis und Homer: Studien zur poetischen Technik Vergils mit Listen der Homerzitate in der Aeneis* (Hypomnemata 7). Göttingen

—— (1981). 'Vergil and Homer', *ANRW* 2.31.2.870–918.

Kölblinger, G. (1971). *Einige Topoi bei den lateinischen Liebesdichtern* (Dissertationen der Universität Graz 15). Vienna

König, A. (1970). *Die Aeneis und die griechische Tragödie: Studien zur imitatio-Technik Vergils.* Diss. F.-U. Berlin

Kopff, E.C. (1981). 'Virgil and the Cyclic Epics', *ANRW* 2.31.2.919–47

Koster, S. (1983). *Tessera: Sechs Beiträge zur Poesie und poetischen Theorie der Antike* (Erlanger Forschungen: Reihe A Geisteswissenschaften 30). Erlangen

Kraggerud, E. (1968). *Aeneisstudien* (*SO* Fasc. Supplet. 22). Oslo

—— (1987). 'Perusia and the Aeneid', *SO* 62.77–87

Kramer, H. (1915). *Quid valeat ὁμόνοια in litteris Graecis.* Diss. Göttingen

Krischer, T. (1977). 'Eine Eigenheit homerischer Darstellung: Lessings Beobachtungen und ihre Deutung', *Antike und Abendland* 23.77–95

—— (1979). 'UnHomeric scene patterns in Vergil', *Papers of the Liverpool Latin Seminar* 2.143–54

—— (1985). 'Phäaken und Odyssee', *Hermes* 113.9–22

Kroll, W. (1968). *C. Valerius Catullus: Herausgegeben und erklärt* (5th edn). Stuttgart

Lattimore, R. (1962). *Themes in Greek and Latin epitaphs.* Urbana

Lausberg M. (1983). 'Iliadisches im ersten Buch der Aeneis', *Gymnas.* 90.203–39

Lawrence, A.W. (1972). *Greek and Roman sculpture* (2nd edn). London

Lefèvre, E. (1978). *Dido und Aias: ein Beitrag zur römischen Tragödie* (Akad. d. Wiss. und der Lit.: Abh. der Geistes- und Sozialwiss. Kl. 2). Wiesbaden

Liebing, H. (1953). *Die Aeneasgestalt bei Vergil.* Diss. Kiel

Lier, B. (1914). *Ad topica carminum amatoriorum symbolae.* Progr. Gymn. Stettin

Lissberger, E. (1934). *Das Fortleben der römischen Elegiker in den Carmina Epigraphica.* Diss. Tübingen

Litchfield, H.W. (1914). 'National *exempla virtutis* in Roman literature', *HSCPh* 25.1–71

Lloyd, R.B. (1957). 'The character of Anchises in the *Aeneid*', *TAPA* 88.44–55

Lloyd-Jones, H. and Parsons, P. (1983). *Supplementum Hellenisticum* (Texte und Kommentare 11). Berlin–New York

Lobel, E. and Page, D. (1955). *Poetarum Lesbiorum fragmenta.* Oxford

Lockyer, C.W. Jr. (1967–8). 'Horace's propempticon and Vergil's voyage', *CW* 61.42–5

Luce, J.V. (1975). *Homer and the heroic age.* London

Luck, G. (1983). 'Naevius and Virgil', *Ill. Cl. St.* 8.267–75

Lundström, S. (1977). *Acht Reden in der Aeneis* (Acta Universitatis Upsaliensis: Studia Latina Upsaliensia 10). Uppsala

Luterbacher, F. (1904). *Der Prodigienglaube und Prodigienstil der Römer: eine historisch-philologische Abhandlung in neuer Bearbeitung* (2nd edn). Burgdorf (repr. (Libelli 190) Darmstadt 1967)

Luther, W. (1935). *"Wahrheit" und "Lüge" im ältesten Griechentum*. Diss. Göttingen

Lyne, R.O.A.M. (1983). 'Vergil and the politics of war', *CQ* 33.188–203

(1983a). 'Lavinia's blush: Vergil, *Aeneid* 12.64–70', *GR* 30.55–64

MacCormack, S. (1976). 'Latin prose panegyrics: tradition and discontinuity in the later Roman empire', *Revue des Etudes Augustiniennes* 22.29–77

(1981). *Art and ceremony in late antiquity*. Berkeley–Los Angeles

McGann, M.J. (1969). *Studies in Horace's first book of epistles* (Coll. *Latomus* 100). Brussels

McGushin, P. (1964). 'Virgil and the spirit of endurance', *AJPh* 85.225–53

McKay, A.G. (1966). 'The Achaemenides episode: Vergil, Aeneid III, 588–691', *Vergilius* 12.31–8

Mackay, L.A. (1957). 'Achilles as a model for Aeneas', *TAPA* 88.11–16

McKeown, J.C. (1984). 'Fabula proposito nulla tegenda meo: Ovid's *Fasti* and Augustan politics' in Woodman–West (1984), 169–87, 237–41

(1987–). *Ovid: Amores. Text, prolegomena and commentary in four volumes*. Liverpool

Macleod, C.W. (1974). 'A use of myth in ancient poetry: (Cat. 68; Hor. *Od.* 3. 27; Theoc. 7; Prop. 3. 15)', *CQ* 24.82–93 (= (1983) 159–70)

(1976). 'Propertius 2.26', *SO* 51.131–6 (= (1983) 196–201)

(1979). 'The poetry of ethics: Horace, *Epistles* I', *JRS* 69.16–27 (= (1983) 280–91)

(1982). *Homer: Iliad book XXIV*. Cambridge

(1983). *Collected essays*. Oxford

MacMullen, R. (1986). 'Judicial savagery in the Roman empire', *Chiron* 16.147–66

Mähl, E. (1974). *Gymnastik und Athletik im Denken der Römer* (Heuremata 2). Amsterdam

Maltby, R. (forthcoming). *A lexicon of ancient Latin etymologies* (Arca). Vols. 1–3. Liverpool

Mandra, R. (1934). *The time element in the Aeneid of Vergil: an investigation*. Williamsport PA

Marg, W. (1973). 'Zur Eigenart der Odyssee', *Antike und Abendland* 18.1–14

Maronitis, D.N. (1981). 'Die erste Trugrede des Odysseus in der Odyssee: Vorbild und Variationen' in *Gnomosyne: menschliches Denken und Handeln in der frühgriechischen Literatur: Festschrift für Walter Marg zum 70. Geburtstag* (edd. G. Kurz, D. Müller and W. Nicolai), 117–34. Munich

(1983). 'Références latentes de l'Odyssée à l'Iliade' in *Mélanges Edouard Delebecque*, 277–91. Aix-en-Provence

Marquardt, J. (1881–5). *Römische Staatsverwaltung* (Handbuch d. röm. Alterthumer 4–6). Vols. 1–3 (2nd edn). Leipzig

Martin, P.-M. (1978). 'L'image et la fonction du roi-tyran dans l'"Enéide"', *Caesarodunum* 13 (bis). (Numero spécial: Présence de Virgile: Actes du Colloque des 9, 11 et 12 Décembre 1976 (Paris E.N.S., Tours), ed. R. Chevallier), 63–72. Paris

(1982). *L'idée de royauté à Rome: de la Rome royale au consensus republicain* (Miroir des civilisations antiques 1). Vol. 1. Clermont-Ferrand

Mason, H.J. (1974). *Greek terms for Roman institutions: a lexicon and analysis* (American Studies in Papyrology 13). Toronto

Matakiewicz, H. (1930–1). 'De regis notione Vergiliana', *Eos* 33.67–99

Maurach, G. (1968). 'Der Pfeilschuss des Ascanius: zum 9. Buch der Aeneis', *Gymnas.* 75.355–70

Meincke, W. (1965). *Untersuchungen zu den enkomiastischen Gedichten Theokrits: ein Beitrag zum Verständnis hellenistischer Dichtung und des antiken Herrscherenkomions.* Diss. Kiel

Mendels, D. (1979). '"On Kingship" in the "Temple Scroll" and the ideological *Vorlage* of the seven banquets in the *"Letter of Aristeas to Philocrates"*', *Aegyptus* 59.127–36

Meuli, K. (1968). *Der griechische Agon: Kampf und Kampfspiel im Totenbrauch Totentanz Totenklage und Totenlob.* Cologne

Millar, F. (1973). 'Triumvirate and Principate', *JRS* 63.50–67

(1977). *The Emperor in the Roman world (31 BC–AD 337).* London

Minar, E.L. (1951). Review of Höistad (1948), *AJPh* 72.433–8

Moles, J. (1978). 'The career and conversion of Dio Chrysostom', *JHS* 98.79–100

(1983). '"Honestius quam ambitiosus?" an exploration of the Cynic's attitude to moral corruption in his fellow men', *JHS* 103.103–23

(1984). 'Aristotle and Dido's *Hamartia*', *GR* 31.48–54

(1986). 'Cynicism in Horace *Epistles* 1', *Papers of the Liverpool Latin Seminar* 5.33–60

Momigliano, A. (1942). 'Camillus and Concord', *CQ* 46.111–20

Mommsen, T. (1887–8). *Römisches Staatsrecht* (Handbuch der röm. Alterthumer 1–3). Vols 1–3 (3rd edn). Leipzig

Mondi, R. (1980). 'Σκηπτοῦχοι Βασιλεῖς: an argument for divine kingship in early Greece', *Arethusa* 13.203–16

Monti, R. (1981). *The Dido episode and the Aeneid* (*Mnem.* Suppl. 66). Leiden

Moritz, L.A. (1968). 'Some "central" thoughts on Horace's *Odes*', *CQ* 18.116–31

Morland, H. (1956). 'Der Hyrtacide in der Aeneis', *SO* 32.69–80

(1957). 'Nisus, Euryalus und andere Namen in der *Aeneis*', *SO* 33.87–109

Moseley, N. (1926). *Characters and epithets: a study in Vergil's Aeneid.* New Haven–London

Moulton, C. (1977). *Similes in the Homeric poems* (Hypomnemata 49). Göttingen

Muecke, F. (1983). 'Foreshadowing and dramatic irony in the story of Dido', *AJPh* 104.134–55

Müller, Raimar (1984). 'Zur Staatsauffassung der frühen Stoa' in *Actes du VIIe*

Congrès de la Fédération Internationale des Associations d'Etudes Classiques (ed. J. Harmatta), I.303–11. Budapest

Müller, Richard (1952). *Motivkatalog der römischen Elegie: eine Untersuchung zur Poetik der Römer*. Diss. Zurich

Murgatroyd, P. (1981). 'Seruitium amoris and the Roman elegists', *Latomus* 40.589–606

Murray, O. (1965). 'Philodemus on the Good King according to Homer', *JRS* 55.161–82

(1967). 'Aristeas and Ptolemaic kingship', *JTS* 18.337–71

(1968). Review of Dvornik (1966), *JTS* 19.673–8

(1970). 'Hecataeus of Abdera and Pharaonic kingship', *JEA* 56.141–71

(1975). 'Aristeas and his sources', *Studia Patristica* XII, *T.U.* 115.123–8. Berlin

(1984). Review of Dorandi (1982), *JRS* 74.235f.

(1987). 'The Letter of Aristeas' in *Studi Ellenistici II* (ed. B. Virgilio) 15–29. Pisa

Murray, R.J. (1964–5). 'The attitude of the Augustan poets toward *rex* and related words', *CJ* 60.241–6

Mynors, R.A.B. (1969). *P. Vergilii Maronis opera*. Oxford

Nadeau, Y. (1982). 'Caesaries Berenices (*or*, the Hair of the God)', *Latomus* 41.101–3

(1984). 'The lover and the statesman: a study in apiculture (Virgil, *Georgics* 4.281–558)' in Woodman–West (1984), 59–82, 211

Nauhardt, W. (1940). *Das Bild des Herrschers in der griechischen Dichtung* (Neue Deutsche Forschungen 255). Berlin

Németh, B. (1981–2). 'Ariadne–Dido–Ariadne: Interpretationsgedanken über ein dramatisches Triptychon', *Acta Class. Univ. Scient. Debrecen* 17–18. 149–59

Nethercut, W.R. (1968). 'Invasion in the Aeneid', *GR* 15.82–95

Newman, J.K. (1967). *Augustus and the new poetry* (Coll. *Latomus* 88). Brussels–Berchem

(1985). 'Pindar and Callimachus', *Ill. Class. St.* 10.169–89

Newton, F.L. (1957). 'Recurrent imagery in *Aeneid* IV', *TAPA* 88.31–43

Nisbet, R.G.M. (1978–80). '*Aeneas Imperator*: Roman generalship in an epic context', *PVS* 17.50–61

Nisbet, R.G.M. and Hubbard, M. (1970). *A commentary on Horace: Odes book 1*. Oxford

(1978). *A commentary on Horace: Odes book II*. Oxford

Ogilvie, R.M. (1965). *A commentary on Livy books 1–5*. Oxford

Oksala, P. (1962). 'Das Aufblühen des römischen Epos: Berührungen zwischen der Ariadne-Episode Catulls und der Dido-Geschichte Vergils', *Arctos* 3.167–97

Oppermann, H. (1974). *Römische Wertbegriffe* (Wege der Forschung 34). Darmstadt

Otis, B. (1963). *Virgil: a study in civilized poetry*. Oxford

Page, D.L. (1941). *Greek literary papyri: poetry*. London–Cambridge MA.
(1955). *Sappho and Alcaeus: an introduction to the study of ancient Lesbian poetry*. Oxford
(1962). *Poetae Melici Graeci: Alcmanis Stesichori Ibyci Anacreontis Simonidis Corinnae Poetarum Minorum Reliquias Carmina popularia et convivialia ...* Oxford

Page, T.E. (1894–1900). *The Aeneid of Virgil: edited with introduction and notes*. Vols. 1–2. London

Paladini, M.L. (1958). *A proposito della tradizione poetica sulla battaglia di Azio* (Coll. *Latomus* 35). Brussels (= *Latomus* 17.240–69, 462–75)

Pani, M. (1975). 'Troia resurgens: mito troiano e ideologia del principato', *Annali della Facoltà di Lettere e Filosofia: Università degli Studi di Bari* 18.65–85

Parsons, P.J. (1977). 'Callimachus: Victoria Berenices', *ZPE* 25.1–50

Paschalis, M. (1982). 'Two Horatian reminiscences in the proem of Lucan', *Mnem.* 35.342–6

Pasquali, G. (1920). *Orazio lirico: studi*. Florence

Pavlock, B. (1985). 'Epic and tragedy in Vergil's Nisus and Euryalus episode', *TAPA* 115.207–24

Pease, A.S. (1935). *Publi Vergili Maronis Aeneidos liber quartus*. Cambridge MA. (repr. Darmstadt 1967)

Perutelli, A. (1972). 'Similitudini e stile "soggettivo" in Virgilio', *Maia* 24.42–60
(1977). 'La similitudine nella narrazione virgiliana', *Rivista di cultura classica e medioevale* 29.597–607

Pfeiffer, R. (1968). *History of classical scholarship: from the beginnings to the end of the Hellenistic age*. Oxford

Pichon, R. (1902). *De sermone amatorio apud Latinos elegiarum scriptores*. Diss. Paris

Pietrusiński, D. (1980). 'L'apothéose d'Octavien Auguste par le parallèle avec Jupiter dans la poésie d'Horace', *Eos* 68.103–22

Pighi, G.B. (1941). *De ludis saecularibus populi Romani Quiritium libri sex* (Pubblicazioni dell' Università cattolica del S. Cuore Ser. 5, scienze filologiche 35). Milan

Pöschl, V. (1970). 'Dido und Aeneas' in *Festschrift Karl Vretska* (edd. D. Ableitinger and H. Gugel) 148–73. Heidelberg
(1977). *Die Dichtkunst Virgils: Bild und Symbol in der Äneis* (3rd edn). Berlin–New York

Pötscher, W. (1977). *Vergil und die göttlichen Mächte: Aspekte seiner Weltanschauung* (Spudasmata 35). Hildesheim–New York
(1983). 'Motivationsprobleme bei Vergil' in *Festschrift für Robert Muth* (edd. P. Händel and W. Meid) 361–74. Innsbruck.

Pohlenz, M. (1906). 'Das dritte und vierte Buch der Tusculanen', *Hermes* 41.321–55

Poliakoff, M.B. (1985). 'Entellus and Amycus: Virgil, *Aen.* 5.362–484', *Ill. Class. St.* 10.227–31

Pomeroy, S.B. (1975). *Goddesses, whores, wives, and slaves: women in classical antiquity.* New York

Powell, I.U. (1925). *Collectanea Alexandrina: reliquiae minores poetarum Graecorum aetatis Ptolemaicae 323–146 A.C. epicorum, elegiacorum, lyricorum, ethicorum.* Oxford

Prendergast, G.L. (1962). *A complete concordance to the Iliad of Homer* (2nd edn rev. B. Marzullo). Hildesheim

Preshous, J.D.M. (1964–5). 'Apollonius Rhodius and Virgil', *PVS* 4.1–17

Preston, K. (1916). *Studies in the diction of the sermo amatorius in Roman comedy.* Diss. Chicago

Price, S.F.R. (1984). *Rituals and power: the Roman imperial cult in Asia Minor.* Cambridge

Pucci, P. (1987). *Odysseus polutropos: intertextual readings in the Odyssey and the Iliad.* Ithaca–London

Puelma, M. (1977). 'Die Selbstbeschreibung des Chores in Alkmans grossem Partheneion-Fragment (fr. 1 P. = 23 B., 1 D. v.36–105)', *Mus. Helv.* 34.1–55

Putnam, M.C.J. (1965). *The poetry of the Aeneid.* Cambridge MA.–London

Quinn, K. (1968). *Virgil's Aeneid: a critical description.* London

Qviller, B. (1981). 'The dynamics of the Homeric society', *SO* 56.109–55

Radermacher, L. (1951). *Artium scriptores (Reste der voraristotelischen Rhetorik)* (Österreichische Akademie der Wissenschaften Phil.-hist. Kl. SB 227.3). Vienna

Rank, L.P. (1951). *Etymologiseering en verwante Verschijnselen bij Homerus.* Diss. Utrecht

Rawson, B. (1986). *The family in ancient Rome: new perspectives.* London–Sydney

Rawson, E. (1973). 'Scipio, Laelius, Furius and the ancestral religion', *JRS* 63.161–74

(1975). 'Caesar's heritage: Hellenistic kings and their Roman equals', *JRS* 65.148–59

(1985). *Intellectual life in the late Roman republic.* London

Reesor, M.E. (1951). *The political theory of the Old and Middle Stoa.* New York

Rehm, B. (1932). *Das geographische Bild des alten Italien in Vergils Aeneis* (*Philol.* Suppl. 24.2). Leipzig

Reinsch-Werner, H. (1976). *Callimachus Hesiodicus: die Rezeption der hesiodischen Dichtung durch Kallimachos von Kyrene.* Berlin

Renger, C. (1985). *Aeneas und Turnus: Analyse einer Feindschaft* (Studien zur klassischen Philologie 2). Frankfurt am Main–Berne–New York–Nancy

Richardson, N.J. (1980). 'Literary criticism in the exegetical scholia to the *Iliad*: a sketch', *CQ* 30.265–87

(1984). 'Recognition scenes in the *Odyssey* and ancient literary criticism',

Papers of the Liverpool Latin Seminar 4.219–35

Rieks, R. (1981). 'Die Gleichnisse Vergils', *ANRW* 2.31.2.1011–110

Ringeltaube, H. (1913). *Quaestiones ad veterum philosophorum de affectibus doctrinam pertinentes.* Diss. Göttingen

Rocca, S. (1983). *Etologia Virgiliana* (Pubblicazioni dell'istituto di filologia classica e medievale dell'università di Genova 80). Genova

Rohde, E. (1914). *Der griechische Roman und seine Vorläufer* (3rd edn). Leipzig (repr. Hildesheim 1960)

Ronconi, A. (1972). 'Omero nella interpretazione di Orazio' in *Studi classici in onore di Quintino Cataudella*, 3.295–306. Catania

Rose, G.P. (1969). 'The unfriendly Phaeacians', *TAPA* 100.387–406

Rose, H.J. (1933). *Hygini Fabulae: recensuit, prolegomenis commentario appendice instruxit.* Leiden

(1948). *Aeneas Pontifex.* London

Rosivach, V.J. (1980). 'Latinus' genealogy and the palace of Picus (*Aeneid* 7. 45–9, 170–91)', *CQ* 30.140–52

Ross, D.O. Jr. (1975). *Backgrounds to Augustan poetry: Gallus elegy and Rome.* Cambridge

(1987). *Virgil's elements: physics and poetry in the Georgics.* Princeton N.J.

Rudd, N. (1976). *Lines of enquiry: studies in Latin poetry.* Cambridge

Russell, D.A. (1964). *'Longinus': on The Sublime.* Oxford

Russell, D.A. and Winterbottom, M. (1972). *Ancient literary criticism: the principal texts in new translations.* Oxford

Rutherford, R.B. (1986). 'The philosophy of the Odyssey', *JHS* 106.145–62

Santirocco, M.S. (1986). *Unity and design in Horace's odes.* Chapel Hill–London

Schaps, D. (1977). 'The woman least mentioned: etiquette and women's names', *CQ* 27.323–30

Schenk, P. (1984). *Die Gestalt des Turnus in Vergils Aeneis* (Beiträge zur klassischen Philologie 164). Königstein/Ts.

Schiebe, M.W. (1981). *Das ideale Dasein bei Tibull und die Goldzeitkonzeption Vergils* (Acta Universitatis Upsaliensis: Studia Latina Upsaliensia 13). Uppsala

(1983). 'Der Black-out des Aeneas: Zur Frage der Diskrepanz zwischen zweitem und drittem Buch der Aeneis', *Eranos* 81.113–16

(1986). 'The Saturn of the *Aeneid* – tradition or innovation?', *Vergilius* 32.43–60

Schlunk, R.R. (1974). *The Homeric scholia and the Aeneid: a study of the influence of ancient Homeric literary criticism on Vergil.* Ann Arbor

Schmidt, E.G. (1983). 'Achilleus–Odysseus–Aeneas: zur Typologie des vergilischen Helden', *Listy Filologické* 106.24–8

Schneider, C. (1967–9). *Kulturgeschichte des Hellenismus.* Vols. 1–2. Munich

Schubart, W. (1937). 'Das hellenistische Königsideal nach Inschriften und Papyri', *Archiv für Papyrusforschung* 12.1–26

Schweizer, H.J. (1967). *Vergil und Italien: Interpretationen zu den italischen Gestalten der Aeneis.* Aarau

Schwenn, F. (1915). *Die Menschenopfer bei den Griechen und Römern* (Religions-geschichtliche Versuche und Vorarbeiten 15.3). Giessen

Scott, K. (1929). 'Octavian's propaganda and Antony's *De sua ebrietate*', *CP* 24.133–41

(1933). 'The political propaganda of 44–30 B.C.', *Mem. Amer. Acad. Rome* 11.7–49

Seager, R. (1984). 'Some imperial virtues in the Latin prose panegyrics: the demands of propaganda and the dynamics of literary composition', *Papers of the Liverpool Latin Seminar* 4.129–65

Severyns, A. (1938–63). *Recherches sur la Chrestomathie de Proclos* (Biblio-thèque de la Faculté de Philosophie et Lettres de l'Université de Liège 78, 79, 132, 170). Vols. 1–4. Paris–Liège

Skard, E. (1932). *Zwei religiös-politische Begriffe: Euergetes–Concordia* (Av-handlinger Utgitt av Det Norske Videnskaps-Akademi i Oslo. 2: Hist.-Filos. Klasse. 2). Oslo (part. repr. in Oppermann (1974), 173–208)

Skulsky, S. (1985). '"*Invitus, regina ...*": Aeneas and the love of Rome', *AJPh* 106.447–55

Skutsch, O. (1985). *The Annals of Quintus Ennius: edited with introduction and commentary*. Oxford

Slater, W.J. (1969). *Lexicon to Pindar*. Berlin

(1981). 'Peace, the symposium and the poet', *Ill. Class. St.* 6.205–14

(1982). 'Aristophanes of Byzantium and problem-solving in the Museum', *CQ* 32.336–49

Smith, K.F. (1913). *The elegies of Albius Tibullus: the Corpus Tibullianum edited with introduction and notes on books I, II, and IV, 2–14*. New York (repr. Darmstadt 1967)

Snell, B. and Maehler, H. (1975). *Pindari carmina cum fragmentis: pars II: fragmenta*. Leipzig

Speyer, W. (1971). *Die literarische Fälschung im heidnischen und christlichen Altertum: ein Versuch ihrer Deutung* (Handbuch der Altertumswissenschaft 1.2). Munich

Stabryła, S. (1970). *Latin tragedy in Virgil's poetry* (Polska Akademia Nauk-Oddzial w Krakowie Prace Komisji Filologii Klasycznej 10) (tr. M. Abrahamowicz and M. Wielpolska). Wrocław

Stahl, H.-P. (1981). 'Aeneas – an 'unheroic' hero?', *Arethusa* 14.157–77

(1985). *Propertius: "love" and "war": individual and state under Augustus*. Berkeley–Los Angeles–London

Stanford, W.B. (1959). *The Odyssey of Homer: edited with general and gram-matical introduction commentary, and indexes*. Vols 1–2. London–Basing-stoke

(1968). *The Ulysses theme: a study in the adaptability of a traditional hero* (2nd edn). Oxford

Stégen, G. (1971). 'Un match de pugilat vu par Virgile (Enéide V, 362–472)' in *Vergiliana: recherches sur Virgile* (edd. H. Bardon and R. Verdière) (Roma Aeterna 3), 344–57. Leiden

Steidle, W. (1962). 'Das Motiv der Lebenswahl bei Tibull und Properz', *WS* 75.100–40

Steinhauser, K. (1911). *Der Prodigienglaube und das Prodigienwesen der Griechen*. Diss. Tübingen.

Stewart, D.J. (1972). 'Morality, mortality and the public life: Aeneas the politician', *Antioch Review* 32.649–64

Strasburger, H. (1983). 'Vergil und Augustus', *Gymnas.* 90.41–76

Stroh, W. (1971). *Die römische Liebeselegie als werbende Dichtung*. Amsterdam

Strong, D. (1976). *Roman art*. Middlesex

Suerbaum, W. (1967). 'Aeneas zwischen Troja und Rom', *Poetica* 1.176–204
(1980–1). 'Hundert Jahre Vergil-Forschung: eine systematische Arbeits-bibliographie mit besonderer Berücksichtigung der Aeneis', *ANRW* 2.31. 1.3–358, 2.31.2.1359–99

Syme, R. (1939). *The Roman revolution*. Oxford
(1956). 'Seianus on the Aventine', *Hermes* 84.257–66
(1986). *The Augustan aristocracy*. Oxford

Szastyńska-Siemion, A. (1981). '*dapana* und *ponos* bei Pindar' in *Aischylos und Pindar: Studien zu Werk und Nachwirkung* (ed. E.G. Schmidt) (Schriften zur Geschichte und Kultur der Antike 19), 90–2. Berlin

Tarn, W.W. (1948). *Alexander the Great*. Vols 1–2. Cambridge

Taylor, L.R. (1931). *The divinity of the Roman emperor* (American Philological Association: Philological Monographs 1). Middletown Connecticut (repr. New York–London 1979)

Thesleff, H. (1961). *An introduction to the Pythagorean writings of the Hellenistic period* (Acta Academiae Aboensis: Humaniora 24.3). Åbo
(1965). *The Pythagorean texts of the Hellenistic period: collected and edited* (Acta Academiae Aboensis: Humaniora 30.1). Åbo
(1972). 'On the problem of the Doric pseudo-Pythagorica: an alternative theory of date and purpose', in *Fondation Hardt, Entretiens sur l'antiquité classique* 18.57–87. Vandoeuvres–Geneva

Thomas, R.F. (1982). *Lands and peoples in Roman poetry: the ethnographical tradition* (Cambridge Philological Society Suppl. Vol. 7). Cambridge
(1983). 'Callimachus, the *Victoria Berenices*, and Roman poetry', *CQ* 33.92–113
(1986). 'Virgil's *Georgics* and the art of reference', *HSCPh* 90.171–98

Thome, G. (1979). *Gestalt und Funktion des Mezentius bei Vergil: mit einem Ausblick auf die Schlussszene der Aeneis* (Europäische Hochschulschriften Reihe 15 (Klassische Philologie und Literatur) 14). Frankfurt am Main–Berne–Las Vegas

Thornton, A. (1976). *The living universe: gods and men in Virgil's Aeneid* (Mnem. Suppl. 46). Leiden

Thornton, M.K. (1985). 'The adaptation of Homer's Artemis–Nausicaa simile in the *Aeneid*', *Latomus* 44.615–22

Thuillier, J.-P. (1985). *Les jeux athlétiques dans la civilisation étrusque* (Bibliothèque des Ecoles françaises d'Athènes et de Rome 256). Rome

Thummer, Erich (1968–9). *Pindar: die Isthmischen Gedichte: textkritisch heraus- gegeben, übersetzt und kommentiert, mit einer Analyse der pindarischen Epinikien.* Vols 1–2. Heidelberg
Tilly, B. (1969). *P. Vergili Maronis liber XII.* London
Timpanaro, S. (1986). *Per la storia della filologia virgiliana antica* (Quaderni di 'filologia e critica' 6). Rome
Todd, R.W. (1980). 'Lavinia blushed', *Vergilius* 26.27–33
Toher, M. (1985). 'The date of Nicolaus' Βίος Καίσαρος', *GRBS* 26.199–206
Tränkle, H. (1963). 'Elegisches in Ovids Metamorphosen', *Hermes* 91.459–76
Treu, M. (1955). *Von Homer zur Lyrik: Wandlungen des griechischen Weltbildes im Spiegel der Sprache* (Zetemata 12). Munich
Trüdinger, K. (1918). *Studien zur Geschichte der griechisch-römischen Ethno- graphie.* Diss. Basel
Tupet, A.-M. (1976). *La magie dans la poésie latine I: des origines à la fin du règne d'Auguste.* Paris

Van Nortwick, T. (1979). 'Penelope and Nausicaa', *TAPA* 109.269–76
Vatin, C. (1970). *Recherches sur le mariage et la condition de la femme mariée à l'époque hellenistique* (Bibliothèque des Ecoles françaises d'Athènes et de Rome 216). Paris
Versnel, H.S. (1970). *Triumphus: an inquiry into the origin, development and meaning of the Roman triumph.* Leiden
Vessey, D.W.T.C. (1971). 'Thoughts on two poems of Catullus: 13 and 30', *Latomus* 30.45–55
Vollmer, F. (1898). *P. Papinii Statii Silvarum libri.* Leipzig

Walbank, F.W. (1984). 'Monarchies and monarchic ideas' in *The Cambridge Ancient History* (2nd edn edd. F.W. Walbank, A.E. Astin, M.W. Frederik- sen, and R.M. Ogilvie) 7.1.62–100. Cambridge
Wallace-Hadrill, A. (1981). 'The Emperor and his virtues', *Historia* 30.298–323
(1982). 'Civilis Princeps: between citizen and king', *JRS* 72.32–48
Warwick, H.H. (1975). *A Vergil concordance.* Minneapolis
Weber, O. von (1955). *Die Beziehungen zwischen Homer und den älteren griechischen Lyrikern.* Diss. Bonn
Weinstock, S. (1971). *Divus Julius.* Oxford
Wender, D. (1978). *The last scenes of the Odyssey* (*Mnem.* Suppl. 52). Leiden
Werner, J. (1963). 'Astyanax, Telemachos und Verwandtes', *Linguistique Balkanique* 6.47–60
West, D. (1969). 'Multiple-correspondence similes in the *Aeneid*', *JRS* 59.40–9
(1970). 'Virgilian multiple-correspondence similes and their antecedents', *Philol.* 114.262–75
(1974). 'The Deaths of Hector and Turnus', *GR* 21.21–31
West, D. and Woodman, T. (edd.) (1979). *Creative imitation and Latin literature.* Cambridge
West, G.S. (1975). *Women in Vergil's Aeneid.* Diss. U. of California, Los Angeles
(1983). 'Andromache and Dido', *AJPh* 104.257–67

West, M.L. (1980). *Delectus ex iambis et elegis Graecis.* Oxford

Wheeler, A.L. (1930). 'Tradition in the epithalamium', *AJPh* 51.205–23

Whitman, C.H. (1958). *Homer and the heroic tradition.* Cambridge MA.–London

Wigodsky, M. (1965). 'The arming of Aeneas', *Class. et Med.* 26.192–221

(1972). *Vergil and early Latin poetry (Hermes* Einzelschr. 24). Wiesbaden

Willcock, M.M. (1973). 'The funeral games of Patroclus', *BICS* 20.1–11

(1983). 'Antilochos in the Iliad' in *Mélanges Edouard Delebecque,* 477–85. Aix-en-Provence

Williams, F. (1978).*Callimachus Hymn to Apollo: a commentary.* Oxford

Williams, G. (1968). *Tradition and originality in Roman poetry.* Oxford

(1983). *Technique and ideas in the Aeneid.* New Haven–London

Williams, R.D. (1960). *P. Vergili Maronis Aeneidos liber quintus: edited with a commentary.* Oxford

(1962). *P. Vergili Maronis Aeneidos liber tertius: edited with a commentary.* Oxford

(1963). 'Virgil and the *Odyssey', Phoenix* 17.266–74

(1973). *The Aeneid of Virgil: books 7–12: edited with introduction and notes.* Basingstoke–London

Willis, W.H. (1941). 'Athletic contests in the epic', *TAPA* 72.392–417

Wilson, J.R. (1969). 'Action and emotion in Aeneas', *GR* 16.67–75

Wimmel, W. (1960). *Kallimachos in Rom: die Nachfolge seines apologetischen Dichtens in der Augusteerzeit (Hermes* Einzelschr. 16). Wiesbaden

(1973). *'Hirtenkrieg' und arkadisches Rom: Reduktionsmedien in Vergils Aeneis* (Abh. der Marburger Gelehrten Gesellschaft 1972.1). Munich

Winnington-Ingram, R.P. (1971–2). 'Digna atque indigna relatu: observations on Aeneid IX', *PVS* 11.61–74

Wirszubski, Ch. (1960). *Libertas: as a political idea at Rome during the late Republic and early Principate.* Cambridge

Wiseman, T.P. (1971). *New men in the Roman senate 13 B.C.–A.D.14.* Oxford

(1974). 'Legendary genealogies in late-republican Rome', *GR* 21.153–64

(1985). *Catullus and his world: a reappraisal.* Cambridge

Wistrand, E. (1984). 'Aeneas and Augustus in the Aeneid', *Eranos* 82.195–8

Wlosok, A. (1976). 'Vergils Didotragödie: ein Beitrag zum Problem des Tragischen in der Aeneis' in *Studien zum antiken Epos* (edd. H. Görgemanns and E.A. Schmidt), 228–50. Meisenheim am Glan

(1980). 'Nihil nisi ruborem – über die Rolle der Scham in der römischen Rechtskultur', *Graz. Beitr.* 9.155–72

(1985) 'Bimillenarium Vergilianum 1981/1982 (1983): Wissenschaftliche Kongresse, Symposien, Tagungen, Vortragsreihen, Jubiläumsbände – ein Überblick', *Gnomon* 57.127–34

(1986). *'Gemina doctrina*: on allegorical interpretation', *Papers of the Liverpool Latin Seminar* 5.75–84

Woodhouse, W.J. (1930). *The composition of Homer's Odyssey.* Oxford (repr. 1969)

LIST OF MODERN WORKS CITED

Woodman, A.J. (1977). *Velleius Paterculus: the Tiberian narrative (2.94–131): edited with an introduction and commentary* (Cambridge Classical Texts and Commentaries 19). Cambridge

Woodman, T. and West, D. (edd.) (1984). *Poetry and politics in the age of Augustus*. Cambridge

Woodworth, D.C. (1930). 'Lavinia: an interpretation', *TAPA* 61.175–94

Wülker, L. (1903). *Die geschichtliche Entwicklung des Prodigienwesens bei den Römern: Studien zur Geschichte und Überlieferung der Staatsprodigien*. Diss. Leipzig

Yardley, J.C. (1972). 'Comic influences in Propertius', *Phoenix* 26.134–9

Young, D.C. (1968). *Three odes of Pindar: a literary study of Pythian 11, Pythian 3, and Olympian 7* (*Mnem.* Suppl. 9). Leiden

(1971). *Pindar Isthmian 7, myth and exempla* (*Mnem.* Suppl. 15). Leiden

(1984). *The Olympic myth of Greek amateur athletics*. Chicago

Zetzel, J.E.G. (1981). *Latin Textual Criticism in Antiquity*. Salem N.H. (repr. 1984)

INDEX LOCORUM

271

GENERAL INDEX

Cloanthus, 224, 225
concord, 22-3, 26, 27, 35, 60, 85-108,
 124-5, 156, 188-90, 207-8, 213-14
 history of concept, 89-90
 in games, 220-1, 228, 236-48
 of Jupiter and Juno, 98-9
 spheres of application, 90-2
Concordia Augusta, 88, 90, 108
Concordia Nova, 90, 108
concordia, 107-8
conflation (of episodes or characters), 87
 and n. 5, 134, 137, 147, 150, 175-6,
 195-6, 201, 212-13, 232-3
contaminatio, *see* conflation
convivium, 141-2
correction, 73 n. 40, 103, 106 n. 57, 126
 and n. 43, 127 n. 47, 131, 182 and n.
 19, 191, 193, 196, 207, 232, 234 n. 72,
 242, 244, 246 n. 93, *see also aemulatio*
councils, 58-9, 73, 102, 207-8
courage, 19, 29, 39
Creusa, 39, 105, 155
cruelty (in war), 81-2
cura, of good king, 20, 31-3
 of love, 44
cyclic epics, 178
cynic, philosophy, 25, 33-8, 50, 182, 190
 king, 34-6, 38, 51
 view of Odysseus, 87, 88, 182, 190
Cyrus, 7, 11

Dardanus, 63, 116 and n. 15
Dares, 225, 227-8
decreasing explicitness, 62 n. 10
Demetrius of Phaleron, 15
Diana, 27, 130-1
Dido, 47, 84, 99, *see also under* analogues
 kingship of, 2, 38, 39-46, 49, 52, 67, 68
 as lover, 27, 48-54, 56, 83, 137-50
Dio Chrysostom, 17
 Orationes, 25
Diomedes, 74, 77, 122
'Diotogenes' 13, 22-3
Dis, 27
discord, *see* concord
dithyramb, 102
divine machinery, 69 n. 26, 106
Drances, 73-4

Egypt, 5
'Ekphantus', 13
elegy, 54, 56, 136-50
 lover/beloved distinction, 137-9
 topics, 147-9
Ennius, 9

Entellus, 225, 227, 240
Epeius, 225
epicurean philosophy, 14, 79
Epicurus, 14
 Περὶ βασιλείας, 14
epinician poetry, 216
 athletic values in, 218-22
 influence on Augustan poets, 217
epithalamium, 106-7
erotic causation, 106
ethnographic theory, 121, 125, 128
etymology, 30 n. 3, 63 and n. 15, 67 and
 n. 24, 118 and n. 19, 213 and n. 110,
 230 and n. 67
Euripides, *Medea*, 49
Euryalus, 242, 243, *see also* Nisus
Evander, 122

Fama, 49, 50
fate (*fata*), 25, 26, 27, 50, 193
Faunus, 63, 64, 119, 123
foresight, 20
Foundation (Κτίσις), 184
furor (*furo* etc.), 27, 33, 39, 52, 68, 69,
 70, 71, 74, 75, 76, 77, 82-4

Galaesus, 101
galliambics, 175
Gallus (Cornelius), 136, 146
games, 58, 118, 178
 Actian, 215
 difference between Greek and Roman,
 216-17
 in *Argonautica*, 215, 241
 in Homer and Virgil, Ch. 9 *passim*, esp.
 230-48
generosity, 20
good king stereotype, 17-21, Chs. 2-3
 passim
 history of, 10-17
good looks (of king), 21, 30
Gracchus (Ti.), 8
greed, analogous to love, 140
 cause of discord, 99
Gyas, 238 n. 82, 225, 242

hard work (*labor*, πόνος), 20, 31, 32-3,
 222, 226
Hector, 185
Helen, 154, 155
Heracles, 35-6, 220-1
Hercules, 51, 84, 101-2
Hermesianax, *Leontion*, 144
Hesiod, *Works and Days*, 11
Hieron II of Syracuse, 12

Homer, 106 n. 57, 150, 177
homeric epics, ancient comparisons
  between, 179–84, 197, 209
  Augustan poets' use of, 183
  concord/discord in, 188–90
  kingship in, 2, 3–4, 10
  moralising views of, 86, 182, 185, 209
  structures of, 198–200
homerica imitatio, 177
Horace, 34, 88, 174, 176, 217
  Epistles, 37
human sacrifice, 80–1 and n. 63
hunting, 31, 35, 46, 142–3

Iambulus, 87
Ilioneus, 29, 41, 42, 120
imitation, 2, 80, 87, Chs. 8 and 9 *passim*,
  see also aemulatio, analogues,
  conflation, correction, looking
  through, self-imitation
imperium (imperator), 5 and n. 11
inconsistencies in *Aeneid*, 115
ira, 26, 27, 39, 71, 74, 76, 77
Isocrates, 11, 87
Italy, 52, 58, 113–14, 128
  true *patria* of Aeneas, 114–15
Iuno Pronuba, 46, 47

Jason, 47–9, 185, 195
Julia (daughter of Julius Caesar), 96
Julian (emperor), 17
Julian house, 4, 28, 156, 157, 225–6
Julius Caesar, 4, 8, 28, 30, 60–3, 95–7
Juno, 1, 8, 26–7, 45–6, 94–5, 98, 99–100,
  157, 202–4
Jupiter, 1, 21, 25–6, 41, 42, 49, 50, 63,
  103, 124
justice, 19, 22, 29, 64

kindness (philanthropy), 20, 35
king/god equivalence, 21–5, 63
kings of Rome, 60–2
kingship, Chs. 1–3, 208
  and concord, 87–8
  Roman attitudes to, 2, 6–8
komos, 143–4

Latinus, 62–6, 74, 76–7, 119, 120
Latium, 63 and n. 15
Lavinia, characteristics, 162–3
  marriage to Aeneas, 96, 99
  role in *Aeneid*, 151, 155–9, 174–6
Libanius, 17
literature, part of 'real life', 229
Livius Andronicus, translation of
  Odyssey, 182

looking through, 194–5
  Aeneid 5 through *Odyssey* 8 to *Iliad* 23,
    233–44
  Aeneid through *Argonautica* to *Odyssey*,
    195, 206
  Aeneid through *Odyssey* to *Iliad*,
    202–14
  Acestes through Odysseus to Nestor,
    245
  Aeneas through Jason to Odysseus,
    195–6
love, 54–7, 68–9, 221–2, 228–9
  furtivus amor, 48
  and idleness, 45–6
  and marriage, 105–7
  in open air, 142–3
love affair, of Aeneas and Dido, 46–54,
  99, 195, 204–5
lusus Troiae, 118, 229, 236, 246–8
lyric (early Greek), 137, 154
  Roman interest in
  and virgins, 160–2, 163–73

M. Antonius, 57, 66, 95, 102
Maecenas, 34, 67, 140, 176
magic, 144–6
marriage, 46–9, 152, 205
  brother–sister, 98–9, 104–5
  and love, 140
  of Jason and Medea, 47–8
Mars, 27
Medea, 55, 135, 143, 152–3, 196
Mercury, 50–1
Mezentius, 9, 35, 72
miser, 140
Mnestheus, 224, 225
monsters, destruction of, 35

narrative structure of *Aeneid*, 58
Nausicaa, 130, 131–4, 152
neo-pythagorean philosophy, 13–14,
  22–4, 37, 87
Neptune, 95 n. 38
Nicopolis, 99 n. 45
Nisus, and Euryalus, 224, 228–9, 242
Numanus Remulus, speech of, 125,
  126–7, 226

Odysseus, 86, 155, 184–8, *see also under*
  analogues
  and Nausicaa, 131–4
  as cynic hero, 35, 36
  boasts of athletic prowess, 233–4, 245
  in *Iliad*, 185, 197–8
  primacy of in *Odyssey*, 184–5